ORDER AND DISORDER IN MODERN BRITAIN

Victor Bailey

Order and Disorder in Modern Britain

Essays on Riot, Crime, Policing and Punishment

BREVIARY STUFF PUBLICATIONS
2014

Published by Breviary Stuff Publications,
BCM Breviary Stuff, London WC1N 3XX
www.breviarystuff.org.uk
Copyright © Victor Bailey, 2014
The centipede device copyright © Breviary Stuff Publications

A CIP record for this book is available from
The British Library

ISBN: 978-0-9570005-5-1

Contents

Images

Abbreviations

CAB	Public Record Office, Cabinet Office
CM	Cabinet Minutes
CP	Cabinet Papers
DNB	*Dictionary of National Biography*
HO	Public Record Office, Home Office Papers
Hansard	*Hansard Parliamentary Debates*
ILP	Independent Labour Party
LCO	Public Record Office, Lord Chancellor's Office
LP	Lord President's Committee
MEPO	Public Record Office, Metropolitan Police Papers
MPR	Metropolitan Police Records
OED	*Oxford English Dictionary*
P. Com.	Prison Commission
Parl. Deb.	Parliamentary Debates
PP	*Parliamentary Papers*
PREM	Prime Minister's Private Office
PRO	Public Record Office
QBD	Queen's Bench Division
VC	Report of the Departmental Committee on Vagrancy, 1906

Acknowledgements

The essay, *Salvation Army Riots, the 'Skeleton Army' and Legal Authority in the Provincial Town*, originally appeared in A. P. Donajgrodzki (ed.), *Social Control in Nineteenth Century Britain* (London, 1977); the essay, *The Metropolitan Police, the Home Office and the Threat of Outcast London*, first appeared in V. Bailey (ed.), *Policing and Punishment in Nineteenth Century Britain* (London, 1981); the essay, *'In Darkest England and The Way Out': The Salvation Army, Social Reform and the Labour Movement, 1885-1910*, first appeared in *International Review of Social History*, vol. XXIX (Cambridge University Press,1984). The essay, *The Fabrication of Deviance: 'Dangerous Classes' and 'Criminal Classes' in Victorian England* originally appeared in J. Rule and R. Malcolmson (eds.), *Protest and Survival: Essays for E. P. Thompson* (London, 1993); the essay, *English Prisons, Penal Culture, and the Abatement of Imprisonment, 1895-1922*, first appeared in *Journal of British Studies*, vol. 36 (Cambridge University Press, 1997); the essay, *The Shadow of the Gallows: The Death Penalty and the British Labour Government, 1945-51*, first appeared in *Law and History Review*, vol. 18 (Cambridge University Press, 2000).

I would like to thank Cambridge University Press, The Merlin Press, Taylor & Francis Books (UK), and A. P. Donajgrodzki for permission to republish the essays in this book.

Introduction

I

Any historian who republishes essays available elsewhere needs to offer readers an explanation. The justification for this volume of papers, which were originally published in the quarter century between 1977 and 2000, is the theme that pervades them all, which is the relationship between order and disorder in England over the space of a century beginning around 1850. The thread running through the essays, to adapt Peter Berger, is the belief that social history 'leads to the understanding that order is *the* primary imperative of social life'.[1] 'Society, in its essence,' Berger insists, 'is the imposition of order upon the flux of human experience'.[2] But exactly who or what is responsible for the imposition of order or social stability? Few if any historians now tout coercion or active repression to explain order in the second half of the nineteenth century. The police force was unarmed and decentralized, the intelligence services were small and less than competent, and when troops were called in they typically acted at the behest of the civil authorities. Anyway, the post-1850 years were noted for their low level of political and industrial violence. The relative absence of active repression was linked to the absence of serious threats of popular revolt. In response to this evidence, many historians in the 1970s adopted the concept of 'social control', and in particular the notion that the incorporation of working-class communities into middle-class standards and values came not via coercive law and police, but via a whole range of activities from religion to 'rational recreation', from education to charity.[3] These strategies were, said Jose Harris, 'a central theme of nineteenth-century reformist liberalism'.[4]

In what seemed like the blink of an eye, the idea of social control was soon recast to mean state control. In *Discipline and Punish*, Foucault posited the emergence of a hegemonic disciplinary ideology, which served to reinforce the dominance of the ruling elite, and to prevent the 'criminal class' from infecting the workforce with its habits of idleness and theft. In prisons and cognate disciplinary institutions (factories, schools, asylums, and workhouses), the population was "subjected to habits, rules,

---

1   Berger used Sociology not Social History in his sentence, hence the adaptation: P. L. Berger, *Facing Up To Modernity: Excursions in Society, Politics, and Religion* (New York, 1977), p. xv. Emphasis in the original.

2   Ibid.

3   See A. P. Donajgrodzki (ed.), *Social Control in Nineteenth Century Britain* (London, 1977); F. M. L. Thompson, 'Social Control in Victorian Britain', *Economic History Review*, vol. XXXIV (1981), pp. 189-208; J. Mayer, 'Notes towards a Working Definition of Social Control in Historical Analysis', in S. Cohen and A. Scull (eds.), *Social Control and the State* (Oxford, 1985), pp. 17-38.

4   J. Harris, *Private Lives, Public Spirit: Britain, 1870-1914* (London, 1994), p. 212.

orders … The human body was entering a machinery of power that explores it, breaks it down and rearranges it… This discipline produces subjected and practised bodies, 'docile' bodies.'[5] This is not the approach to be found in the present essays. I have always sought to shift the balance from the state and 'moral entrepreneurs' as the exclusive sources of social order, towards what has been termed 'the consensual and voluntary aspects of human behaviour'.[6] I part company with those historians who argue that Victorian society was held together predominantly by social control, or the active conditioning of the working poor into a set of desirable moral norms and behaviours. The grounds of my dissent, which are now common to many historians, are as follows.

For a start, the belief that positive conditioning was needed commonly rests on exaggerated accounts of the threat of popular revolt, especially in the first half of the nineteenth century. This is the argument to be found in my essay on the 'dangerous and criminal classes'.[7] The supposed threat of a conjunction of the labouring and criminal poor, for which the term 'dangerous classes' was invented, was exploited by utilitarian reformers to persuade government to establish a professional police force and the penitentiary. The fear that the categories of criminal, pauper, and labouring poor were part of an interlocking social continuum was wildly exaggerated, however, and was always overpowered by a more sober taxonomy of the moral distinctions that were believed to separate the criminal from the working classes, the world of crime from the world of labour. Moreover, it was a taxonomy to which many members of the working class both subscribed and contributed. The evolution in their own forms of social identity and consciousness led workers to distance themselves from criminals. It is the argument, also, of my essay on the threat of Outcast London in the 1880s.[8] The Pall Mall riot of February 8, 1886, in London's West End failed to provoke fears of a combination of the 'residuum' of criminal and casual poor with the 'respectable working class'. Public, press, and parliament never doubted that the rioters in Pall Mall were drawn from the rough and criminal classes, and that the riot was the product of a temporary lapse on the part of the metropolitan police force. The social trenches dug in the mid-Victorian years held fast in these later Victorian years.

Secondly, the evidence we have of disorder in the mid-to-late Victorian years suggests neither a peaceable kingdom nor any serious threat of violence, which challenges both the effectiveness of social control and the need for it. If positive conditioning was so effective, how do we explain the fact that England after 1850 was hardly strife free? The peace was periodically disturbed by strike violence, by

---

5   See M. Foucault, *Discipline and Punish* (New York, 1978), pp. 128-9. See also M. Ignatieff, *A Just Measure of Pain: The Penitentiary in the Industrial Revolution, 1750-1850* (New York, 1978).

6   M. Ignatieff, 'State, Civil Society and Total Institutions: A Critique of Recent Social Histories of Punishment', in Cohen and Scull, *Social Control*, p. 99.

7   'The Fabrication of Deviance: 'Dangerous Classes' and 'Criminal Classes' in Victorian England.'

8   'The Metropolitan Police, the Home Office and the Threat of Outcast London.' See also M. Brodie, 'Artisans and Dossers: The 1886 West End Riots and the East End Casual Poor', *London Journal*, vol. 24 (1999), pp. 34-50; J. Welshman, *Underclass. A History of the Excluded 1880-2000* (London, 2006), pp. 11-16.

electoral partisanship, and by attacks on adherents of the Catholic Church and the Salvation Army.[9] There were a number of large demonstrations, some involving damage to property, the most renowned being the Black Monday and Bloody Sunday riots of 1886 and 1887, which led to a ban on public meetings in central London until 1892.[10] Yet rioting post-1850 was mostly a collusive, conservative undertaking, with rioters acting more to enforce than challenge conventional opinion. The essay in the present volume on the riots in the 1880s against the Salvation Army, written for the first collection of papers on English history to make explicit use of the concept of social control, adopted the contrarian view that the riots posed no threat to the social order.[11] The riots were inspired by an alliance of dominant and subordinate classes upholding a traditional conception of order against the disruptive challenge of militant methodism.

Thirdly, there were marked internal differences within the governing elite in their approach to popular disorder. These differences led both to inconsistency in the application of controls and restraint on the use of law enforcement. In towns that experienced riots against the Salvation Army, local magistrates would often decline to uphold the law of public processioning and meeting, even when pressed to do so by central government, in favour of demonstrations against the Salvation Army that were backed by community interests and opinion. In some towns, magistrates and town councils were divided over the legal response to disorder. Some gave informal sanction to the rioters and used the law to rid the streets of Army processions; others sought to protect the Army in its legal right to process. Likewise, in London, in the aftermath of the Pall Mall riot, and during the discussion about closing Trafalgar Square to all meetings of the unemployed and others, there was a bitter dispute between the chief commissioner of the metropolitan police, who wanted closure at any price, and the Home Secretary, who sought an incontestable legal right of closure. As the final essay in the present volume also argued, the attempt in the aftermath of the Second World War to abolish the death penalty failed in the face of elite dissension.[12] The bulk of the House of Lords, including the high court judges, used the post-war crime wave and other arguments to defeat the abolitionists in the House of Commons, where the Labour party, which had long advocated abolition, was in power. To this elite division, we should add the fact that little success attended many of the campaigns to bring control to bear over, say, popular pastimes, alcohol use, or gambling, because police forces were reluctant to sour public relations

---

9   See D.C. Richter, *Riotous Victorians* (Athens, 1981). For a thinly researched survey of civil disturbance, see I. Hernon, *Riot: Civil Insurrection from Peterloo to the Present Day* (London, 2006), chaps. 10 & 11; and for a breathless conspectus, see C. Bloom, *Violent London. 2000 Years of Riots, Rebels and Revolts* (Basingstoke, 2010), chaps. 10 & 11.

10   A number of historians have argued that the new sense of order in late Victorian England was symbolized by the London Dock Strike of 1889, when tens of thousands of workers marched peaceably through the central streets of London. See G. Stedman Jones, *Outcast London* (Harmondsworth, 1984), chap. 17.

11   'Salvation Army Riots, the 'Skeleton Army' and Legal Authority in the Provincial Town'.

12   'The Shadow of the Gallows: The Death Penalty and the British Labour Government, 1945-51'.

over the enforcement of essentially venial offences.[13]

Fourthly, the findings of historians who have examined the workings of social control agencies suggest less that behavioural change was effectively imposed on the labouring poor, and more that the original intent of the controllers was frequently deflected or even overwhelmed by the norms of those for whom control was meant. The urgent needs of urban life generated independent working-class values and attitudes. These owed little or nothing to middle-class instruction, yet frequently moulded the form and function of middle-class control agencies — as well as leading to the creation of new institutions of self-help. This was especially true of ethnic communities, which developed indigenous institutional support — religious, educational, recreational, and charitable — and a strong tradition of popular self-regulation in the sphere of socialization.[14] The Salvation Army is another case in point. As the essay on the Army and the labour movement argued, both organizations were expressions of an independent working-class consciousness.[15] Those who joined trade unions and socialist clubs and those who became Salvation Army officers understood the connection between character reform and social reform; self-restraint, notably by avoiding alcohol, equipped them to take control of their lives, to reshape them towards increased autonomy and effectiveness.

And, lastly, social control historians have had an unfortunate tendency to rack the Victorians on the Procrustean bed of their own ideological making. They are too impatient to assess the moral imagination of the Victorians with any scrupulousness or accuracy. The essay in the present collection that examines the supposed sea-change in 'penality', from 'classical' Victorian principles of retribution and deterrence to the 'positivist' credo of individualism and rehabilitation, argued instead for the influence of humanitarianism, idealist philosophy and ethical socialism, and hence for the continued role of a 'just proportion' between crime and punishment, and a continued belief in the moral causation of crime and the moral force of punishment.[16]

What, then, needs to replace the theory of social control? We require a theory, or simply an approach, that shifts the emphasis from formal control mechanisms to informal and intimate groups, and that frees historical actors from the shackles of social control. As Thomas Bender argued over thirty years ago, the sociological tradition associated with Ferdinand Tonnies, who gave us the 'gemeinschaft und gesellschaft' model of social solidarity, was perverted by the likes of Louis Wirth and Edward A. Ross to mean that communal and associational bonds of social cohesion — the traditional basis of solidarity — were entirely replaced in modern society by formal mechanisms of social control. No longer were the two forms, communal and institutional, allowed to co-exist, as Tonnies's model required; communal

---

13 See V. Bailey, *Charles Booth's Policemen: Crime, Police and Community in Jack-the-Ripper's London*, (Breviary Stuff: London, 2014).

14 See the section on the Jewish community in the East End of London in ibid.

15 "In Darkest England and the Way Out': The Salvation Army, Social Reform and the Labour Movement, 1885-1910'.

16 'English Prisons, Penal Culture, and the Abatement of Imprisonment, 1895-1922'.

forms were said to have weakened, declined, eroded, disappeared. All legitimacy was thus denied to such solidary forces as neighbourhood, ethnic culture, or social class. Far more convincing is a theory of social fields in which there are multiple social groupings; a theory of social worlds that are diverse and interacting. We are better employed probing the relative importance to people's lives of these different sources of solidarity.[17]

This approach requires a focus on the social field in which order was maintained and deviance was contained. In a recent study of the East End of London I have tried to do exactly this. The hypothesis is that the police operated within what Pierre Bourdieu called a 'force field', a social arena endowed with its own rules and forms of authority, imposing specific determinations of variable intensity on those within the space, yet also allowing improvisation and even escape from social conditioning.[18] The main agents within this zone of struggle — occupying positions within the field by virtue of shared 'habitus' or their collective view of the world — included the beat policemen with their own operational practices, the 'moral entrepreneurs' with their 'civilizing efforts', the police court magistrates who scrutinized the policing of street crime, and inhabitants with their own codes, customs and culture, including the large Jewish community with its own forms of self-regulation. Without a full appreciation of this force field, historians run the risk of overestimating the extent to which the police were able or willing to intervene in the daily behaviour of inhabitants in order to suppress law breaking, and the extent to which 'moral missionaries' were successful in imposing social control. The commission and repression of crime and disorder are dependent variables. They are linked not only to the structures of law enforcement and moral zealotry, but also to levels of community solidarity, associational life, family integration, and parental authority.[19]

This approach to the history of social order is in accord with the conclusions of a number of labour historians who see the defining characteristic of working-class life to be the rich associational world of trade unions, friendly societies and working-men's clubs. It is this communal life that prompted Jose Harris to argue that social control was 'a horizontal as well as a vertical process, and some of the most law-abiding and disciplined communities in Edwardian England were those which were most contemptuous of upper-class patronage, most fiercely loyal to the autonomous culture and institutions of the independent working class.'[20] Working people voluntarily participated in the main institutions of public life, whether a willingness to bargain over wages and conditions, or agreement to use the criminal courts for arbitration of disputes.[21] The result was what Harris described as 'the extraordinary

---

17   T. Bender, *Community and Social Change in America* (New Brunswick, 1978), pp. 35-43. See also Mayer, 'Notes', p. 17.

18   P. Bourdieu, *The Field of Cultural Production* (New York, 1993); R. Jenkins, *Pierre Bourdieu* (London, 1992), chap. 4 at pp. 84-91.

19   See V. Bailey, *Charles Booth's Policemen: Crime, Police and Community in Jack-the-Ripper's London*, (Breviary Stuff: London, 2014).

20   Harris, *Private Lives, Public Spirit*, p. 212.

21   J. Davies, 'A Poor Man's System of Justice: The London Police Courts in the Second Half of the Nineteenth Century', *Historical Journal*, vol. 27 (1984), pp. 309-35.

coexistence of extreme social inequality with respect for and observance of the law, of growing public order with fierce defence of civil liberties, and of endemic structural and economic change with social and institutional cohesion, that characterized British society for most of the period 1870 to 1914'.[22]

This approach, moreover, draws upon what we might call a new sociology of action, a new view of individual agency. Gone: is the constancy and predictability of behaviour patterns in thrall to economic logic. Gone: is the image of actors imprisoned in the reified identities of class, race or gender. In: is a view of actors operating strategically in the face of varied and contradictory norms. In: is a view of actors reflectively and voluntarily negotiating ethnic and cultural differences to find agreement or consensus, albeit within constraints and contexts that fence them in. This is all best encapsulated in Stedman Jones's description of the new social history in France:

> The stress is upon active, self-conscious, knowing, manipulating, and ambivalent actors, preserving their freedom of manoeuvre at every moment of their participation in social life. Society is held together by conventional rather than juridical means. But these conventions and rules are the product of constant and arduous social labour and have never been other than provisional, ephemeral, and unstable. They are implemented by complex social actors with an ability to justify themselves by resorting simultaneously to several different and often contradictory social worlds.[23]

In these ways, it is possible to escape the notions of domination and social control, which distinguished radical social theory, and to examine instead the diversity of sources of social solidarity, the role of communal forms of social cohesion, and the strategic improvisation adopted by reflective individuals.

II

Next, we assess how the essays collected in this volume have fared at the hands of other historians, starting with the two essays that deal with the Salvation Army. Glenn Horridge believed that the 'mere arrival of the Army in itself was not enough to cause widespread disorder', and hence he challenged my assertion that there was a rough correspondence in time between the direction of the Salvation Army's geographic expansion and the riots. His plot of physical assaults on Army members suggests that between 1878 (when the Army first adopted its military trappings) and 1883, there was 'an increasingly strong 'rough-musicing' reaction nationally', reaching its apex in 1882.[24] The point is well taken, though it does not alter my claim that there was much more violence in the small towns of Southern England

---

22 Harris, *Private Lives, Public Spirit*, p. 38. See also R. McKibbin, 'Why was there no Marxism in Great Britain?', in idem, *The Ideologies of Class. Social Relations in Britain 1880-1950* (Oxford, 1990), pp. 12-16.

23 G. Stedman Jones, 'The New Social History in France', in C. Jones and D. Wahrman (eds.), *The Age of Cultural Revolutions. Britain and France, 1750-1820* (Berkeley, 2002), p. 99.

24 G. K. Horridge, *The Salvation Army. Origins and Early Days: 1865-1900* (Godalming, 1993), pp. 97-8.

than in the Midlands and the north of England (with the exception of Sheffield, Birkenhead, and Liverpool), an account that Horridge confirms. This leads him to suggest 'that 'rough-music' was dying out in the industrial towns and villages', which speaks to my main point that the Army's assault on popular culture was most violently resisted in exactly those areas (small and middling towns of the South) where working-class consciousness was weakest. The riots were a last stand of the 'rough' working class against the tide of Victorian character reform. By the same token, the Army's arrival was less disruptive in industrialized areas like Manchester, precisely because it posed less of a threat to their already-modernized and moralized way of life.[25]

Pamela Walker accepted my argument concerning the riots and the law, but disagreed with my assessment of 'the Army's place in working-class communities'. The disorders, she argued, were not alone an issue of 'unctuous outsiders imposing their values on lively working-class neighbourhoods', but were 'very much part of urban street life'.[26] If I understand her point, it is that Salvationists and Skeletons were alike in terms of occupation, age, and streets of residence, and that Salvationism was a 'neighbourhood religion', grounded in the realities of urban working-class life. I would be willing to accept that the Army was neither fully part of the communities it evangelized nor totally outside them. Yet I would still insist that in the initial stages of the Army's 'invasion' or 'bombardment' of a town, in the early attempts to site a 'fort in enemy territory' (terms they used in advertising their imminent arrival), acting in ways that were critical of the male world of pub and pipe, 'sacralizing' public space in an assertive manner (as Paul O'Leary and Diane Winston have convincingly argued), the Army purposely filled the streets with the sights and sounds of a conquering army.[27] In Honiton, where an organized Skeleton Army met the invading evangelists, it is surely significant that 'Captain' Lomas's report to Army headquarters (which introduced my essay) was penned in the Swan Temperance Hotel, indicating that at this stage he had no lodgement in any working-class neighbourhood. In subsequent years, Salvationists doubtless settled into neighbourhood life, but it was the very fact of doing so that allowed opposition to their work to subside. In the early riotous years, the Army's religion and its antics were antithetical to the host culture.

For Gertrude Himmelfarb 'social control' is the red rag to the bull. She is always ready to rattle the cages of those who would suggest that charitable and other organizations were instruments of social

---

25 For Manchester, see G. K. Horridge, "Invading Manchester': Responses to The Salvation Army 1878-1900', *Manchester Region History Review*, vol. VI (1992), pp. 16-29.

26 P. J. Walker, *Pulling the Devil's Kingdom Down: The Salvation Army in Victorian Britain* (Berkeley, 2001), p. 224. Also idem, "A Carnival of Equality': The Salvation Army and the Politics of Religion in Working-Class Communities', *Journal of Victorian Culture*, vol. 5 (2000), pp. 65-8, 77.

27 P. O'Leary, *Claiming the Streets. Processions and Urban Culture in South Wales, c. 1830-1880* (Cardiff, 2012), pp. 152-61; D. Winston, "The Cathedral of the Open Air': the Salvation Army's Sacralization of Secular Space, New York City, 1880-1910', in R. A. Orsi (ed.), *Gods of the City* (Bloomington, 1999), pp. 370-4; idem, *Red-Hot and Righteous. The Urban Religion of the Salvation Army* (Cambridge, 1999), chap. 1. See also B. Beaven, *Leisure, citizenship and working-class men in Britain, 1850-1945* (Manchester, 2005), pp. 37-8.

control. I was charged with inconsistency, however, arguing first that the Salvation Army was an enemy of the working class, only later to contend that it was an ally of the working class.[28] I would like to think my arguments had greater consistency and were more nuanced than she allowed. The first essay suggested that the riotous opposition to the Army was strongest in non-industrialized towns where the working class was most traditional and where the labour movement and working-class consciousness were least developed; the second essay pointed to some areas of compatibility between the Salvationists and the organized labour movement in the first phase of development of both groupings. Lynne Marks provided comparative support for this last essay by examining the Salvation Army and the Knights of Labour in Ontario, Canada. Workers at Kingston's largest factories organized both Salvation Army prayer-meetings and Knights of Labor strikes. There may even have been some overlap in membership, with a few being simultaneously Knights and soldiers; but 'many more may have been touched by both movements over the course of the 1880s'. The Army's appeal to a spiritual (and gender) equality, Marks argued, 'may have tapped into or strengthened an emerging class consciousness'. The Army provided a space for 'a class-based challenge to respectable middle-class churchgoing', 'an assertion of working-class dignity and independence'.[29]

The links I described between Salvationism and Socialism would have been strengthened, if only marginally, had I known about novelist Margaret Harkness, who lived with cousin Beatrice Webb in Katharine Buildings, a tenement for casual labourers, and who veered between the twin influences of Socialism and Salvationism.[30] In March, 1888, in *Justice*, the mouthpiece of the Social Democratic Federation, Harkness described the Salvation Army Hostel in West India Dock Road, established a month before to lodge and feed the East End poor, as 'probably the most communistic place in London'. She called it communistic, 'because it is carried on in the socialist spirit'. The day before her visit, 4,000 people had been fed, and 500 farthings (a quarter of a penny) had been taken from children for basins of soup. Harkness concluded: 'The two organizations [socialists and salvationists] ought to work more together than they do at present, for they have many points of common interest.' The Salvation Army,

---

28 G. Himmelfarb, *Poverty and Compassion. The Moral Imagination of the Late Victorians* (New York, 1991), pp. 228-30.

29 L. Marks, 'The Knights of Labour and the Salvation Army: Religion and Working-Class Culture in Ontario, 1882-1890', *Labour/Le Travail*, vol. 28 (1991), pp. 97, 102, 112-14. See also L. Taiz, 'Applying the Devil's Works in a Holy Cause: Working-Class Popular Culture and the Salvation Army in the United States, 1879-1900', *Religion and American Culture*, vol. 7 (1997), pp. 200-1; P. J. Walker, "I Live But Not Yet I For Christ Liveth In Me": Men and masculinity in the Salvation Army, 1865-90', in M. Roper and J. Tosh (eds.), *Manful Assertions. Masculinities in Britain since 1800* (London, 1991), pp. 96, 104; Beaven, op cit., pp. 33-5. For the interesting possibility that the Army's home colonies scheme (which was an integral part of the Darkest England project) 'might well have spoken to rising sections of the working class who would otherwise be lumped in with the urban residuum', see S. Joyce, *Capital Offenses: Geographies of Class and Crime in Victorian London* (Charlottesville, 2003), p. 231.

30 See J. Goode, 'Margaret Harkness and the socialist novel', in H.G. Klaus (ed.), *The Socialist Novel in Britain* (Brighton, 1982), p. 62; D.E. Nord, *Walking the Victorian Streets: Women, Representation, and the City* (Ithaca, 1995), pp. 185-96; S. Ledger, 'In Darkest England: The Terror of Degeneration in *Fin-de-Siecle* Britain', *Literature and History*, vol. 4 (1995), pp. 79-81. For two of Harkness's novels, see J. Law, *A City Girl* (New York, 1984; first pub., 1887); *In Darkest London: A New and Popular Edition of Captain Lobe, A Story of the Salvation Army* (London, 1891).

she said, 'is one large labour union'.[31]

For one historian, finally, 'implacable resistance from urban ghetto neighbourhoods', whether in the East End of London or among the Liverpool Irish, to the Salvation Army's revivalist message is what truly inspired William Booth to launch the 'Darkest England' social scheme.[32] Norman Murdoch is particularly persuaded by the 1888 *British Weekly* survey of London churches, which indicated that Salvation Army services attracted only 0.7 per cent of the metropolitan population, a figure that went lower still in the poor East End districts of Whitechapel and Bethnal Green. The Army, Murdoch concluded, was failing to recruit what Booth would call 'the submerged tenth'. I am not persuaded of a clear-cut shift from spiritual to social work, from soul to social salvation. The figures of the formation of new Salvation Army corps and of numbers of Army officers are notoriously imprecise, but for what they are worth, they suggest that the Army peaked around 1889, not 1886 as Murdoch argued, and thus the social scheme was launched from a position of strength not weakness. In addition, the Darkest England scheme did not appear out of nowhere. Murdoch himself acknowledges that as early as the 1870s, Booth had sponsored soup kitchens, free breakfasts, and free clothing, and that by 1884 the Cellar, Gutter, and Garret Brigade of the slum sisters was visiting, cleaning, and nursing in London's tenements. This was six years before the big scheme for social regeneration. Moreover, Booth himself never talked of a break or turn around 1890 with the launch of the Darkest England scheme. He saw no tension between religious and social work. The only war he truly understood was the war on sin.[33]

In the essay on the fabrication of deviance, I was concerned to evaluate the discursive and political distinction between the category of 'dangerous classes' — 'a threatening amalgamation of poverty, vagrancy and crime' — and that of the 'criminal classes' — no longer associated with political subversion and social breakdown; and to link this distinction to the project of establishing moral boundaries within different groups of the lower classes. The world of labour and the world of crime, I argued, became discrete realms for the mid-Victorian criminologist. The late David Philips took

---

31 M. Harkness, 'Salvationists and Socialists', *Justice*, 24 March 1888, p. 2. See also Harkness's letter to editor, *Justice*, 14 April 1888, p. 6. Cf. L. Hapgood, 'Urban utopias: socialism, religion and the city, 1880 to 1900', in S. Ledger and S. McCracken (eds.), *Cultural Politics at the Fin De Siecle* (Cambridge, 1995), p. 186-8; M. Bevir, 'The Labour Church Movement, 1891-1902', *Journal of British Studies*, vol. 38 (1999), pp. 223, 244.

32 N. H. Murdoch, 'Salvation Army Disturbances in Liverpool, England, 1879-1887', *Journal of Social History*, vol. 25 (1992), pp. 575, 586; idem, 'From Militancy to Social Mission: The Salvation Army and Street Disturbances in Liverpool, 1879-1887', in J. Belchem (ed.), *Popular Politics, Riot and Labour: Essays in Liverpool History 1790-1940* (Liverpool, 1992), pp. 160-72; idem, *Origins of the Salvation Army* (Knoxville, 1994), pp. 79-81, 103, 120-3, 133-4. For other examples of the Salvation Army's invasion of Irish Catholic districts, see J. Reed-Purvis, '"Black Sunday": Skeleton Army Disturbances in Late Victorian Chester', in R. Swift (ed.), *Victorian Chester. Essays in Social History 1830-1900* (Liverpool, 1996); J. Holmes, 'Gender, Public Disorder and the Salvation Army in Ireland, 1880-82', in R. Raughter (ed.), *Religious Women and Their History* (Dublin, 2005).

33 See A. R. Higginbotham, 'Respectable Sinners: Salvation Army Rescue Work with Unmarried Mothers, 1884-1914', in G. Malmgreen (ed.), *Religion in the Lives of English Women, 1760-1930* (London, 1986), pp. 217-19; A. M. Eason, *Women in God's Army: Gender and Equality in the Early Salvation Army*, Studies in Women and Religion, vol. 7 (2003), pp. 47-8; note 49, pp. 175-6; A. M. Woodall, *What Price the Poor? William Booth, Karl Marx and the London Residuum* (Aldershot, 2005), pp. 148-53, 162-4, 181-2.

exception to my argument, on the grounds that there was no 'clear qualitative change between [Patrick] Colquhoun's alarmist picture of the 'dangerous classes', and the image of crime and criminals projected by [Edwin] Chadwick (with [W. A.] Miles)'.[34] I am willing to accept that the middle-class fear of the growth of pauperization and of the related descent of the labouring classes into the dangerous classes raised its head periodically, as in G. W. M Reynolds's fictional *The Mysteries of London* (1844-48) or in some of Henry Mayhew's mid-Victorian writings.[35] I am willing to accept (why wouldn't I?) that the idea that crime was the product of a 'criminal class' was 'already strongly embedded in the writings of commentators in the first half of the century'. Yet I also beg to differ. I persist in thinking that there was a difference between the fear of an anarchic alliance of labour and crime, which is what made the 'dangerous classes' dangerous, and which was heard mainly in the first half of the nineteenth century (though never as frequently as some historians have alleged), and the term 'criminal classes', which dominated discourse by the mid-Victorian years, and which marked a clear social and moral distinction between the working and criminal classes.[36]

In *Punishment and Welfare*, David Garland argued that between 1895 and 1914, under the impact of a new 'positivist' scientific discourse or criminology, which emphasized the force of environmental and biological determinism, there was a major transition in England's penal-welfare system.[37] Official penal policy shifted from the retributive and deterrent effect of sanctions to techniques for rehabilitating offenders, using penal dispositions that drew upon the medical, psychological, and social sciences. Offenders were seen less as free and rational subjects and more as individuals whose actions were determined by social and psychological forces. Late Victorian penal policy, moreover, was deemed to be only one cog in a larger transition in the role and reach of the state, and in the provision of welfare to the wider citizenry.[38] Garland's argument rarely descended from the level of ideas to that of penal practice. For this reason, my essay on this subject looked carefully at the degree to which penal practice

---

34 D. Philips, 'Three 'moral entrepreneurs' and the creation of a 'criminal class' in England, c. 1790s-1840s', *Crime, History & Societies*, vol. 7 (2003), p. 103.

35 See D. Englander, 'Henry Mayhew and the Criminal Classes of Victorian England: The Case Reopened', *Criminal Justice History*, vol. 17 (2002), pp. 93, 103; A. L. Beier, 'Identity, Language, and Resistance in the Making of the Victorian 'Criminal Class': Mayhew's Convict Revisited', *Journal of British Studies*, vol. 44 (2005), p. 504.

36 For endorsement of my approach to this issue, cf. C. Aguirre, *The Criminals of Lima and Their Worlds* (Durham, 2005), pp. 61-4.

37 In my essay, 'English Prisons, Penal Culture, and the Abatement of Imprisonment, 1895-1922', I defined positivism as follows: 'The main tenets of 'positivist' criminology were, first, that criminal behaviour was determined by factors and processes that could be discovered by observation, measurement, and inductive reasoning, the methods used by the natural and social sciences. Second, since people were impelled to commit crime by constitutional and environmental forces beyond their control and, thus, were not responsible for their actions, treatment, not punishment, was the most appropriate legal response. Third, the delinquent was fundamentally different from normal, law-abiding citizens.'

38 D. Garland, *Punishment and Welfare. A History of Penal Strategies* (Aldershot, 1985). Martin Wiener takes a different tack from Garland, insofar as he looks for the shared elements or consensus within penal thought about the perception of the criminal. Nevertheless, Wiener's conclusion that a shift in the perception of the criminal personality from 'willfulness to wreckage', and a shift in outlook or mental frame from 'moralism to causalism', occurred from the 1870s onwards, surely cogs with Garland's view that positivism underlay the formation of a new penal estate: M. J. Wiener, *Reconstructing the Criminal: Culture, Law, and Policy in England 1830-1914* (Cambridge, 1990), pp. 10-13 and chap. 9.

bore the imprint of the new ideas. But even at the level of ideas, I differed with Garland over the main influences on penal policy. I was more convinced by the role of humanitarianism, idealism, and ethical socialism than by the 'positivist' ideas of individualized rehabilitation. Penal policy and practice continued to emphasize, in my view, the classical principles of a just proportion between crime and punishment, and the disciplinary moralism of the Victorian years.

I was unaware when I wrote the essay that Bill Forsythe had already directly challenged the Garland thesis, though more with regard to the preceding years, 1835-1890, than of the period from 1890 to 1920, which I focused upon.[39] Since then, Alyson Brown, on the basis of her work on Victorian prisons, prisoners, and prison staff, has endorsed the general approach to be found in Forsythe's and my work.[40] The main riposte to our evidence of the gap between positivist aspiration and penal practice in the period 1895 to 1922 came from Neil Davie, whose main challenge, however, was to the more extreme argument in favour of continuity in 'classical' notions of moral responsibility for crime, to be found in Leon Radzinowicz and Roger Hood's *History of English Criminal Law and its Administration* (1986).[41] Davie takes me to task for underestimating the persistence in thinking to be found among criminal justice professionals, especially the psychiatric and medical staff, who kept alive the mid-Victorian idea of an hereditary criminal-type, associated with the 'habitual criminal' or 'recidivist' — an idea that structured research and policy in Britain as profoundly as it did on the continent. Davie's allied point — that senior and lower-level officials 'drew on both classical and positivist explanations of criminal behaviour, according to the category of offenders concerned' — I would not cavil with.[42] I have always accepted that determinist models of criminal behaviour were influential in the treatment of juveniles, the insane, and the feeble-minded. Where we differ, therefore, is in the significance we attach to the habitual criminal. Davie emphasizes the consensus in official thinking that habitual offenders 'were drawn disproportionately from a mentally *and physically* defective category of the population: a 'criminal type' in all but name'.[43] I stress the fact that whatever the official thinking about the recidivist, it did not lead to the widespread or effective use of specialized, individualized, penal and medical solutions, in large part because of judicial unwillingness to depart from the just proportion between crime and punishment.

In fairness, independent of the challenges to his 1985 book, Garland soon recognized the limitation

---

39   W. J. Forsythe, 'The Garland Thesis and the Origins of Modern English Prison Discipline: 1835 to 1939', *The Howard Journal*, vol. 34 (1995), pp. 259-71. See also idem, *Penal discipline, reformatory projects and the English Prison Commission, 1895-1939* (Exeter, 1990).

40   A. Brown, *English Society and the Prison: Time, Culture and Politics in the Development of the Modern Prison, 1850-1920* (Woodbridge, 2003), chap. 6.

41   N. Davie, *Tracing the Criminal. The Rise of Scientific Criminology in Britain 1860-1918* (Oxford, 2005), p. 185. See L. Radzinowicz and R. Hood, *A History of English Criminal Law and its Administration from 1750*, vol. 5: *The Emergence of Penal Policy* (London, 1986), pp. 15-16.

42   Ibid, p. 187.

43   Ibid, p. 192. See also N. Davie, 'Criminal Man Revisited? Continuity and Change in British Criminology, c.1865-1918', *Journal of Victorian Culture*, vol. 8 (2003) pp. 1-24.

of *Punishment and Welfare* in 'its tendency to view penal change only from the point of view of its implications for class domination and the control of the poor'. He has since retreated from a full-blooded social control framework, in favour of one that allows for the exploration of 'the webs of cultural meaning within which modern punishment actually operates'.[44] In a 1997 article, Garland's change of heart was expressed as follows: 'The story of penal policy is one of compromise and accommodation, of ambivalence and poorly implemented policy. It is necessary to look at the whole configuration of practices, and not just the rationalities, or programmes, or even the selected practices that best instantiate them.'[45]

Finally, my essay on the campaign to abolish the death penalty in the wake of the Second World War has been challenged, after a fashion, by Kevin Manton.[46] I am said to have underestimated the role of Herbert Morrison, a Labour minister in the Cabinet, in his opposition to abolition, and the significance of the post-war crime wave. In the early part of my essay, I wrote that the postwar world was much less hospitable to penal reform than the abolitionists had anticipated. For a start, the war crimes trial at Nuremberg 'lent justification to a retributive approach to indigenous murder'. More important, I continued, 'was the rise in officially recorded crime and the 'moral panic' the figures generated', concluding: 'This crime-wave narrative had an effect upon penal thought, notably by reinvigorating the belief that punitive measures could not be surrendered.' I returned to the influence of the post-war crime wave in my conclusion. Perhaps Mr. Manton could try reading an essay before he critiques it. As for Morrison, I made it clear that his role in Cabinet was staunchly abolitionist, I referred to his decisive role in the decision to allow ministers only to abstain rather than be free to vote their conscience on the amendment for the abolition of the death penalty (which Manton implies I also neglect), and I noted that Morrison was willing to accept a compromise clause at the eleventh hour which would have at least limited the operation of the death penalty. More to the point, had I written acres more about Morrison's role in Cabinet, the main arguments in my paper as to what went wrong for the abolitionists and why, would have been unaffected. I stand by the explanations offered for the failure to abolish capital punishment in the 1940s.[47]

---

44   D. Garland, *Punishment and Modern Society* (Chicago, 1990), pp. 125-9. See also A. Howe, *Punish and Critique. Towards a Feminist Analysis of Penality* (London, 1994), pp. 66-70. Garland's cultural turn influenced Philip Smith whose *Punishment and Culture* (Chicago, 2008) interprets punishment as a 'cultural expression'. In the decoding of penal activity, Smith rejects Foucault in favour of Durkheim, especially the latter's insight that punishment 'is an act of imaginative reordering or expiation that offers a way of thinking and reinforcing moral boundaries, thereby re-building solidarity'. (p. 16).

45   Garland, "Governmentality' and the problem of crime: Foucault, criminology, sociology', *Theoretical Criminology*, vol. 1 (1997), p. 202. I should add, finally, that when it comes to explaining the abatement of imprisonment during these years, I am now more persuaded by Wiener's point that new forms of heightened social regulation, new levers of intervention by social agencies like the National Society for the Prevention of Cruelty to Children, lessened the need for formal criminal sanctions, making it possible to begin emptying the jails: M. Wiener, 'The March of Penal Progress?', *Journal of British Studies*, vol. 26 (1987), pp. 83-96.

46   K. Manton, 'Labour Governments and Capital Punishment, 1924-1970', *Labour History Review*, vol. 76 (2011), pp. 17, 20, 22.

47   Manton also implies that historians have overlooked the reactionary influence of the permanent officials in the Home Office. How else can we explain the fact that professed abolitionists went retentionist as soon as they became Home Secretary? In fact, I addressed this very point over two

III

The six papers in this book were deeply influenced by my time and training at the Centre for the Study of Social History at Warwick University. A few months before matriculation, I was given a copy of 'History from Below', E. P. Thompson's state-of-the-discipline review, which appeared in *The Times Literary Supplement* of April 7, 1966, and which began with characteristic bite:

> It is one of the peculiarities of the English that the history of the 'common people' has always been something other than — and distinct from — English History Proper. ... In English History Proper the people of this island (see under Poor Law, Sanitary Reform, Wages Policy) appear as one of the problems Government has had to handle.

Thompson, Director of the Centre for the Study of Social History, wished to rewrite the national story around the struggles of ordinary people, focusing on their experiences and perspectives, along the lines of his formative 1963 study, *The Making of the English Working Class*. History from below differed not only from traditional political history, but also from traditional labour history, in that its exponents were more interested in popular protest and culture, including the social history of crime, than in the institutions of the organized working class. If history from below swept all before it for twenty years or more, in recent decades the lived experience of working people has been neglected for the disembodied analysis of 'discourse', or a focus on the language of the middling sort and elite. Fortunately, there are still historians who continue to mine the rich archives of the working poor — court records, pauper and charitable petitions, and plebeian autobiographies — and persist in writing a history from below.[48] I count myself among their ranks.

---

pages, concluding that Home Secretary, James Chuter Ede, was 'a mite "captive" of the departmental view. That said, I think the retentionist culture of the department can be exaggerated. The influence on Home Secretaries of Cabinet, party, and public opinion was always more salient. Finally, for work that is supportive of my argument, see D. Hay, 'Hanging and the English Judges. The Judicial Politics of Retention and Abolition', in D. Garland *et al.* (eds.), *America's Death Penalty* (New York, 2011), p. 154; T. J. Wright, 'Arguing for the Death Penalty: Making the Retentionist Case in Britain, 1945-1979', M.A. thesis, 2010, University of York, section I; A. Hammel, *Ending the Death Penalty. The European Experience in Global Perspective* (Basingstoke, 2010), chap. 5.

48 See, for example, A. Davin, *Growing Up Poor. Home, School and Street in London 1870-1914* (London, 1996); T. Hitchcock, P. King, and P. Sharpe (eds.), *Chronicling poverty: the voices and strategies of the English poor, 1640-1840* (New York, 1997); T. Hitchcock, *Down and out in eighteenth-century London* (London, 2004); P. King, *Crime and law in England, 1750-1840: remaking justice from the margins* (Cambridge, 2006); J. Marriott, *Beyond the Tower. A History of East London* (New Haven, 2011).

1

Salvation Army Riots

The 'Skeleton Army' and Legal Authority in the Provincial Town

There was a meeting of the Councillors yesterday and from reliable information that has reached me the Mayor has promised to hold aloof. The leading business men of the Town, with few exceptions are members of the Skeleton Army who have notices printed inviting members to join the Skeleton Army. Their programme on Sunday next, at a given signal is to cut open the drum end and put in the drummer, cover the processionists with red ruddle and flour and keep us from the Barracks. Oh! Hallelujah, the town is on a blaze from end to end, and much spiritual awakening in every chapel, glory be to Jesus! His name shall be praised! Bless Him! The employers promise their people that if they get saved they will not employ them any longer. But Hallelujah they are getting saved in spite of the Devil. The Superintendent has flatly refused either protection outside or inside. The Sergt. but grins and indirectly encourages them. On Sunday last when I got knocked down a policeman was by my side. He simply grinned and walked on. 30 Barrels of Beer were given to the roughs to prime them. A great many of these Dear misguided men have withdrawn and there will be grand results shortly Hallelujah! here we have clearly established our right of processioning. The publicans grind their teeth at me, their trade here is shaken to its very foundation. It is a fact that about 6 pm. on Sunday last there were not 6 men in 23 public houses. The week-night services are well attended. The offerings are better & if the police would only do their duty, all would be well, as the dear people are just beginning to understand us.

'Captain' Lomas, 23 November 1882, Swan Temperance Hotel, Honiton, Devon

I

In the late Victorian period the British economy underwent a major transition in response to the international challenge to its industrial and commercial supremacy. At the same time, the outlook and demeanour of the workforce pointed to the break-up of working-class liberalism and to a revival of

---

I am grateful to Professor Royden Harrison, Mr Edward Thompson, Dr Tony Mason and Dr Sheridan Gilley for their valuable criticisms of earlier drafts of this article.

labour's own political aspirations. But throughout these years, there was a marked absence of the social disorder of a widespread, semi-revolutionary nature, characteristic of earlier economic and social transitions. With the onset of economic depression in the 1880s, London's propertied classes suspected the emergence of a revolutionary threat, but it was fired by a city-bred 'residuum', not an organised and rebellious working class.[1] Only the outlying rural areas in the Celtic fringe were at all affected by extensive social protest: the tithe riots in Wales and the crofting riots in Scotland, in the 1880s. In late Victorian England, the threat to public order came only from transient outbreaks of election, anti-Catholic and labour disturbances.[2] It was evident that the governmental acquiescence in alternative ways of 'handling' protest, notably trade unions and political associations, and the development of a system of preventive policing had done what was required of them. Riots no longer performed a crucial role in the articulation of social and economic grievances.

One effect of this undoubted decline of social protest from the mid-nineteenth century has been that historians have neglected the isolated outbreaks of riot in the late Victorian period.[3] The present study of the riots against the Salvation Army, between 1878 and 1890, is intended partially to correct that neglect. It alters in no way the overall view of the depleted role of social protest: indeed, it sustains the argument that riots in this period posed no substantial threat to the social order. But the riots of the late Victorian period can tell us a great deal about legal authority, and the use of discretionary legal powers — in this instance, by the local authorities of the smaller provincial towns of the southern counties. Previous references to the Salvation Army riots have come from the hands of criminal lawyers, but have said nothing about the administration of the law by local magistrates, even though the majority of offences relating to public order were tried summarily. Instead, the emphasis has been on the Queens Bench judgements (regarding the law of public meeting and processioning) which have formed precedents in the warehouse of case law.[4] If much greater generosity is shown to the historical context in which the Salvation Army riots occurred, it becomes possible to reach behind these abstract legal decisions to the husbandry of the law by the local authorities. This examination reveals, above all, the unreality of the venerable notion of 'good law' which is seen as wholly autonomous in relation to human interests, and entirely independent of all social agencies.

---

1   See G. Stedman Jones, *Outcast London* (Oxford, 1971), chap. XVI. For an estimate of the middle-class perspective on the urban 'dangerous classes' and the threat of social disturbance, over the longer period from 1840-90, see V. Bailey, 'The Dangerous Classes in Late Victorian England' (Univ. of Warwick, PhD thesis, 1975), chap. V.

2   See J. P. D. Dunbabin, *Rural Discontent in Nineteenth-Century Britain* (London, 1974), chaps. IX, X, XII and XIII. For references to election and anti-Catholic riots in the late Victorian period, see V. Bailey, op.cit., chap. III. For labour riots, see e.g., HO 144/73872 (Lancs. cotton riots, 1878); HO 144/X41472 (Hull dock riots, 1893).

3   However, see Dr Richter, 'The Role of Mob Riot in Victorian Elections, 1865-1885', *Victorian Studies*, vol.15 (1971), pp. 19-28; R. Price, *An Imperial War and the British Working Class* (London, 1972), chap. IV.

4   See D. G. T. Williams, *Keeping the Peace* (London, 1967), chap. II.

II

The Christian faith has often confronted hostility, 'mobbing' and violent persecution. Opposition to an alien faith affected the growth and recruitment of early Methodism, Primitive Methodism and the Bible Christians. Persecution only strengthened the incipient movements. Anti-Methodist mobs were confirmation that at least the religious message was not ignored, and that the breakaway sect was reaching the large section of the ungodly who were excluded 'by the increasing respectability' of the established congregations.[5] Formed in 1878, the Salvation Army similarly provoked physical opposition from organised 'Skeleton Armies' who tried to drive it out of the towns, just as protestant 'mobs' evicted newly established Catholic missions.[6] The attitude of the Salvationists to the 'Skeleton Armies' was inevitably ambiguous. The 'Skeletons' were their harshest critics, but also testimony that the missionaries were reaching the 'social residuum'. 'It was very hard', said Mrs Booth, 'when the members of the Army were facing these dangerous classes. They had no other motive but to save them.'[7]

The earliest incidents which revealed an organised resistance to the Salvation Army were in East London. In the summer of 1880 'Captain' Payne of the Whitechapel corps told the *War Cry* of an opposition army entitled, 'The unconverted Salvation Army', which held open-air meetings and processions in imitation. But the 'real, original, first skeleton army', according to George Railton (first Commissioner of the Salvation Army) was organised in Weston-super-Mare (Somerset) in 1881.[8] As a term, 'Skeleton Army' was quickly taken up and used in other towns where the Salvationists were attacked.[9] Not all of the incidents in which the term was used, however, involved an organised 'Skeleton Army'. In Sheffield in January 1882 the Salvationists were attacked by irregular crowds of working men.[10] More strictly, the 'Skeleton Armies' were a social phenomenon of the Southern and Home Counties. The term itself seems to have derived from groups like the 'Skull and Crossbones Boys', organisations which celebrated Guy Fawkes' night.[11] Recruits came mainly from the working-class quarters of towns; predominantly young labourers, shop assistants or semi-skilled workers.[12] In most towns the public houses had a hand in the recruitment. Surrounding villages often contributed to the opposition army, as in Honiton (Devon) in 1882. Occasionally, 'Skeleton Armies' supported each other,

5   See J. Walsh, 'Methodism and the mob in the eighteenth century', in *Studies in Church History*, no. 8, eds. G. J. Cuming and D. Baker (Cambridge, 1972), pp. 213-27.

6   See J. F. Ede, *History of Wednesbury* (Wednesbury, 1962}, p. 318.

7   *Daily Telegraph*, 23 April 1883, p. 3.

8   R. Sandall and A. R. Wiggins, *The History of the Salvation Army* (London, 1950), vol.II, pp. 194-5; *The Times*, 15 Nov. 1881, p. 10.

9   e.g., in Exeter: *The Times*, 21 Oct. 1881.

10   *The Times*, 17 Jan. 1882, p. 6.

11   *Worthing Gazette*, 17 July 1884. Cf. E. Rowan, *Wilson Carlile and the Church Army*, 3rd edn. (London, 1928), pp. 66-7. The latest known reference to a 'Skeleton Army' was in 1893 in Egham, Surrey: 4 *Hansard* 17, 21 Sept. 1893, col. 1780.

12   The occupational data is drawn from press reports of court cases, mainly of rioters in Basingstoke (1881) and Worthing (1884).

as between towns along the Sussex coast in 1884.[13] The 'Skeletons' often wore elaborate costumes, and their processions were executed with care, incorporating parodied elements of the Salvationist parades. Through subscriptions from publicans, beersellers and other tradesmen, the 'Skeleton Armies' became a well-organised secular imitation, and a unique instrument of social pressure.[14]

The 'Skeleton Armies' used a variety of tactics to intimidate the preachers. In Folkestone (Kent) as the Salvation Army came out of its barracks, seven hundred 'roughs' formed up across the street, 'moving as slowly as it was possible for them to do without stopping altogether'. At Basingstoke 'rough music' was played alongside the Salvationist processions. The borough magistrates believed the aim was, 'by marching in front and at the sides of the [Salvation] Army, making discordant noises, beating old kettles, trays, etc., and blowing horns, to bring that body into odium and disrepute'.[15] Most commonly, the 'Skeletons' indulged in rough 'horse-play', hustling the preachers as they marched through the streets, pelting them with lime dust and refuse. At times, brutal assaults were inflicted on the 'soldiers',[16] but the intimidation was meant to insult more than injure. In 1886, the 'Hallelujah Lasses' visited Ryde (Isle of Wight) where 'liquid manure and sewer contents were freely thrown at them'. At Honiton when the Salvationists left a prayer meeting, they were showered with turnips; and the female evangelists 'not only had their clothes smeared with cow dung but their faces covered with mud'. In St Albans (Herts) 'officers' were ducked in a water-trough. In Eastbourne (Sussex) the Salvationists had bullocks driven into their procession, and they were also nearly forced into the sea by a crowd.[17] The 'Skeleton Armies' were artists in devising intimidating and humiliating sanctions, emphatically telling the Salvation Army to take its religious excesses out of the borough.

Salvation Army riots affected at least sixty towns and cities between 1878 and 1891. There was a rough correspondence in time between the direction of Salvation Army expansion and the riots.[18] North and North-western England, the Midlands and South Wales experienced riots between 1879 and 1882. There were disturbances in the Home Counties, Hampshire, Wiltshire, Somerset and Devon between 1881 and 1883; whilst the Southern counties of Sussex and Kent were affected between 1883 and 1885. Most of the riots, approximately one half, occurred in the years of greatest growth of the Salvation Army: 1882 and 1883. In relation to the distribution of 'Army' corps, the riots were over-represented in southern England. Disturbances broke out in Basingstoke (Hants, 1881); Salisbury (Wilts, 1881);

---

13 Honiton: HO 45/A2241S/5; *Sussex Coast Mercury*, 27 Sept. 1884, p. 4.

14 Honiton: HO 45/A22415/10; R. Sandall, op.cit., II, p. 193.

15 H. Castle, 16 April 1883: HO 45/A23941/5: Return containing Copies of any Correspondence which has passed between the Home Office and the Local Authorities of Basingstoke or other Places, with reference to the Suppression of Disturbances, *PP*, 1882 (Cd. 132), vol. 54, p.17 at pp. 29-30.

16 Folkestone, Jan. 1883: HO 45/A23941/3.

17 *Ryde and Isle of Wight News*, 24 Sept. 1886; Honiton: Dec. 1882; HO 45/A22415/4; St Albans: *Pall Mall Gazette*, 4 June 1888; Eastbourne, 1891: HO 144/X32743.

18 The Salvation Army's development is examined in C. Ward, 'The Social Sources of the Salvation Army 1865-1890' (Univ. of London, M Phil thesis, 1970), chap. IV.

Exeter and Honiton (Devon, 1881-2); Poole (Dorset, 1882); Weston-super-Mare and Yeovil (Somerset, 1882); Guildford (Surrey, 1882); Maidstone, Folkestone and Gravesend (Kent, 1883); and Worthing and Hastings (Sussex, 1884). In contrast, the Midlands, Yorkshire, Northumberland and Lancashire were much less affected by the disturbances.[19] A variety of urban environments experienced riots, but one half of the outbreaks occurred in towns of between 3,000 and 20,000 population: in seaside resort towns like Worthing, Ryde and Weston-super-Mare; in declining manufacturing towns like Honiton and Frome; and in old provincial capitals like Salisbury.[20]

Salvationist riots did break out in larger towns above 50,000 population, in industrial cities like Sheffield (Yorks, 1881), Oldham (Lancs, 1882) and Birkenhead (Cheshire, 1882), and in some regions of London (between 1879 and 1883).[21] But in absolute numbers the riots were a product of small and medium-sized towns, especially in the South. Even in the 1880s, these towns were a vital proportion of urban England, and only gradually adjusting to nineteenth-century patterns of industrial and urban expansion.[22] Interpretation of the disturbances must especially admit such townships, where a large number of Salvation Army riots took place, and where, significantly, the legal authorities were implicated in the religious disorder.

There follows an examination of the different forms the impetus to riot could take — the conduct of the brewery trade; popular resentment against the social content of Salvationism; and community disapproval of an organisation extraneous to the local society. This assessment has the virtue of depicting the setting in which the legal authorities of the provincial southern towns acted. But it is useful, first, to highlight those features of the Salvation Army which assist in elucidating the intense opposition which emerged in these towns.

III

The Salvation Army was one variant of late Methodist revivalism. As with earlier schisms, there had been a charismatic preacher straining under the old discipline, eager to return to the outcast and their purity of heart. William Booth had originally intended creating a 'bridge' between the 'unchurched' and

---

19 There were few disturbances, and no organised 'Skeleton Armies' in strong Nonconformist areas like the Black Country or West Yorks: see *The Advertiser* (South Staffs), 23 Aug. 1884, p. 4. I am indebted to Ms Sheila Bailey of the University College of Swansea for the information on the Black Country.

20 Additionally, one fifth of the riots occurred in urban districts of 20,000-50,000 population, e.g. Exeter, Hastings, Eastbourne, Maidstone and Reading.

21 In London, the major disturbances took place in Hounslow, Walworth, Clapham, Stoke Newington and in the Whitechapel and City Roads: MEPO 2/168; Metropolitan Board of Works Papers, MBW 1023.

22 As a percentage of total population in 1891, urban sanitary districts of under 20,000 population contributed 26.3 per cent: S. J. Low 'The Rise of the Suburbs', *Contemporary Review*, 60 (Oct. 1891), p. 548.

the nonconformist Church, but this adjusted to the formation of a separate religious organisation.[23] To attract what Booth termed the 'submerged tenth', the Nonconformists were too conventional. His work was a continuous protest against the religious sects which remained remote from the lives of the poor, and which stressed man's intellect above his soul.

Salvationism was defined by the emphasis upon a personal relationship with a personal God; and by an intense congregational participation in the service. There was no intellectualism and little theology. Nor was there confirmation, communion or other festivals, preparatory to salvation. The sacraments and the implication of a priesthood were thought to interfere with the essential transition from 'sinner' to 'saved'. The all-important theological tenet of Salvationism was complete faith in the atoning work of Christ, a faith which would lead to conversion, to an instant flight from the terror of hell to the assurance of heaven. In their meetings emotional appeals were repeatedly made for an immediate 'Closing with Christ'. In the 'closing' appeared the intense fervour characteristic of revivalist sessions.[24] Following conversion, the Salvationist dedicated himself to the spiritual welfare of other sinners. He was asked to adapt his religious message to the requirements of his own deprived inheritance; to call upon his own personal experience rather than upon authorised or established learning. He was thrust forward to testify to the effects of salvation in his indigenous language and style. The public confessional arrayed 'Blood Washed Colliers' and 'Hallelujah fishmongers' with the 'Milkman who has not watered his milk since he was saved'. The Army's success, albeit limited, was due to this employment of all converts in the subsequent work, and to the recognition of the value of personal testimony presented on a popular cultural level, in vivacious language 'understanded of the people'.[25] Essential ingredients of any popular religion thus lay at the centre of Salvationism: the interleaving of religious and vernacular effect, and a trust in the flexible, anarchic quality of revivalist meetings.

In 1878 the Christian Mission transformed itself into the 'Salvation Army', with a centralised system of organisation and government, and with the full 'military' trappings of uniforms, bands and official titles.[26] The application of this military form to the 'Army's' evangelistic work took place amid a wave of imperialist feeling at the time of the Russian-Turkish war; and it was an opportunist extension of this mood.[27] As befitted an 'Army' of Christian Soldiers, it concentrated on the 'war' to be waged against the

---

23 I am not attempting, here, to provide a full assessment of the Salvation Army as a religious and social organisation. For the detailed history of the movement, there is the Army's official history by R. Sandall and A. R. Wiggins, *The History of the Salvation Army*, 4 vols. (London, 1947-65). These volumes are no substitute, however, for the required work of historical sociology. The best historical critique of the Army is K. S. Inglis, *Churches and the Working Classes in Victorian England* (London, 1963), chap. V. See also, R. Robertson, 'The Salvation Army; the Persistence of Sectarianism', in *Patterns of Sectarianism*, ed. B. R. Wilson (London, 1967), pp. 49-105.

24 See Bramwell Booth, 'Salvation Army', in *Encyclopaedia of Religion and Ethics*, XI, ed. J. Hastings (Edinburgh, 2nd impress., 1934), p. 157; R.Robertson, op.cit., pp. 58-68.

25 Rev. Randall Davidson, *The Times*, 29 June 1882, p. 5. Cf. G. B. Shaw, *Major Barbara* (London, 1958), p. 89.

26 See *The Doctrines and Discipline of the Salvation Army* (London, 1881), section 29; R. Sandall, op.cit., II, chaps. VI-XVII. Cf. O. Anderson, 'The Growth of Christian Militarism in Mid-Victorian Britain', *English Historical Review*, vol. 86 (1971), pp. 66-7.

27 See R. Sandall, op.cit., I, pp. 226, 285-7; H. Cunningham, 'Jingoism in 1877-78', *Victorian Studies*, XIV (1971), pp. 429-53.

'dangerous classes' of urban society — 'men as essentially heathen', declared Mrs Booth, 'as any in the centre of Africa'.[28] Salvationist publications emphasised that the ruffianism met by the 'soldiers' and 'officers' indicated the existence of an outlying 'continent' of evil, where irreligious masses were drowning in a sea of drunkenness and crime. It was a national benefit to civilise such people, 'to preserve the country from mob-violence and revolution'.[29] It all represented a belief that along with missionary activity in the outskirts of the Empire (and the Salvation Army became the most advanced exponent of religious colonisation), the civilising mission against all sinners had also to be carried on at home. As a great empire required an imperial race, so a Christian empire required a Christian populace.[30]

The adjustment of the Salvation Army's organisation and style to the military form enhanced the dichotomy of piety and aggression which distinguished its work. A spiritual offensive was to be waged against the 'Devil's Kingdom' — that great mass of urban demoralised held captive by the publican, the brewer and other satanic subordinates. A comprehensive code of directions was quickly available to field officers on how to bombard, capture and hold fresh territory.[31] It was recommended that the Army's 'invasion' of new towns and cities be publicised in the most elaborate and antagonistic manner, luridly dramatised as an imminent contest between Sin and Redemption.[32] This militant evangelism was to rely on regular street meetings and processions to reach the depressed strata of urban districts. A procession through the working-class streets of the town and an open-air meeting was held on most work-day evenings, varied by lunchtime meetings at the gates of factories and workshops. On Sundays, when the urban poor were at their leisure, the Salvationists went into the streets on two or even three separate occasions, singing hymns adapted for their audience — 'Out of the Gutter we pick them up' — led by officers in red guernseys ornamented with religious texts. 'Open-airs' always ended with an invitation to the audience to return to the barracks for an indoor service. Alternatively, the procession alone was used as a 'beat-up' for recruits, collecting a crowd of people 'with whom', the Queen's Bench judges were told, 'attended by much shouting and singing, uproar and noise, they eventually return to the hall, where a meeting is then held'.[33]

The overall aim was not merely to hold a temporary mission, or conduct a few revival services. 'We desire', proclaimed a Salvationist pamphlet, 'to make a permanent lodgement, and to raise up a force

---

28 *The Times*, 26 May 1880, p. 7.

29 20 Oct. 1881, in HO 45/A9228/3. See also, Catherine Booth, *Aggressive Christianity* (London, 1880), pp. 11-12; Catherine Booth, *The Salvation Army in relation to the Church and State* (London, 1883), pp. 1-4.

30 A few years later, in its elaborate scheme of farm and overseas colonies, the Salvation Army became an important constituent of the social-imperial movement: W. Booth, *In Darkest England and the Way Out* (London, 1890), *passim*; J. Harris, *Unemployment and Politics. A Study in English Social Policy 1886-1914* (Oxford, 1972), pp. 124-35.

31 *Orders and Regulations for field Officers of the Salvation Army* (London, 1886; first published in 1878), p. 302.

32 R. Sandall, op.cit., II, Appendix I, pp. 326-7.

33 *Beatty V. Gillbanks*, *The Times*, 14 June 1882, p. 4. See also, MEPO 2/168; Charles Booth, *Life and Labour of the People in London*, 3rd series (London, 1903), Vol. 7, p. 328.

that shall continue the war… To make a raid, and capture a few prisoners, is a far less difficult task than the establishment and maintenance of a fort in the enemy's territory.'[34] This required carrying an aggressive Christianity into the slums and working-class quarters of towns. In this drive to become, in Booth's phrase, 'a great Hallelujah press-gang', opposition was inevitably provoked. The 'Army' gave notice to the Gravesend police in October 1884 that they would 'enter and occupy'. *The Times* observed: 'A portion of the inhabitants have intimated their intention of banding themselves together to oppose the invasion.'[35]

IV

'My work', William Booth promised, 'is to make war on the hosts that keep the underworld submerged.'[36] The Salvation Army's militant, evangelistic campaign centred particularly on the cultural distractions to a truly religious life. All symbols of spiritual degeneration — theatres, boxing booths, pubs and music halls — were attacked in print and on the platform. They were also 'invaded', like St Giles' Fair in Oxford, the racecourse at Northampton, or the new havens of cheap recreation, the seaside resort towns, where the entertainments of the music hall were repeated on the seashore.[37] General Booth was convinced that the 'Worthings' and 'Hastings' contained their own social residuum, contaminated by drink and the popular amusements, and were the weekend nurseries of London's thriftless pauperism. He was determined that the Salvation Army should pit its own literature, songs and recreations against the attractions of the tavern and music hall. Accordingly, the Salvationists sang outside public houses; touted the *War Cry* around tap rooms and music halls; and arranged religious 'free-and-easies'. Poverty, they largely attributed to drunkenness; spiritual and moral weakness, they laid at the door of the public house. They preached total abstinence from alcohol, and took as a major test of their success (celebrated in the reports sent into the *War Cry* each week) the estimated decline in public house patronage.[38] In numerous towns, theatres or halls of entertainment were purchased, and loudly proclaimed as a victory for Salvationism. In London the best-known attack on popular amusements took place around the Eagle Tavern in City Road, with its Grecian theatre and dancing gardens.[39] A moral imperialism looked to colonise spaces in which 'savage' entertainments were performed. In all, the Salvationists reinforced the Nonconformist 'social gospel' which traced human evils to drink, gambling

---

34   *All About the Salvation Army* (London, 1882), p. 25.

35   *The Times*, 15 May 1882, p. 8.

36   Quoted in A. G. Gardiner, *Prophets, Priests and Kings* (London, 1914), p. 192.

37   See S. Alexander, *St Giles Fair, 1830-1914* (Oxford, 1970), p. 30; *The Times*, 19 Nov. 1886, p. 5.

38   *Daily Telegraph*, 31 Oct. 1881, p. 2; H. S. Hume, *The Temperance Movement and the Salvation Army* (London, 1883), *passim*.

39   *The Times*, 30 June 1882, p. 10; *Daily Chronicle*, 13 Aug. 1882. When the 'Army' took possession of the Eagle Tavern, they were mobbed by large crowds in the surrounding streets: *The Times*, 23 Sept. 1882, p. 5.

and low music halls.[40]

This determined onslaught against public houses and forms of cheap entertainment like the music hall (commonly extensions of public houses), led to a recreational or cultural rivalry between the representatives of the brewery trade and the Salvation Army. Publicans immediately set about remunerating local 'roughs' for attacking the Salvationist processions. No explanation of the anti-Salvationist 'mobbing' was more commonly endorsed than the financing of 'Skeleton Armies' through the public houses.

The Salvation Army always held the 'trade' responsible for the organised opposition. A memorandum was prepared for the Home Secretary in 1881 in which it was claimed that

> …in nearly every town where there has been any opposition we have been able to trace it more or less, to the direct instigation, and often open leadership of either individual Brewers or Publicans, or their *employes* [sic].
>
> The plan adopted is by treating and otherwise inciting gangs of roughs… to hustle and pelt, and mob the people.[41]

The document was based on the reports sent into 'Army' headquarters by 'officers' in the field. It was validated by a good deal more evidence in the next few years. Local Salvationists accused the 'trade' of instigating riots in Chester, Salisbury, Stamford, Maidstone, Gravesend, Honiton, Basingstoke, Luton and Eastbourne.[42] In Honiton, judging from court depositions, the publicans and leading shopkeepers were employing men from miles around. George Wood (a local farmer, who had allowed the Salvationists to meet in his cottage in 1882) deposed that the 'Skeleton Army' was 'supported strongly by the publicans. They have issued papers ridiculing the Salvation Army and by their papers as well as by words declare their intention of driving the Salvation Army from Honiton.'[43] It was not only the Salvationists and their sympathisers who blamed the 'trade' for the disturbances. The Basingstoke magistrates explained to the Home Secretary that once the Salvationists began to empty the public houses and diminish drunkenness, 'roughs' from the town and surrounding villages were organised through the pubs into a 'Skeleton Army', and paid by the main brewers in the town.[44]

It is unlikely that even the Salvationists anticipated the degree to which the brewers and publicans would go to stifle their campaign. The 'trade', however, was well-versed in organising intimidation,

---

40   See B. Harrison, *Drink and the Victorians* (London, 1971), p. 333.

41   Enclosed in HO 45/A2886/13. And see Bramwell Booth, *Echoes and Memories* (London, 1925), pp. 28-9.

42   *Chester Chronicle*, 1 April 1882, p. 6; Salisbury, 1881: HO 45/A1775/ 2; Gravesend, 1884: HO 45/A32518/4; Honiton, 1883: HO 45/A22415/3; Basingstoke, 1881: HO 45/A2886/1; Luton, 1883: HO 45/A30742/1; Eastbourne, 1891: HO 144/X32743/61. London publicans were also said to be financing the 'Skeleton Army' in Whitechapel (1879) and in City Road (1883): *Saturday Review*, 5 July 1879; HO 45/A9275/26 (Jan. 1883).

43   HO 45/A22415/3. The paper referred to was a publication entitled 'The Skeleton', circulated in Honiton.

44   18 Aug. 1881: *PP* 1882, vol. 54, p. 17 at pp. 29-30; *Hants. and Berks. Gazette*, 24 Sept. 1881; HO 45/A2886/23. Cf., Gravesend, 1883: HO 45/A32518/1.

whether against harmful licensing legislation or on behalf of political patrons in election campaigns.[45] In the early 1880s the brewers mobilised their lower-class 'rowdies' to silence a religion which challenged their profits and their prestige.

Like other temperance reformers, the Salvation Army sought not only to free the 'unchurched' from the grips of the publican, but also to modify indigenous working-class mores. Implicit in the Salvationist crusade against the public houses and music halls was an arrogant attack on popular leisure habits and life-styles. The opposition to the Salvation Army included, in consequence, the so-called 'rough' working class who were determined to defend their entertainments, and who were hostile to the self-righteous cult of respectability.[46]

Contempt for particular working-class mores and behaviour patterns was an integral facet of the Salvationist creed. Dramatic conversions were claimed, conversions which were said to involve an instant switch in lifestyle from drunkard to preacher, and occasion an improvement in work and self-discipline. Abstention from working-class sports and pastimes, from theatre entertainment, and from drinking, swearing and smoking were all announced to be the results of 'finding the Lord'. In Sheffield there was the 'man who when converted hardly knew himself'.[47] The penitent seat, itself, placed in front of the platform, not only tested the sincerity of the 'calling', but also (as Bramwell Booth recognised) 'is conspicuous enough to register a distinct break in a man's life'.[48] Outspoken confession on the public platform, before other companions, was arranged to serve the same purpose. The major emphasis of Salvationism was on moral improvement, but the effects of being 'born again' were expected to leaven social as well as moral careers. Salvationists were not so conscious of the need to be industrious and to progress as previous generations of Methodists had been, but the conversion was promised to lead, in every case, to a 'self help' which offset poverty and engendered social respectability.[49]

No sooner was a good convert found than he was turned into a recruiting officer and sent into his native street to drum up fresh recruits. At open-air meetings, the new moral and social outlook was conceitedly advanced. In an unerring evocation of the earnest convert in close association with old friends, Wiliiam Pett-Ridge in *Mord Em'ly* had Miss Gilliken testify to her recent criminal past:

> Many a time 'ave I with my ongodly companions, roamed about these streets, seeking what I might devour ... thank the Lord, I 'ave been washed whiter than SNOW, and purified of my sins. . . and I do so

---

45 See B. Harrison, op.cit., p. 276; B. L. Crapster, '"Our Trade, Our Politics". A Study of the Political Activity of the British Liquor industry, 1868-1910' (Univ. of Harvard, PhD thesis, 1949). chap. III.

46 For the traditional attack by social or religious philanthropists on popular culture and life styles, see R. W. Malcolmson, *Popular Recreations in English Society 1700-1850* (Cambridge, 1973), pp. l00-7; I. Bradley, *The Call to Seriousness — the Evangelical Impact on the Victorians* (London, 1976), chap. V.

47 *The Times*, 5 April 1882, p. 8.

48 B. Booth, 'Salvation Army', in J, Hastings, op.cit.

49 *The Salvation Army as a Money-Making Concern* (London, 1881).

want all you other sinful people to come and do likewise and not to 'old back, becos' you think you're too black, or too wicked, or too sinful; for b'lieve me, my friends, BAD as you may be, and no doubt are...[50]

It was this self-righteous unction, the arrogation of a new-found respectability which provoked stern resistance from the working-class communities which the Salvationists persistently entered. Many Salvationists were 'tin kettled' and otherwise intimidated by workmates alarmed at their 'going over'. Salvationist hymns and proceedings were ridiculed, according to Charles Booth, the social investigator, at public houses and in the music halls. And in London and other towns defensive barriers were erected at the ends of working-class streets to prevent the Salvationists' entry.[51]

An articulate working-class response to the Salvation Army was a feature of urban areas like London where working people, impervious to the evangelical crusade, clung to fixed drinking habits and leisure patterns.[52] Yet I would argue that working-class 'mobbing' of the Salvationists was most typical of the small southern towns. In these urban areas there was no radical working-class culture which had strongly adopted certain values of social respectability. This description would better fit the politically conscious strongholds of Lancashire and the West Riding, which were resistant to the Salvation Army, and which also showed few disturbances. Instead, there was an 'old culture' which in some ways was less inhibited and 'non-respectable', rudely rejecting the values of temperance and respectability, but which was equally often deferential and jingoist. It is beyond the scope of this essay, but the plebeian response to the Salvation Army reveals, at least in part, a confrontation *within* working-class culture.[53]

The Chief Constable of West Sussex, in correspondence with William Booth in 1884, admitted that, besides the opposition from 'the rougher portion of the inhabitants', the Worthing tradesmen and residents objected to the disruption of 'the customary quiet of the town'. The result was that 'the persons who form the 'Skeleton Army' have received and do receive considerable encouragement from those in a higher social position'.[54] In other middle-class watering places the complicity of more senior townsmen in the opposition to the Salvation Army was based on the anxiety that noisy bands and processions would ruin the fashionable season.[55] But something larger was involved than the reputations

50 W. Pett-Ridge, *Mord Em'ly* (London, 1898), pp. 135-6.

51 *The Salvation War* (London, 1883), p. 35; C. Booth, op.cit., VII, p. 325; Folkestone: HO 45/A23941/3. Street barriers were put up in Birkenhead: *Birkenhead and Cheshire Advertiser*, 28 Oct. 1882; and Hounslow: *The Times*, 25 Sept. 1884. And for contemporary reference to a conflict between the 'rough' and 'respectable' working class, see *Pall Mall Gazette*, 29 March 1881, p. 3; *Saturday Review*, 20 Oct. 1883; *The Month*, vol. 44 (1882), p. 480.

52 Cf. G. Stedman Jones, 'Working-Class Culture and Working-Class Politics in London, 1870-1900; Notes on the Remaking of a Working Class', *Journal of Social History*, VII, (Summer, 1974), pp. 472-9 and 491.

53 Working-class opposition to the Salvation Army occasionally derived from religious sentiment, especially in Lancs. and Cheshire. Irish Catholics were responsible for riots in Bolton, 1882: H. Begbie, *The Life of General William Booth* (London, 1920), II, p. 5; Chester, 1882: *Chester Chronicle*, 1 April 1882; Birkenhead, 1883: *Birkenhead and Cheshire Advertiser*, 6 Jan. 1883; and Tredegar, 1882: HO 144/A18355/27.

54 11 Aug. 1884: HO 45/X2676/12.

55 May 1883, Folkestone: HO 45/A23941/9.

of seaside resorts. Behind the 'Skeleton Armies' there was a wider community sanction against an intruding religious organisation which disturbed customary religious and social patterns. In safely Conservative boroughs like Guildford and Eastbourne, in declining towns like Honiton and Frome, or in cathedral towns like Salisbury and Exeter, the pattern of social relationships retained a deferential character. Social ties sustained local rather than national loyalties. It was in such towns, portrayed so authentically by Robert Tressell in his 'Mugsborough' (based on Hastings), that the Salvation Army's entrance could release a wider outbreak of enraged traditionalism.[56]

Salvationist street processions and open-air meetings were thought to coarsen religion, and offended respectable townsmen.[57] Community hostility was intensified by stories of strange ceremonials and revivalist excesses inside the Salvationist barracks. Sexual rumours were rife, sustained by the evening revivalist meetings, and the ritual, 'Creeping for Jesus' when the lights were turned low and kneeling men and women groped with their hands in the darkness.[58] Imagination and guilt fed the community's fears for established morality. The Salvationists also intensified a number of fundamental strains in the local society. They challenged traditional views of the woman's role in the church and family by refusing distinctions in rank, authority and duty between men and women preachers. In their campaign to forge a new cultural identity for the young, they defied parental authority.[59] Work relationships in the local society were also strained when employees were sent packing for joining the Salvationist processions. Tradesmen who supported the 'Army' were boycotted and put out of business.[60] Religious ill-feeling could develop, as in Basingstoke in 1881 when church and chapel took opposing sides. In other towns, the Salvationists rekindled the political rivalry between Tory and Liberal factions, an integral facet of which could be the respective allegiance to the drink trade and the temperance cause.[61] In all, there was the realistic anxiety that the Salvationists would divide families and the community.

Many of the 'Skeleton Armies' were embodiments of these fears of change and disruption in the traditional structure and control of the community.[62] Once established, social legitimacy was imparted to the 'Skeleton Army' in a number of ways. Pulpit speeches gave clerical sanction to mob violence in Basingstoke (1881) and in Eastbourne (1892). Local newspapers were believed to have incited

---

56   See H. Pelling, *Social Geography of British Elections 1885-1900* (London, 1967), pp. 85-6, 172; R. Tressell, *The Ragged Trousered Philanthropist* (London, 1968; first published 1914), *passim*.

57   Folkestone, Jan. 1883: HO 45/A23941/1.

58   H. Begbie, op.cit., II, p. 17.

59   See O. Anderson, 'Women Preachers in Mid-Victorian Britain: Some reflexions on Feminism, Popular Religion and Social Change', *Historical Journal*, XII (1969), pp. 467-84; H. Begbie, op.cit., I, p. 479; Anon., *The Salvation Army: Is it a Good or an Evil? The Question Calmly Considered* (London, 1882), p. 8.

60   Basingstoke: *Hants. and Berks. Gazette*, 23 April 1881, p. 5; Honiton, Nov. 1882: HO 45/A22415/1; Whitchurch, 1888: HO 45/X24164/21; Eastbourne, 1891: HO 144/X32743/123.

61   *PP*, 1882, vol. 54, p. 17 at pp. 27-29; HO 45/A2886/16; Guildford, 1882: HO 45/A19890/8.

62   Guildford, Sept. 1882: HO 45/A19890/4. Cf., Salisbury, 1881: HO 45/A1775/4. Wealthier inhabitants sometimes worked vicariously through the publicans, as at Honiton: HO 45/A22415/5.

disturbances in Gravesend (1883) and Worthing (1884). Special constables recruited from the tradesmen of Basingstoke refused to act against a 'Skeleton Army' which took the Union Jack as its colours.[63] If the 'Skeletons' were encouraged to evict the Salvation Army, they were also directed against those people in the community who welcomed or assisted the 'Army'.[64]

Whilst working men and 'roughs' constituted the 'Skeleton Armies', the wider community approved of them. The 'Skeletons' assisted the collective defence against anticipated religious and social change. In these towns there was a strong 'parochial consciousness', defined by a network of personal relations, and by a physically limited neighbourhood. It produced an insularity which inspired a xenophobic outburst against as well-defined a body of outsiders as the Salvation Army. In the anti-Salvationist riots in the southern towns there was a demonstration of fidelity to customary national values (which found another outlet for expression in the jingo riots against the pro-Boers at the end of the century).

In time, the Salvation Army was counted among the churches of most towns, and carried on its work without arousing physical opposition.[65] Its advance between 1878 and 1885, however, was met with sustained and organised 'mobbing', impeding, yet also firing its religious 'war' against the urban 'submerged'. The existence of fully-organised 'Skeleton Armies' in the provincial towns of the southern counties was, in part, an expression of the hostility of the brewery trade to an assault on popular entertainments which it provided. The opposition was also a lower-class reflex to an arrogant religiosity which lauded the social and moral values of 'respectability'. But these separate strands were often constituents of a larger community disquiet at the social and religious alterations which the 'Army' induced. It was in this context of the southern provincial town that the performance of the legal authorities was notoriously unsatisfactory. By May 1882 it led John Bright to regret 'the foolish and unjust magistrates to whom in some districts the administration of the law is unfortunately committed'.[66]

V

A crucial dimension to the Salvation Army riots was the role of the authorities who were responsible for the maintenance of public order. From a large number of towns affected by riots, the Home Secretary received complaints about the reluctance of the police and the magistracy to act firmly against the 'mobbing'. Most criticism was levelled at the authorities of the small towns of the southern counties,

---

63 *Hants. and Berks. Gazette*, 17 Sept. 1881, p. 5; HO 144/X32743/121; HO 45/A32518/3; *Sussex Coast Mercury*, 20 Sept. 1884, p. 4; *Worthing Intelligencer*, 6 Sept. 1884. In Poole and Basingstoke (1881), imprisoned 'Skeletons' were escorted back into town by bands and a procession: HO 45/A2886/13.

64 Worthing, 1884: HO 45/X2676/21; Basingstoke: *Hants. and Berks. Gazette*, 18 June 1884, p. 5.

65 I have no strong explanation for the cessation of riots against the Salvation Army, except to suggest that familiarity bred indifference, and that the Army's adoption of social work from the mid-1880s attracted the support of the middle classes.

66 Quoted in R. Sandall, op.cit., II, p. 171.

where the religious disorder was most extensive.[67] In these provincial towns, law enforcement policy had the same character. The 'Skeleton Army' was officially endorsed in the hope that the Salvationists would tire of being rabbled; and more permanent prohibition of Salvationist meetings and processions was improvised through administrative action. Above all, the authorities seemed determined to curb the disorders without having either to repress the 'Skeleton Army' or to protect the Salvationists in their provocative missionary work.

Judicial and police behaviour in the towns of the southern counties clearly encouraged the mobbing of the Salvationists. Legitimacy was imparted to the 'Skeleton Armies' of Poole and Eastbourne by police court magistrates delivering public and abusive attacks on the beliefs and practices of the evangelists.[68] Magistrates at Worthing refused to issue summonses applied for by the Salvationists against members of the 'Skeleton Army', making comments, attested William Booth, 'calculated to encourage the mob, and to assure them of immunity from penal consequences'.[69] Well-publicised refusals by the Ryde and Salisbury magistrates to grant police protection to Salvationist processions similarly incited disturbances. In Exeter, Guildford, Gravesend and Folkestone, police constables openly refused to interfere to prevent the assaults, and declined to summons rioters whom they obviously recognised.[70] In Honiton at the end of 1882, the 'Skeleton Army' was even more evidently endorsed by the magistracy and police authority. After another day of disrupted meetings and processions in November, 'Captain' Lomas went to see Honiton's Mayor, an *ex officio* magistrate. The latter stated that 'he would not protect [the Salvationists] any more than he would the Skeleton Army'. Further, according to Lomas: 'He [the Mayor] said that it would be always like that while the Salvation Army remained, and he, with the Superintendent of Police would like to see us out of the town.' A week later, Lomas alleged in a sworn deposition that the ex-Mayor, also an *ex officio* magistrate, had recently informed the town council that 'if a hundred cases were brought before him by the Salvation Army he would dismiss them all'.[71] After court appearances in which the ex-Mayor deliberately refused to convict a number of rioters in spite of sufficient evidence, the Home Secretary notified the Lord Chancellor, who agreed that the Mayor and ex-Mayor were justly charged 'with having practically encouraged, and afforded impunity to these disturbances'.[72]

In many of the provincial towns where official licence was extended to the 'Skeleton Army', the legal authorities also looked to more effective administrative means of suppressing the outdoor work of the Salvationists. In the nineteenth century there was no nationwide statutory power to prohibit public

67   *The Times*, 4 Oct. 1883.

68   HO 45/A2886/13; HO 144/X32743/28.

69   16 July 1884: HO 45/X2676/1. Cf., Basingstoke, 2 April 1881: *PP* 1882, vol. 54, p. 17 at p. 25; Folkestone: HO 45/A23941/4.

70   *Ryde and Isle of Wight News*, 24 Sept. 1886; HO 45/A1775/6; HO 45/A18238/1; HO 45/A19890/1; HO 45/A32518,/3; HO 45/A23941/3.

71   27 Nov. 1882: HO 45/A22415/3.

72   28 Dec. 1882, Lord Selborne to Sir William Harcourt (Home Secretary): HO 45/A22415/8.

meetings and processions. There were, however, statutory enactments applicable to a large number of individual towns which could be adapted to allow the suppression of street meetings and processions.[73] In particular, there were borough bye-laws and provisions in Local Acts. In response to the disorders, numerous Watch Committees and Local Boards utilised the discretionary powers afforded by this array of local enactments.

At the beginning of the 1880s, however, borough authorities attempted first to impose a *common law* power of prohibition over processioning. If there were disturbances as a result of Salvation Army processions, magistrates simply announced that no more processions could be held because they would lead to breaches of the peace. The Salvation officers, if they persisted, were fined and imprisoned. In so far as the prohibitory proclamation was dependent on the threat of disorder, it even made possible the direct exploitation of the 'Skeleton Army' by the authorities. The magistrates of Basingstoke, William Booth claimed, were party to a conspiracy 'to encourage the mob in the creation of a state of things which can then be used as an excuse for attempting by law to stop our work in the streets'.[74] In March, 1881, when the 'Skeleton Army' assaulted a Sunday procession, the Mayor read the Riot Act, and called out a battery of artillery billeted in the town. In his report to the War Office, Major Curson maintained that, whilst met by large crowds in the streets, 'I did not see any rioting, and the mob seemed to me to be remarkably good tempered.' But the day's proceedings were to validate the proclamation, issued in April, which forbade the Salvation Army from holding processions or open-air meetings.[75]

In April, 1882, however, the Salvation Army succeeded in getting a high court judgement on the validity of these proclamations. At Weston-super-Mare, where the magistrates had likewise prohibited processioning, the Salvation Army officer refused to disperse his procession on the orders of the police, and submitted to arrest. The magistrates convicted him of unlawful assembly, and bound him over to keep the peace for twelve months. On appeal to the Divisional Court, this conviction was reversed, the court stating that no crime had been committed since the disturbances were caused by other people whom the 'Army' did not incite.[76] This decision, in *Beatty v. Gillbanks*, which effectively denied any nationwide common law power to prohibit processions, forced the Home Office to issue different directions to the magistracy.[77] By no means all local authorities acted in accordance with this advice. Guildford's Mayor told 'Captain' Bryan in September, 1882, that the bench had decided to give no police protection 'adding that he knew the Salvation Army had a legal right to procession in the streets, which they could exercise if they liked, but if they did so it would be on their own risk and

---

73   A fuller assessment of the law of public meeting and processioning is in D. G. T. Williams, *Keeping the Peace* (London, 1967), *passim*.

74   2 April 1881: HO 45/A2886/13.

75   *PP* 1882, vol. 54, p. 17 at pp. 19-21; HO 45/A2886/10.

76   *Beatty v. Gillbanks*, 1882, QBD, vol. 9, p. 308.

77   HO 45/A9275/17.

responsibility'.[78] Other authorities pressed the Home Secretary for amendments to the Town Police Clauses Act to give justices the general discretionary power to prohibit processions.[79] Nevertheless, after 1882, this avenue was largely abandoned, especially as subsequent legal judgements gave confirmation to *Beatty v. Gillbanks*.[80] Instead, the authorities turned to the remedies available through local enactments.

Between 1883 and 1891, bye-laws and Local Acts were used by a number of provincial authorities in an attempt to repress the outdoor work of the Salvation Army. In Ryde and Truro, bye-laws which prohibited singing and the playing of music, under certain conditions, were enforced by the authorities against the 'Army's' processions. To give body to the Ryde enactment, all police protection of street parades was withdrawn, and the Salvationists were left to the mercy of the 'Skeleton Army'.[81] At the end of 1884, when the Sussex watering places came under attack from the Salvation Army, a conference of coastal towns approved the inclusion of clauses prohibiting Sunday processions in the Local Acts of Hastings and Eastbourne.[82] In 1886, the Torquay authorities inserted a similar clause in their Improvement Act. This led to protracted struggles between the Salvationists and the local authorities in Torquay (1888) and Eastbourne (1891). For a period of two months in 1891, Eastbourne's Watch Committee prosecuted Sunday processionists; leading councillors called upon the 'Skeleton Army' to champion this administrative policy; whilst the magistrates refused to suppress the attacks made by the 'Skeleton Army' on the street processions and meetings.[83]

In conjunction with officially endorsed 'mobbing', then, a series of administrative powers was exploited by a large number of provincial authorities to put down the activities of the Salvation Army.[84] The 'Army' soon learned to expect and resist the authorities' opposition, the upshot being a fierce and varied legal battle during the 1880s in which the Salvationists earned a place alongside the Socialist groups as the defenders of the rights of processioning and meeting. Their struggle in the smaller provincial towns was the counterpart to the London fight to retain similar freedoms. But the struggle was not merely over the abstract legal rights of processioning and meeting, any more than was the fight in London in the mid-1880s. The provincial authorities were resisting a larger challenge to social order and to legal prestige, which requires closer assessment.

---

78   8 Sept. 1882: HO 45/A19890/4.

79   Worthing: HO 45/X2676/19; Folkestone: HO 45/A23941/2.

80   See *M'Clenaghan and others v. Waters*, *The Times*, 18 July 1882, p. 4; HO 45/A16004/8 (Whitchurch); *Stone's Justices Manual*, 25th edn. (London, 1889), p. 824; *Justice of the Peace*, vol. 48 (1884), p. 659.

81   HO 45/X4230/1; *R. v. Powell*, 1884, *Law Times*, vol. 51, p. 92.

82   *The Times*, 18 Nov. 1884, p. 10; G. F. Chambers, *Eastbourne Memories of the Victorian Period 1845-1901* (Eastbourne, 1910), pp. 209-10.

83   HO 45/X18313; HO 144/X32743; Eastbourne Improvement Act, 1885 (Prosecutions for Open-Air Services), *PP* 1892 (Cd. 103), vol. 65, p. 115.

84   Additionally, some authorities exploited the Highway Act (1835) to repress Salvationist street meetings — Stamford: HO 45 /A47490B; Whitchurch: HO 45/X24164.

VI

The particular character of the authorities' response to the disturbances was a result, in part, of magistrates joining, or being exhorted to join, with other businessmen and tradesmen to defend the special economic interests of the town. Official indulgence of 'mobbing', along with legal prevention of processioning, seemed directly related to the defence of the brewery trade in towns where the latter had representatives in authority.[85] In seaside towns, the authorities were more pressed to defend local interests in the tourist trade.[86] But the avoidance of damage to town economies was only part of the explanation. The authorities' actions were also determined by the difficulties of restoring public order once it was broken in these smaller provincial settings.

Small-town police forces were generally unprepared to deal with disturbances which raged around the street meetings and parades, held each evening and throughout the weekend.[87] Rather than overwork their police forces, or go to the expense and inconvenience of borrowing outside police or enrolling special constables, the authorities, in the first instance, often struck an informal bargain with the 'Skeleton Army' in the hope that the Salvationists would be forced by the 'mobbing' to restrict their work to indoor meetings.[88] For the same reason of maintaining public order, the authorities sought to prevent the Salvationists' outdoor work by taking premature administrative action against their meetings and processions. Fears that serious riots would result in Weston-super-Mare in March 1882, led the magistracy to prohibit the Salvationist processions.[89] A year later, at Folkestone, the authorities displayed a similar urgency to stop the disorders by acting against the Salvation Army. The clerk to the justices informed the Home Secretary that it was generally understood that 'if the Salvation Army will cease to parade the public streets the Skeleton Army will also discontinue their processions'. Therefore, despite the decision in *Beatty v. Gillbanks*, the clerk urged the government to give the justices discretionary power to prohibit processions.[90] In all, the authorities in many provincial towns agreed with the ex-Mayor at Honiton, who refused to act against the 'Skeleton Army', 'as he considered the Salvation Army were to blame and caused all the disturbances in the Town'.[91]

There was a more significant reason for the attitude and behaviour of the legal authorities to the Salvation Army. Salvationism challenged their social and legal influence. In its early years the Salvation Army must have appeared an awesome organisation: a body with effective national coordination, despatching, replacing and rearing disciplined cadres who spoke directly to the poor, who were

---

85   Basingstoke, 1881: HO 45/A2886/2.

86   Worthing: HO 45/X2676/1; Folkestone: HO 45/A23941/9.

87   Salisbury, July 1882: HO 45/A18238/5; Folkestone, Feb. 1883: HO 45/A23941/4.

88   Worthing: *Sussex Daily News*, 15 July 1884. Cf., Honiton, Nov. 1882: HO 45/A22415/2.

89   1 April 1882: HO 45/A15220/2.

90   Feb. to May 1883: HO 45/A23941/2-9.

91   HO 45/A22415/6.

unamenable to the local patterns of social discipline. Field officers stubbornly maintained their incessant missionary work in the streets, despite the disturbances it caused. They took unfavourable summary decisions to the higher courts; they refused to accept legal sanctions short of imprisonment.[92] Escorts were provided for convicted preachers on their way to prison; prisoners were welcomed home by a band and procession. And magisterial policy was denounced at indoor meetings and by way of public demonstrations.[93]

Moreover, just as the Salvation Army splintered religious and political communities, they could also divide, and thereby undermine the authorities in their administration of discretionary legal power. At Basingstoke in 1881, the magistrates initially employed both the 'Skeleton Army' and prohibitory proclamation to repress the Salvationists. But after the appointment of new justices to the bench, the Mayor lost control of magisterial policy. Thereafter, different policies were enforced by the Mayor and Watch Committee (supported by two more magistrates) on the one hand, and the rest of the bench on the other. Whilst the Mayor tried to put down the 'Army's' processions, the bench defended the preachers by imprisoning members of the 'Skeleton Army'. For this firmness, the pro-Salvationist magistrates were escorted to and from the police court by 'Skeletons' playing 'rough music'.[94] Again in February 1882, when riots recurred, the main bloc of magistrates used the county police to protect the Salvation Army; the Mayor and Watch Committee reissued the proclamation banning Salvationist processions.[95] This occasion illustrates how the Salvation Army's entrance into one provincial community led by stages from officially endorsed 'mobbing' and administrative prohibition of the Salvationist processions, to public dissension between the administrative and judicial arms of the law. At the same time as the Salvation Army uncovered latent religious and political rivalries, it provoked an associated conflict among the Basingstoke authorities, which, in turn, engendered an inconsistent policy of law enforcement. As in many other towns, the Salvation Army's intransigence in the recruitment of the poor depreciated the authority and standing of the law's representatives.

'The special sphere for the Salvation Army', explained Catherine Booth in an address to London businessmen, 'is no doubt what are termed the dangerous classes, and that there is great *need* for some such agency recent events make but too manifest. The inability of the authorities to cope with the ruffianly element … ought to awake everybody to the necessity for something being done.'[96] The Salvation Army's assertion that the organised 'Skeleton Armies' were a portent of the revolutionary threat from the mass of urban demoralised, relied too heavily on observation of metropolitan conditions. It did not accord with the social configuration of the southern provincial towns. Fashionable

---

92   Worthing: *The Salvation War* (London, 1884), p. 12

93   Frome: *The Times*, 30 Aug. 1884, p. 4; Whitchurch: HO 45/A2886/20.

94   7 Sept. 1881: HO 45/A2886/20; *PP* 1882, vol. 54, p. 17 at p. 31.

95   March 1882: HO 45/A2886/25 and 29.

96   C. Booth, *The Salvation Army in Relation to the Church and State* (London 1883), p. 1 (emphasis in original).

watering places and old provincial centres concealed aggregations of badly housed, severely impoverished urban workers. But the poor were still enclosed in social structures where personal influence and social ties retarded class solidarities. The 'Skeleton Armies' were manifestations of these integrated social communities, more than of socially segregated cities. They were participants in 'reactionary' riots on behalf of established moral and social codes, not in disorder which presaged social insurrection. Moreover, the Salvationists' submission that their work was required to strengthen the inadequate forces of social order did not accord with the attitude and behaviour of judicial authority in many of the provincial towns where the 'Army' disembarked. Indeed, an essential facet of the outbreak and continuation of the riots against the Salvation Army was the role of the authorities. Provincial towns were not controlled by the professional agents of a dispassionate legal system. The juridical system was incestuously recruited from townsmen possessed of social and economic influence in the community. This urban elite enjoyed unhindered discretionary power, administering peacekeeping measures according to its personal assessment of the threat to public order. Hence, unlike London's legal system, relatively distanced from the community it policed, provincial authority retained a more intimate understanding of the nature of different species of disorder.[97] The informed basis of the authorities' behaviour was evident in the 'reactionary' riots against the Salvation Army. The authorities handed towns over to organised 'Skeleton Armies', approving and encouraging 'mobbing' in the hope of deterring a revivalist sect which disturbed the social peace. They buttressed the 'mobbing' by discriminative legal prohibitions of religious processions and meetings. The magistracy and Watch Committees sought, in these irregular ways, to disable what they perceived as a challenge from the Salvation Army to the social influence and authority of their class. In the consequent riots, there was frequent illustration of how the provincial authorities could regulate disorder which served as a form of social control rather than a challenge to it.

---

97   See, V. Bailey, op.cit., chap. I, 'The Magistracy and the Urban Elite'.

2

The Metropolitan Police, the Home Office and the Threat of Outcast London

What is the true view of Home Office history for the last six years I do not know — that history remains to be written at a date safer for sound judgement than the present. At all events no chronicle will be of value unless it relies upon the testimony which you and I alone can supply.

(A Home Office clerk to E. Ruggles-Brise, Principal Private Secretary to the Home Secretary, 1892; in *Sir Evelyn Ruggles-Brise. A Memoir*, compiled by Shane Leslie (1938), p. 79.)

I

In what sense did Victorian society feel threatened by 'outcast London'? According to Dr Stedman Jones, public concern about poverty and the London poor re-emerged in the 1880s out of fear of the 'dangerous classes' and of the disaffection of the adjacent social stratum, the 'respectable working class'. Middle-class London feared, in particular, an insurrectionary alliance between the casual 'residuum' and the 'true working classes'. The real depth of these fears, we are told, was revealed by the disturbances of 1886 and 1887 when, for a brief but significant moment, the urban poor represented a social menace to propertied Londoners.[1]

The present essay submits a reassessment of the threat of revolution in the 1880s by examining, in the main, the response of the Home Office and the Metropolitan police force to the unemployed disturbances. This reconstruction of the viewpoint of Metropolitan authority draws extensively upon departmental papers hitherto unavailable under the Official Secrets Act. The essay argues, first, that the fears aroused by the Trafalgar Square riot of 8 February 1886, related to the casual residuum, not to an alliance of the 'outcast' and 'respectable' poor. Contemporaries spoke of a spontaneous outburst of the East End barbarians, not a movement which included *bona fide* unemployed and 'decent' workmen. The social distinction which had been forged in the mid-Victorian years between the 'dangerous' and the 'respectable' classes was not thawed by the economic and social crisis of the 1880s. It is further

---

1   G. Stedman Jones, *Outcast London* (Oxford, 1971), pp. 235, 290-1.

submitted that the level and durability of middle-class alarm about the casual residuum has been exaggerated. The practical initiatives of the propertied and of authority, in the sequel to the riot, do not reflect an abiding fear of social insurrection. It was quickly recognised that the outbreak and continuance of the riot owed considerably more to the inflexibility of existing police organisation, than to any premeditated iconoclasm on the part of the 'mob'.

The essay also assesses the response of the legal authorities to the disorders of 1887, which reached their apogee in the clash of police and poor around Trafalgar Square on 'bloody Sunday'. Previous work has presented too simple a model of a unified governmental strategy to repress the protest of the unemployed and the attendant campaign to maintain the right of public meeting. In fact, police determination to deal with the threat from the unemployed was hedged round with important constraints. There was manifest disagreement over the policy of public order between the Chief Commissioner of Police and the Home Secretary. To this disharmony was added the inhibiting effect of the 'rule of law' on executive action. Too much mythology, then, has grown up around the events of Trafalgar Square in 1886-7. It has masked an understanding of the threat posed by these events to middle-class London, and of the complexity of the attitudes of those involved in administering the law of public order.

II

By 1886, a largely socialist-led unemployment movement was holding regular open-air meetings, at times challenged by a protectionist agitation under the auspices of the Fair Trade League.[2] The meeting in Trafalgar Square on 8 February was called by the League in support of protectionist tariffs. An opposing platform was organised by the Social Democratic Federation. Some ten to twenty thousand unemployed dockers and building workers assembled in the square later in the afternoon, a confused contingent of socialists, anti-socialists and unemployed moved off towards Pall Mall, the 'street of the big political, aristocratic and high-capitalist clubs'.[3] The march-past brought club members to the balconies and windows, from where they derided the 'great unwashed'. The outcome was extensive damage to the clubs from stone-throwing, a mere prelude to a general attack on visible wealth in the form of shops and passing carriages. The black banner of the unemployed lent its name to 'Black Monday' in the annals of propertied London, a few hours of rioting within the hallowed precincts of the West End producing an estimated £50,000 of damage.[4]

---

2   See D. Torr, *Tom Mann and His Times* (2 vols., London, 1956), vol. 1, pp. 226-9; B. H. Brown, *The Tariff Reform Movement in Great Britain, 1881-1895* (New York, 1943), chap. 2.

3   D. Torr (ed.), *The Correspondence of Marx and Engels, 1846-1895* (London, 1934), p. 447.

4   *The Times*, 9 Feb. 1886, p. 6. For other descriptions of the riot, see E. P. Thompson, *William Morris* (London, 1977), pp. 406-7 ; C. Tsuzuki, *H.M. Hyndman and British Socialism* (Oxford, 1961), pp. 73-4.

Worse riots had occurred in the course of labour disputes, anti-Catholic affrays or at election time.[5] London, however, was the centre of government and of Empire, the headquarters of the *ancien régime* of landed wealth, the heart of the country's commercial and financial system — and extremely vulnerable to disorder. It was difficult to assert complete control of the casual labour force of this largely non-factory city, yet London had gradually acquired a reputation as the special home of security. Hence, disturbances which revealed that the principal streets of the capital were inadequately policed sent shock-waves through the nervous system of the propertied. There followed the days of 9 and 10 February when, according to George Bernard Shaw, there was ample material for 'a study of West End mob panic'.[6] Rumours of predatory mobs marching on the West End were increased by the heavy fog of the next days.[7] That stout Tory, Beatrix Potter, could think of little else. She recorded that on the 10th there had been absolute panic caused by the rumours of 10,000 roughs marching from Greenwich and Deptford: 'The bridges were guarded, the troops held in readiness at the barracks, and a guard at the banks'[8] The whole was a self-inflicted 'grande peur'.

In post-Chartist England, the rich feared most not an organised movement of rebellion, but sudden mob disorder as portrayed by Dickens in *Barnaby Rudge* or *A Tale of Two Cities*. What the wealthy now found dangerous about the 'dangerous classes' was 'an undefined yet serious misgiving on the score of safety to life and limb — to say nothing of property'.[9] Doubtless the Paris Commune of 1871 had refreshed the fears of irresponsible tumult. Following the 8 February incident, Beatrix Potter queried 'are we to have something like the Gordon Riots again?' She also sketched the standard interpretation of the riots: 'no one seems to lay the blame on the working men, it is the Jacobins, roughs and thieves'.[10] In press accounts, police reports and parliamentary speeches, the blame was put squarely on the criminal and dangerous classes. The honest workman or the *bona fide* unemployed were exonerated. Press and parliamentary comment emphasised, indeed, that the riots were deprecated by the respectable work force.[11] As the *Pall Mall Gazette* concluded:

> It was no Socialist demonstration. It was no hunger raid upon food. It was simply the surging up to the

---

5   See e.g., HO 144/73872 (Lancs. cotton riots, 1878); HO 45/A36317 (anti-Catholic riot, Cleator Moor, 1884); HO 144/A41348P (Nottingham election riot, 1885).

6   G. B. Shaw (ed.), *Fabian Essays in Socialism* (London, 1962; first published 1889). pp. 226-7.

7   *The Times*, 10 Feb. 1886, p. 5; 11 Feb. 1886, p. 6; *Justice*, 13 Feb. 1886, p. 3.

8   *The Journal of Beatrix Potter from 1881-1897*, transcribed by L. Linder (London, 1966), p. 175. See also, G. Cronje, *Middle Class Opinion and the 1889 Dock Strike* (London, 1975), p. 6; HO 144/A42380/ 1-4; MEPO 2/182; *The Times*, 10 Feb. 1886, p. 6. The panic in London was probably reinforced by news of the riots in Leicester on 11 February, which accompanied a hosiery workers' strike: *The Times*, 13 Feb. 1886, p. 8.

9   A. Fleishman, *The English Historical Novel* (London, 1971), chap. 4; Anon. 'How to Deal with the Dangerous Classes', *Leisure Hour* (Jan. 1869), p. 53.

10 *The Journal*, op. cit., pp. 173-4.

11 See *Spectator*, 13 Feb. 1886; *Saturday Review*, 13 Feb. 1886; *Fortnightly Review*, March 1886, p. 298; 3 *Hansard* 302, 18 Feb. 1886, cols. 555-77; 26 Feb. 1886, cols. 1412, 1426-9, and 1437; HO 144/A42380/16 & 40.

surface of the bandits of civilization.[12]

'Low-life' pamphleteers and social investigators advanced the same interpretation. So, too, George Gissing and W. H. Mallock, novelists who, *inter alia*, evaluated the revolutionary threat in the 1880s, described the rioters as a great urban *lumpenproletariat*.[13]

The middle-class interpretation of the Trafalgar Square riot was based on confidence in the social differentiation of the 'real working class', including those who were unemployed, from the casual 'residuum'. But what of the Socialists, the organisers of the unemployed agitation? In fact, they affirmed the contemporary distinction. In the subsequent trial of the leading members of the Social Democratic Federation, Henry Hyndman blamed the riot on 'the anti-sugar bounty mob', the tools of protectionist intrigue.[14] Frederic Engels, the doyen of English Socialism, had believed this all along. The procession to Hyde Park, he told Bebel, was composed of 'the masses of the Lumpenproletariat, whom Hyndman had taken for the unemployed'.[15] Engels felt only contempt for crude street looting. The criminal and slum rowdy were not the recruits vital to an organised labour movement. In the assessment of the West End riot, then, the Socialists also insisted on distinguishing between 'respectable labour' and the 'residuum'.

Contemporary interpretation was leavened by the Metropolitan economy. A 'dangerous class' of intimidating proportions was fashioned out of the distinctive features of London's industrial structure. The capital was the haven of seasonally-required, casual and unskilled labour, particularly in the building, transport and service sectors. This pool of underemployed labour, moreover, was thought to shade imperceptibly into those social groups more clearly unattached to the industrial economy — paupers, vagrants and criminals. H. E. Hoare, voluntary worker for the Charity Organisation Society, spoke of 'the casual labourers who live on the brink of starvation and crime, and who are a disgrace and may easily become a danger to London.'[16] Whilst in other cities, vast portions of the labouring class had been withdrawn from membership of the 'dangerous class', in London it was more difficult to separate the casual labour force from the semi-criminal, pauperised residuum. Yet if the London 'residuum' incorporated the unskilled workforce, the entire social stratum was thought to be morally and socially

---

12 *Pall Mall Gazette*, 9 Feb. 1886, p. 9.

13 A. S. Krausse, *Starving London* (London, 1886), pp. 163-4; H. Solly, 'Our Vagrant and Criminal Classes', *Leisure Hour* (1887), pp. 761-7, 830-3; G. Gissing, *Demos* (London, 1886), vol. 3, pp. 244 and 251; W. H. Mallock, *The Old Order Changes* (London, 1886), vol. 3, pp. 31-2, 43 and 46-9.

14 D. Walker-Smith and E. Clarke, *The Life of Sir Edward Clarke* (London, 1939), p. 202; R. Hyndman, *The Record of an Adventurous Life* (London, 1911), pp. 400-7; HO 144/A42380/40. Cf. the Liberal attempt to establish a connection between the Tories and the Trafalgar Square riot through the 'fair trade' activities of Peters and Kelly: A. B. Cooke and J. Vincent, *The Governing Passion* (Brighton, 1974), p. 375.

15 *Marx-Engels, Correspondence*, op. cit., p. 447. Cf. *Engels-Lafargue, Correspondence* (Moscow, 1959),vol. 1, p. 334.

16 See G. Stedman Jones, op. cit., Part I; H. E. Hoare, 'Homes of the Criminal Classes', *National Review*, vol. 1, March 1883, p. 838. Londoners were often reminded of the prospect of marauding mobs from the metropolitan slums: George Sims, *How the Poor Live and Horrible London* (London, 1889; first published 1883), p. 44; Henry George, *Progress and Poverty* (London, 1881), pp. 474-88.

distinct from the 'respectable working class'. Mid-century social investigations, many of which were based on the East End of London, had redefined the bottom rung of the social ladder as the 'residuum', distinguished as much for their incompetence as their rebelliousness, and had identified a distinct stratum of respectable workers.[17] It was a social differentiation which was not undermined in the 1880s, even in the face of the Trafalgar Square riot.

It has been argued that the main component of middle-class anxiety in the days following the riot was the threat of social insurrection on the part of the city residuum. Related to this was the comforting judgement that the riot had not been supported by the respectable working class or the *bona fide* unemployed. Equally significant is the fact that the Socialist organisations endorsed the middle-class description of aimless rioting. In a city which retained 'pre-industrial' forms of production, a 'pre-industrial' definition of a semi-criminal mob coloured public discussion of the threat of social upheaval.

III

'Throughout the rest of 1886 and 1887', according to Dr Stedman Jones, 'fear of a "sansculottic" insurrection remained strong.'[18] What evidence is there for such a claim? There are the pamphlets of contemporary social reformers, in which, however, the fear of disorder was so often manipulated to disturb an indifferent public into contributing money. There are the warnings of impending catastrophe to be found in the newspapers, yet as early as 4 March 1886, William Morris of the Socialist League stated that the 'cool-headed people of the middle-classes rather smile at the ravings of the *Telegraph*'.[19] The testimony of anxious social workers or excitable London dailies could never act as an exhaustive source of evidence on which to base an estimate of the fear of revolution. A more reliable, and largely neglected, way of assessing the level and persistence of alarm about the 'dangerous classes' is to document the practical response of the propertied and the authorities to the Trafalgar Square riot.

Riots commonly remind the propertied of their social responsibility to the poor. The immediate reaction of one gentleman in Brooks's Club was far from charitable, according to the Liberal MP for York:

> As the windows crashed in he shouted, 'This'll do 'em no good!' ... and as the fire got hotter his language

---

17 See V. Bailey, 'The Dangerous Classes in Late Victorian England' (Univ. of Warwick, Ph.D. thesis, 1975), chap. 5 ; E. P. Hennock, 'Poverty and social theory in England: the experience of the eighteen-eighties', *Social History*, No. 1 (1976), pp. 77-8; E. M. Yeo, 'Social Science and Social Change: A Social History of Some Aspects of Social Science and Social Investigation in Britain 1830-1890' (Univ. of Sussex, Ph.D. thesis, 1972), chap. 8.

18 G. Stedman Jones, op. cit., p. 295.

19 *Commonweal*, March 1886.

grew stronger, and he finally was swearing that he would stop 'all his subscriptions to everything'.[20]

In fact, there was a rapid increase in subscriptions to the Mansion House Relief Fund in the wake of the riots. Was this an attempt by the propertied 'to assuage the threatening discontent of the poor'?[21] On 8 February the fund stood at £3,300; by 23 February at £60,000. The lessons taught by the Charity Organization Society, particularly the prescribed distinction between the 'deserving' and 'undeserving' poor, were neglected. The money was doled out without system by emergency committees.[22] But after the initial spurt of donations, little more came in. If this was 'ransom' money to disarm the threat of outcast London, the sum seems pitifully small.

A more considered proposal to alleviate the social distress which was felt by some to underlie the riot, was a temporary relaxation of the conditions for granting outdoor relief in London.[23] But no other welfare measures were conceded. The riot was not, according to Jose Harris, responsible for Joseph Chamberlain's circular of 15 March which sanctioned public relief works for the unemployed.[24] If the riot brought the problem of unemployment into public discussion, therefore, it had little direct impact on social policy for the relief of the unemployed. As Harris put it, the unemployed were still seen 'as a problem of public order rather than of social distress — as the responsibility of the Home Office rather than of the Local Government Board.'[25]

What, then, was the response of metropolitan authority? Some 20 rioters were dealt with by the police courts, charged with being disorderly or riotous, or with committing wilful damage. The convicted were either bound over in recognisances to be of good behaviour, or fined between 5s and £1, or (in the cases of wilful damage) imprisoned for between one and two months. A dozen more cases were committed for trial to the Middlesex Sessions, where they were generally indicted for breaking and entering, and stealing items of jewellery, food or wine. Apart from one sentence of five years' penal servitude, the guilty were mostly given short sentences of imprisonment of between three and twelve months.[26] A more significant proceeding was the State prosecution of the speakers at the Trafalgar Square meeting. Perhaps in order to avoid conferring notoriety on the Socialists, the government initially sought to prosecute them summarily, but the Law Officers advised against it. By 12 February, the Attorney General, Sir Charles Russell, believed that there was sufficient evidence against Hyndman, Burns, Champion and Williams to indict them for unlawfully uttering seditious words with intent to

---

20 Sir Alfred E. Pease, *Elections and Recollections* (London, 1932), p. 106.

21 G. Stedman Jones, op. cit., p. 298. Cf. B. B. Gilbert, *The Evolution of National Insurance in Great Britain* (London, 1966), pp. 32-9.

22 *Charity. A Record of Philanthropic Enterprise*, vol. 1, Dec. 1886, p. 119; *Pall Mall Gazette*, 23 Feb. 1886, p. 10; C. L. Mowat, *The Charity Organisation Society 1869-1913* (London, 1961), p. 132; G. Stedman Jones, op. cit., pp. 298-300.

23 *Pall Mall Gazette*, 10 Feb. 1886, p. 1; *The Times*, 10 Feb. 1886, p. 6.

24 Jose Harris, *Unemployment and Politics. A Study in English Social Policy 1886-1914* (Oxford, 1972), pp. 75-6.

25 Ibid., p. 56.

26 *The Times*, 10 Feb. to 10 March, 1886. The arrested rioters, mostly under 30 years of age, were drawn mainly from London's casual trades and associated residual occupations.

incite to riot, and for conspiring together to effect the same. A conviction for the crime of seditious speech was often difficult to obtain, however, as subsequent events proved. Unswayed by the excitement aroused by the disturbances, the jury found all the defendants not guilty.[27] There is little evidence, then, of a stern legal response to the riot. The sentences passed on the rioters were unexceptional in severity, and the one State prosecution ended in ruin.

Nor was there any haste to assert greater police control over the assemblages of unemployed in the centre of London. Insurance against further disorder was sought, by some, in a tougher policy towards out-door demonstrations which, it was thought, attracted the 'roughs' and criminal classes.[28] The Queen suggested to Hugh Childers, the Liberal Home Secretary, that since public meetings in Trafalgar Square were, in strict law, illegal, disorderly meetings there might be forbidden. However, Childers was not prepared to restrict the places of holding meetings — 'To withdraw a permission, granted or recognised by successive Governments, would be a very grave step.'[29] Moreover, whilst firm precautions were taken to avoid disorder ensuing from an SDF meeting in Hyde Park on 21 February, the Home Office refused to disturb the public mind by swearing in special constables. Significantly, too, military support was arranged by the Chief Commissioner of Police because of 'a very strong feeling among the "unemployed" against the Social Democrats which might possibly lead to a collision'.[30] Again, these do not seem like the actions of a government under threat from a revolutionary situation.

Indeed, judging from a close assessment of the concerns of the parliamentary community in the first months of 1886, there was remarkably little governmental attention devoted to the Trafalgar Square riot. The Cabinet acceded to the pressure from shopkeepers to secure proper compensation for the damage to their property.[31] But politicians and the government were, and remained, considerably more engrossed with the Irish question than with working out why economic depression and unemployment had led to disturbances under Socialist leadership.[32] The riot, in fact, was seen less as a problem of government, a concern of parliamentary life, than a simple matter of police. This position was reinforced when it became clear that the 'dangerous classes' had not been on the verge of mass uprising, but that a street riot had developed out of police incompetence.

---

27 *The Letters of Queen Victoria*, ed. G. E. Buckle, 3rd set. (London, 1930), vol. 1, p. 54; HO 144/A42380/15 and 24; *R. v. Burns and others*, 16 Cox C.C. (1886), pp. 355-67. Burns doubtless eased public anxiety by emphasising the peaceful intentions of the SDF speakers, and insisting that they had tried to stop the looting: Central Criminal Court, *Sessions Paper*, vol. 103 (1886), p. 681 at . pp. 693-4.

28 3 *Hansard* 302, 25 Feb. 1886, cols. 1174-81; 26 Feb. 1886, cols. 1405-6; 3 *Hansard* 303, 15 March 1886, cols. 758-9; MEPO 2/182.

29 *Letters Q.V.*, loc. cit.; 3 *Hansard* 303, 20 March 1886, col. 16.

30 HO 144/A42380/3-7. The SDF made it clear to the authorities on more than one occasion that they were anxious to avoid further disorder, and they asked for police assistance on 21 February: MEPO 2/182; HO 144/A42380/21.

31 MEPO 2/182; 3 *Hansard* 305, 20 May 1886, cols. 1612-4; A. B. Cooke and J. Vincent, op. cit., p. 376.

32 Cooke and Vincent, op. cit., p. 4-7. Cf. Viscount Chilston, *Chief Whip. The Political Life and Times of Aretas Akers-Douglas. 1st Viscount Chilston* (London, 1961), p. 137.

IV

The pre-eminent response of the propertied to the riot was one of indignation at the obvious inertia of the Metropolitan police force. It was quickly recognised that the rioters could have been routed by a handful of police had they been in the right place. Indignation was increased by the fact that the panic of the days following the riot had been fuelled by the police advising shops to close, thus admitting their inability to keep order.[33] So indecisive had the police appeared, in fact, that Engels was not alone in suggesting that 'the row was *wanted*'.[34] The evidence points rather to the incapacity of the force to respond efficiently to a sudden emergency. Ironically, the Metropolitan force was originally formed as a para-military organisation in response, not only to crime *per se*, but also to the possibility of riot by the 'dangerous classes'. Its power of mobility and co-ordination had become revered as a successful antidote to mob disturbance. So confident were the chiefs of police that the technique developed of keeping the police in reserve in order not to antagonise the demonstrators.[35] The riot came, therefore, as a severe blow to public confidence. It was one of the rare occasions since the establishment of the modern force in 1829 that a crowd had got the upper hand of a large body of constables.[36]

The Home Secretary's first act was to set up a Committee of Inquiry into the disturbances and the conduct of the police authorities. It met in the Home Secretary's room, taking evidence from 15-20 February.[37] The most important witness, inevitably, was Sir Edmund Henderson, Chief Commissioner of Police.[38] Henderson had clearly been very conscious of his responsibilities during the interregnum between Home Secretaries, but, lulled by the previous security of London, he had displayed little foresight and assumed no overall command. His evidence illuminated two main facts about police

---

33   See editorials in *The Times*, 10 Feb. 1886; *Daily Telegraph*, 9 Feb. 1886; *Pall Mall Gazette*, 10 Feb. 1886. See also, HO 144/A42380C/10; R. F. V. Heuston, *Lives of the Lord Chancellors;1885-1940* (Oxford, 1964), p. 103; E. S. E. Childers, *The Life and Correspondence of the Right Hon. Hugh C. E. Childers 1827-1896* (London, 1901), vol. 2, p. 240.

34   *Engels-Lafargue, Correspondence*, op. cit, vol; 1, p. 336. (emphasis in original); *Marx-Engels, Correspondence*, op. cit., p. 447. Engels's interpretation has been endorsed recently by Y. Kapp, *Eleanor Marx* (London, 1976), vol. 2, p. 77, and R. Mace, *Trafalgar Square* (London, 1976), p. 167. But for a contemporary rejection of the theory that Henderson was ordered not to act, see the letter of Sir William H. Russell, 10 Feb. 1886, in *Wolseley Papers*.

35   See A. Silver, 'The Demand for Order in Civil Society: A Review of Some Themes in the History of Urban Crime, Police and Riot', in D. Bordua (ed.), *The Police: Six Sociological Essays* (London, 1967), pp. 7-8. See also, Anon., 'The Police System of London', *Edinburgh Review*, vol. 96, July 1852, pp. 9-10; Anon., 'The Police of London', *Quarterly Review*, vol. 129, July 1870, pp. 91 and 122; A. Wynter, *Curiosities of Toil*, vol. II (London, 1870), pp. 96-7; W. R. Miller, *Cops and Bobbies: Police Authority in New York and London, 1830-1870* (London, 1977), p. 13.

36   See B. Harrison, 'The Sunday Trading Riots of 1855', *Historical Journal*, vol. 8 (1965), pp. 219-45; R. Harrison, *Before the Socialists* (London, 1955), chap. 3.

37   The Committee members were Hugh Childers (the new Home Secretary, who acted as Chairman), Lord Edward Cavendish, Henry T. Holland, C. T. Ritchie and Viscount Wolseley. The last three were Conservatives. It is important to establish the political chronology of these years. In February 1886, a Liberal government under W. E. Gladstone took over from the Conservative government of Lord Salisbury. The West End riot coincided with this change of ministries. The defeat of the Irish Home Rule bill, however, led to an early dissolution of Parliament in July 1886 and to the return of a Conservative ministry under Salisbury. The Conservatives remained in office until 1892.

38   On Henderson, see *The Times*, 10 Dec. 1896, p. 8; *Royal Engineers Journal*, vol. 27 (1897), pp. 32-5.

arrangements. First, CID information suggested that any disorder would take place between the rival contingents within Trafalgar Square. Accordingly, Henderson took adequate precautions for the management of the crowd in the square.[39] Secondly, experience suggested that crowds invariably went back by the routes on which they had come, usually eastwards, past Whitehall. Therefore, the superintendents of those police divisions through which the crowd would return on 8 February were asked to keep order. The flaw in the arrangements was that no precautions were taken in the event of the crowds going westwards, and the police in the square saw no evidence of the crowd moving in that direction. All that happened was the belated despatch of the police reserve in St George's Barracks to Pall Mall. The message was confused and the reserve set off for the Mall.[40]

The other police witnesses revealed a most unexpected state of affairs in Trafalgar Square. The Chief Commissioner was there, but not in command of police action. That responsibility was given to a 74-year-old District Superintendent. Dressed in civilian clothes and jammed in the densest part of the crowd (during which his pockets were picked), he had found it difficult to transmit any orders. It had been equally difficult for other policemen to find him.[41] The evidence also pointed to a decided lack of initiative among the subordinate officers. The superintendents adhered rigidly to their orders, refusing to shift position, even when, in one case, the riotous mob could be seen in Piccadilly.[42] Finally, the system of telegraphic communication between the police on the ground and headquarters was clearly deficient. As Godfrey Lushington, the Permanent Under Secretary of State, said to Childers, after the Committee had reported, the riot showed

> that it was possible for a riotous crowd to make a raid through the streets of the Metropolis for more than an hour without any intimation of their proceedings reaching Scotland Yard.[43]

The Report of the Committee condemned the lack of overall leadership, the poor communication between different sections of the force and the inflexibility of the police response to an unexpected occurrence. It identified, as the main single fault, the lack of arrangements made for managing the mob after it had broken up, 'although it was well understood that a large element of a very dangerous class was present'. As the Committee recognised:

---

39   Report of a Committee to Inquire and Report as to the Origin and Character of the Disturbance which took place in the Metropolis on Monday 8 February, with Minutes of Evidence, *PP*, 1886 (Cd. 4665), vol. 34, p. 381 at p. 392 (q. 9); p. 397 (q. 177), p. 403 (qq. 331-5) and p. 489 (Appendix VII). Cf. evidence of Lieut-Col. R. L. O. Pearson, Assistant Commissioner of Police: p. 405 (q. 382), p. 411 (q. 537), p. 417 (q. 677); and James Monro, Assistant Commissioner in charge of CID: p. 418 (q. 722).

40   Ibid., p. 384, p. 386 (para. 22), p. 387 (para. 29), p. 398 (qq. 178-9, 187), and p. 403 (q. 334). Cf. James Monro: p. 419 (q. 728), p. 484 (Appendix II); R. L. O. Pearson: p. 411 (q. 538), p. 418 (qq. 695-702). Henderson insisted that the riot was an unexpected event: 'I am perfectly assured it was wholly unpremeditated…' p. 401 (q. 303).

41   Ibid., evidence of Robert Walker, one of four District Superintendents appointed in 1869: p. 426 (qq. 978-83), p. 429 (q. 1083), pp. 437-8 (qq. 1303-30). See also p. 388 (para. 40).

42   Ibid., Superintendent Hume: p. 448 (q. 1602), p. 449 (q. 1661); Inspector Knight: p. 470 (qq. 2517-22).

43   HO 45/B158/1.

had the police authorities shown greater resource, acting upon a good and well-understood system, the mob might have been effectively headed, and easily broken up at an early period of their progress.[44]

The Report went on to identify briefly the defects in the police system which the riot had exposed. Emphasis was put on the inadequate number of 'officers of superior rank and education, or of experience in the habit of command'; on the defective chain of responsibility in the force; and on the lack of a settled system for dealing with large meetings. Its final proposal, therefore, was for a second inquiry into the administration and organisation of the police force.[45]

Yet by no means all senior statesmen were convinced of the need to interfere with police organisation. Only a few days after the riot, Gladstone, the Prime Minister, 'expressed himself against any great alteration in the metropolitan police as a consequence of the West End riots'. R. A. Cross and Sir William Harcourt, both previous Home Secretaries, also discouraged any drastic reorganisation in the system of police administration. For Harcourt, indeed, the riot was a 'most lamentable accident', unlikely to recur.[46] Despite the speed with which the first Committee of Inquiry completed its task, it was not until July that the second Committee started work. Even then, their recommendations were hardly thoroughgoing — development of the telegraphic system, the use of mounted police, and clearer regulations for the guidance of officers at public meetings.[47] Another proposal was the appointment of more senior officers. The moribund posts of District Superintendent were revived, in order to enhance the element of 'educated control' and to provide another link in the chain of responsibility between Commissioner and constable.[48] These appointments exhausted the drive for reform. They were little indemnity against an undue centralisation of administration and hardly affected materially the actual system of control.

The only other facet of the legal system which came under scrutiny as a result of the riot was the working relationship of the Home Secretary and the Chief Commissioner of Police. On 8 February, Childers, the new Home Secretary, had received a message from his wife in Piccadilly which mentioned riot damage to neighbouring houses. He asked to know the meaning of this passage, which, said his

---

44 Report, p. 386 (para. 28), p. 387 (para. 32), p. 388 (para. 39). Cf. Henderson: p. 400 (qq. 260-4). See also Eleanor Marx to Lavrov, 9 March 1886, quoted in Y. Kapp, op. cit, p. 78. Wolseley first drafted a Report of the Police Committee, but Childers 'cut the Report to pieces before approving it': *Sir Evelyn Ruggles-Brise. A Memoir*, compiled by Shane Leslie (London, 1938), p. 57.

45 Ibid., pp. 289-90 (paras. 45-9), p. 490 (Appendix IX): MEPO 2/174; Copy of a Memorandum by the Secretary for the Home Department on the Report of the Committee appointed to inquire into the Origin and Character of the Disturbances...', *PP* 1886 (Cd. 132),vol. 53, p. 351.

46 Cooke and Vincent, op.cit., p. 375; 3 *Hansard* 302, 26 Feb. 1886, cols. 1446-8; 3 *Hansard* 330, 14 Nov. 1888, col. 1166.

47 Report of the Committee appointed by the Secretary of State for the Home Department to Inquire into the Administration and Organisation of the Metropolitan Police Force, *PP* 1886 (Cd. 4894), vol. 34, p. 493 at pp; 497-8. The Committee members were Hugh Childers, Sir Charles Warren, Henry James, J. T. Ingham and E. Leigh Pemberton. See also C. T. Clarkson and J. Hall Richardson, *Police!* (London, 1889), pp. 81-2.

48 Ibid., pp. 495-6. For the history of the District Superintendents, see Sir John Moylan, *Scotland Yard and the Metropolitan Police* (London, 1934), pp. 146-9; HO, 45/74577A; 'Custos', *The Police Force of the Metropolis* (London, 1868), pp. 14-27. The riots were also followed by an augmentation of constables: Report of the Commissioner of Police of the Metropolis for 1889, *PP* 1890-91 (Cd. 6237).; Vol. 42, p. 307 at p. 376.

private secretary:

> I was unable to do, having had no communication from the police, and having no idea that any riot had occurred. I at once telegraphed to Scotland Yard. No one in the Home Office had the remotest idea of what had occurred.[49]

The conjunction of the riot with the changeover of governments had not helped an interchange of information. But advocates of reform in the government of the Metropolitan police seized their chance. Municipal rather than Home Office control of the police was recommended as a better way of directing the police to maintain order.[50] Nevertheless, in the parliamentary debates on the riot, Childers argued for continued Home Office authority over the Metropolitan police, and defended the existing distribution of duties between Home Secretary and Chief Commissioner. A Home Secretary, said Childers, would be unwise to interfere in police arrangements. There might be joint discussion about the level of policing, but thereafter responsibility for public order rested with the Commissioner. Nor was it usual, the House was told, for communications to pass between Scotland Yard and the Home Office during the course of a meeting.[51] Other parliamentary speakers agreed that the Commissioner should have the power to act on his own responsibility without hindrance from the Home Office. The second Committee of Inquiry into the police confirmed that the primary responsibility for public order rested with the Commissioner. It simply recommended that the Home Office ought to be kept informed of abnormal circumstances, especially if it seemed that military aid might be needed.[52] Otherwise, the West End riot only reinforced the sense of need for Home Office oversight of executive police action, and largely endorsed the respective spheres of responsibility of Home Secretary and Chief Commissioner.

It has been submitted that the evidence for a crisis of middle-class confidence in the face of the Trafalgar Square riot does not exist in the active response of the propertied or of governmental and legal authority. Faced with a coincidence of economic depression, a Socialist-led unemployed campaign, and riotous expression of proletarian discontent, it is not too surprising to find that the propertied were momentarily haunted by the spectre of upheaval. But in the aftermath of the riot, there was little sense of an urgent mission to alleviate the economic and social distress of unemployment by charitable donations or by welfare measures. Few, if any, exemplary sentences were imposed to deter further rioting. There was little parliamentary support for a more coercive policy towards the unemployed

49   E. S. E. Childers, op. cit., vol. 2, p. 239.

50   3 *Hansard* 302, 26 Feb. 1886, cols. 1394. *The Times*, 27 Feb. 1886, p. 11.

51   3 *Hansard* 302, 18 Feb. 1886, cols. 594-6, 600, 603-6; HO 45/B158/23; MEPO 2/X7215/31a; E. S. E. Childers, op,. cit., vol. 2, pp. 242-4; *PP* 1886, vol. 34, p. 381. at p. 389 (para. 43).

52   3 *Hansard* 302, 26 Feb. 1886, cols. 1438; HO 144/A48409/2; Y. Kapp, op. cit., pp. 80-1; S. H. Jeyes and F. D. How, *The Life of Sir Howard Vincent*, (London, 1912), p. 188. See also R. Plehwe, 'Police and Government: The Commissioner of Police for the Metropolis', *Public Law* (1974), p. 332.

demonstrations; no Home Office pressure to alter markedly the policing of open-air meetings. Even widespread criticism of police incompetence, public demands for the reform of the force, plus two departmental enquiries which revealed deficiencies in police organisation, led only to a few minor changes, along with a measure of decentralisation which had previously failed. Moreover, no change was made in the government of the Metropolitan police; no greater restraint was placed on the Chief Commissioner's freedom of action. Middle-class nerves were largely soothed, it seems, by the resignation of Sir Edmund Henderson, and by placing police administration in the more vigorous charge of Sir Charles Warren.[53] The extreme reluctance to countenance more radical responses to the Trafalgar Square riot is explained by the fact that it was seen merely as an unfortunate lapse on the part of the Metropolitan police, not as the thin end of the revolutionary wedge.[54]

V

Yet the Trafalgar Square riot inevitably cast a shadow over subsequent policing arrangements whenever the outcast poor converged on the West End.[55] This was notably so in the autumn months of 1887. Seasonal unemployment in a year of severe depression turned Trafalgar Square into an encampment of the homeless poor. Soon there were daily meetings of the unemployed in the square, forays of beggars into the surrounding streets and spontaneous marches on the Mansion House and the Local Government Board. The effect of such disorderly events, according to Lady Monkswell, was that 'all law-abiding people began to fear that any day we might have an incursion by the roughs as we had 18 months ago when they broke the windows in St. James's Street and Pall Mall, and looted shops.' Engels, writing on 12 November, took up the story:

> After a deal of hesitation and vacillation the police have at last forbidden all meetings on Trafalgar Square; the radical clubs have answered by calling a great meeting thither for tomorrow afternoon... I do not anticipate a serious collision. But it is just possible that Matthews and his colleagues of the Tory government for once show fight; especially as the daily Liberal press have taken the side of the police, and there is no general election in sight just now...[56]

---

53 Lord George Hamilton, *Parliamentary Reminiscences and Reflections 1886-1906* (London, 1922), vol. 2, p. 14. See also, Shane Leslie, op. cit., p. 56; MEPO 2/166; HO 144/A42552; *The Times*, 243 Feb. 1886, p. 9.

54 The metropolitan authorities were similarly unmoved by the threat of unemployed disorder in 1894: HO 45/B13077C/1; J. Harris, op.cit. pp. 81-3.

55 Warren was vigilant towards processions and meetings of the unemployed. See HO 144/A45155; HO 144/A42480; HO, 144/A45225; HO 144/B862; HO 144/A46834; MEPO 2/173.

56 See B. Burleigh, 'The Unemployed', *Contemporary Review*, vol. 52, Dec. 1887, pp. 770-80; Charles Booth, *Life and Labour of the People in London*, 1st ser. (London, 1902),vol. 1, p. 231; MEPO 2/181; *A Victorian Diarist. Extracts from the Journals of Mary, Lady Monkswell 1873-1895*, ed. Collier (London, 1944), pp. 145-6; *Engels-Lafargue Correspondence* (Moscow; 1960), vol. 2, pp. 71-2. Henry Matthews was Home Secretary in the Salisbury administration from July 1886 until July 1892.

There was never any likelihood that Trafalgar Square would be successfully entered on what has become known as 'bloody Sunday'. The police and military were husbanded too well for unarmed and unorganised demonstrators; Ernest Bax described the ensuing scene in Northumberland Avenue and Parliament Street:

> The police were in strong force and the military behind. As the contingents of the various Radical clubs, branches of the Socialist organizations, and Irish Societies of London debouched through the streets leading into the Square, they were attacked and mostly dispersed by the police.[57]

In the history of the working-class movement, 'bloody Sunday' is celebrated as the climax to the struggle between the Socialists and the authorities in the 1880s over the issue of free speech and free assembly. The argument is that the police, encouraged by the unorganised state of the unemployed agitation, deliberately forced to a head the issue of free speech in the metropolis.[58] Undoubtedly, 'bloody Sunday' had the trappings of a set-piece confrontation, reminiscent of other significant episodes in the past — Kennington Common in 1848, Hyde Park in 1866. Its importance is only underlined by the readiness of the propertied classes to steel the government's resolve, in the aftermath, by serving as special constables. However, the implication of previous assessments is that the Metropolitan authorities were as one in their determination to move against the 'direct action' of the unemployed. A more scrupulous examination of the role of the Metropolitan police and the Home Office suggests that the mainsprings of social control were more complex and confused. Why else were meetings in the square between mid-October and mid-November alternately allowed and dispersed? The high point of inconsistency was reached when, on 6 November, the morning meeting in the square was banned, whilst the one in the afternoon was allowed.[59] What explains this vacillation in policy? The answer emerges from a reconstruction of the attitudes of Metropolitan authority in the prelude to 'bloody Sunday'. In the following sections of this essay, it is argued that the dilemma of the Conservative administration, which had been in office since July 1886, arose from a conflict over approach to the threat of the outcast poor between the Police Commissioner and the Home Secretary, and, relatedly, from the constraints imposed on the executive by the need to legitimise the policy of public order by appeal to the law.[60]

Sir Charles Warren's appointment as Chief Commissioner of Police had been applauded as restoring lost confidence in the force and reassuring the public. Warren was a strong-willed, opinionated and combative man, a stern disciplinarian with an imperious military attitude. He saw his role as being 'to

---

57 E. B. Bax, *Reminiscences and Reflexions of a Mid and Late Victorian* (London, 1918), p. 87.

58 See E. P. Thompson, op. cit., pp. 484-5; R. Mace, op. cit, pp. 178-9; D. Torr, op. cit.,vol. 1, pp. 259-62.

59 B. Burleigh, loc. cit.; 'Remember Trafalgar Square', *Pall Mall Gazette Extra*, No. 37, p. 3.

60 The same events have been examined, to little effect, in L. Keller, 'Public Order in Victorian London' (Univ. of Cambridge, Ph.D. Thesis, 1977), chap. IV. There is a more suggestive appraisal in B. Lewis, 'The Home Office, the Metropolitan Police and Civil Disorder 1886-1893' (Univ. of Leeds, M.Phil. Thesis, 1975), chap. III.

bring into order and reorganise the Police of the Metropolis'.[61] Warren's short tenure of office has been described by Sir John Moylan as 'a signal instance of the failure of a military administration of the Metropolitan police'.[62] This statement rests primarily on Warren's 'militarisation' of police organisation and discipline, his impatience of 'civilian' interference at the Home Office and Scotland Yard, and his ferocious campaigning attitude towards the unemployed disorders in 1887. These separate strands of the description are worth closer examination in so far as they disclose a distinct police attitude to social disturbance, and a strategy which was pursued often without Home Office sanction.

Warren's period of office did not mark a wholly new venture into militaristic discipline and organisation. A common indictment of the Metropolitan force, indeed, was that it was too militarised to perform the duties of a civil body. Since 1869, according to one MP, the police had been transformed into 'a quasi-military force, drilled, distributed and managed as soldiers', a 'cumbrous and badly-organised army, which was never required as a whole, and was nearly useless in detail.'[63] Nevertheless, it was felt that Warren considerably advanced the tendency towards militarism by his appointment of ex-Army men to the new positions of Chief Constable and Assistant Chief Constable, as well as by the severe enforcement of internal regulations, further abbreviating personal initiative. To an inflexible discipline was added a renewed emphasis on squad drill with the despatch to all inspectors of copies of the handbook, *Field Exercise and Evolutions of Infantry*.[64]

Police administration was assimilated to military administration in other ways. Warren resolved that his efforts to reorganise the Metropolitan police should not be impeded by officials at Scotland Yard and the Home Office. He fought implacably against any restraint on his operational independence, seeking to limit the Metropolitan Police Receiver's functions to purely financial matters, and to make the Receiver an equivalent of the War Office's Accountant General. This was because he resented the Receiver's reports on the financial implications of his reform proposals being sent to the Home Secretary.[65] Warren also considered that his relationship with the Home Secretary should resemble the one which existed between the Secretary of State for War and the commanding officer of an overseas expedition. In a series of petulant letters to the Home Secretary, Warren complained about the

---

61 Watkin Williams, *The Life of Sir Charles Warren* (Oxford, 1941), pp. 195-7; C. Pulling, *Mr. Punch and the Police* (London, 1964), pp. 109-10
   Letters Q.V., op. cit., vol. 1, pp. 65-6; HO 144/A47288; HO 144/A42763; *DNB* (Supplement 1922-30), p. 889; E. S. E. Childers, op. cit., vol. 2,
   p. 241. In 1885 Warren had contested unsuccessfully the Hallam Division of Sheffield as a Liberal candidate. He was summoned from a military
   command in Africa to be Commissioner of Police. The main candidates for the job, apart from Warren, were Sir Redvers Bullet and Lord Charles
   Beresford (both of whom declined the post when it was offered by Childers), and James Monro, Assistant Commissioner in Charge of the CID.

62 J. Moylan, op. cit., p. 49. See also, D. Ascoli, *The Queen's Peace* (London, 1979), pp. 157-63.

63 Ibid., pp. 42-3; W. Miller, op. cit., pp. 2, 40 and 116-7; 3 *Hansard* 330, 13 Nov. 1888, cols. 1146-8 (Mr. Lawson).

64 HO 45/A49455; HO 45/A46751; MEPO 2/257; MEPO 2/170; MEPO 7/48; *Pall Mall Gazette*, 9-13 Oct. 1888; Charles Warren, 'The Police of
   the Metropolis', *Murray's Magazine*, Nov. 1888, pp. 592-4. Dissatisfactions among the constabulary concerning the system of police
   administration led to meetings in Hyde Park: MEPO 2/171; Anon, *The Metropolitan Police and its Management* (London, 1888).

65 HO 144/A47600; HO 144/A46998; HO 45/A46889; MEPO 5/306. See also, R. M. Morris, 'The Metropolitan Police Receiver in the XIXth
   Century', *The Police Journal*, vol. 47 (1974), pp. 70-2. A similar conflict of authority broke out between Warren and James Monro, Assistant
   Commissioner in charge of CID: HO 144/A464728; HO 144/A46472C; HO 144/A48606.

interference of the permanent Home Office officials in his reforming efforts and in what ought, in his opinion, to be a personal relationship with the Secretary of State. Such interference, he even implied, by producing disorganisation in the police force, had been the main cause of the Trafalgar Square riot in 1886.[66] Warren's pretensions to be in no way subordinate to the Home Office had practical import. Having asserted his independence of any 'civilian' control, he was in a strong position to act unilaterally against the threat of the unemployed demonstrations.

Beginning in the warm summer nights of 1887, homeless unemployed and vagrants camped out in Trafalgar Square. Initial reluctance on the part of the police and the First Commissioner of Works to remove the squatters, along with indiscriminate food donations, increased the scale of the problem.[67] Police reports reveal the gradual formation of opinion that leaving the casual poor in the square could prove troublesome.[68] On 17 October, Trafalgar Square was, in fact, cleared by Chief Constable Howard, who later advised Warren to prevent 'these roughs from entering the Square at all'. On the 18th, Warren kept the square clear all day.[69] A few days later, Warren urged the Home Secretary, Henry Matthews, to close the square against the next day's meeting and to break up processions *en route*, rather than risk disturbances. His argument was as follows:

> We have during the last month in my opinion been in greater danger from the disorganised attacks on property by the rough and criminal element than we have been in London for many years past. It is not that I apprehend any organised movement from the Socialists themselves or from any other organised body, but it is from the roughs and criminals who always attach themselves to large processions and meetings that I anticipate serious damage to property.[70]

Warren was pressed by the Home Secretary to allow the meetings for the next few days, but on 25 October he again claimed the right to disperse what he described as 'the veriest scum of the population':

> a mob of these people may be innocuous in their own district; but very dangerous when among the houses of the opulent classes to which they do not belong and to which they have no ties.[71]

---

66 HO 144/A47288/1; E. Troup, *The Home Office*, 2nd. ed. (London, 1926), p. 105; R. Plehwe, op. cit., pp. 326-32. The situation came to a head, finally, in November 1888, when Warren wrote a controversial article criticising the general organisation of the police force (see n. 64 above). When Warren's response to Home Office criticism of this action was to insist that the Home Secretary had no authority to interfere in the exercise of powers expressly conferred on the Chief Commissioner by statute, Lushington minuted to the Home Secretary that 'the Commissioner is and has long been out of hand, in a state of complete insubordination, ignoring the Secretary of State': HO 144/ A48043/3 and 4. See also, Matthews, 1 May 1888, in Salisbury MSS, Class E; *Letters Q.V.*, op. cit., vol. 1, p. 448; MEPO 5/256. Warren resigned in November 1888. Unlike his previous letter of resignation of March, it was accepted by the Home Secretary: HO 144/A47288/3; HO 144/A48043/4.

67 3 *Hansard* 319, 25 August 1887, col. 1804; MEPO 2/185; Report of the Commissioner of Police of the Metropolis for 1887, *PP* 1888, vol. 57 , p. 349.

68 MEPO 2/181; HO 144/A47976/43D. See also, *R. v. Graham and Burns*, 4 *Times Law Reports* 212 (1888).

69 HO 144/A47976/43D.

70 HO 144/A47976/8: quoted in W. Williams, op. cit., pp. 209-10.

71 HO 144/A47 976/ 14. Matthews's reply to Warren's letter of 22 October was: 'I think you should not attempt to prevent any orderly body of persons from meeting or making speeches in Trafalgar Square tomorrow' (A47976/8).

His fears were sharpened when it seemed that the once-disorganised 'mobs' were developing an element of cohesion:

> It is now apparent that the policy of the mob leaders is to settle in private their tactics for each day how to elude the Police, and I think it more than probable that they will get out of hand in a very short time if they are not dispersed ... [By] some private signal they appear to be able to get together now to the number of two or three thousand in two or three minutes about the region of Charing Cross.[72]

The Chief Commissioner was clearly anxious to avoid being caught by a spontaneous burst of rioting, as had occurred in 1886, especially since it would be said that earlier intervention was warranted.

Warren was certainly not prepared to wait upon the Home Office's deliberations. He had already written to the Office of Works to obtain their authority for closing Trafalgar Square if disorder broke out — a letter which the Home Secretary, himself, would not have sent without Cabinet endorsement.[73] At the same time, the Chief Commissioner put pressure on the Home Secretary by sending him memorials from tradesmen and others complaining of the riotous proceedings.[74] Eventually, on 1 November, Warren issued a notice which warned that disorderly crowds would be dispersed. Although he recommended such a notice to the Home Office, he was too impatient to wait for a reply and issued the notice without prior submission to it.[75]

Warren's approach was evident. In the absence of legal justification, where the 'mob' terrorised the West End, the police should vigorously intervene. Haunted by the doings of the 'London mob' in February 1886, Warren's strategy was to strike quickly at the wandering bands of unemployed. By his unilateral action, however, the Chief Commissioner carelessly interfered in policy-making. Putting expediency before legality, Warren remained insensitive to the Home Office exploration of the question — partly one of policy, partly one of law — whether and how the unemployed could be brought to heel.

VI

The Home Office was not entirely unsympathetic to Warren's interpretation of the threat to public order. Henry Matthews wrote to the Prime Minister on 22 October to gain Treasury sanction for an increase in the police force, which, said the Home Secretary, was under excessive strain in dealing with the Socialist meetings and with 'a continuance of this Carnival of roughs urged on by statesmen to set

---

72 Warren to Lushington, 31 Oct. 1887, MEPO 2/182. See also *R. v. Graham and Burns*, Central Criminal Court, *Sessions Paper*, vol. 107 (1888), p. 377 at pp. 394-6; MEPO 7/49, P.O. 258.

73 HO 144/A48043/1 and 2.

74 HO 144/A47976H; A47976E/1; A47976/43D.

75 HO 144/A47976/l8 and 19; A479761/20 and 23a; MEPO 2/182. Warren, however, was without a Legal Adviser at this time: HO 45/A4747 1/2; MEPO 5/302.

law and order at defiance'.[76] Departmental memoranda similarly displayed anxiety at the condition of the West End. This is Godfrey Lushington's view of Warren's letter of 25 October: 'The state of things depicted … is a chronic condition of semi-disorder in the streets'. Along with the unemployed, the Under Secretary continued, there was invariably a portion of 'ill-disposed Socialists, roughs, thieves and wild mischievous youths', and, as witness the riots of 1886, 'in a town like London full of shops, it requires but a very few minutes for a very few men to do a vast amount of actual mischief'. Lushington was likewise convinced that the matter should not drift, especially considering the possible political effects of disorder in the Metropolis:

> The political consequences that may arise might of course be most serious looking to the strong party animus now existing. Any disorder or looting of shops arising from the inactivity of the police on one hand or any violent conflict with the mob on the other, would undoubtedly lead to grave political embarrassment to the Government.[77]

Despite this state of affairs, the Home Office papers indicate that the formulation of a policy to diminish the threat of the outcast poor was held back by the search for statutory or common-law justification for executive action. There were very distinct mentalities at work in the department. Henry Matthews was a distinguished lawyer but a cautious administrator.[78] At his side was Godfrey Lushington, the Permanent Under Secretary of State, industrious, painstaking, with a meticulous legal mind.[79] These two shared the burden of decision-making. Above all, they wanted a defensible legal case before acting against the bands of unemployed. The division between the administrative and judicial wings of the legal system ensured a scrupulous attention by the Home Office to the legal validity of police prosecutions. It proved difficult, however, to find legal backing for the immediate dispersal of street 'mobs'. One way of acting against them was to prohibit meetings in Trafalgar Square. Here again there were legal difficulties. Organised meetings could be regulated but not prohibited by the police. Moreover, encroachment on the right of public meeting invariably aroused intense political emotion. Yet the unpredictable behaviour of the 'wandering mobs' posed a threat which had to be dealt with. In short, Home Office acceptance of a prohibition on meetings in the square seems to have developed out of the legal difficulties experienced in dealing with the riotous potential of these disorganised bands, not from a politically-motivated determination to crack down on an important outdoor forum of organised protest.

---

76 Salisbury MSS, Class E. Matthews refused to swear in special constables because of the alarm it would cause: Viscount Chilston, *W.H. Smith* (London, 1965), p. 266.

77 HO 144/A47976/ 14.

78 *DNB* (Supplement 1912-21), p. 370; Shane Leslie, op. cit., pp. 57-8; Cooke and Vincent, op. cit., p. 452; Shane Leslie, 'Henry Matthews Lord Llandaff', *Dublin Review*, vol. 168 (1921), p. 13.

79 *Positivist Review*, vol. 15, 1st March 1907, pp. 70-1; Sir L. Guillemard, *Trivial Fond Records* (London, 1937), p. 14; Sir A. West, *Contemporary Portraits* (London, 1920), pp. 151-2; HO 45/B17626; J. Pellew, 'Administrative Change in the Home Office 1870-1896' (Univ. of London, Ph.D. thesis, 1976), pp. 60-6.

The problem was that bands whose conduct was not riotous, and who could only with great difficulty be proved to be unlawful assemblies, were really beyond the reach of the law.[80] There was only the Metropolitan Police Act of 1839, which allowed police interference with a wide array of street activities in order to prevent obstructions or breaches of the peace.[81] The chief magistrate of Bow Street had informed the Home Office that he had no judicial objection to a police notice, based on section 54 of the Act, declaring that, for the space of a month, such bands would be dispersed.[82] The Attorney- and Solicitor-General (Sir Richard Webster and Sir Edward Clarke) insisted, however, that such a notice would be *ultra vires* in relation to the statute, since it would practically prohibit groups of men wandering through the streets. The section of the Act in question gave power to the police to make special arrangements on particular occasions when the streets were liable to be obstructed; it did not justify any general prohibition. They reiterated their opinion when asked to consider the prohibitory notice of 1 November which Warren had issued without Home Office sanction. They remained convinced that objective conditions still did not justify the Home Secretary instructing the police to interfere with meetings or processions coming within the description in the police notice.[83]

Significantly, the need to act in accordance with the rule of law soon imposed itself upon executive government. Increasing pressure was being put on Matthews to alleviate the deteriorating state of affairs by prohibiting the meetings of the unemployed. It came from West End tradesmen and property-owners, in the form of memorials and deputations, complaining of the disruption of trade caused by leaving the streets in the hands 'of roughs, and thieves whose only object is to promote disorder for their own purposes'. In the same idiom, came criticism from the press, Liberal as well as Conservative; from the Chief Commissioner of Police; and from within the Cabinet.[84] The Cabinet finally resolved to prohibit meetings in the square, a police notice to that effect being issued on 8 November.[85] But the notice had no legal basis. It was certainly not a regulation order under the 1839 Police Act. This became evident when, on 11 November, William Saunders, late liberal MP for Hull, addressed a meeting in Trafalgar Square, where he was arrested and charged with disorderly conduct and obstructing the police. In effect, that is, he was charged with a breach of the Commissioner's notice of 8 November.[86] Yet this notice made no reference to any statutory regulation which, when knowingly

---

80 MEPO 2/182. The following section has been guided by the 'Memo as to Law Officers' Opinions (1867-1905) on regulation of meetings and processions' (1906), in HO 45/136764.

81 2 and 3 Vict. c. 47, ss. 52, 54 and 64.

82 HO 144/A47976/15.

83 HO 144/A47976/17-21; HO 144/A47976l/23a.

84 MEPO 2/182; HO 144/A47976H/30; HO 144/A47976/26; *Commonweal*, 12 Nov. 1887, p. 360; *The Times*, 18 Oct. 1887, p. 9; E. A. A. Douglas, loc. cit.; *Letters Q.V.*, op. cit., vol. 1, p. 357.

85 *Letters Q.V.*, op. cit., vol. 1, p. 358.

86 The Rev Stewart Headlam (English Land Restoration League and founder in 1877 of the Socialist Guild of St Matthew) had told Warren: 'I wish by peaceable means to get a legal decision as to the legality of your proclamation': MEPO 2/182. On Headlam, see M. B. Reckitt, *Maurice to Temple* (London, 1947), pp. 124-36.

disobeyed, could be dealt with summarily in the police courts. Before the chief magistrate on the next day, therefore, the case was adjourned to allow the government to state the legal grounds for the arrest.[87] At the adjourned hearing on 17 November, Henry Poland, acting for the Treasury, withdrew the prosecution. Saunders could have been *indicted* for attempting to hold an unlawful meeting, but for a summary prosecution there was only the charge of obstruction.[88] For the latter charge, however, the admission would have been necessary that Trafalgar Square was a thoroughfare. At this stage, the government did not want to make such an admission, since they thought they might ultimately have to argue that Trafalgar Square was Crown property and that the Crown had the right to prohibit meetings held there.[89] Saunders' case illustrated that the law did not allow the permanent prohibition of meetings, for which there was power of arrest and summary disposal of offenders, and that the publication of a police notice would not make illegal a meeting which in law was not so.[90]

The authorities had eventually decided to forestall the threat of the 'wandering hands' by prohibiting all meetings in the square. Even then, the Home Secretary felt it necessary to emphasise, before a deputation, that he was acting against 'tumultuous assemblages that … threaten to attack and destroy property', not *bona fide* gatherings. The effect of these ambiguous words was to leave it still open to question as to whether *bona fide* meetings in the square were illegal (including that called by the Metropolitan Radical Federation for 13 November 1887, to protest against the prohibitory notice).[91] The Home Office now asked the Law Officers whether processions *en route* to the square could be dispersed. The Officers still believed that the 1839 Police Act would not justify such action, but they tentatively advised another police regulation prohibiting processions from approaching the square. As to the Commissioner's right to prevent public meetings in the square, the Law Officers postponed judgement. They simply recommended that, since the meeting had been prohibited, the police ought to occupy the square in force.[92] In this equivocal manner, the government faced the Radical and Socialist organisations, which traditionally united in the defence of free speech. If the Home Office was ultimately impelled by the consideration that public safety and public opinion would justify the action of the police, it had hung fire in the knowledge that the law would have to be strained to the utmost.

---

87 HO 144/A47976G/ 2. Cf. HO 144/A47976F/1.

88 *Weekly Dispatch*, 20 Nov. 1887, p. 4; *The Times*, 18 Nov. 1887, pp. 4 and 9; HO 144/A47976G/1; 3 *Hansard* 322, 1 March 1888, col. 1896; Anon., *Right of Meeting in Trafalgar Square* (London, 1887).

89 Matthews, in fact, told a deputation on 11 November that the square was Crown property and the Queen had a legal right to withdraw permission to meet there: HO 144/A47 976/26. It was only on 17 November that the Law Officers declared that the square could be taken to be a thoroughfare.

90 Cf . A. V. Dicey, 'On the Right of Public Meeting', *Contemporary Review*, vol. 55, April 1889, p. 509.

91 HO 144/A47976/26; *Pall Mall Gazette*, 12 Nov. 1887, p. 1; C. T. Clarkson and J. Hall Richardson, op. cit., pp. 208-9. Home Secretary Matthews claimed subsequently that the 'bloody Sunday' demonstrators did not constitute a *bona fide* gathering. Judging from an examination of 55 court cases, however, those who tried to enter Trafalgar Square were workmen in the staple trades and industries of east and south London, such as the building and finishing trades: 3 *Hansard* 322, 1 March 1888, cols. 1908-9; *The Times* and *Weekly Dispatch*, November and December, 1887 ; HO 144/A479760; HO 144/A47976/63-8.

92 HO 144/A47976/34 and 35.

VII

In the wake of 'bloody Sunday', the success of government policy was celebrated by the press and the propertied classes. Thus encouraged, the police bridled the bands of unemployed and forestalled renewed attempts to meet in Trafalgar Square. The Radicals and Socialists, meanwhile, astonished at the facility with which the police dispersed the demonstrations, seemed reluctant to instigate further mass action. Yet despite every indication that the authorities had secured and consolidated an unqualified victory in the streets around Trafalgar Square, it was, as the Home Office had anticipated, preface to a longer contest over the legality of public-order policy. These reactions to 'bloody Sunday' require closer assessment.

Not quite everyone in respectable circles approved of the manner in which the demonstrators had been put to rout. 'My own feeling', wrote the Rev Samuel Barnett, founder of Toynbee Hall, 'is that repression has been ill managed. The crowds should have been sternly controlled but grievances should not have been created.[93] A fiercer epistle came from Henry Scott Holland, leader of the Christian Social Union:

> I never saw a crowd look more innocent of revolution in my life: and there was no disturbance to London
> ... until the Police smashed their heads. The Government seem *bent* on manufacturing a Revolution — I
> have seldom felt so sad, or so mad, at a political wickedness.[94]

Such dissent was drowned in a sea of public rejoicing. *The Times* applauded Warren's defeat of 'a deliberate attempt to set aside the elementary safeguards of civilized society and terrorize London by placing the control of the streets in the hands of the criminal classes'. The same editorial convinced itself that the demonstrations had been composed of 'all that is weakest, most worthless, and most vicious in the slums of a great city'.[95] On the 15th, *The Times* reported that the West End was rejoicing at the police victory, and that the London working classes were 'foremost in expressions of satisfaction that the noisy faction has been debarred from making a mockery of public meeting in Trafalgar-square'.[96] Members of the Stock Exchange expressed their gratitude by opening a subscription list to reimburse the police.[97] Others offered to raise drilled volunteers in the event of further trouble.[98]

The Chief Commissioner of Police had already asked the Home Office for 3,000 special constables to occupy Trafalgar Square on 20 November, and 20,000 more to protect the suburbs while the regular

---

93 Barnett Papers, F/BAR/61. I am grateful to the Greater London Record Office for permission to quote from this document.

94 Quoted in P. d'A. Jones, *The Christian Socialist Revival 1877-1914* (New Jersey, 1968), p. 195 (emphasis in original).

95 *The Times*, 14 Nov. 1887, p. 9. Cf. E. P. Thompson, op. cit., p. 491.

96 *The Times*, 15 Nov. 1887, p. 10.

97 Ibid. £400 was raised.

98 HO 144/A479761/1A.

police defended the approaches to the square. Warren feared that another attempt might be made to enter Trafalgar Square. He told Godfrey Lushington:

> I think that if anything does take place on Sunday it will either be something small by way of protest, or else it will be organised on a very extensive scale as a supreme effort; and I think it is necessary to be prepared with an overwhelming force to frustrate the most vigorous effort that the combined roughs and anarchists can possibly make.[99]

The Home Secretary agreed. 'If we are to have another battle,' Matthews minuted to Lushington, 'we should have some of the public on our side.'[100] It was with difficulty that some 6-7,000 specials were recruited, but they were employed on the 20th to defend the square.[101] In harassing the straggling crowds, however, the mounted police fatally injured Alfred Linnell, a Radical law-writer. If this mishap embarrassed the authorities, it did not deter them from keeping the massive funeral procession, which was subsequently arranged by the Radicals and Socialists, away from Trafalgar Square.[102]

Delegates from the London Radical clubs had met on 16 November to decide whether a second assault should be made on the square. However, little confidence remained in the power of unorganised demonstrators to resist the police. Instead, the Metropolitan Radical Federation, pressured by the Gladstonian Liberals, agreed to rely on legal action to open the square to public meetings.[103] Shortly afterwards, a Law and Liberty League was formed on the initiative of W. T. Stead, editor of the *Pall Mall Gazette*. Its ultimate aim was to bring the Metropolitan police under popular control, but in the short term it represented political offenders in court and, more significantly, started litigation in the cause of free assembly.[104] The League was as aware as the authorities that the police notice of 8 November had done nothing to resolve the uncertainties in the law of public meeting.

Not until after 'bloody Sunday' did the Law Officers adjudicate on the right to prohibit meeting in the square. They stated that neither the Crown nor the Police Commissioner had the power to prevent 'user' of the square as a public place. But they considered that section 3 of the Trafalgar Square Act (1844) put the square in the position of a thoroughfare for the purpose of the 1839 Police Act. As such, if the Commissioner felt the meetings were causing serious obstruction to the thoroughfare, directions could be given under section 52 of the Police Act to prevent such meetings. On the 18th, therefore, a police notice prohibited meetings in and processions approaching Trafalgar Square, 'until further

---

99   HO 144/A479761/1. Cf. MEPO 2/174.

100   HO 144/A47976/36. Matthews already knew that the Prime Minister was averse to the employment of soldiers in and around the square.

101   *Annual Register*, 1887, p. 177; A. Liddell, *Notes from the Life of an Ordinary Mortal* (London 1911), p. 254; W. S. Adams, *Edwardian Portraits* (London, 1957), p. 6.

102   HO 144/A17976P/2-7.

103   HO 144/A49014/8; Y. Kapp, op. cit., p. 232; H. Hamilton Fyfe, *Annals of Our Time* (London, 1891), vol. 3, p. 17.

104   Y. Kapp, op. cit., p. 235; G. Williams, *The Passionate Pilgrim. A Life of Annie Besant* (London, 1932), pp. 170-3.

notice'.[105] A permanent ban on meetings and processions had finally been worked from the existing statutes. Above all, the Law Officers estimated that it would hold up in the law courts.

Already, the initiative in judicial proceedings had been taken by the Home Office. Matthews made it clear to Lushington, the day after 'bloody Sunday', that he wanted a jury's verdict in favour of the government. He insisted that a case 'of an aggravated kind' for which there was sufficient proof should be sent to the Old Bailey. As he explained:

> Throughout all these meetings I have not had brought before me a report of a single case of the kind one
> would wish to try. It will not do to rest on decisions of Police Magistrates.[106]

The anticipated prosecution became *R. v. Cunninghame Graham and John Burns*. Both defendants had tried to force their way into the square on 13 November, when they were arrested and charged with riot, unlawful assembly and assaulting the police. At the trial, the Crown's case was that there was no right of public meeting in the square. For the defence, H. H. Asquith concentrated on the uncertainty shown by the authorities as to the legal basis of the prohibitory notices. The trial judge, Mr Justice Charles, took the view that the duty of preserving the peace fell upon the Chief Commissioner who, in consequence, had the right to issue police notices prohibiting meetings and processions. Accordingly, both defendants were found guilty of unlawful assembly and sentenced to six weeks' imprisonment.[107] The decision was hardly the express adjudication upon the question of a right of public meeting in Trafalgar Square which the Home Secretary hankered after, but it served, nevertheless, as authority for subsequent judicial decisions.

The decision in *Graham and Burns* influenced a succession of cases promoted by the Law and Liberty League.[108] The stipendiary magistrates took the law to be laid down by Mr Justice Charles and generally refused to state a case for the opinion of Queen's Bench.[109] In the case of Antonio Borgia, a member of the Clerkenwell Patriotic Club, even the Home Secretary looked forward to a high court

---

105 HO 144/A47976/35 and 39. See also Return giving the Regulations issued by the Chief Commissioner of Police with respect to Trafalgar Square, issued 12 and 18 November 1887, *PP* 1889, vol. 61, p. 265.

106 HO 144/A47976/36.

107 4 *Times Law Reports* 212 (1888); 16 Cox C.C. 420 (1888); HO 144/A479760/1; Sir Richard Webster, *Recollections of Bar and Bench* (London, 1914), p. 173; D. G. T. Williams, *Keeping the Peace* (London, 1967), p. 80; C. Watts and L. Davies, *Cunninghame Graham: A Critical Biography* (Cambridge, 1979), pp. 71-6. Another 55 demonstrators were arrested during 'bloody Sunday' and charged mainly with assaulting the police. Of these, 28 were sentenced to imprisonment with hard labour for periods varying between 14 days and six months. Two more were tried at the Middlesex Sessions — one was sentenced to 12 months' imprisonment; the other to 5 years' penal servitude, for wounding a constable. Another 16 were fined between 20s and 40s each; the rest were bound over to keep the peace or were discharged: HO 144/A47976/60-68.

108 E. Reed, 'Remember Trafalgar Square', *Pall Mall Gazette Extra*, no. 37, p. 2; A. Hutt, *This Final Crisis* (London, 1935), p. 111. Annie Besant was particularly active in the attempt to test the legality of the prohibition issued by the Chief Commissioner: HO 144/A47976/53, 55, 82, 83.

109 E.g., the case of Hicks, *Pall Mall Gazette*, 23 Jan. 1888, p. 4. One case, however, went before the Divisional Court, where the judges affirmed that there was no right of public meeting in Trafalgar Square: *Ex parte Lewis*, 21 QBD. 191 (1888); HO 144/A49014/4; 'The Trafalgar Square Question', *St. James's Gazette*, 29 June 1888. For criticism of the decision in *ex parte Lewis*, see B. L. Mosely, 'Trafalgar Square', *Law Magazine and Review*, vol. 13 (1888), p. 260.

judgement on the question of public meeting. Prior to the hearing, Evelyn Ruggles-Brise, Principal Private Secretary to the Home Secretary, wrote to the Treasury Solicitor:

> Mr. Matthews wishes me to tell you privately that he would be extremely glad if the question of a 'right of public meeting' in Trafalgar Square could be directly raised in a special case. However clear this point may be, it will do good to have an express adjudication upon it.[110]

But the stipendiary, Mr Vaughan, would not allow the issue to be raised.[111] In short, throughout 1888, the courts deflected all attempts to challenge the prohibitory notice of 18 November 1887. Trafalgar Square was seen, in effect, as a direct responsibility of executive government.

Even with judicial opinion running in the required direction, however, the Home Office was made to feel uneasy about the legal basis of the police notice. In September 1888, the Treasury Solicitor advised the Home Office that it was unlikely the police notice allowed the continued closure of Trafalgar Square, given that it referred to a state of public unease specific to the previous November. He went on to suggest that, under the authority of the Trafalgar Square Act (1844), the Commissioner of Works should frame regulations to prohibit all meetings in the square.[112] But this did not meet with Home Office approval. It failed to incorporate what Lushington considered were two necessary features — that the police should have the power to arrest without warrant those who disregarded the prohibition; and that it should be possible to proceed summarily against those arrested. There were other deficiencies, too. 'This would be an admission', said Lushington, 'that hitherto the Police had been acting without sufficient authority: and it seems to me very doubtful whether the Trafalgar Square Act gives this power to the Commissioner, and at all events the point would be disputed.'[113] Lushington, himself, was attracted to a bill which would prohibit all meetings in the square, but he knew that this would be rejected by the Commons. Once again, therefore, the opinion of the Law Officers was canvassed. They advised that it was unwise to rely on the police notice of 18 November, and that a better course was to give the Commissioner of Works statutory power to make regulations to deal with meetings.[114] Again, the Home Office was unconvinced. Lushington thought that such a bill would succeed only if it carried a pledge that meetings would be allowed, a pledge which the government would not wish to give.[115]

At this point, James Monro, Warren's successor as Chief Commissioner of Police, added his voice to the internal deliberations on the question of Trafalgar Square. He asked the Home Office whether the proclamation of 18 November was defensible in relation to *bona fide* political meetings, when there was no reason to fear disturbances. He also declared that if the enforcement of the proclamation could be

---

110 HO 144/A49014/11. Cf. HO 144/A47976/100.

111 Ibid.; *Pall Mall Gazette*, 13 Aug. 1888.

112 HO 144/A49014/13. Cf. HO 144/A47976/106.

113 Ibid.

114 HO 144/A49014/15.

115 Ibid.

justified in such circumstances, 'the police practically acquire the power of stopping meetings anywhere in London at discretion, and this is a power which will not I take it be conceded to them'.[116] At the beginning of 1889, Monro pressed the Home Office for legislation to clarify the position. He thought the time was opportune because of the dissension within the Metropolitan Radical Federation. At a meeting of the Federation, the London Liberal MPs had opposed fresh moves to arrange a meeting in Trafalgar Square. The Chief Commissioner went on:

> With the prospect of legislation by Government in view, the hands of the Police will be enormously strengthened, as they will then only have to deal with the faction of disorder, who apparently will not be content with any course but asserting their supposed right by force to hold meetings in the Square.[117]

By this time, however, the Home Office seemed to think it unwise to rekindle the emotions surrounding the issue of Trafalgar Square, which the introduction of legislation would have brought about.

For quite some time after 'bloody Sunday', then, the Home Office had periodically to review the strengths and limitations of the prohibitory notice of 18 November. The legal basis of the police notice was section 52 of the Metropolitan Police Act (1839), a provision which allowed the regulation of meetings and processions, but which did not authorise their permanent prohibition. It was fortunate for the executive that no objection to this formation of law by administrative decree was ever sustained by the judiciary. But the prospect that the courts might not remain so favourably disposed to executive policy impelled the Home Office to examine more reliable defences. Legislation to prohibit meetings in Trafalgar Square on a permanent basis was the most desirable but also the least obtainable. Only legislation which would allow meetings under prescribed regulations stood any chance of success. With the Liberal and Radical parties pressing for exactly this, however, such a measure would have been interpreted as a political concession on the part of the government.[118] In the face of these difficulties, the Home Office abandoned the idea of legislation. It again took shelter behind the police proclamation, which managed to see out the remaining years of the Salisbury administration. The abrogation of the prohibitory notice of 18 November had to wait for the Liberal Home Secretary, H. H. Asquith, who, in 1892, instructed the Commissioner of Works to make regulations allowing meetings in the square on specified days and under certain conditions.[119]

---

116 HO 144/A49014/16.

117 HO 144/A49014/17-18.

118 'A Bill for the Regulation of meetings in Trafalgar Square', *PP* 1888, vol. 7, p. 449; HO 144/A49014/4; HO 144/A47976/90. In July 1889, the London County Council's request to be given control of Trafalgar Square was turned down: D. Torr, *Tom Mann and His Times* (London, 1956), vol. 1, p. 344.

119 HO 144/A47976U/9.

VIII

Judging from the Trafalgar Square riots of 1886/7, it is unwise to pre-suppose the relationship between the state and the legal system. This requires concrete examination in every specific case, and never more so than in relation to the distinctive socio-legal context of London. The Metropolitan juridical system was characterised by three main features — a semi-military, highly centralised police system which conferred immense discretionary authority on the Chief Commissioner; a Minister of State whose direct control over this crucial agency for law enforcement in the nation's capital gave a political aspect to every lapse in public order; and a pronounced separation of police and judicial functions. The indecision and hesitancy in law enforcement in the autumn of 1887 was the product of the tensions between these factors. Exploiting the ill-defined relationship between Chief Commissioner and Home Secretary, Sir Charles Warren sought support for decisive action against the disorderly groups of unemployed, however politically or legally inappropriate. His *modus operandi*, that of a high-handed military campaigner in the outskirts of Empire, inevitably pre-empted Home Office decisions.[120] Matthews, the Home Secretary, was, in fact, well aware of the damaging political repercussions if the government were held responsible for renewed damage to property in the centre of London; but there were political risks, too, in the illegal suppression of unemployed demonstrations, given the commitment of many parties to freedom of speech and assembly. The very division of police and judicial duties and the consequent impossibility of predicting the outcome of court hearings also obliged the executive to construct meticulously a sustainable legal case for the suppression of meetings in Trafalgar Square. These divisions and stresses within the policy of public order make existing evaluations of 'bloody Sunday' appear inadequate. The government, of course, eventually used the police to rid the West End of the threat of further riot, illustrating that the courts and the 'rule of law' do not alone define the role and conduct of the police force. But the depiction of a unified state repression of 'outcast London' masks both the conflict of personalities which distracted the enforcement of law, and the constraint, if only in the sense of outer limits, which the rule of law imposed upon the use of authority.

---

120 Lest it be thought that Warren's personal contribution alone explains the 'divided counsels' in public-order policy, the next Chief Commissioner, James Monro, was to have his troubles with the Home Office when, in 1890, he claimed the right to prohibit peaceable processions: HO 45/A48160; MEPO 2/248; D. Ascoli, op. cit., pp. 163-5.

In Darkest England and the Way Out: Whitechapel Road, 1890

Salvation Army Barracks Courtyard

Salvation Army Social Campaign

3

'In Darkest England and the Way Out'

The Salvation Army, Social Reform and the Labour Movement, 1885-1910

The British bourgeois [...] finally [...] accepted the dangerous aid of the Salvation Army, which revives the propaganda of early Christianity, appeals to the poor as the elect, fights capitalism in a religious way, and thus fosters an element of early Christian class antagonism, which one day may become troublesome to the well-to-do people who now find the ready money for it.

F. Engels[1]

In the past decade a prominent theme in the historiography of nineteenth-century Britain has been the imposition of middle-class habits and attitudes upon the populace by means of new or re-invigorated mechanisms of 'social control'. To the apparatus of law enforcement and to the disciplines of the factory and wage labour, historians have added the less overt instruments of social welfare, education, religion, leisure and moral reform. Philanthropists, educators, clergymen and moralizers have all become soldiers in a campaign to uproot the 'anti-social' characteristics of the poor and to cement the hegemony of the elite.[2]

Not surprisingly, the concept of 'social control', and the depiction of the activities and institutions of the propertied as effective instruments of social discipline, have run into opposition. Most significant, for present purposes, is F. M. L. Thompson's objection that the idea of social control ignores the possibility that 'the working classes themselves generated their own values and attitudes suited to the

The research for this paper was greatly facilitated by the R. T. French Visiting Professorship, which links the University of Rochester, New York, and Worcester College, Oxford. A preliminary version of the paper was presented at a conference on Victorian Outcasts at the Victorian Studies Centre, University of Leicester. I would like to thank Simon Stevenson of Exeter College, Oxford, for research assistance; Lieut.-Col. Cyril Barnes for guidance with the archives in the International Headquarters of the Salvation Army, London; and Clive Fleay, Tina Isaacs, Ellen More, K. O. Morgan, Rosemary Tyler and Martin Wiener for their helpful comments. Finally, for her advice and encouragement, I am indebted to Jennifer Donnelly.

1   F. Engels, *Socialism, Utopian and Scientific* (London, 1892), p. xxxi.

2   See *Social Control in Nineteenth Century Britain*, ed. by A. P. Donajgrodzki (London, 1977); *Popular Education and Socialization in the Nineteenth Century*, ed. by P. McCann (London, 1977); J. R. Hay, 'Employers' Attitudes to Social Policy and the Concept of 'Social Control', 1900-1920', in *The Origins of British Social Policy*, ed. by P. Thane (London, 1978), pp. 107-25.

requirements of life in an industrial society'. Thompson instructs us to 'pay more attention to the workers' own history as something with a life of its own', and he suggests that the transformation in Victorian social habits and social relations owes as much to the 'autonomous development of working-class culture' as to 'embourgeoisement by social control'. A similar view was put forward by Martin Wiener when reviewing the first collection of essays on British history to refer explicitly to the concept of social control. Victorian moral reform, argued Wiener, not only represented efforts at social engineering from above, but also 'efforts by vast numbers of ordinary individuals to reshape their lives — as individuals and together with their fellows — towards increased autonomy and effectiveness'.[3] In harmony with this critical response to the idea of social control, the present article examines the Salvation Army as an expression of independent working-class cultural development, and not as an agency of middle-class domination.

The trend of previous historical work on the Salvation Army has been to represent it as part of a middle-class onslaught on the 'uncivilized' poor: a middle-class evangelism and philanthropy which sought to re-create the poor in its own image, to establish a new paternalism; in all, to restore class harmony and class control to the threatening urban areas. For Bentley Gilbert, the Salvation Army was one of several representatives of indiscriminate charity, used as 'vehicles to transmit the ransom' which the propertied were eager to pay to subdue the menace of the poor in the wake of the Trafalgar Square riots. Gareth Stedman Jones has described the reforming effort of middle-class London in the same years, manifested in the proliferation of missions, shelters and settlement houses, dispensing an Evangelicalism that sought to mould working-class culture and conduct. There is, of course, evidence in favour of such an interpretation. The Salvation Army was party to an ambitious effort of cultural reconstruction, in the best tradition of the temperance movement. Its flaunted purchase of the Grecian Theatre and Eagle Tavern in City Road, London, in 1882 prompted *The Times* to ask if the Salvationists intended 'to wage war upon all amusements save those provided by the religious "free-and-easies" of their meeting rooms?' Seemingly the London working class believed so, since they came out in force to resist physically the Army's colonization of their former haunt.[4]

The aim in what follows, however, is to argue for a modification of this conventional image of the Salvation Army, and thus to begin the construction of the more adequate work of historical analysis that the Army deserves. The focus is on the phase of the Salvation Army's history, from the mid 1880s to the early twentieth century, which E. P. Thompson rightly described as 'a profoundly ambiguous moment

---

3   F. M. L. Thompson, 'Social Control in Victorian Britain', in *Economic History Review*, second series, XXXIV (1981), pp. 189-208; M. Wiener, review of *Social Control in Nineteenth Century Britain*, in *Journal of Social History*, XII (1978-79), p. 318. See also *Popular Culture and Class Conflict 1590-1914*, ed. by E. and S. Yeo (Brighton, 1981), chap. 5.

4   B. B. Gilbert, *The Evolution of National Insurance in Great Britain* (London, 1966), p. 32; G. Stedman Jones, 'Working-Class Culture and Working-Class Politics in London, 1870-1900: Notes on the Remaking of a Working Class', in *Journal of Social History*, VII (1973-74), pp. 466-69; also R. D. Storch, 'Introduction', in *Popular Culture and Custom in Nineteenth-Century England*, ed. by id. (London, 1982); *The Times*, 19 August 1882, p. 7; also 22 September, p. 8; 7 February 1883, p. 7

when Salvationism ran in double harness with London Radicalism' and with the early labour movement.[5] Throughout these years, in particular, the Army developed a definite rapport with the labour movement in the sphere of social reform. The subsequent sections seek to document the origins and progress of this relationship between the Salvation Army and the various components of labour. More crucially, they strive to demonstrate the social and ideological affinities between the Army, on one hand, and the most emancipated and self-sustaining movement of the working class, on the other. First, however, it is useful to provide a brief outline of the Salvation Army's evolution.

The emergence of the Salvation Army in 1878 from the cocoon of the Christian Mission represented a significant development in the attitude of Nonconformity to the depressed strata of late-Victorian England. From below 5,000 in 1878, 'Army' membership grew rapidly to an estimated 100,000 in 1900 and 115,000 by 1911. The number passing through Salvationist hands was considerably greater: between 1886 and 1906, probably no fewer than four million people knelt at the Army's penitent-forms. Religion, it appeared, could break new ground among the urban poor. The number of full-time officers likewise increased from 127 in 1878 to 2,868 in 1906; the number of corps rose from 81 to 1,431 between the same years.[6] The Salvation Army was particularly strong in Bristol, in the working-class wards of Nottingham and Leicester, and in the Northern towns of Hull, Barnsley, Darlington and Scarborough. It was always much tougher going in London, where, according to the social investigator Charles Booth, 'the mental life of the average working man' was ever more occupied by sport, leisure and secular societies, to the exclusion of religious interests.[7]

The first phase of the Salvation Army's history, *circa* 1865 to 1885, saw the development of one more variant of late Methodist revivalism: the charismatic preacher, in the shape of William Booth, frustrated by the discipline of the Methodist New Connexion, eager to return to the intuitive virtue of the pure in heart, determined to minister to the outcast poor excluded by the more respectable denominations.[8] From the mid 1880s, however, the Army gradually supplemented its soul-saving mission with various forms of social relief work: night shelters, rescue homes for fallen women, a prison-gate brigade, and a detachment of slum sisters to nurse the sick and assist with child care. The Army's social work expanded considerably following the publication in October 1890 of William

---

5   E. P. Thompson, 'Blood, Fire and Unction', in *New Society*, No 128 (1965), p. 25.

6   A. D. Gilbert, *Religion and Society in Industrial England* (London, 1976), pp. 42-3; R. Robertson, 'The Salvation Army: The Persistence of Sectarianism', in *Patterns of Sectarianism*, ed. by B. R. Wilson (London, 1967), p. 102; R. Sandall, *The History of the Salvation Army* (3 vols; London, 1947-55), II, p. 338.

7   H. McLeod, 'Class, Community and Region: The Religious Geography of Nineteenth-Century England', in *A Sociological Yearbook of Religion in Britain*, VI (1973), p. 57; id., *Class and Religion in the Late Victorian City* (London, 1974), pp. 27, 60; K. S. Inglis, *Churches and the Working Classes in Victorian England* (London, 1963), pp. 196-7; Ch. Booth, *Life and Labour of the People in London* (London, 1902-3), Third Series, VII, p. 425; also I, p. 82; V, pp. 67-68. The Salvation Army was also well represented in Bradford, Sheffield, Barrow and Runcorn: Robertson, 'The Salvation Army', p. 91.

8   Sandall, *The History of the Salvation Army*, op. cit., I, pp. 15-18; H. Begbie, *The Life of General William Booth* (2 vols; New York, 1920), I, chap. 18; S. J. Ervine, *God's Soldier. General William Booth* (2 vols; London, 1934), I, Book II.

Booth's *In Darkest England and the Way Out*. Extrapolating from the figures in Charles Booth's *Life and Labour of the People* (1889), 'General' Booth estimated that three million men, women and children in the United Kingdom, or one-tenth of the entire population, languished in a state of abject destitution and misery. The General intended to guide the 'submerged tenth' out of the jungle of 'Darkest England', or, changing the metaphor, to launch Salvation lifeboats into the sea of drunkenness, want and crime, there to rescue the 'shipwrecked' unemployed and sweated, as the lithograph in the frontispiece to *Darkest England* so garishly depicted. The instrument of deliverance was to be a threefold scheme of 'self-helping and self-sustaining communities, each being a kind of co-operative society, or patriarchal family, governed and disciplined on the principles which have proved so effective in the Salvation Army'. The City Colony would gather up the outcast poor, give them food, shelter and work, and start the process of 'regeneration'. This process would continue in the Farm Colony, situated in the countryside, where colonists would be trained to begin a new life of economic independence in the Over-Sea Colony.[9]

I

Stephen Yeo has convincingly described a distinct stage in the social history of socialism, characteristic of the years 1883-96, which he terms 'the mass conversion, 'making socialists', religion-of-socialism phase'.[10] Significantly, the main features of the socialism of this period — the outdoor 'missionary' activity; the importance of *being* socialists and of having socialism inside you; the expectation of personal and social change in the wake of 'conversion' — were strikingly replicated in early Salvationism. The present section examines these resemblances in detail. For a start the main methods of transmitting the respective 'gospels' coincided. In the 1880s, both movements took to the streets and parks to rally recruits. Both groups occupied the main urban pitches for street preaching, or stump oratory, leading on some occasions to physical conflict between them.[11] At this stage, socialists no less than Salvationists believed that socialism (or Salvationism) would come if the gospel were preached sufficiently: it was all a matter of proselytising. Both bodies also, it seems, suffered attack from sections of the London working class. The so-called 'Skeleton Army', which dogged the footsteps of the Salvationists in London and in many provincial towns, 'tried a fall with the Radical workers of East London', according to George Lansbury, a founding father of the Labour Party, who as a boy belonged to the Salvation Army.[12] Both movements also used the street procession to some effect. More crucially,

---

9   Sandall, *The History of the Salvation Army*, III, *passim*; W. Booth, *In Darkest England and the Way Out* (London, 1890), pp. 91-93.

10   S. Yeo, 'A New Life: The Religion of Socialism in Britain, 1883-1896', in *History Workshop*, No 4 (1977), p. 42.

11   For one instance of conflict, in Norwich between the 'Army' and the Socialist League, see *Daylight*, 8 January 1887; also 15 January.

12   G. Lansbury, *My Life* (London, 1928), p. 85; S. Mayor, *The Churches and the Labour Movement* (London, 1967), pp. 322-23. See also chap. 1 above.

real accord developed between Salvationists and socialists in the 1880s around the struggle with the London authorities to maintain the freedom to hold open-air meetings and processions. In September 1890, Commissioner Frank Smith crossed swords with the Metropolitan Police when he led a procession of Salvationists to Exeter Hall in the Strand, and refused to disperse in Savoy Street, thereby falling foul of the Trafalgar Square regulation of November 1887, for which Smith served three weeks in prison.[13] Well might Friedrich Engels, by then a doyen of English socialism, counsel Paul Lafargue thus: 'You should also stand up for the *Salvation Army*, for without it the right to hold processions and discussions in the street would be more decayed in England than it is.'[14]

There were compelling similarities, too, between religious and political conversion. The 'faith' was commonly revealed by individual 'evangelists', the latter exhorting members of the audience to join the faithful. There were converts struggling to resist the appeal before finally succumbing; there were individual confessions of faith from the platform, with both types of proselyte proclaiming visions of a new world, a Kingdom of God on earth. It was not unknown for socialists to testify to having been 'born again', a crucial canon of Salvationism's meagre theology. In South Wales, according to Tom Jones, 'Socialism swept through the valleys like a new religion, and young men asked one another, Are you a Socialist? in the same tone as a Salvationist asks, Are you saved?' The literature of the two movements adopted an equally vivid vocabulary. If the *War Cry* spoke of converted drunkards and thieves, the *Clarion* cited instances of 'converted Tories'; if the *War Cry* announced enthusiastic receptions and successful 'invasions' of virgin territory, the *Workers' Cry* described open-air meetings at which officers were appointed 'and many new members enrolled amidst much enthusiasm'.[15]

Following conversion, there was the intense fervour of committed converts and a strong sense of calling to do good to others. Salvationists and socialists alike sought not only their own spiritual and social welfare, but also the deliverance of their neighbourhoods and workmates from personal vices and denigrating social conditions. Making a bold stand for Christ or for socialism, however, was just as likely to lead to alienation from family, friends and workmates, with converts sorely tested by those who felt challenged by divergent beliefs and habits.[16] Converts to both faiths commonly abandoned strong

---

13 MPR 2/254, Public Record Office, London.

14 *Engels Lafargue Correspondence*, 11 (Moscow, 1960), p. 85. Cf. *Pall Mall Gazette*, 29 March 1888, p. 4; *Clarion*, 6 February 1892, p. 4. Other methods coincided; Captain Irons of Portsmouth recorded in his diary for 1 March 1879: 'took 1500 handbills to the Dock gates, to distribute to workmen as they went home', G. S. Railton, *Captain Ted* (London, 1880), p. 65.

15 Jones is quoted in P. Joyce, *Work, Society and Politics* (Brighton, 1980), p. 229. See Yeo, 'A New Life', loc. cit., pp. 10-13, 17, 28; *Workers' Cry*, 15 August 1891. The *Workers' Cry* was the organ of the Labor (sic) Army, founded by Frank Smith, formerly of the Salvation Army, for whom see below, pp. 72f., 83f. The *War Cry* was the Salvation Army's weekly paper; the *Clarion* was an openly Socialist weekly, edited by Robert Blatchford.

16 Yeo, 'A New Life', p. 13; W. Bramwell Booth's contribution to *Christianity and the Working Classes*, ed. by G. Haw (London, 1906), p. 155; S. Pierson, *Marxism and the Origins of British Socialism* (Ithaca, 1973), pp. 228-9; J. Kent, 'Feelings and Festivals. An interpretation of some working-class religious attitudes', in *The Victorian City: Images and Realities*, ed. by H. J. Dyos and M. Wolff (2 vols; London, 1973), II, pp. 862-4.

drink. At this date of course many socialists were still closely identified with the moral cause of temperance: George Lansbury, Tom Mann, Ben Tillett, Keir Hardie, all temperance reformers before joining the labour movement, saw in drink an explanation of the inertia of the poor.[17] At times, it was more than simply new habits that were adopted, but a new sense of personal worth leading to a complete change in life-style, including what the Salvation Army called an 'improved temporal condition'. In the *War Cry* for February 1888, General Booth commended 'the Socialism of Salvation', whereby moralized people created improved material circumstances. A decade later, a Salvationist officer from Peckham informed Charles Booth: 'Conversion has a wonderful effect on a man; he is very soon decently clothed; his home becomes better, and, although he still remains a working man, outwardly he might pass with the clerks'.[18] Early socialism also looked to these individual changes of personal character and circumstance. The central creed of the Fellowship of the New Life, from which the Fabian Society emerged, was the creation of social change through the perfection of individual character. 'Man building' was seen as an integral part of constructing the co-operative commonwealth.[19] Other labour pioneers, particularly those from an Evangelical background, considered that new standards of personal conduct — self-discipline, self-respect, self-sacrifice — would equip working-class individuals to take control of their own lives, to throw off the shackles of patronage and manipulation. There was, in their view, a connection between character or moral reform and social reform.[20] It was this whole conversion and post-conversion syndrome that Bernard Shaw both elucidated and encapsulated in *The Illusions of Socialism* (1897), at a time when backsliding was increasing, with earnest converts burning themselves out through overwork.

> we are told of the personal change, the transfigured, lighted-up face, the sudden accession of self-respect, the joyful self-sacrifice, the new eloquence and earnestness of the young working man who has been rescued from a purposeless, automatic loafing through life, by the call of the gospel of Socialism.
>
> These transfigurations [...] are as common in Socialist propaganda campaigns as in the Salvation Army.[21]

Inevitably there were similarities in the social-class appeal and constitution of both movements. If

---

17 B. Harrison, *Drink and the Victorians* (London, 1971), pp. 395-7; W. Kendall, *The Revolutionary Movement in Britain 1900-21* (London, 1969), p. 8.

18 Yeo, 'A New Life', pp. 8, 13; Booth, *Life and Labour*, op cit., Third Series, V1, p. 78. Cf. C. Booth, *The Salvation Army in relation to the Church and State* (London, 1883), pp. 20-1. Catholicism similarly gave the Irish poor in New York an internal discipline and a 'militant respectability'. I owe this international comparison to Sheridan Gilley.

19 A. M. McBriar, *Fabian Socialism and English Politics 1884-1918* (Cambridge, 1962), pp. 2-3; D. Douglas-Wilson, 'The Search for Fellowship and Sentiment in British Socialism, 1880-1914' (M. A. thesis, Warwick University, 1971), *passim*; S. Rowbotham and J. Weeks, *Socialism and the New Life* (London, 1977), pp. 15-16; M. J. Wiener, *Between Two Worlds. The Political Thought of Graham Wallas* (Oxford, 1971), chap. 2; J. Clifford, *Socialism and the Churches* [Fabian Tract No 139] (London, 1908), p. 12.

20 Storch, 'Introduction', loc. cit.

21 B. Shaw, 'The Illusions of Socialism', in *Forecasts of the Coming Century* (Manchester, 1897), p. 158.

William Booth penned *How to Reach the Masses with the Gospel*, the early socialist journals, *Justice* and *Commonweal*, spoke of the awakening of 'the masses' — a relatively new term in social discourse, descriptive of an industrial-urban working class, including those who could find no work.[22] In one sense, the class appeal was stronger in the Salvation Army than in the labour movement. The tract *All About the Salvation Army* (1882) insisted that the masses must be evangelized by those of their own class. Unlike, say, the Wesleyans, the Army stressed that working-class people could find leaders from among themselves, that evangelists could be drawn from the same social strata as the non-worshippers. Not for Booth the bridges to the poor of the settlement movement; class divisions were too wide, he believed, for such social closures. Instead, the Salvation Army worked for a genuine participatory movement, a 'priesthood of believers', albeit a highly undemocratic one in terms of decision-making. As an organization of the poor, it thus bore some resemblance to the labour movement, including the Labour Churches.[23]

As for the social composition of the leadership and membership, there were undoubted parallels. If the Fabian Society was an exclusive body of middle-class teachers, journalists and clerks, the Social Democratic Federation and the Socialist League drew most of their recruits from the lower middle class (clerks and shopmen) and from amongst skilled artisans.[24] The most detailed estimate of the social background of approximately one-third (or 500 officers) of the Salvationist leadership in 1884 also discovered regular wage-earners in skilled manual or lower clerical employment. A sufficient number had been colliers, navvies and labourers, however, to suggest that the Army was to some degree plumbing the lower reaches of the urban poor. Almost half of all Salvationist officers were women, drawn mainly from domestic service and the clothing industry (dressmaking, weaving): the smaller range of skills reflecting the kind of jobs which were available to female labour.[25] The stable centres of Salvationism were thus to be found in the solid working-class communities of London, not in the poorer quarters of Bethnal Green or Whitechapel, where the Army was not conspicuously successful. Charles Booth's massive survey of religious influences at the turn of the century found the Salvation Army recruiting from among gas-workers in Camberwell, railwaymen in Kentish Town and 'the decent working class, earning from thirty shillings to fifty shillings a week' in Peckham. In Camberwell, moreover, where the Army split into two rival camps, both corps grew into regular congregations, having 'more the character of working-men's churches than militant missions'.[26] By 1906, Bramwell

22 A. Briggs, 'The Language of 'Mass' and 'Masses' in Nineteenth-Century England', in *Ideology and the Labour Movement*, ed. by D. E. Martin and D. Rubinstein (London, 1979), *passim*.

23 Inglis, *Churches*, op. cit., p. 95; S. Meacham, 'The Church in the Victorian City', in *Victorian Studies*, XI (1968), p. 361. The Labour Churches were usually organized by branches of the Independent Labour Party, Inglis, ch. 6; Pierson, *Marxism*, op. cit., p. 235.

24 McBriar, *Fabian Socialism*, op. cit., p. 6; Pierson, *Marxism*, p. 88; W. Wolfe, *From Radicalism to Socialism. Men and Ideas in the Formation of Fabian Socialist Doctrines, 1881-1889* (London, 1975), p. 303.

25 C. Ward, 'The Social Sources of the Salvation Army, 1865-1890' (M.Ph. thesis, London University, 1970), chap. 5.

26 Booth, *Life and Labour*, Third Series, 1, pp. 176-7; VI, pp. 25, 32, 77; VII, p. 327; *The Times*, 19 August 1882, p. 7; Ward, 'The Social Sources',

Booth could declare that ninety-five percent of male officers were 'formerly mechanics, operatives, and labourers. [...] It is a working-man's Church, with a working-man's ritual, and a working-man's clergymen — and clergywomen!'[27]

It is surely not over-extending the analysis, therefore, to suggest that the Salvation Army corps, no less than temperance bands or trade-union and co-operative-society branches, was the beneficiary of an emerging working-class consciousness. Working-class individuals, becoming aware of their potential status as citizens, expressed and formalized this new status by joining the Salvation Army as much as by attaching themselves to the labour movement.[28] The fact that working-class political and industrial organizations were still in an early stage of development made it more likely that proletarian aspiration would also be expressed through religious structures. This seems especially to have been the case with women: at this date they were hardly represented at all within the labour movement, yet the Salvation Army recruited them and gave them a measure of equality and accomplishment few other women of their generation obtained. To a certain extent, we are talking of a new generation of 'joiners', since most Salvation Army officers enlisted in their late teens and early twenties.[29] It would of course be helpful to know the extent to which Salvationists were concurrently involved in Friendly Societies or in the trade-union movement, and the extent to which Salvationists moved off entirely into other social and political channels. The evidence is hardly overwhelming, but one Salvationist in Northampton was the treasurer of the Boot and Shoe Operatives Union, and at a public meeting protesting the unfair competition of the Salvation Army's workshops, he urged in defence that the Parliamentary Committee of the Trades Union Congress had found the workshops in good order.[30] Frank Smith is an example of the passage from Salvation Army to socialist movement, as are the working-class women, former Salvationists, who served with Sylvia Pankhurst in the East London Federation of the Suffragettes (later, Workers' Socialist Federation).[31] The contention, in short, is that the background to the origin and early progress of the Salvation Army, no less than that of the early socialist movement, was an emerging working-class consciousness.

A new self-awareness and status was fortified by membership of bodies with a strong group consciousness and *esprit de corps*. Just as the socialist groups generated a sense of unity, fellowship and fraternity, the rescue mission induced a tenacious corporate identity, based on immense self-denial and

---

p. 118; P. Thompson, *Socialists, Liberals and Labour* (London, 1967), pp. 18-19.

27   W. B. Booth in *Christianity and the Working Classes*, op. cit., p. 152.

28   Cf. Ward, 'The Social Sources', pp. 154-5, 167, 270-2.

29   Ibid., pp. 148-50.

30   *Northampton Daily Echo*, 10 and 12 September 1910, cutting in the Gertrude Tuckwell Collection, Trades Union Congress Library.

31   For Frank Smith, see below, pp. 73f., 83ff. For the suffragettes (Mrs Jessie Payne, Mrs Baines, Mrs Schlette and Harriet Bennett) see E. S. Pankhurst, *The Home Front* (London, 1932), p. 97; id., *The Suffragette Movement* (London, 1931), pp. 475-9; id., *The Suffragette* (London, 1911), p. 324; *The Workers' Dreadnought*, IV (1917-18), p. 938. I am indebted to Carolyn Stevens of the University of Rochester, New York, and to Rosemary Tyler for this information.

a desire to save others. Many factors served to reinforce commitment to the Salvation Army: a distinctive uniform and the military paraphernalia; the reality and memory of persecution; and an authoritarian organization which insisted that cadres rely on the locality for subsistence, requiring young Salvationists to 'live very hardly and work hard'.[32] Not that corporate identity survived all pressures. If the socialists had their differences (with the Socialist League breaking away from the SDF), schisms and secessions likewise afflicted the Salvation Army, due mainly to the disciplined, not to say despotic, character of Army government. In 1886, *The Times* reported that 'the whole of the southern division staff have resigned or been dismissed and serious defections have followed among the rank and file.'[33] Even so, Charles Booth's informed judgement was that the Army 'is before everything a religious community', binding people together 'whose faith it has strengthened, and whom it has set diligently to work for the social and religious welfare of the world'.[34]

Associated with the Salvation Army, especially in the earliest years of the establishment of foreign missions, was finally an internationalism that commands some respect. Later on, perhaps, the Army became more associated with imperial service, with the development of native power along non-insurrectionary paths. Protests against the Boer War were certainly forbidden to its officers in 1900.[35] But then the labour movement hardly stood four-square against either imperialism or the Boer War.[36] And of one thing there is little ambiguity, the Salvation Army maintained a resolutely pacifist stance throughout these years.

II

The argument on behalf of a correspondence in certain social and organizational details between the Salvation Army and the labour movement would seem to break down, however, when it comes to the approach taken towards poverty, unemployment and the outcast poor. For the best part of the 1880s, the Salvation Army expressed a traditional evangelical attitude to poverty — one inimical to radical social reform. In 1883, during the controversy over the revelatory pamphlet *The Bitter Cry of Outcast London*,

---

32   Booth, *Life and Labour*, Third Series, III, p. 209; Inglis, *Churches*, p. 45; S. Yeo, 'Religion in Society: a view from a provincial town in the late nineteenth and early twentieth centuries' (Ph.D. thesis, Sussex University, 1971), p. 137, note 49; *Saturday Review*, LIII (1882), p. 763; *My Adventures with General William Booth*, Henry Edmonds 1877-1889 (Private circulation, 1930); Robertson, 'The Salvation Army', pp. 55-56.

33   *The Times*, 10 May 1886, p. 6; Robertson, 'The Salvation Army', p. 76; *Saturday Review*, LIV (1882), p. 243; J. J. R. Redstone, *An Ex-Captain's Experience of the Salvation Army* (London, 1888).

34   Booth, *Life and Labour*, Third Series, VII, pp. 337, 345; Inglis, *Churches*, p. 184.

35   G. S. Railton, *The History of Our South African War* (London, 1902), p. 129; S. H. Swinny, 'John Wesley and General Booth', in *Positivist Review*, XX (1912), pp. 217-22. Arthur Clibbom and Kate Booth, the General's daughter, pleaded for permission to condemn the Boer War, without success, C. Scott, *The Heavenly Witch: The Story of the Marechale* (London, 1982).

36   B. Baker, *The Social Democratic Federation and the Boer War* [Our History Pamphlet No 59] (London, 1974), *passim*; N. Etherington, 'Hyndman, the Social-Democratic Federation, and Imperialism', in *Historical Studies* (Melbourne), XVI (1974), pp. 89-103. For a different interpretation of popular attitudes, however, see R. Price, *An Imperial War and the British Working Class* (London, 1972), *passim*.

General Booth wrote to the *Pall Mall Gazette* to warn against 'the attempt to deal with the great social difficulty as though it had no deeper cause than a want of bricks and mortar'. A belief that sin was the authentic source of poverty bred an indifference to material conditions, which was again revealed when Bramwell Booth, Chief of the Staff, proclaimed the Salvation Army's belief in 'the Divine power of the Gospel as the quickest and completest means of raising up the poor from the dunghill'.[37] Yet here, too, the concerns of the Salvation Army and the labour movement began to converge. Raising the living standards of the poor assumed a new urgency for the Salvation Army in the late 1880s. The present section traces this increasing intersection in the realm of social welfare.

Let us first dispose of the charge, still made by some historians, that in the late 1880s the Salvation Army exacerbated the problem of sweating in the matchbox making industry of the East End of London.[38] The accusation first surfaced in 1888 when the Reverend William Adamson, Vicar of Old Ford (Bow), told the House of Lords Select Committee on the Sweating System that the Salvation Army was known to have offered to make matchboxes at $2\frac{1}{4}d$ per gross, undercutting the going rate of $2\frac{3}{4}d$. He even stated, in subsequent correspondence, that the opposition of the East End poor, including that of the 'Skeleton Army', had been actuated by 'the supposed complicity of the Salvation Army with the reduction'. Yet Adamson clearly knew little about the Salvation Army's reputed operations, even suggesting that Salvationists supported themselves by making matchboxes in their barracks.[39] Not surprisingly, Bramwell Booth leapt to the defence of the Salvation Army, informing the editor of *The Times* that the Army had 'never either made or offered to make matchboxes at $2\frac{1}{2}d$ per gross, nor at any other price'. The Army, he said, so disapproved of the 'sweating system' — which he described as 'an abominable and scandalous iniquity' — that 'we will not employ firms who profit by it to supply us with uniforms, however advantageous to our funds the contract might be'. Later, Bramwell Booth appeared before the Select Committee to denounce Adamson's evidence as a complete fabrication.[40] Of course the Army entered the matchbox-making trade in the 1890s; they also crashed into the organized trade-union movement over the sweating of 'unemployables' in the carpenters' shop of the Hanbury Street Elevator between 1907 and 1910.[41] But these later facts ought not to influence judgments, as they seem to have done, on the Army's work in the 1880s.

By this date the Salvation Army had begun, however, to expand its social-relief work. In January

---

37 Cited in Inglis, *Churches*, pp. 175-6. See also *War Cry*, 29 February 1886; *The Times*, 26 July 1882, p. 6 (Mrs Booth speaking at Blackheath). Cf. K. S. Inglis, 'English Nonconformity and Social Reform, 1880-1900', in *Past & Present*, No 13 (1958), pp. 83-6; H. Pelling, 'Religion and the Nineteenth-Century British Working Class', ibid., No 27 (1964), pp. 128-33.

38 E.g., R. Beer, *Matchgirls Strike 1888. The Struggle Against Sweated Labour in London's East End* [National Museum of Labour History Pamphlet No 2] (London, n.d.), pp. 19-20.

39 First Report from the Select Committee of the House of Lords on the Sweating System, with Minutes of Evidence [C. 361] (1888), pp. 248, 254, 353; *The Times*, 10 May 1888, p. 6.

40 First Report from the Select Committee of the House of Lords on the Sweating System, pp. 1005-6; *The Times*, 7 May 1888, p. 16; 12 May, p. 17; also *War Cry*, 13 April 1889; Ervine, *God's Soldier*, op. cit., II, pp. 694-6.

41 See below, pp. 85f., 91ff.

1888 a food depot was opened near the West India docks. By April 1889, the Army also had three night shelters, two of which were for men.[42] One was at St John's Square, Clerkenwell, where the first two floors each contained 100 coffin-like boxes, 6 feet long by one foot 9½ inches wide, containing a bed: what William Booth himself described as 'a shake-down on the floor in the packing-boxes'.[43] Temporary assistance was given without discrimination between 'deserving' and 'undeserving' — the central division in Victorian philanthropy. Any such categorization, Booth believed, ought to wait until the submerged had first been offered a way out. This displayed a much less censorious attitude to the urban 'residuum' than that shown either by the Charity Organization Society or, indeed, by the labour movement.[44]

The first practical convergence of social salvationism with the labour movement came with the London Dock Strike of 1889, when the food depots supplied cheap provisions to the dockers' families. Ben Tillett, leader of the dockers' union, later recalled that 'Booth's organisation was destined to serve a very useful purpose of a commissariat character in the great upheaval in 1889.' From Australia, the Salvation Army sent the proceeds of the sale of *War Cry* to the London dockers' strike fund, supplementing the donations from the Australian labour movement.[45] It all secured an enduring commitment to the Salvation Army's social work on the part of the New Unionist leaders.

A more important mode of bringing Salvationism and socialism together was the personal influence of Frank Smith. Born of lower-middle-class parents in Chelsea, apprenticed as an upholsterer (in which trade he ultimately set up in business), Smith was a part-time evangelist at the Chelsea Mission from 1879, before deciding to devote all his time to the Salvation Army. In true Salvationist style, he developed into an energetic and unorthodox evangelist, whether in 'capturing' the Eagle tavern in London or when 'invading' Liverpool, riding through the streets on horseback, facing the animal's tail, in order to attract a crowd.[46] As Keir Hardie revealed, in a portrait of Smith a few years later, 'The old campaigners in the S.A. still speak with delight of those days. Wherever hard fighting in the most literal sense of the word had to be done, Frank Smith was sure to be in the midst of it.'[47] In 1884 Booth sent Frank Smith to take charge of the Salvation Army in the United States, during which time he read and was deeply influenced by *Progress and Poverty*, written by Henry George, the American radical and land reformer, a book which proved to be a crucial stepping-stone to socialism for not a few English

---

42 HO 45/9802/B5587/1. In December 1888, General Booth asked the Home Office for £15,000 to provide cheap shelters for the outcast poor, *Hansard*, Third Series, CCCXXXII (1888), c. 648; *The Times*, 11 December 1888, p. 5; 25 December, p. 9.

43 MPR 2/203; Booth, *In Darkest England*, op. cit., pp. 99-100.

44 Inglis, *Churches*, p. 201; G. Stedman Jones, *Outcast London: A Study in the Relationship between Classes in Victorian Society* (Oxford, 1971), pp. 289, 345-6; See above, p. 38.

45 *War Cry*, 29 November 1890; B. Tillett, *Memories and Reflections* (London, 1931), p. 92; A. Stafford, *A Match to Fire the Thames* (London, 1961), pp. 24, 139-40, 185.

46 Inglis, *Churches*, p. 202; E. I. Champness, *Frank Smith, M.P. Pioneer and Modern Mystic* (London, 1943), pp. 6-11.

47 J. K. Hardie, 'Frank Smith, L.C.C.', in *Labour Prophet*, III (1894), p. 113. The *Labour Prophet* was the organ of the Labour Church.

radicals.[48]

Back in England by 1887, Smith, now in his early thirties, began to link up with the early socialist movement, addressing meetings of the unemployed, where he would stress that Christ had always fed the hungry, and assisting the Law and Liberty League, formed in the aftermath of Bloody Sunday to fight the ensuing court cases. At the public funeral of Alfred Linnell (a victim of police aggression), which the League organized, Frank Smith was one of the pall-bearers, touching shoulders with other key figures in the radical and socialist movement: Annie Besant, Herbert Burrows, Cunninghame Graham, W. T. Stead and William Morris. Until 1890, moreover, Smith was at the forefront of the Salvation Army's contribution to the defence of the freedom to meet and process.[49] Smith's direct political involvement irritated General Booth, and for a brief period Smith left the Salvation Army. As the Army's involvement in social work filled out, however, Booth recalled Smith and in May 1890 gave him direction of the Social Reform Wing. Smith set about the implementation of 'Social Christianity' with characteristic zeal, increasing the number of food depots and shelters, organizing a labour exchange, establishing a factory or 'elevator' in Whitechapel, and planning a match factory with the aim of undermining the large match firms. If the trade-union movement harboured any fears that the factory, opened in June 1890, would be a source of cheap labour and unfair competition, it was reassured by Smith himself, who, in correspondence with the London Trades Council, guaranteed that no such situation would arise.[50]

In August 1890, Smith attracted Henry George to come and inspect the various components of the Social Reform Wing. Addressing a noon prayer meeting in the Whitechapel shelter and workshop, George explained that he had come to see for himself

> the beginning of The Salvation Army's noble attempt to grapple with this great social problem. He was rejoiced to see that the Army at any rate recognised that it was not by virtue of God's law that any man willing to work should be unable to find work. He was sure The Almighty never intended destitution, starvation or poverty to be the lot of mankind [...].[51]

George's visit coincided with the first of five articles which Smith contributed to *War Cry* (out of a planned eight 'volleys' on the Lord's Prayer), under the general title of 'Sociology'. In these articles Smith wrote of the Kingdom of Justice that had to be founded, and of 'the right to live without the

---

48 Champness, *Frank Smith*, loc. cit.; W. H. G. Arrnytage, *Heavens Below. Utopian Experiments in England 1560-1960* (London, 1961), p. 317. *Progress and Poverty* was published in America in 1879, in England in 1881. George lectured energetically in Britain to publicize his single-land-tax plan, H. Ausubel, *In Hard Times. Reformers Among the Late Victorians* (New York, 1960), pp. 106-8.

49 *Methodist Times*, VI (1890), p. 1077; Inglis, *Churches*, p. 202; E. P. Thompson, *William Morris* (London, 1977), pp. 493-4. See also note 13.

50 Champness, *Frank Smith*, p. 12; Inglis, *Churches*, p. 202; *The Star*, 24 September 1890, p. 1; *Justice*, 30 August, p. 2; R. A. Woods, *English Social Movements* (London, 1892), pp. 171-2; N. H. Murdoch, 'Salvationist-Socialist Frank Smith, M.P.: Father of Salvation Army Social Work', unpublished paper delivered at the Fourth Annual Salvation Army Historical Conference, New York, September 1978.

51 *War Cry*, 30 August 1890. In January 1887, Catherine Booth had told Henry George that 'privately she would further his ideas as much as she could but that her position made it impossible for her to advocate his views publicly', Ausubel, *In Hard Times*, op. cit., p. 115.

pangs of hunger, the right of an opportunity to honest toil, and the right to maintain themselves and theirs in a position worthy of the creation of God' — and not on the verge of starvation, where so many people were to be found. It was not God's will, he maintained, 'that the fruits and flowers of life should be in the sole possession of one class, while to another should be given the thorns and thistles only'. The medium was religious, but the message had important social, not to say political, implications. Poverty was gradually represented not simply as a bulwark against individual salvation (which would better describe William Booth's position), but as a social injustice in itself.[52]

Through Frank Smith's agency, a limited rapport had developed between the Salvation Army and the labour movement. This rapport was doubtless strengthened by the fact that the early labour movement had not yet turned its face against charitable social work. As Stephen Yeo wrote, 'ILP branches and even the SDF in places like Battersea, Clerkenwell, and South Salford, were not afraid of direct charity work as part of their presence in a locality'.[53] In Manchester in the early 1890s, Robert Blatchford started his 'Cinderella' work for poor children, whilst the Pankhurst family persuaded their local ILP branch to organize the cooking and distribution of food to the unemployed. A little later, through the efforts of Fred Brocklehurst, the ILP attempted to establish an annual 'Self-Denial Week', during which socialists would fast to help the needy: a straight 'lift' from the Salvationist practice of the same name.[54] At least until the First World War, the ultimate goals of socialism did not exclude attempts to work for reforms that would create a juster society in the present.

It has been argued, then, that an informal understanding between the Salvation Army and the labour movement materialized in the 1880s. Here were two groups using similar open-air methods to bring their respective gospels to the labouring masses. Both movements bound new converts together into a committed and zealous fellowship; inspired them to energetic missionary activity on behalf of the unsaved; and commonly impelled changes in personal character and environment. Both movements, furthermore, drew from and in turn invigorated an emerging working-class consciousness. It is a comparison which confirms that the Salvation Army was a movement both of the working class and in intimate relationship with the submerged, and which suggests that it warps historical reality to bracket the Army with organizations bent simply on imposing middle-class values on the uncultured poor. A closer evaluation of this uniformly proletarian evangelism lends credence to the view that the change in the social habits of the urban masses in late-Victorian England owes much to self-discipline,

---

52 *War Cry*, 30 August, 13 and 27 September, 1 and 29 November 1890. Smith left the Salvation Army before the final three articles were written, see below, p. 83ff. See also Inglis, *Churches*, p. 209; C. Parkin, 'The Salvation Army and Social Questions of the Day', in *A Sociological Yearbook of Religion in Britain*, VI, p. 111. It would be interesting to know if any accord between the Salvation Army and the labour movement developed in the United States. My impression, for what it is worth, is that there were similar linkages: *Labour Leader*, IX (1897), p. 355; P. Boyer, *Urban Masses and Moral Order in America, 1820-1920* (Cambridge, Mass., 1978), pp. 140-1.

53 Yeo, 'A New Life', p. 39.

54 Ibid., pp. 14, 51, note 34; R. Blatchford, *My Eighty Years* (London, 1931), pp. 189-90; Pankhurst, *The Suffragette Movement*, op. cit., pp. 128-29; Pierson, *Marxism*, p. 228. Brocklehurst was a key figure in the Labour Church movement.

self-respect and self-help: in short, to the independent transformation of working-class customs and culture.[55]

The relationship between the two movements was built around the provision of charitable relief, both during and after the celebrated London Dock Strike. At the centre of this dialogue was Frank Smith, a Salvationist on his way to becoming a socialist. Under Smith's influence, the Army departed from the plain evangelical tradition and turned to ways of improving the material environment of the depressed poor. Admittedly the connections between the Salvation Army and the labour movement rested heavily upon Frank Smith. The cross-talk also relied, however, upon a labour and socialist movement which refused to erect impassable barriers between itself and other groups that were doing comparable work under different banners with contrasting credos. The arteries between the different political and religious organizations had not yet fully hardened. In these ways the stage was set for the Salvation Army's dramatic entrance on to the stage of social reform, heralded by the publication in October 1890 of *In Darkest England and the Way Out*.

III

Frank Smith's articles in the *War Cry*, coinciding as they did with William Booth's announcement in *Darkest England* of new proposals to help the outcast poor, plus public knowledge of Smith's activity as head of the Social Reform Wing, meant that he was initially credited with the employment of the Salvation Army as 'an instrument of social reform'. According to W. T. Stead, Smith was 'one of the leading spirits of the new departure', and had been pressing the social scheme on Booth for the past three years. The labour press endorsed this view: Keir Hardie was in no doubt that 'the social side of the Army's work is largely due to Mr. Smith's initiative and activity'.[56]

As far as the content of *Darkest England* is concerned, however, Frank Smith's was not the only imprint. W. T. Stead — Congregationalist editor of the *Pall Mall Gazette*, publicist of *The Bitter Cry of Outcast London*, 'partner in crime' in the covert investigations that resulted in the 'Maiden Tribute of Modern Babylon', whom Bramwell Booth described as 'a Salvationist in mufti' — was a vital influence on the design and detail of the Darkest England scheme as it appeared in General Booth's book. Stead's biographer has described how the radical editor offered to act as amanuensis, converting Booth's disordered material into a manageable manuscript, to which Booth then added his own evocative vernacular and some of the singular proposals. There is a Boothian touch to the scheme to transfer salvage from London to the farm colony. 'I see, as in a vision', declared Booth, 'barge loads upon barge

---

55 Cf. Thompson, 'Social Control in Victorian Britain', loc. cit.

56 Inglis, *Churches*, p. 209; Hardie, 'Frank Smith', loc. cit.; also *Star*, 24 September 1890, p. 1. A *Times* correspondent believed that 'the ideas of the substantial parts of the scheme — that is to say, of the city colony and the farm colony — had their origin in the mind of Mr. Frank Smith', *The Times*, 26 December 1890, p. 5.

loads of bones floating down the Thames to the great Bone Factory.'[57] Stead was influential in other ways, too. He probably called Booth's attention to W. L. Rees's *From Poverty to Plenty: or, the Labour Question Solved* (1888), which informed the General's views on emigration; and he most certainly introduced Booth to Arnold White, who had experience of colonization in South Africa, and with whom Booth compared notes.[58] Stead himself was clearly satisfied with the results of his intercession; he wrote to Lord Milner, then at the Ministry of Finance in Cairo, predicting a new era of social reform:

> You remember, of course, the first great *coup* which we made in the *Pall Mall Gazette* — The Bitter Cry of Outcast London. General Booth's Book may be regarded as a bigger and a better "Bitter Cry", and in order to make the apostolic succession quite clear I took care to incorporate in the first page the greater part of that famous Leader which began everything.[59]

Stead sent Milner a copy of *Darkest England*, assured that he would recognize Stead's 'fine Roman hand in most of the chapters', and closed the letter thus:

> You will be delighted to see that we have got the Salvation Army solid not only for Social Reform but also for Imperial Unity. I have written to Rhodes about it and we stand on the eve of great things.[60]

To Stead's undoubted influence should be added the Reverend Herbert Mills's *Poverty and the State or Work for the Unemployed* (1886), whose proposal to transform the workhouses into Home Colonies for co-operative production (which, in turn, may have been taken from the Dutch and German labour colonies for the incorrigibly idle), underlay Booth's Farm Colony. Mills was a somewhat disillusioned Unitarian minister, a Socialist, and founder of the Home Colonization Society in 1887, with the aim of substituting co-operative estates for the existing poor law. When Booth appeared on the scene, however, Mills agreed to transfer the £5,000 which he had so far raised, to the Darkest England fund.[61]

In view of the different tributaries feeding into *Darkest England*, it is perhaps unwise to be too

---

57 W. B. Booth, *Echoes and Memories* (London, 1926), pp. 141-3; F. Whyte, *The Life of W. T. Stead* (2 vols; London, 1925), II, p. 12; Begbie, *General William Booth*, op. cit., II, pp. 92-3; Murdoch, 'Salvationist-Socialist Frank Smith', op. cit., p. 5; Booth, *In Darkest England*, p. 136. In the Preface to *In Darkest England*, Booth acknowledged 'valuable literary help' from a friend of the poor. Professor J. O. Baylen of Georgia State University, Atlanta, is about to publish what promises to be the definitive biography of W. T. Stead.

58 Inglis, *Churches*, p. 203; W. Booth to A. White, 24 October 1890, to be found in the copy of A. White, *The Great Idea* (London, 1910), in the archives of the Salvation Army.

59 Whyte, *W. T. Stead*, op. cit., II, p. 13. Milner had previously been on the staff of the *Pall Mall Gazette*, A. M. Gollin, *Proconsul in Politics. A Study of Lord Milner in Opposition and in Power* (London, 1964), pp. 10-11, 19.

60 Whyte, *W. T. Stead*, II, p. 13.

61 P. d'A. Jones, *The Christian Socialist Revival 1877-1914* (Princeton, 1968), p. 398; Inglis, *Churches*, pp. 203-4; J. Harris, *Unemployment and Politics* (Oxford, 1972), pp. 119-21. It is unknown whether Booth ever consulted the pamphlet *Our Tramps*, issued by the Church Army (the Church of England's imitation Salvation Army) in March 1890, in which a threefold scheme of City, Farming and Over-Sea colonies was first propounded, K. Heasman, *Evangelicals in Action* (London, 1962), pp. 59-60. It seems unlikely, finally, that Charles Booth's scheme of labour colonies influenced *In Darkest England*, J. Brown, 'Charles Booth and Labour Colonies, 1889-1905', in *Economic History Review*, Second Series, XXI (1968), p. 357; Harris, loc. cit., p. 119.

categorical about its true source. Nonetheless, the book seems to emerge from the fusion of the ideas of the social-imperialist movement, anxious to use the Empire to combat urban degeneration, and the 'social gospel' wing of Nonconformity, notably its emphasis on rural panaceas.[62] Without question, a strong anti-urbanism runs through *Darkest England*, not least in the prefatory chart, where the city is obviously the source of evil, the countryside 'the way out'. Now, it would be strange if the anti-urbanism of Booth's study had failed to find an appreciative audience within at least sections of the labour movement, given the pro-country sentiments which found expression in William Morris's *News from Nowhere* (1890) or, later, in Robert Blatchford's *Merrie England* (1894). More specifically, Annie Besant had already put the Fabian imprimatur on a scheme for 'County Farms' as one way of assisting unemployed labour; and Keir Hardie and the Scottish Labour Party were attracted at this date to Home Colonies as a remedy for unemployment.[63]

However, historians invariably interpret *Darkest England* as a highly conservative and backward-looking document, and hence by implication anti-socialist. Christine Parkin underscored Booth's 'conservative, patriarchal approach to human misery'.

> Here was no blue-print for a social revolution, no encouragement for the breakdown of the social order. The prevailing class structure is made the focal point of fruitful co-operation, rather than an element of friction.[64]

Roland Robertson detected in the Darkest England scheme 'a feudal conception of the social structure, in which each person's position in society was clearly defined and ascribed on the basis of a system of authority gradations'. One could add K. S. Inglis's opinion that Booth introduced the social scheme as merely a new strategy of salvation once it became evident that 'poverty itself was a grave impediment to salvation'. Booth did indeed affirm: 'it is primarily and mainly for the sake of saving the soul that I seek the salvation of the body.' For the democrat, finally, there was much to deter in the undemocratic administration envisaged for the various colonies. Without discipline and unquestioning obedience, declared Booth, 'your Utopians get to loggerheads, and Utopia goes to smash'.[65] Yet William Booth did,

---

62   D. W. Bebbington, 'The City, the Countryside and the Social Gospel in Late Victorian Nonconformity', in *The Church in Town and Countryside* [Studies in Church History, XVI] (Oxford, 1979), pp. 418-23; J. Kent, 'The Role of Religion in the Cultural Structure of the Later Victorian City', in *Transactions of the Royal Historical Society*, Fifth Series, XXIII (1973), pp. 153-73; Stedman Jones, *Outcast London*, op. cit., pp. 308-12, 311, note 20. I agree with Jones when he says that General Booth and Frank Smith 'were probably not motivated by any particular ambition to advance the cause of social imperialism'.

63   McBriar, *Fabian Socialism*, p. 27; A. Besant, 'Industry Under Socialism', in *Fabian Essays in Socialism*, ed. by G. B. Shaw (London, 1889), p. 154-5. Annie Besant was also clearly influenced by the Rev. H. V. Mills's *Poverty and the State*. Keir Hardie proposed Home Colonies at the inaugural conference of the ILP in Bradford, in January 1893, which was held in the Labour Institute, formerly a Salvation Army 'citadel'. H. Pelling, *The Origins of the Labour Party 1880-1900* (Oxford, 1965), p. 119.

64   Parkin, 'The Salvation Army', loc. cit., p. 116.

65   Robertson, 'The Salvation Army', pp. 65, 83; Inglis, *Churches*, p. 195; Booth, *In Darkest England*, pp. 45, 232. The Darkest England scheme was certainly the beginning of Booth's widespread popularity, following a decade of opposition, and it revived a flagging Salvation Army, A. M. Nicol, *General Booth and the Salvation Army* (London, 1911), pp. 192-3.

after all, set out to fight poverty on a massive scale; he dramatized the war against want like no one before him, provoking a new awareness of social conditions and a new desire for social reform. For these reasons alone, *Darkest England* deserves closer textual analysis than it is usually accorded.

The title of the book was an acknowledged paraphrase of the explorer Stanley's *In Darkest Africa*, the intended analogy being that between the equatorial forest and Darkest England, 'alike in its vast extent [...], its monotonous darkness, its malaria and its gloom, its dwarfish dehumanized inhabitants, the slavery to which they are subjected, their privations and their misery'.[66] The General first presented, in a racier manner, many of the facts and figures in Charles Booth's more systematic and sombre survey, enriching them with case records and personal statements that bear comparison with those to be found in *Life and Labour of the People*. In the early sections, indeed, *Darkest England* is a serious work of sociological testimony. Here is the statement of a 54 year old homeless man who was found sleeping on the Embankment.

> I've slept here two nights; I'm a confectioner by trade; I come from Dartford, I got turned off because I'm getting elderly. They can get young men cheaper, and I have the rheumatism so bad. I've earned nothing these two days; I thought I could get a job at Woolwich, so I walked there, but could get nothing. I found a bit of bread in the road wrapped up in a bit of newspaper. That did me for yesterday. [...] When it's wet we stand about all night under the arches.[67]

No high moral tone is adopted towards the outcast, not even towards prostitutes.

> there is no doubt it is a fact that there is no industrial career in which for a short time a beautiful girl can make as much money with as little trouble as the profession of a courtesan. [...] the number of young women who have received £500 in one year for the sale of their person is larger than the number of women of all ages who make a similar sum by honest industry.[68]

It was rare for prostitution to be described with such matter-of-factness in the late-Victorian period, but then the Salvation Army had more experience than most religious organizations in the etiology of prostitution.

More significantly, Booth traced the source of individual distress, as of the entire 'social problem', to the want of employment. Existing schemes to improve the condition of the workforce were founded, Booth contended, not upon 'rock', nor even upon 'sand', but upon the 'bottomless bog of the stratum of the Workless'. Reversing the equation so beloved of the Charity Organisation Society, unemployment was said to cause drunkenness, sickness and depravity (although as to what caused the want of

66   Booth, *In Darkest England*, p. 12; Armytage, *Heavens Below*, op. cit., p. 318; W. S. Smith, *The London Heretics 1870-1914* (New York, 1968), p. 14.

67   Booth, *In Darkest England*, p. 27.

68   Ibid., p. 50. For the Army's rescue work with prostitutes, see F. K. Prochaska, *Women and Philanthropy in Nineteenth Century England* (Oxford, 1980), pp. 190, 202-3.

employment, if not the personal failings of workmen, the book provided no adequate answer). The corollary of this analysis was a denunciation of individualist attitudes towards, and individualist solutions of, poverty. Booth was no defender of a *laissez-faire* political economy which simply let men sink; he gave short shrift to 'those anti-Christian economists who hold that it is an offence against the doctrine of the survival of the fittest to try to save the weakest from going to the wall, and who believe that when once a man is down the supreme duty of a self-regarding Society is to jump upon him'.[69] He strongly chastised the ineffective alliance of a deterrent Poor Law and organized charity, the latter ministering exclusively to the thrifty and industrious — what Booth termed 'the aristocracy of the miserable'.

> We have had this doctrine of an inhuman cast-iron pseudo-political economy too long enthroned among us. It is now time to fling down the false idol, and proclaim a Temporal Salvation as full, free, and universal, and with no other limitations than the "Whosoever will" of the Gospel.[70]

Following these opening shots, Booth carried the war into the enemy's camp by proposing elementary remedial welfare for the submerged, however undeserving. The standard of life to be gained was modest (although more generous than that of the COS), to wit, that of the London Cab Horse.

> These are the two points of the Cab Horse's Charter. When he is down he is helped up, and while he lives he has food, shelter and work. That, although a humble standard, is at present absolutely unattainable by millions [...] of our fellow-men and women in this country.[71]

Finally, Booth sought to convince the labour movement that his scheme of social salvation need not conflict with its own panaceas for poverty and unemployment. He declined to endorse such plans as Henry George's single tax on land values, preferring a more practical scheme of immediate help for the hungry and workless, but, as he also emphasized, 'There is nothing in my scheme which will bring it into collision either with Socialists of the State, or Socialists of the Municipality'. Booth also believed that the most knowledgeable trade unionists would recognize that 'any scheme which could deal adequately with the out-of-works and others who hang on to their skirts and form the recruiting ground of blacklegs [...] would be [...] most beneficial to Trades Unionism.' As for the workshops of the City Colony, no unjust competition would emanate from them (as was the case with pauper and criminal labour), since the Army was 'pledged to a war to the death against sweating in every shape and form',

---

69 Booth, *In Darkest England*, pp. 18, 34; Harris, *Unemployment and Politics*, op. cit., pp. 124-5. For a critical response to Booth's view that unemployment caused distress, by the economic historian W. J. Ashley, who preferred the sentiments of the COS, see 'General Booth's Panacea', in *Political Science Quarterly*, VI (1891), p. 546. I accept of course that the assault upon *laissez-faire* attitudes towards poverty was, at this date, a characteristic also of the writings of the social imperialists, Stedman Jones, *Outcast London*, p. 311.

70 Booth, *In Darkest England*, pp. 36, 67-72. Cf. S. and B. Webb, *The Prevention of Destitution* (London, 1916), pp. 234-5.

71 Booth, *In Darkest England*, p. 20. Booth regretted that a prison standard would be to set things too high: 'Some time, perhaps, we may venture to hope that every honest worker on English soil will always be as warmly clad, as healthily housed, and as regularly fed as our criminal convicts — but that is not yet.' Ibid., p. 19.

and since anti-sweating experiments were an essential part of the social scheme.[72]

But how, in fact, did the different sections of the labour movement respond to this chariot of philanthropic fire? Herman Ausubel and K. S. Inglis have documented the response to *Darkest England* from the so-called experts on London pauperism and from the main political and religious journals. Clearly, *Darkest England* aroused more public interest than any other book since Henry George's *Progress and Poverty*. By December 1890, some 115,000 copies had been sold; within four months, the £100,000 which Booth requested as a token of public commitment to the social scheme had been contributed.[73] But we still know very little of the response of the labour movement and the labour press to *Darkest England*.

According to the American social investigator, Robert A. Woods, New Unionism 'formally expressed confidence in the Salvation Army's scheme, and offered all possible assistance.' Both Tillett and Mann thought the social scheme deserved a fair trial; and Tillett was in the audience when Booth sought financial support for the scheme at an Exeter Hall meeting in November 1890.[74] Evidently, the Army's work during the Dock Strike was paying dividends. What of the labour press, in its widest sense? Among the Radical Weeklies, none was more supportive of Booth's plan than the widely read working-class journal, *Reynolds's Newspaper*. 'As a scheme', it declared, 'it is in one sense the most socialistic that has ever been brought out', a commendable ground-plan for the improvement of the condition of the masses. Two months later, *Reynolds's Newspaper* looked forward to the residue which would be left once the 'fantastic side of Salvationism' had evaporated, *viz.*,

> A large number of men and women who have been organised, disciplined, and taught to look for something better than their present condition, and who have become public speakers and are not afraid of ridicule. There you have the raw materials for a Socialist Army.[75]

The radical London daily, the *Star*, described the social scheme as 'an ingenious, a large, a resourceful

---

72 Ibid., pp. 18, 77-80, 108, 110, Appendix 2. Anti-sweating experiments were an integral part of the scheme, whether it was the proposal to enter the matchbox-making industry or the labour exchange for the employment of sandwich men, bill-distributors and messengers.

73 H. Ausubel, 'General Booth's Scheme of Social Salvation', in *American Historical Review*, LVI (1950-51), pp. 519-25; Inglis, *Churches*, pp. 204-9; Mayor, *The Churches and the Labour Movement*, op. cit., p. 52. For a sample of responses to *In Darkest England*, see *Review of Reviews*, II (1890), pp. 382ff., 492ff.; *Economist*, XLVIII (1890), p. 1468; F. Peek, 'General Booth's Social Work', in *Contemporary Review*, LXII (1892), pp. 59-84. Most 'experts' on London pauperism, with the exception of Peek, denounced the scheme as impractical, financially prohibitive, over-ambitious and a duplication of existing schemes to aid the submerged. C. S. Loch, *An Examination of 'General' Booth's Social Scheme* (London, 1890), *passim*, but esp. p. 94, for the COS, predictably criticized the absence of all discrimination and the neglect of inquiry in the demoralizing provision of free food and shelter. The reaction of the main London newspapers to *In Darkest England* was generally very favourable. See the *Daily Telegraph*, *Daily News* and *Daily Chronicle* for 20 October 1890.

74 Woods, *English Social Movements*, op. cit., p. 19; *Review of Reviews*, II, p. 652; *Commonweal*, V11 (1891), p. 5; *Reynolds's Newspaper*, 23 November 1890, p. 4. The Executive Council of Tillett's Dock, Wharf, Riverside and General Labourers Union congratulated Booth 'for the efforts he is now making on behalf of the downtrodden and helpless', *Docker's Record*, December, p. 12. There was a favourable reaction also from the *Workman's Times*, 31 October, and the *English Labourers Chronicle*, 22 November.

75 *Reynolds's Newspaper*, 26 October, p. 4; 23 November, p. 2; also Armytage, *Heavens Below*, p. 321. Cf. *Weekly Dispatch*, 23 November.

method for transplanting the slum population'.[76] Turning to ultra-radical opinion, the *Labour World* (Henry Georgian in outlook) heralded the plan as 'the most important step that has yet been taken in England in the direction of thorough social reform. It is the most marvellous scheme for the reformation of society that this generation has been called upon to study.' As crucially, it would illustrate that 'State or municipal organisation of labour […] are not Utopian dreams.'[77] In short, a substantial section of the labour press gave a warm welcome to *Darkest England*, if for the moment judgement was reserved on the actual efficacy of the social scheme.

In the socialist press, in contrast, divergence was soon apparent between the Salvation Army, basically suspicious of centralist collectivism, and the main socialist groups. The *Christian Socialist*, representing a melange of Christian social conscience and ethical socialism, considered *Darkest England* to be the most notable book of the year, the Army to be well-fitted for its task, and the plans to be well-drawn. If the journal entered the caution that Booth's palliatives inevitably fell short of 'the drastic cure of collective action', it nonetheless welcomed the Salvationists to the ranks.

> To the Socialist the chief cause for rejoicing is that General Booth's corps has changed front and is now
> an attacking brigade of the Great Army which fights under the banner of "Social Salvation".[78]

The socialist pamphleteer "Elihu" (Samuel Washington) similarly invited Booth 'to unfurl the standard of *practical* Christianity', a reformed Christianity which would fashion a juster set of social arrangements. This plea, however, came at the end of a lengthy indictment of the Darkest England scheme, in which it was claimed that Booth had misunderstood the true reasons for the existence of the submerged tenth. Finding employment for the submerged, "Elihu" argued, would merely increase the size of the labour market and decrease the level of wages, such was the law of supply and demand, and Booth would quickly become 'general-in-chief of a huge nest of organised blacklegs'.[79] Henry Hyndman, leader of the SDF, likewise accused Booth of ignoring the real causes of poverty. In the opening sections of *Darkest England*, Hyndman found little to which to object: 'a well-ordered indictment of our present social system, and a careful statistical tabulation of its results'. Nor could he do anything but admire Booth's denunciation of the prevailing relief schemes and of the 'narrow limitations and inefficiency of trade unions'. This was preface, however, to a critique of the social

---

76 *Star*, 20 October, pp. 1-2; 21 October, p. 1. In the 1890s, the *Star* was the organ of the 'Progressives' on the London County Council.

77 *Labour World*, 25 October, p. 8; 15 November, p. 3 (letter). Cf. the response to *In Darkest England* of Durant, an English single-taxer, in a letter to Henry George, 27 October: 'You will be pleased with it. It seems to me the most important thing that has occurred for some time', cited in Ausubel, *In Hard Times*, p. 108.

78 *Christian Socialist*, December 1890, January and March 1891. For more critical expressions of Christian Socialist opinion, see T. Hancock, *Salvation by Mammon. Two Sermons on Mr. Booth's Scheme* (London, 1891), p. 16; *Church Reformer*, IX (1890), p. 286; Jones, *The Christian Socialist Revival*, op. cit., pp. 108-11, 121.

79 "Elihu", *Is General Booth's Darkest England Scheme a Failure? A Word of Protest and Advice* (Manchester, London, 1893), *passim*, but esp. pp. 11-12.

scheme as 'but a supplement to philanthropy', and as a strategy destined to intensify competition and sweating. In short, an anti-socialist dodge that the capitalist class would readily support.[80] *Justice*, the SDF's paper, lent weight to Hyndman's indictment, as did *Commonweal*, the organ of the Socialist League, where William Morris condemned the new scheme as 'Workhouse Socialism, [...] which casts about for devices at once to get [the workers] better rations and to lower the cost of keeping them to the capitalists'.[81]

But if the socialist press almost unanimously joined the anti-Boothite camp, the critical stance was due, to some extent at least, to the fact that Booth was being described as a new socialist ('here is General Booth turning Socialist', exclaimed the *Methodist Times*), and to the fact that he was employing the language and commandeering some of the proposals of a programme that both movements referred to as 'social salvationism'.[82] The socialist bodies doubtless recognized that a sturdy competitor was setting up shop in the same street to sell some of the same wares. Little wonder that they wished to point the differences between 'Salvation Socialism' (as William Morris termed it) and 'Scientific Socialism'. Other sections of the labour movement, more practical and proletarian in orientation, to whom socialism essentially meant economic justice, greeted *Darkest England* as an important addition to the library of social reform. One additional proof of this fact appeared when W. T. Stead asked the Labour MPs elected in 1906 to list the books which had helped to define their political creed. Thomas Summerbell, MP for Sunderland, a former printer, and member of the Church of England, listed Charles Dickens, the books and leaflets issued by the ILP and the Fabians — 'not forgetting Mr. Booth's *Darkest England*'.[83]

IV

The first few years of the Darkest England scheme were not dramatically successful. After only eight months as head of the Social Reform Wing, Frank Smith resigned, on the grounds that the promised separation of his section from the Army's other departments was being trenched upon, thus making the

---

80 H. M. Hyndman, *General Booth's Book Refuted* (London, 1890), *passim*, but esp. pp. 4, 6, 8, 11.

81 *Justice*, 17 January 1891, p. 3; 24 January, p. 2 (H. Quelch spoke of Booth's 'policy of pigwash and piety'); 9 April 1892, p. 2; *Commonweal*, VI (1890), pp. 345-6, 365. Cf. John Burns's critical response to the social scheme in an address to a Battersea Music Hall, *Labour World*, 1 November 1890, p. 2. Burns maintained a critical view of the Farm Colony, as he gradually abandoned the socialists for the Liberal Party, K. D. Brown, *Labour and Unemployment 1900-1914* (Newton Abbot, 1971), p. 81; J. Marsh, 'The Unemployed and the Land', in *History Today*, April 1982, p. 20; *The Times*, 7 February 1908, p. 12. For a less hostile Socialist response, see the opening quotation to this chapter from Friedrich Engels.

82 *Methodist Times*, V1, p. 956, cited in Inglis, *Churches*, p. 194.

83 W. T. Stead, "The Labour Party and the Books that helped to make it", in *Review of Reviews*, XXXIII (1906), pp. 568-82, quote at p. 580. For Summerbell, see D. Martin, "The Instruments of the People?': The Parliamentary Labour Party in 1906', in *Ideology and the Labour Movement*, op. cit., pp. 128-9; Brown, *Labour and Unemployment*, op. cit., *passim*. The Webbs recommended *In Darkest England* for information on the most destitute, in *The Prevention of Destitution*, op. cit., p. 13.

social movement a 'mere sectarian agency' for the benefit of the Salvation Army. In fact, Smith was wrong to suggest that the finances of the social and religious operations had been amalgamated. But the whole incident was a sign of General Booth's unwillingness to allow Smith to administer the Social Reform Wing as a semi-independent outfit.[84] Shortly afterwards, the work of the section, renamed the 'Social Wing', was put in the hands of Elijah Cadman, who, if less eager than Smith to grapple with the root causes of poverty, nonetheless worked energetically, making a direct appeal to the Home Secretary in 1892, for example, for state assistance to help both the submerged and 'the respectable unemployed'.[85]

The response to Smith's resignation was disappointment all round. 'It may well be', said the *Times* Correspondent, who was greatly impressed by Smith, 'that his resignation is destined to be the death-blow to Mr. Booth's more ambitious schemes.' For the socialist press, the resignation confirmed its fears that Booth would exert too large a control over the social scheme. There was one man, claimed *Justice*, who,

> though he could not possibly save the blatant Booth's scheme from failure in the long run, might have managed to keep it afloat for a season. That man Social Democrats have always spoken well and thought well of [...]. If our Government had any sense they would give Frank Smith carte blanche to reorganise the Poor Law on a Socialistic basis.[86]

In fact, Smith's first undertaking, after leaving the Salvation Army, was to form the 'Labor [sic] Army' and edit its paper, the *Workers' Cry*, the latter sporting a Salvationist-like crest with the words 'Truth and Right' instead of 'Blood and Fire'. The Labor Army was to fight the causes rather than the results of the social system, and to this end planned a countrywide democratic organization to get workers' representatives into Parliament. The venture was short-lived, but it was Smith's stepping-stone to election to the London County Council and to energetic service on behalf of the ILP and ultimately the Labour Party, which reinforced his close friendship with Keir Hardie. In 1901, Smith rejoined the Salvation Army, saying he was disillusioned at the lack of unity and purpose among the secular political groups, but not for long. He was soon back in harness, a veritable workhorse of the labour movement. At last, in 1929, at 75 years of age, Frank Smith won his first Parliamentary election in Nuneaton, as Labour took office for the second time in its history.[87]

The practical implementation of the Darkest England scheme also had its share of difficulties. An Essex estate of over 1,000 acres was purchased in 1891, the heart of the Hadleigh Farm Colony. Within

---

84 *War Cry*, 3 January 1891; *Daily Chronicle*, 2 January; 5 January (letter); *The Times*, 6 January, p. 5; Champness, *Frank Smith*, pp. 14-16.

85 Inglis, *Churches*, pp. 209-10; Harris, *Unemployment and Politics*, p. 128; HO 45/9861/13077D/1-2.

86 *The Times*, 26 December 1890, p. 5; 29 December, p. 4; 30 December, p. 5; 2 January 1891, pp. 5, 7; *Justice*, 3 January, p. 1.

87 *Workers' Cry*, 2 May 1891; *Labour Prophet*, I (1892), p. 24; III, p. 114; *War Cry*, 30 November 1901; *All the World*, December 1901; Armytage, *Heavens Below*, p. 320; Murdoch, 'Salvationist-Socialist Frank Smith', p. 10; Champness, *Frank Smith*, pp. 19-49. See also K. O. Morgan, *Keir Hardie* (London, 1975), pp. 45-6, for Smith's unique brand of ethical socialism.

a year, 200 colonists were employed in mixed farming (particularly market gardening and fruit growing) and in brick manufacture. Unfortunately, a combination of late frosts, dry seasons, depressed farm prices and inefficient labour led to substantial losses on the colony in each year between 1892 and 1895. Harold Moore, brought in to advise on farming matters, had resigned at the end of 1891 over the Army's determination to make an industrial concern as well as a farming colony of Hadleigh. Thereafter, poor leadership and supervision added to the colony's burdens. At the close of 1895, Bramwell Booth considered that 'mismanagements and mistakes' rather than 'misfortunes' best described the tribulations of the past year.[88]

Meanwhile, in the so-called City Colony, the Army had declared war on sweating by opening a match factory in May 1891. The intention was to make matches without using yellow phosphorus (the toxic substance which created the ravages of 'phossy jaw'), and to pay the matchbox makers 4d per gross instead of 2¼d or 2½d. The Army's 'safety matches' were more expensive than the strike-anywhere type however, and sales began to plummet; even Salvationists were said to be buying the cheaper brands. The best consumers of the Army's matches, according to the *Officer*, 'are members of other denominations, Co-Operatives, and Trade Unions.' Eventually, in December 1894, the match factory had to be temporarily closed.[89] Nor were the city shelters proving too acceptable. In addition to being criticized for attracting destitute persons to East London, the level of hygiene of the shelters led the Chief Commissioner of Metropolitan Police and a number of metropolitan boards of guardians to press the Home Office to have them registered as common lodging houses and regularly inspected. The Medical Officer of Health for Southwark described the shelter in Blackfriars Road as 'a dangerous hot-bed of infection, not only from small-pox, but from other infectious diseases'. The *Clarion* newspaper joined the campaign, with the editor, Blatchford, complaining that the end product of subscriptions to the tune of £120,000 was 'a series of shelters where the submerged tenth are herded together under the most indescribably noisome and filthy conditions, and the shelters are simply disseminators of vermin'. At this date, however, the Home Office took the view that the shelters did not come within the definition of Common Lodging Houses.[90]

88 W. B. Booth to General Booth, 9, 11 and 14 April 1891, 7 December 1894, 18 October 1895; id. to Commissioner Pollard, 13 December 1895; letters to General Booth, 29 September 1894, 8 November 1895, Salvation Army archives. See General Booth to W. B. Booth, 29 November 1905: 'Your letter made me very sad last night, but Hadleigh has ever been a trial to us.' See also *Hadleigh Official Journal*, 1908-9; A. S. Swan, *The Outsiders* (London, 1905-6), p. 61; *Selected Papers on the Social Work of the Salvation Army* (London, 1907-8); Third Report from the Select Committee on Distress from Want of Employment [C. 365] (1895), qq. 9607-9 (H. E. Moore); C. Fleay, 'Hadleigh: A labour colony and its problems, 1891-1914', in *Middlesex Polytechnic History Journal*, 11 (1981), *passim*. I am extremely grateful to Mr Fleay for sending me an offprint of this article. For descriptions of the Farm Colony, see Booth, *Life and Labour*, Third Series, V1, pp. 178-81; Report on Agencies and Methods for Dealing with the Unemployed (Board of Trade, Labour Department) [C. 7182] (1893-4), pp. 549-52. However, a favourable account of Hadleigh Colony appeared in the *Clarion*, 16 June 1892, p. 7.

89 D. C. Mitchell, *The Darkest England Match Industry* (Camberley, 1976), *passim*;

90 Heasman, *Evangelicals in Action*, op. cit., pp. 60-1; Booth, *Life and Labour*, First Series, I, p. 127; Third Series, VI, pp. 174-85; VII, p. 342; HO 45/9729/A52912; *Clarion*, 27 August 1892, p. 6; 3 September, p. 6; 17 September, p. 4; 24 September, p. 5; W. B. Booth, *Light in Darkest England in 1895* (London, 1895), p. 25. There were shelters in Bristol, Leeds, Bradford and Manchester, and one for women in both Edinburgh

If this were not enough, there were accusations of underselling in the woodchopping and printing trades. 'The Salvation Army is a misnomer', declared the *Clarion* in September 1892, 'it should be called the Sweating Army.' The censure appeared in response to the complaint of the secretary of the Woodchoppers Union that the competition of the Salvation and Church Armies had reduced the number of union members from 2,000 to 800. The union's case was also taken up by the Reverend Stewart Headlam, Christian Socialist, Fabian and member of the London School Board. Headlam became convinced that the Salvation Army was securing tenders for firewood for use in Board schools by declining to pay 'union wages' to the men employed in its shelters and 'elevators'. The Army had, however, signed the contract clause, agreeing to pay the trade-union rate of wages, by which the Army presumably meant the wage *equivalent* in the form of food and shelter. This only led to the additional charge of violating the Truck Act. Headlam thus tried to get Sidney Webb, recently elected to the London County Council, to pursue the issue, but Webb said he was too busy. The London *Star* agreed to help, only to back-track by stating that the accusations of unfair competition had been disproved.[91] Nor did anything come of the charge of sweating made against the Army in 1895 by the Printers' Federation, and investigated by the printing trades group of the London Trades Council. Beatrice Webb, who was party to the discussion at an LTC meeting, later commented thus:

> Quite obvious that the delegates of the Printing Federation had made numberless exaggerated statements: equally clear that the printing trades group had given a clean bill of health to the Salvation Army in spite of manifold signs of sweating in the past, if not in the present.[92]

Even so, it was a worrying sign for the Army's 'accord' with the labour movement that, at ground level, conflict was developing with some trade unions over the employment of 'unemployables' at wages below the trade-union minimum.

Beyond these isolated criticisms, the Darkest England scheme *qua* scheme was far from operative. The city-colony workshops and shelters were of little value as feeders to the rural colony; an Over-Sea

---

and Cardiff, in addition to the London shelters. For more favourable comments on the Salvation Army shelters, see Report of the Inter-Departmental Committee on Physical Deterioration [Cd 2175] (1904), qq. 3669 (D. Eyre), 7876 (W. H. Libby).

91 "Elihu", *General Booth's Darkest England Scheme*, op. cit., p. 11; R. B. Roxby, *General Booth Limited. A Lime-Light on the "Darkest England" Scheme* (London, 1893), p. 5; *Clarion*, 30 April 1892, p. 2; 21 May, p. 8; 27 August, p. 6; 3 September, p. 6; 15 October, p. 5; 26 November, p. 5. See ibid., 1 October, p. 8, letter from a firewood cutter: 'Now, when Commissioner Smith was head of the Salvation Army he received our deputation, and promised us that he would discontinue the practice of Firewood Cutting in the Salvation Army.' See also *Church Reformer* (edited by Headlam), XI (1892), pp. 210, 227-9, 249, 277; S. Headlam, *Christian Socialism* [Fabian Tract No 42] (London, 1892), p. 10. For Bramwell Booth's reply to these charges, and to the related charges of underselling on the Farm Colony, see Third Report from the Select Committee on Distress from Want of Employment, op. cit., qq. 9911, 9913. There were workshops in Bradford, Bristol, Manchester, Leeds and Hull, as well as in London. By 1903, there were 64 'elevators' in operation, *Living Epistles: Sketches of the Social Work of the Salvation Army* (London, 1903), p. 36.

92 B. Webb, *Our Partnership* (London, 1948), pp. 125-6; Ervine, *God's Soldier*, II, p. 729. In consequence, the London Trades Council refused to join a demonstration against the Salvation Army organized by the Printers Federation.

Colony, the ultimate aim of the whole venture, was proving extremely difficult to establish.[93] Yet the individual segments of the social scheme continued to function, and between 1892 and 1910 to expand. This expansion was due, in part, to the Salvation Army's increasing acceptance of social work as an end in itself, once it became evident that the spiritual profits to be gleaned from the social scheme were relatively meagre. From the 1890s, therefore, as Jose Harris has shown, the social wing acted 'as both a 'laboratory' for social administration and as a pressure group for intervention by the State'.[94] It is necessary to re-tread some of this terrain in order to establish the main point of this section, that the rapport between Labour and the Salvation Army, if strained by the events of the early 1890s, re-affirmed itself around the pole of welfare politics. More strictly, the Fabian and increasingly predominant wing of the labour movement, with its ideology of social engineering by administrative fiat, viewed favourably a Salvation Army that began to look to state action on behalf of the unemployed and the 'unemployable' as a framework in which its own work could be set.

The main representatives of Salvationism often highlighted the experimental value of the Army's work. When questioned by a Select Committee in 1895 as to whether Hadleigh Farm Colony could contribute to a solution of the unemployed question, Bramwell Booth responded thus: 'the effort we are making is really in the nature of an experiment in certain principles which, if it can be carried out successfully, we think could be extended to an unlimited degree. What we are trying to show is that they are sound.'[95] His overall view of the experiment, moreover, was that it had shown that male colonists, 'even the most unfortunate class', would submit to the life of discipline and labour.[96] From 1894, the Mansion House Relief Fund Committee and a number of poor-law authorities sent groups of able-bodied paupers to the Hadleigh colony. The most important supplier was the Poplar Union, under the influence of George Lansbury, elected on a socialist platform, and Will Crooks, a right-wing Fabian and active trade unionist; both were advocates of setting the unemployed on the land.[97] The human material that the parochial bodies sent to Hadleigh was very poor, and the experiment was an unmitigated failure, with many paupers refusing to stay in the colony. Even so, Colonel David Lamb, governor of the colony, still defended the arrangement: 'when you consider the larger questions bearing on the unemployed', he told the Departmental Committee on Vagrancy, 'we could not well object. We had the facilities for an effective demonstration of what could be done'.[98] The colony was indeed inspected by social reformers and politicians for evidence of ways to rehabilitate the unemployed.

---

93 VC [Cd 2891] (1906), p. 96 (para 332), qq. 7414-16 (D. C. Lamb). In 1895, the Argentine looked like a possible site for an oversea colony, W. B. Booth to General Booth, 18 October 1895, Salvation Army archives.

94 Harris, *Unemployment and Politics*, pp. 124-35, quote at p. 128.

95 Third Report from the Select Committee on Want of Employment, q. 9963.

96 Ibid., q. 9911.

97 Fleay, 'Hadleigh', loc. cit., p. 6; Booth, *Life and Labour*, Third Series, I, p. 108; VII, p. 341; VC, q. 5371 (Crooks); McBriar, *Fabian Socialism*, pp. 120, 198, 202.

98 VC, q. 7322 (Lamb).

Henry Chaplin, President of the Board of Agriculture, visited Hadleigh in 1895; Cecil Rhodes spent an energetic day there in 1898.[99] Occasionally the Salvation Army's experimental role was facilitated by outside sympathizers. The Countess of Warwick (converted to socialism by Blatchford's *Clarion* and a patron of schools for the training of rural occupations) contracted with the Army to improve her garden at Easton. She and her head gardener were said to be impressed with the job of work done by sixty 'unemployables' under Salvationist foremen.[100]

As for pressure-group diplomacy in the cause of state subsidy, the Salvation Army was active on two main fronts: the foundation of an overseas colony for surplus unemployed, and penal-labour colonies for vagrants and 'unemployables'. On the first front, a real advance seemed imminent when the agricultural reformer, Henry Rider Haggard, who had inspected the Salvation Army colonies in England and North America on behalf of the Colonial Secretary, recommended that the government should fund Booth's scheme of overseas colonization, as a way of avoiding the 'race-ruin' that urban conditions fostered. Unfortunately, a Colonial Office committee immediately rejected Rider Haggard's scheme of state-aided colonization, on the grounds that religious bodies were ill-suited to levying regular re-payments from the settlers.[101] The financial disorder of the Darkest England scheme (not to mention the paucity of evidence for the success of Hadleigh colony) probably added to the Committee's fears.[102] If dispirited by what it felt to be a one-sided report, the Army responded positively by redoubling its efforts in sponsored emigration, becoming a sort of Cook's agency for the respectable working class.[103]

The second sphere of policy in which the Salvation Army wanted state assistance is, for present purposes, much more significant. In the provision of compulsory-labour colonies for the detention, discipline and reclamation of vagrants and 'unemployables', the Salvation Army and the labour movement found themselves once more in substantial agreement. In February 1904, Colonel Lamb, governor of Hadleigh, informed Booth that the work of the land colony was being hampered by 'the residuum of 'won't works' and 'unemployables'', for whom he proposed powers of detention along the

---

99 Armytage, *Heavens Below*, p. 321; Booth, *Echoes and Memories*, op. cit., pp. 148-50. In 1895, W. T. Stead also visited Hadleigh and was 'captured by what he saw' according to Bramwell Booth, Begbie, *General William Booth*, II, p. 204.

100 Blatchford, *My Eighty Years*, op. cit., pp. 209-13; *Hansard*, Fourth Series, CXVIII (1903), c. 324 (Sir John Gorst); Gilbert, *National Insurance in Britain*, op. cit., p. 99.

101 Report on the Salvation Army Colonies in the United States and at Hadleigh, England [...] by Commissioner H. Rider Haggard [Cd 2562] (1905), pp. 370, 377-9, 430-5; Report by the Departmental Committee appointed to consider Mr. Rider Haggard's Report on Agricultural Settlements in British Colonies [Cd 2978] (1906), p. 545. One of the members of Lord Tennyson's Committee was Sidney Webb. See also M. N. Cohen, *Rider Haggard. His Life and Works* (New York, 1961), pp. 239-43. Rider Haggard's report appeared in popular form as *The Poor and the Land* (1905). which was recommended reading in *More Books to Read on Social and Economic Subjects* [Fabian Tract No 129] (London, 1906).

102 Harris, *Unemployment and Politics*, pp. 131-2; VC, p. 77 (para 264), qq. 7103-24 (Lamb), 10585-86 (H. Lockwood), Appendix XXIV.

103 *Emigration-Colonisation: Proposals by General Booth* (London, 1905), Beveridge Collection, Coll. B, III, item 28, British Library of Political and Economic Science; C. Fleay, 'The Salvation Army and Emigration 1890-1914', in *Middlesex Polytechnic History Journal*, I (1980), pp. 63-64; cf. G. Wagner, *Children of the Empire* (London, 1982). Between 1906 and 1908, however, William Booth was pressing the Liberal Cabinet, particularly Earl Rosebery, for a loan of £100,000 for a Rhodesian colonization scheme, but without success: Begbie, *General William Booth*, II, pp. 362-68; R. Hyam, *Elgin and Churchill at the Colonial Office 1905-1908* (London, 1968), p. 287.

lines of the legislation for habitual drunkards. By the establishment of labour colonies for 'unemployables', Lamb argued, it would be possible 'to regard vagrancy and begging not as a crime, but as a social danger requiring treatment'. Moreover, only by confronting the problem of this residuum, Lamb contended, would it be possible 'to bring the unemployed question within measurable distance of solution'.[104] The proposals set out in *The Vagrant and the Unemployable* were embodied in a draft bill to be introduced in the Commons by Sir John Gorst, who for nigh-on twenty years had championed the Salvation Army and its social enterprises. Magistrates were to be empowered to order the detention of vagrants in state-subsidized colonies for a period of from one to three years. Gorst was an appropriate sponsor for the bill, having tried unsuccessfully for many years to interest the Conservative Party in a social-welfare programme, and having recently assumed leadership of the campaign to promote the recommendations of the Physical Deterioration report. The Interdepartmental Committee on Physical Deterioration, itself part of the 'quest for national efficiency', which dominated the politics of welfare in the aftermath of the Boer War, had visited Hadleigh colony. As a result, it recommended labour colonies along the same lines as Hadleigh (although with powers of compulsory detention), 'for the reclamation of some of the waste elements of society'.[105] The Salvation Army's bill made no progress, however. Its principles were endorsed by the Local Government Board's Committee on Vagrancy in 1906, but the new Liberal government was no more disposed than its predecessor to legislate on the recommended lines.

Meanwhile, the idea of state coercion of the residuum had struck a chord in parts of the labour movement. Between 1905 and 1909, the labour press, from *Reynolds's Newspaper* to the *Labour Leader*, gave open support to the incarceration of habitual tramps and paupers in labour settlements.[106] Labour saw land colonies to be of little value as a way of dealing with the genuine unemployed — *pace* the Poplar guardians, headed by Lansbury and Crooks — and their role was now restricted to reclaiming the down-and-out. In 1907, the 'New Unemployed Bill' of the Labour Party included a clause whereby 'deliberate and habitual disinclination to work' would be penalized by compulsory work.[107] Organized labour was clearly not prepared to allow the 'loafer' to spoil the claims of the

---

104 HO 45/10499/117669/4; W. Booth to W. B. Booth, 29 November 1905, Salvation Army archives; VC, qq. 6189, 7504; *The Vagrant and the 'Unemployable'. A Proposal by General Booth* (London, 1904), pp. 9-18. For William Beveridge's annotations to this pamphlet, see Beveridge Collection, Coll. B, IV, item 38.

105 VC, Appendix XXVII. Gorst's bill was supported by Herbert Gladstone and R. B. Haldane, Liberal MPs, and by D. J. Shackleton and Will Crooks, Labour MPs. See HO 45/10499/117669/10 and 10578/179621/1-2. For Gorst, see McBriar, *Fabian Socialism*, p. 215; Begbie, *General William Booth*, II, p. 361; Gilbert, *National Insurance in Britain*, pp. 94-5, 98-9, 130; J. E. Gorst, 'Governments and Social Reform', in *Fortnightly Review*, LXXVII (1905), p. 848; id., 'Physical Deterioration in Great Britain', in *North American Review*, CLXXXI (1905), pp. 1-10; *Hansard*, Fourth Series, CXXXV (1904), c. 648. See also Report of the Inter-Departmental Committee on Physical Deterioration, p. 24 (para 91).

106 See R. Vorspan, 'Vagrancy and the New Poor Law in late-Victorian and Edwardian England', in *English Historical Review*, XCII (1977), pp. 78-9. See also *Lloyd's Weekly News*, 11 March 1906, p. 14.

107 J. K. Hardie, 'Dealing With the Unemployed', in *Nineteenth Century*, LVII (1905), p. 52; Vorspan, 'Vagrancy and the New Poor Law', p. 79. For Lansbury and Crooks, see Harris, *Unemployment and Politics*, pp. 139-41, 143, 237; Marsh, 'The Unemployed and the Land', loc. cit., pp. 16-20. *The Weekly Dispatch*, 2 February 1908, p. 6, however, was critical of this part of the Labour Party's scheme.

'deserving' unemployed.

For the Fabian section of the labour movement, moreover, the 'elimination' of the 'industrial residuum' through disciplinary or reformative detention was an integral part of a state socialism which, to use George Orwell's later denunciation, "we', the clever ones, are going to impose upon 'them', the Lower Orders'. Sidney and Beatrice Webb, the main spokesmen of this creed of efficiency above equality, tried hard around 1901 to incorporate 'national efficiency' into a party of social reform and imperial strength around the prominent Liberal, Lord Rosebery, but to little practical effect.[108] The Webbs were not easily cowed, however, and with Beatrice Webb's appointment to the Royal Commission on the Poor Laws in 1905, another round of Fabian high-pressure salesmanship began. At the end of 1907, Mrs Webb was bending ears on 'our able-bodied proposals: [...] I am submitting them to General Booth of the Salvation Army to get that organisation on my side.'[109] More interestingly, she visited Hadleigh colony for a weekend in February 1908 and came away full of admiration for the Salvation Army staff and for their ability to arouse the faculty for regular work in the unemployable (which was more than she could say about Hollesley Bay Colony, run by the London Central Committee for the Unemployed). The Salvationist officers represented 'a *Samurai* caste', selfless and self-disciplined.

> The men, and some of the women, are far more cultivated than is usual with persons of the same social status — one can talk to them quite freely —- far more freely than you could talk to an elementary school teacher, or trade union official [...].[110]

The exertions made on the Sunday evening to convert the colonists, Mrs Webb confessed, 'somewhat frightened me off recommending that the Salvation Army should be state- or rate-aided'. She concluded, nonetheless, that as a voluntary agency, linked to a national campaign against destitution, the Salvation Army 'will be a quite invaluable agency to which to entrust the actual treatment of difficult sections of the residuum of Unemployed and Unemployable labour'. Not surprisingly, the Minority Report of the Royal Commission on the Poor Laws (two of the four signatories of which were Beatrice Webb and George Lansbury) recommended that labour colonies, run by voluntary religious bodies, should be used to train the recalcitrant unemployed.[111]

That was as close as the Salvation Army came to getting the coveted powers of compulsory detention and exchequer support. It was always unlikely perhaps that the Liberal social programme

---

108 G. Orwell, *The Road to Wigan Pier* (London, 1937), p. 212; Gilbert, *National Insurance in Britain*, pp. 72-7. See also S. Ball, *The Moral Aspect of Socialism* [Fabian Tract No 72] (London, 1896), p. 5; *The Abolition of Poor Law Guardians* [Fabian Tract No 126] (London, 1906), p. 22.

109 Webb, *Our Partnership*, op. cit., p. 396.

110 Ibid., p. 400.

111 Ibid., p. 401; id. to Mary Playne, 2 February 1908, Passfield Papers, II, 4 d, item 2. Cf. S. and B. Webb, *The Prevention of Destitution*, p. 243. See also Royal Commission on the Poor Laws and Relief of Distress [Cd 4499] (1909), pp. 633 (Majority), 1206-08 (Minority). The Majority Report also proposed labour colonies for the residuum.

would authorize a religious sect to detain and train contingents of 'unemployables'. Nevertheless, the idea of using the Salvationists as agents of social administration was placed on the Liberal agenda, and in this way the Salvation Army helped to force the pace of state interference with the social conditions of the poor. In putting its work into a framework of state action, the Salvation Army was helped by the Fabian wing of the labour movement, who were particularly supportive of the proposal for the compulsory detention of the 'industrial residuum'. Exponents of a socialism of welfare legislation, the Fabians were the midwives of a welfare ideology which increasingly joined punitiveness to compassion.[112]

V

By 1910, however, other sections of the labour movement were rather more disenchanted with the Salvation Army. Around 1903, *Justice* had seriously questioned the efficacy of emigration; in 1905, the London Trades Council had denounced Booth's proposals 'to transport for life thousands of the flower of the working classes as a pretended relief for the unemployment difficulty'.[113] But the attitude of the labour movement was most greatly affected by the renewed and protracted battle between the Salvation Army and the trade unions over the related issues of sweating, truck-payment and under-selling. From 1901, the London branch of the Amalgamated Society of Carpenters and Joiners had been observing the Army's Hanbury Street workshop, which was fitted up as a modern carpenters' and joiners' shop, with working space for eighty men. Finally, in 1907, it brought the problem before the Trades Union Congress, although at this stage adopting a fairly conciliatory attitude. James O'Grady, a socialist member of the Alliance Cabinet Makers, whilst paying tribute to the 'socially regenerative work' of the Salvationists, charged the Army with undermining the rate of wages agreed between the London Master Builders' Association and the Carpenters' and Joiners' Union, and successfully moved that the Parliamentary Committee of the TUC should open negotiations with Booth in order to stop the unfair competition.[114]

Shortly afterwards, a United Workers' Anti-Sweating Committee was formed from London trade-union branches and socialist societies, which for the next three years held protest demonstrations in London and several provincial towns in an attempt to get a public inquiry into the Army's social work.[115] The campaign was backed by the *Daily News*, increasingly eager to publicize the plight of the

112 See Nicol, *General Booth and the Salvation Army*, op. cit., p. 204.

113 Etherington, 'Hyndman, the Social-Democratic Federation, and Imperialism', loc. cit., p. 98; Armytage, *Heavens Below*, p. 326. Cf. R. V. Clements, 'Trade Unions and Emigration 1840-80', in *Population Studies*, IX (1955), pp. 167-80.

114 H. A. Clegg, A. Fox and A. F. Thompson, *A History of British Trade Unions since 1889*, I (Oxford, 1964), p. 403, note 7; *The Times*, 6 September 1907, p. 5.

115 This section is based on work done by Sheila Blackburn of Manchester University on the newspaper cuttings in Folder 207 of the Gertrude Tuckwell Collection. Tuckwell was, amongst other things, the honorary secretary of the Women's Trade Union League. The following items were

low paid, and, in a more limited manner, by the *Labour Leader*, organ of the ILP. For the *Daily News*, the moral of the dispute was 'the ease with which the most disinterested philanthropy may unconsciously degenerate into sweating'. The *Labour Leader* emphasized the fact that skilled work had been done in the Salvation Army workshops by what was a semi-permanent workforce and paid for 'at piece rates that would represent 'starvation level' for any outside worker', adding that the sweating was 'viewed with great disfavour by the rank and file of the Army itself'.[116]

The typical Salvationist response to these charges served only to indicate the distance between the provision of 'labour hospitals' for 'the wounded soldier of labour' on one hand and the canons of organized trade unionism on the other. Trade-union principles, said Commissioner Alex Nicol, could not apply when the men concerned were more in need of 'remaking' than of wages. Colonel Moss put it more provocatively when describing the derelict class of labour which the Army employed:

> They are brought in from the streets and from the Embankment — dirty, ragged, and hopeless — without ambition or inspiration. [...] They are fed and clothed by the army, and they are at liberty, when they choose, to find other employment. Are we to pay a fellow who is picked up out of the gutter the trade union rate of wages, or are we to give him what he is worth?[117]

Accordingly, the argument that the Army's measures of relief work served to undercut the market, and to create as much as to relieve destitution, cut little ice with William Booth, who proved, as on other occasions, an intractable and slippery negotiator.[118]

The whole issue came before the TUC conference in 1908 and again in 1909, when the Parliamentary Committee reported on the outcome of its negotiations with William Booth. To the distress of the representatives of the CJU, the Parliamentary Committee seemed afraid of offending public opinion by demanding an inquiry into the Army's social work. While accepting that the charges of sweating were substantiated, C. W. Bowerman, David Shackleton and James O'Grady wished only to persuade Booth either to close the factory or to put goods on to the market at the price at which they

---

the most helpful: *Morning Post* and *Daily Chronicle* for 7 September 1908; *Nottingham Guardian*, 10 September; *Morning Leader*, 20 January 1909; *Bromley Chronicle*, 18 February; *Eastern Daily Press*, 28 June; *Dulwich Post*, 14 August; *Glasgow Herald*, 27 September; *Derby Telegraph*, 15 August 1910; *Northampton Echo*, 10 September. See also *The Times*, 2 September 1908, p. 10; 13 February 1909, p. 8; 8 March, p. 10; 30 August, p. 2; *Salvation Army Sweating: Manifesto by the United Workers' Anti-Sweating Committee*, Beveridge Collection, Coll. B, IV, item 15.

116 *Daily News*, 26 August 1907; *Labour Leader*, New Series, IV (1907), pp. 152, 178.

117 *Daily Express*, 26 August; *Tribune*, 7 September; *Star*, 16 September; *The Times*, 7 September, p. 7; 22 September 1908, p. 9; *A Calumny Exposed. A Reply to the unfounded charges of Sweating brought against the Hanbury Street Labour Home* (London, 1909), *passim*. Alex Nicol subsequently left the Salvation Army and wrote favourably of state or Fabian socialism. Of the sweating issue, he later said: 'It was alleged that sweating was practised here — I know it was. The Army officials argued to the contrary, and I am rather ashamed that I was among the number.' *General Booth and the Salvation Army*, p. 202.

118 A. G. Gardiner, *Prophets, Priests, and Kings* (London, 1914), p. 193. Booth's intransigence hardly dovetailed with the anti-sweating movement of the early twentieth century, for which see Mayor, *The Churches and the Labour Movement*, pp. 124, 136, 219; N. C. Solden, *Women in British Trade Unions 1874-1976* (Dublin, 1978), p. 65; S. Lewenhak, *Women and Trade Unions* (London, 1977), pp. 119-20.

would be sold if produced by trade-union labour.[119] So, too, the leaders of the Anti-Sweating Committee were dispirited by the lukewarm attitude of the Parliamentary Labour Party. Ramsay MacDonald sent a letter of support to a public meeting in London in May 1908, in which he stated that 'while he for one would not like to stop what good work the Salvation Army was doing, at the same time it must not be allowed to undercut employers working under ordinary conditions'. By February 1909, S. Stennett, the district secretary of the London branch of the CJU, was moved to complain that Ramsay MacDonald, Will Crooks and Keir Hardie had all expressed admiration of the Army's work.[120] The way the issue was finally resolved was also unsatisfactory to the union delegates. Booth agreed to confine Hanbury Street to the production of articles required for the exclusive use of the Army (resembling the compromise that was accepted by the trade-union movement for prison-made goods). No public inquiry was granted, and the union had simply to rely upon the promises of General Booth and his officers. Yet if the trade unionists felt that Booth had been left the master of the situation, there seems little doubt that the compromise arrangement further restricted the Salvationist workshops and colonies in providing for the unemployed.[121]

The conflict between the Army and the trade unions was not the only factor behind the growing rupture between Salvationism and labourism. By 1910 the influence of temperance principles within the labour movement was waning, a symptom of Labour's drift away from radical Nonconformity, which, too often for Labour's liking, still traced the ills of man to drink, and too rarely seemed capable of acting as a source of social change. This loss of confidence in religious institutions eventually contaminated Labour's relations with the Salvation Army.[122] Equally influential, particularly in London, was the development of a working-class culture whose focal points, to judge from Charles Booth's end-of-century survey, were increasingly those of entertainment, trade unionism and, to some degree, political action.[123]

For a couple of decades, however, the labour and Salvationist movements had ploughed parallel furrows towards the same end of the field. Both organizations were 'moralizing' agencies in the sense of appealing to working-class self-respect and self-discipline; both drew their strength from an emerging

---

119 *The Times*, 9 September 1908, p. 12; *Labour Leader*, New Series, V (1908), p. 586; *Our Society's History*, ed. by S. Higenbottam (Manchester, 1939), pp. 176-9; *Report of Proceedings at the Forty-Second Annual Trades Union Congress* (London, 1909), pp. 75-84, 119-22.

120 *The Times*, 28 May 1908, p. 12; 5 February 1909, p. 7. Nor did the Anti-Sweating Committee gain any assistance from the Report of the Departmental Committee on the Truck Acts [Cd 4442] (1908), pp. 17-18. See, however, the Minority Report by Stephen Walsh and Mrs H. J. Tennant at p. 93. Keir Hardie still often visited Salvation Army shelters in order to help the destitute, Pankhurst, *The Suffragette Movement*, p. 179; Morgan, *Keir Hardie*, op. cit., p. 127.

121 *Report of the Forty-Second Annual TUC*, pp. 119-22; *Yorkshire Evening News*, 1910, undated cutting in the Tuckwell Collection; *The Times*, 14 September 1910, p. 8.

122 Harrison, *Drink and the Victorians*, op. cit., pp. 397-405. For the continued strength of the Nonconformist connection, however, see Mayor, *The Churches and the Labour Movement*, p. 339; K. D. Brown, 'Non-Conformity and the British Labour Movement: A Case Study', in *Journal of Social History*, VIII (1974-75), No 2, pp. 113-20.

123 Booth, *Life and Labour*, Third Series, VII, pp. 422ff; Stedman Jones, 'Working-Class Culture and Working-Class Politics', loc. cit., pp. 460-508

sense of self- and class-awareness. Both movements made important and at times complementary contributions to the discussion of social reform and to the search for solutions to poverty and unemployment; both movements were essentially concerned in these years with the welfare of the poor. Gradually, attitudes and directions diverged, and the partial accord between the Salvation Army and the labour movement began to disintegrate. The parting of the ways was foreshadowed, perhaps, by George Bernard Shaw's play *Major Barbara*. It was performed at the Court Theatre, London, in November 1905, before an audience which included Sidney and Beatrice Webb, the Conservative leader Arthur Balfour, and a box of uniformed Salvation Army Commissioners, attending a theatre performance for the first time in their lives. In the play, Shaw, the Fabian socialist, set out to dramatize the capitalist system as so corrupting that Christian virtue and charity became inimical to working-class interests. 'I don't think you quite know what the Army does for the poor', says Major Barbara's *fiancé* and fellow-Salvationist. 'Oh yes I do', replies Undershaft, the armaments manufacturer. 'It draws their teeth: that is enough for me as a man of business.'[124]

---

124 G. B. Shaw, *Major Barbara* (London, 1980), p. 98.

4

The Fabrication of Deviance

'Dangerous Classes' and 'Criminal Classes' in Victorian England

The *Scarman Report* on the Brixton riots of 10-12 April 1981 opens with a graphic description of the weekend's events. Television viewers, it says, 'watched with horror and incredulity ... scenes of violence and disorder in their capital city, the like of which had not previously been seen in this century in Britain'.[1] The national press had sketched more luridly the image of a 'hooligan criminal element', directed by political extremists, the apocryphal 'Four Horsemen of the Apocalypse', hooded motorcyclists with citizens' band radios.[2] The imagery was always far-fetched. The disorders broke out in response largely to the methods used by the police to diminish street crime in Brixton: the exercise of the power to 'stop and search', the use of the 'sus' law to net 'suspected persons and reputed thieves', and the appropriately named 'Swamp '81', the saturation policing operation that was applied in the days immediately preceding the disorders.[3] Accordingly, the rioters' limited objective was to evict the police from the streets of Brixton. Yet the imagery died hard. It coloured reactions to the riots, a few months later, in Liverpool and Manchester; and to the 1985 disturbances in Handsworth (Birmingham) and in the Broadwater Farm Estate (Tottenham, North London), where a policeman was brutally stabbed to death, the first metropolitan constable to be killed in a riot since 1833.[4] The problems of crime, riot and policing were aggregated into a disturbing portrait of what is now fashionably dubbed the 'underclass', what the Victorians labelled the 'dangerous classes'.[5]

These events provide my entrance to the early Victorian era, when the imagery of the 'dangerous classes' — a threatening amalgamation of poverty, vagrancy and crime, aroused to rebellion by radical

I am grateful to the Hall Center for the Humanities, for the research fellowship which made it possible to complete this essay, and to the Department of Special Collections, Kenneth Spencer Research Library, University of Kansas. I would also like to thank the editors of this volume, plus Ann Fidler (UC. Berkeley), Martin Wiener (Rice), Ben Sax and Ann Schofield (Kansas) for their valuable comments on the initial draft of the essay.

1   Lord Leslie George Scarman, *The Scarman Report. The Brixton Disorders 10-12 April 1981* (Harmondsworth, 1982), p. 14.

2   See, e.g., *Daily Mail*, 8 July 1981; *Daily Express*, 8 July 1981. See also Clive Unsworth, 'The Riots of 1981: Popular Violence and the Politics of Law and Order', *Journal of Law and Society*, vol. 9, Summer 1982, p. 77; Graham Murdock, 'Reporting the riots: images and impact' in John Benyon (ed.), *Scarman and After* (Oxford, 1984), pp. 74-78.

3   *Scarman Report*, pp. 94 & 176-7; John Clare, 'Eyewitness in Brixton' in Benyon (ed.), *Scarman and After*, p. 51.

4   See 6 *Hansard* 84, 23 October 1985, cols. 348-88; Brian Robson, *Those Inner Cities* (Oxford, 1988), pp. 37-8.

5   See Robert Reiner, 'Crime and Policing' in S. Macgregor & B. Pimlott (eds.), *Tackling the Inner Cities* (Oxford, 1990), p. 45.

rhetoric — was first deployed, and when many of the attitudes to crime and criminals which we hold today were set in place. If I was one of the early cartographers of this terrain, under the incomparable guidance of the historian honoured by this *Festschrift*, my footprints have long since been obliterated, and more mapping has been done in the intervening years. The aim in returning to this ground is to incorporate the additional evidence into a new chart of how and why this dramatic definition of the Victorian outcast appeared, and how and why the collective construct of the 'dangerous classes' was gradually reduced by social classification and by police and penal routines to the slimmer notion of the 'criminal classes', no longer associated with political subversion and social breakdown.

Above all, the essay is a challenge to the 'political' interpretation of criminal policy as a direct response to burgeoning fears of revolution, and thus as having more to do with class war than with 'crime' *per se*. The centrepiece of this argument is the limited purchase the threatening image of the 'dangerous (and labouring) classes' ever gained in England, compared to the continent, and the fairly rapid shift to the more limited and manageable image of 'criminal classes', distinct from the labouring classes. These two points — Victorian England's 'exceptionalism' and the brief life there of ruling class panic — are, I would contend, neglected truths due for restatement.

As such, the essay is concerned with the discourse of crime: with the terminology used by middle-class Victorians to express the fears and obsessions of their world, and with the way these words, and their meanings, changed over time. It is not only concerned, however, with the discourse of reformers, jurists, and administrators who spoke and wrote about crime. For many of these people not only defined the boundaries of the 'respectable' and the 'dangerous', but also helped to create laws and institutions for dealing with the outcast, which were instrumental in enclosing the dominant meanings within the administrative practice of criminal justice. Over and above the interplay between dominant discourse and law enforcement strategies, the essay seeks to link particular stereotypes of deviance, and the manner in which they were applied, to the wider political project of establishing and reinforcing the moral boundaries between different sections of the vast body of the working population. The emergence and evolution of the discourse of the 'criminal and dangerous classes' is related, in short, to the crucial political and cultural debate on the emerging proletarian 'order'.[6]

---

6 My approach to the subject has been influenced by Martin Wiener's important cultural interpretation of Victorian crime and criminal justice, *Reconstructing the Criminal. Culture, Law, and Policy in England, 1830-1914* (Cambridge, 1990). The book relies too exclusively, in my view, on an individualist, as distinct from a collectivist, reading of crime, and explores only the single cultural image of the wilful, undisciplined and unmoralised criminal. Nonetheless, it reveals how much moral values and distinctions mattered to the Victorian discussion of criminality. For a similar decipherment of the nineteenth-century debate on poverty, see Gertrude Himmelfarb, *The Idea of Poverty. England in the Early Industrial Age* (New York, 1985).

I

Two features of eighteenth-century society warrant immediate attention, as a way of establishing the base line from which we can measure the change in attitudes to crime wrought by the transition to an urban, industrial society. The first is the 'picturesque' description of the underworld of rogues and vagabonds. From Elizabethan times on, the 'rogue literature' conjured up a criminal subculture with its corporative structures and craft subdivisions, its distinct locales and haunts, and its own cant (or dialect), rites and values: a portrait of an anti-society of professional villains, cheats and thieves; one standing in juxtaposition to the world of honest labour. Whether such a 'deviant' underworld existed outside the pamphlet literature is, for present purposes, beside the point. What counts is that perceptions of a bounded netherworld were deeply etched by this traditional 'ethnography' of crime.[7] The second feature is an elite tolerance of crime and riot, displayed both in 'the margin of [minor] illegality', conceded to, and demanded by, the poor (the obverse being the pivotal role accorded the awe-inspiring ritual of public execution), and in the doings of the 'city mob', whether out to force justices to increase wages or to root for Church and King.[8]

Both features of early-modern society were subverted by such long-term 'civilizing' processes as a growing demand for security of daily life and a rising standard of personal self-discipline, and, more specifically, by the change in attitudes caused by the events of the 1780s and 1790s. The portrait of a circumscribed underworld was challenged by a sense of crisis about the levels of violent and property crime, first voiced in Martin Madan's *Thoughts on Executive Justice* (1785), made shrill by the end of transportation and the demobilization of thousands of soldiers and sailors in 1786, and barely muted by the outbreak of war in 1793.[9] The licence granted the city mob was severely curtailed once the Gordon and Priestley riots exemplified the threat that popular turbulence posed to property, and once the French Revolution frightened the elite into viewing the poor as a race of potential revolutionaries.[10]

The person who more than anyone expressed this new perception of crime was Patrick Colquhoun. A Glasgow merchant, Colquhoun had moved to London in 1791 looking for government employment,

---

7   See T. C. Curtis & F. M. Hale, 'English Thinking About Crime, 1530-1620' in L. A. Knafla (ed.), *Crime and Criminal Justice in Europe and Canada* (Ontario, 1981), p. 117; Peter Linebaugh, *The London Hanged. Crime and Civil Society in the Eighteenth Century* (London, 1991), pp. 71-2.

8   See Michael Ignatieff, 'State, Civil Society, and Total Institutions: A Critique of Recent Social Histories of Punishment' in M. Tonry & N. Morris (eds.), *Crime and Justice: An Annual Review of Research* (Chicago, 1981), vol. 3, pp. 166-7; E. Hobsbawm, 'The City Mob' in idem, *Primitive Rebels* (New York, 1965), pp. 111-20.

9   Martin Madan, *Thoughts on Executive Justice, with respect to our criminal laws* (London, 1785), pp. 4-5 & 79. See also J. M. Beattie, *Crime and the Courts in England 1660-1800* (Oxford, 1986), p. 225; Elaine Reynolds, 'The Night Watch and Police Reform in Metropolitan London, 1720-1830', Ph.D. thesis, Cornell University, 1991, pp. 228-32.

10   Allan Silver, 'The Demand for Order in Civil Society: A Review of Some Themes in the History of Urban Crime, Police, and Riot' in D. Bordua (ed.), *The Police* (New York, 1967), pp. 3-4; M. Ignatieff, *A Just Measure of Pain* (London, 1989), p. 89.

which he found the following year as a stipendiary magistrate under the Middlesex Justice Act 1792.[11] His reputation rests, however, on his several treatises on crime, police and indigence, written in the nervous aftermath of the French Revolution.[12] At first blush, Colquhoun's description of the state of crime in the metropolis recalls that of 'picaresque' literature. Crime is a trade, with an infrastructure of receivers and lodging houses; the more daring of 'the Criminal Phalanx' form themselves into gangs or societies to plan and execute robberies.[13] This eighteenth-century image of crime pales into insignificance, however, at the side of Colquhoun's estimates of the size and composition of metropolitan crime.

In a memorandum of 1793, Colquhoun estimated that '[t]he property stolen and pilfered in and about this Metropolis by means of a Systematic plan of Depredation (exclusive of those Thefts Robberys and Burglarys which are committed by common and *professed Thieves*)' came to £800,000 per annum. 'This System,' he continued,

> is Carried on through the medium of *menial Servants & Domestics, — Journeymen, Apprentices, Labourers, Porters and others who are employed in private Houses, Shops, Warehouses, Work shops, Manufactorys* ... and also in the Dockyards.[14]

It is evident also from his more detailed description of those implicated in riverside delinquency, that as much as ninety per cent of all crimes were committed by those employed in loading and discharging the ships and vessels in the River Thames: watermen, lightermen, lumpers and coal heavers; and that almost one-third of the total number of port workers was delinquent.[15] In the *Treatise on Indigence*, the full breadth of Colquhoun's vision is revealed in estimates of those in Great Britain 'presumed to live chiefly or wholly upon the labours of others'. Over 1,320,000 people, or 1 in 8 of the entire population, was indigent (in receipt of parish relief), vagrant, living by prostitution, or criminal.[16] Colquhoun's figures must be taken with a bag of salt, if accurate social observation is the quest.[17] As a reflection of an attitude of mind, however, they are invaluable.

Clearly, Colquhoun found difficulty in distinguishing and demarcating the active delinquent from the poor who were indigent through 'culpable causes'. To meet the threat from the criminal and indigent

---

11 On Colquhoun, see Sir Leon Radzinowicz, *A History of English Criminal Law and its Administration from 1750* (London, 1956), vol. 3, pp. 211-19; D. Philips, '"A New Engine of Power and Authority". The Institutionalization of Law-Enforcement in England 1780-1830' in V. A. C. Gatrell, B. Lenman & G. Parker (eds.), *Crime and the Law* (London, 1980), p. 175; Reynolds, 'The Night Watch', p. 357.

12 Patrick Colquhoun, *A Treatise on the Police of the Metropolis* (London, 1800, 6th. ed; first pub. 1795); idem, *A Treatise on the Commerce and Police of the River Thames* (London, 1800); idem, *A Treatise on Indigence* (London, 1806).

13 Colquhoun, *Treatise on Police*, p. 101.

14 The 1793 memorandum is reproduced in Radzinowicz, *History*, vol. 3, Appendix 5., p. 507.

15 Colquhoun, *Treatise on Police*, pp. 217-43; idem, *Treatise on the Commerce*, pp. 50-80. See also L. Radzinowicz, *A History of English Criminal Law* (New York, 1957), vol. 2, p. 359; E. P. Thompson, *The Making of the English Working Class* (Harmondsworth, 1982), p. 59.

16 See Radzinowicz, *History*, vol. 3, pp. 239-40 and 513-18 (Appendix 5).

17 By estimating the number of women who supported themselves by prostitution at 50,000, Colquhoun condemned every fourth female in London, irrespective of age, to prostitution!

poor, he proposed a regular system of police, whose tasks included regulating those institutions of the urban poor (such as lodging houses) which encouraged crime, and a Pauper Police Institution.[18] With counter-revolutionary zeal, moreover, Colquhoun advised keeping close track of the thousands of 'miscreants' in London, for they, 'upon any fatal emergency, (which GOD forbid!) would be equally ready as their brethren in iniquity were, in Paris, to repeat the same atrocities.'[19] Thus were the 'dangerous classes' linked in this discourse to revolutionary violence. With the exception of the Thames River Police Act 1800, however, Colquhoun made little headway with his vast scheme to invigilate the poorer sections of society. Not even this practised self-publicist was able to gain governmental attention. His conservative critics, moreover, repeatedly attacked his 'disposition to think ill' of what Sir Richard Phillips described as 'the two large classes of poor shop-keepers and labourers'.[20] Yet Colquhoun's vision contrasted markedly with the previous image of a criminal underworld, isolated by its customs, speech and mode of life, and distinguishable from the labouring poor. His alarmist campaign, his strategy of exaggeration, which became a model for other 'moral entrepreneurs' in the cause of police and prison reform, prepared the ground, moreover, for a vocabulary of 'the dangerous classes'.

It is at this point, in my view, that historians of crime and criminal justice go to excess. They have the strong tendency to write the history of the first half of the nineteenth century in terms of the threat of 'the dangerous and labouring classes', and the associated introduction of new instruments of policing and punishment.[21] The logic of the argument is seductive. The first decades of the nineteenth century were ones of extraordinarily rapid population increase. Towns were magnets; England, and a fair bit of Ireland, went to London.[22] Young men between 16 and 25 years of age, the chief protagonists in crime and disorder, formed up to one-third of the adult male population of these towns. While industry summoned these migrants, it could not keep them all in continuous work. Economic crises, unemployment, and a divisive urban structure ripped apart the traditional web of interdependence

---

18   See 28th Report from the Select Committee on Finance, House of Commons Sessional Papers, vol. 112, 1798, Appendix C, pp. 47-53; Report from the Committee on the State of the Police of the Metropolis, *PP*, 1816, V (510), pp. 32-3. See also N. Rogers, 'Policing the Poor in Eighteenth-Century London: The Vagrancy Laws and Their Administration', *Histoire Sociale-Social History*, vol. XXIV, May 1991, pp. 144-5.

19   Colquhoun, *Treatise on Police*, p. 532.

20   Richard Phillips, *Modern London: being the History and Present State of the British Metropolis* (London, 1804), p. 146. See also Ruth Paley, '"An Imperfect, Inadequate and Wretched System?" Policing London Before Peel', *Criminal Justice History*, vol. X, 1989, p. 98.

21   The most important texts, from which the summary in the next two paragraphs is drawn, are Silver, 'The Demand for Order', pp. 3-4; Ignatieff, *A Just Measure*, p. 210; R. D. Storch, 'The Plague of the Blue Locusts. Police Reform and Popular Resistance in Northern England, 1840-57', *International Review of Social History*, vol. 20, 1975, p. 62; idem, 'Policing Rural Southern England before the Police' in D. Hay and F. Snyder (eds.), *Policing and Prosecution in Britain 1750-1850* (Oxford, 1989), pp. 262-3; D. Philips, '"A Just Measure of Crime, Authority, Hunters and Blue Locusts." The "Revisionist" Social History of Crime and the Law in Britain, 1780-1850' in S. Cohen & A. Scull (eds), *Social Control and the State* (Oxford, 1986), pp. 63-5; C. Emsley, *Crime and Society in England 1750-1900* (London, 1987), pp. 58-9; V. A. C. Gatrell, 'The Decline of Theft and Violence in Victorian and Edwardian England' in Gatrell *et al*, *Crime and the Law*, p. 272; idem, 'Crime, authority and the policeman-state' in F. M. L. Thompson (ed.), *The Cambridge Social History of Britain 1750-1950* (Cambridge, 1990), vol. 3, pp. 249-51.

22   The population of London rose as follows: 1801, 1 million; 1830, 1.5 million; 1846, 2.25 million.

between elites and the labouring classes. Cities became breeding grounds of crime and disorder. Elites felt insecure in an urban situation characterised by a growing ungovernability of the poor.[23]

Enter acute political conflict. The popular radical movement recurrently challenged the rule of the governing classes. The position became more volatile still when, in the 1840s, radicalism coincided with Irish discontent and revolution abroad.[24] For many of the propertied classes, we are told, the decay of order not only presaged a rising incidence of crime, but also threatened political catastrophe. In their obsession with the 'dangerous and labouring classes', the propertied amalgamated different kinds of dread — depredation and confiscation, robbery and revolution — and different social strata. Practically the whole of the non-respectable poor was 'criminalised' and collectivised. Finally, the imminent collapse of civilisation at the hands of the 'dangerous and labouring classes' was exploited to great effect by police and prison reformers to scare the ruling classes into abandoning the inadequate police and penal strategies of old.

An undoubted influence on the interpretation of the early nineteenth century in terms of the threat of social revolution has been Louis Chevalier's history of change in the perceptions of crime and disorder in Paris. Chevalier argued that the human invasion of Paris led to acute overcrowding, disease, poverty and starvation. Large swathes of the urban workforce turned to crime or revolution to express an alienation that was rooted in these fundamental biological realities. The result was that Paris became a city in which crime no longer existed on the margins of society, but permeated the mass of the poor. The 'classes laborieuses' rubbed shoulders with the criminals of the 'classes dangereuses'; indeed they became virtually indistinguishable. Vice and poverty, the underworld and the world of labour, were utterly confused.[25] If historians have contested Chevalier's linkage of criminal and revolutionary violence — holding rather that the combatants of 1830 or 1848 were skilled artisans, not the uprooted 'dangerous classes'[26] — they generally accept that bourgeois Parisians obsessively feared the 'dangerous and labouring classes'. Michel Foucault, most notably, confirmed that an increased overlap of politics and crime served

> as a support for the 'great fear' of a people who were believed to be criminal and seditious as a whole, for the myth of a barbaric, immoral and outlaw class which, from the empire to the July Monarchy, haunted the discourse of legislators, philanthropists and investigators into working-class life.[27]

---

23   Cf. Stuart Woolf (ed.), *Domestic strategies: work and family in France and Italy 1600-1800* (Cambridge, 1991), pp. 198-9.

24   See J. Saville, *1848. The British State and the Chartist Movement* (Cambridge, 1987), p. 33.

25   Louis Chevalier, *Labouring Classes and Dangerous Classes in Paris During the First Half of the Nineteenth Century* (London, 1973), pp. 80-120 & 141-2.

26   See, e.g. , George Rudé, *The Face of the Crowd. Studies in Revolution, Ideology and Popular Protest*, ed. by Harvey Kaye (Atlantic Highlands, 1988), pp. 233-8.

27   Michel Foucault, *Discipline and Punish. The Birth of the Prison* (London, 1977), p. 275. See also I. Merriman, *The Margins of City Life. Explorations on the French Urban Frontier, 1815-1851* (New York, 1991), pp. 1445.

Historians of the British scene have too readily assumed that what was feared in Paris was also feared in London and the northern industrial towns. But was it like this? In the following section, I shall suggest (no more) that while the perceived need to reconstitute a stable and orderly society unquestionably underlay police and prison reform, the role of class fear has been exaggerated; that while it is possible to find statements which compare closely with those of Chevalier's informants, and of which historians of criminal justice have made the most, these are distinguished by their rarity. Few English observers saw a close connection between the 'dangerous' and labouring classes; few depicted a 'dangerous class' of subversive significance. Fears of an alliance between the criminal and working classes were neither as potent nor as pervasive as most British historians contend; by implication, class fear was less influential than commonly claimed in creating paid constabularies and the prison system. The evidence suggests, rather, that the Victorians saw in the marginal people among the urban poor — the vagrants, street-folk, prostitutes, and thieves — the main danger to the social and moral order. Considered a problem less of collective social breakdown, however, than of deficient moral restraint, the pre-eminent response of the social and political thinkers of the early- to mid-nineteenth century was to fashion those distinctions for which the Victorians are justly renowned — the ragged, the pauper, the criminal — and to protect the honest and independent poor from the moral infection of these groups.

II

Colquhoun expected his dire warnings to be taken more seriously once the war against France was over, and when, he predicted, the 'phalanx of delinquents' would be supplemented by discharged soldiers and sailors.[28] His forecast came true after 1815, to judge from the published figures of those committed to trial for indictable offences; data which doubtless fuelled the post-war anxiety about a steep increase in crime.[29] Moreover, crime advanced in tandem with political unrest. Once the restraint of war-time patriotism was removed, a working-class Reform movement arose, and assumed revolutionary proportions before the 'Peterloo Massacre' of 1819 led to its abatement.[30] In such times of popular agitation and political turmoil, Colquhoun's alarum also found its seconders. William L. Bowles, chaplain to the Prince Regent and a Wiltshire magistrate, traced 'the dreadful Increase of Crime' to the expansion of the 'pauper population', and to 'the alteration in the reasonings, feelings, and habits of mind, particularly in fermenting populous districts, in consequence of the French Revolution!'[31] Ten years later, the conservative poet and historian, Robert Southey, had the ghost of Sir Thomas More

---

28   Colquhoun, *Treatise on Police*, p. 563.

29   See Gatrell, 'Decline of Theft', p. 239; idem, 'Crime, authority and the policeman-state', pp. 250-1; Ignatieff, *A Just Measure*, pp. 153-8.

30   Harold Perkin, *The Origins of Modern English Society 1780-1880* (London, 1969), pp. 208-13. For the coincidence of 'normal' crime and political unrest, see D. Philips, *Crime and Authority in Victorian England. The Black Country 1835-1860* (London, 1977), p. 83.

31   William L. Bowles, *Thoughts on the Increase of Crimes, the Education of the Poor, and the National Schools* (London, 1819), pp. 6, 12.

(representing tradition against the evils of modern life) warn that the defective state of 'police and order' would exact a high political price:

> [Y]ou have spirits among you who are labouring day and night to stir up a *bellum servile*, an insurrection like that of Wat Tyler, of the Jacquerie, and of the peasants in Germany ... Imagine the infatuated and infuriated wretches, whom not Spitalfields, St. Giles's, and Pimlico alone, but all the lanes and alleys and cellars of the metropolis would pour out; ... the lava floods from a volcano would be less destructive than the hordes whom your great cities and manufacturing would vomit forth.[32]

Yet despite Southey's apocalyptic statement, the post-Peterloo years were not ones in which the propertied classes, even in London, seemed to worry much about a supposed amorphous 'dangerous class', allied with sections of the labouring poor, and incited by political radicals. Rather, these years were characterised by the emergence of the notion (though not yet the phrase) of a 'criminal class', an hereditary 'race', distinct from those who worked for a living, impelled by profligacy not unemployment, and to combat which a permanent police was recommended. If the 1816 Committee on Police could ask about 'that class of persons who ordinarily commit crimes, meaning the poor and indigent', the 1828 Committee, in contrast, asked the Chief Magistrate, Sir Richard Birnie, whether thieves were 'low artizans employed in any trade or business' or 'a class distinct by themselves, who do nothing but thieve', to which Birnie replied that they were 'trained up from what I may call juvenile delinquents', and hence followed no trade.[33] Other magistrates concurred, as did leaders of the radical movement. Francis Place's opinion that thieves formed a separate class of the community is well known; but John Wade also claimed that thieves 'are born such, and it is their inheritance: they form a *caste* of themselves, having their peculiar slang, mode of thinking, habits, and arts of living'.[34] This evidence is in keeping, finally, with the view that the Metropolitan Police Act 1829 was passed in response to rising crime, as distinct from the fear of riot and the 'dangerous classes'.[35]

From 1829, an interpretation in terms of the threat of a subversive 'dangerous class' has a more convincing ring to it. In the next two years, the concurrent though separate movements of rural incendiarism ('Swing'), unemployment and the growth of trade unions, and an extra-parliamentary agitation demanding reform under threat of armed resistance, coming in the wake of revolution in

---

32 Robert Southey, *Sir Thomas More: Or, Colloquies on the Progress and Prospects of Society* (London, 1829), vol. 1, p. 114.

33 Report from the Committee on the State of the Police of the Metropolis, *PP*. 1816, V, p. 226 (evidence of John Gifford, senior magistrate, Worship St. Division); *Report from the Select Committee on the Police of the Metropolis, PP*. 1828, VI (533), p. 45. See also George B. A. Mainwaring, *Observations on the Present State of the Police of the Metropolis* (London, 1821), p. 59; Randle Jackson, *Considerations on the Increase of Crime, and the degree of its extent* (London, 1828), p. 23.

34 John Wade, *A Treatise on the Police and Crimes of the Metropolis* (London, 1829), p. 158. For Place, see Brian Harrison, 'Traditions of Respectability in British Labour History', in idem, *Peaceable Kingdom* (Oxford, 1982), p. 191.

35 Historians disagree on this issue. Some emphasize the role of riot and class fear (see Paley, 'Policing London Before Peel', p. 113; Hay & Snyder, *Policing and Prosecution*, p. 10), some the perception of increasing crime (Reynolds, 'The Night Watch', p. 16), while some hedge their bets and stress both (Philips, 'A New Engine', p. 182). See note 37 below for the role of riot in provincial police reform.

France, and in conjunction with an outbreak of cholera, could not but refresh the imagery of an anarchic alliance of workmen and criminals.[36] The climax came with the reform riots of October 1831. Consider, for example, the reformer E. G. Wakefield's pamphlet, *Householders in Danger from the Populace*. Exploiting the fears aroused by the Bristol riots, Wakefield declared that London could be thrown into revolution by a conjunction between the 30,000 'common thieves', ever ready to sack the capital, 'the Rabble' — (some 60,000 poor and semi-criminal costers, drovers, brickmakers, scavengers, and low prostitutes), and the 'Desperadoes', or Owenite socialists, who would lead this 'populace' against the propertied.[37] Wakefield was probably recognized for what he was — a scaremonger out to frighten the landed elite into conceding reform; his 'dangerous class', moreover, was drawn from the marginal sections of London society, and never ascends beyond the street-folk.[38] But his minatory language doubtless fed alarm concerning what radicals, criminals and the under-employed might jointly do.

Against the fears of an overlap between the labouring and dangerous classes during the Reform crisis must be set the 1834 Poor Law, the conclusions of the statistical societies, and the *Constabulary Report* of 1839: the first contributed to the project of dividing the labouring from the 'dangerous classes', the latter two reinforced the portrayal of a distinct criminal class. The Poor Law Commission grew out of the long-standing debate on how best to halt the 'pauperism' (the state of dependence upon public authorities) of the labouring classes, a pauperism that, it was felt, led to crime. The *Poor Law Report* and subsequent Poor Law Amendment Act aimed to diminish the pauperisation of the labouring classes by fencing off the 'independent poor' from the workhouse pauper, thus promoting 'moral restraint' among the former. If the law had the side effect of making paupers feel like criminals (workhouses were not known as 'bastilles' for nothing), and hence of unintentionally shaping a 'dangerous class' of paupers and criminals, it also withdrew a significant section of the labouring poor from the taint of pauperism and crime and facilitated their eventual integration into the 'moral consensus'.[39]

In their surveys of the social ills of industrialization, the statistical societies increasingly absolved the factory system, placing the blame instead on moral degeneracy and the growth of cities. Crime was ascribed to the moral condition of individuals (idleness, intemperance), not to economic want; and it

---

36 See G. Rudé, 'Why was there no Revolution in England in 1830 or 1848?' in idem, *The Face of the Crowd*, p. 150; Thompson, *Making*, p. 898; D. J. V. Jones, *Crime, Protest, Community and Police in Nineteenth-Century Britain* (London, 1982), p. 17.

37 Edward Gibbon Wakefield, *Householders in Danger from the Populace* (London, n.d. Oct. 1831?), pp. 3-5. Cf. Thompson, *Making*, pp. 894-5. For the Bristol riots, see Joseph Hamburger, *James Mill and the Art of Revolution* (New Haven, 1963), p. 176; George Rudé, 'English Rural and Urban Disturbances on the Eve of the First Reform Bill, 1830-1831', *Past and Present*, no. 37, July 1967, p. 98; Mark Harrison, *Crowds and History. Mass Phenomena in English Towns, 1790-1835* (Cambridge, 1988), p. 303. Harrison also suggests (pp. 309-11) that the reform riots convinced many outside (if not within) Bristol of the case for provincial police reform, which the 1835 Municipal Reform Act introduced.

38 Joseph Hamburger, *James Mill and the Art of Revolution*, pp. 70-73.

39 See Himmelfarb, *Idea of Poverty*, chap. VI.

was linked to the existence of an hereditary criminal class.[40] Edwin Chadwick was equally convinced that crimes against property were not primarily caused by 'blameless poverty or destitution' , but by the criminal's rational estimate of the profitability of 'a career of depredation'. Most crime, he thought, was committed by a class of 'habitual depredators', migratory in habit.[41] Accordingly, the *Constabulary Report* called for a rural police force to assist in making a life of crime less profitable than honest labour. Chadwick was well-versed in the ways of alarming his readers, but unlike Colquhoun (whose inflated estimates of 'malefactors' Chadwick tried to correct), he rarely if ever attempted to construct an image of a 'dangerous class' of indigent and criminal, or to link 'habitual depredators' with the trade union or Chartist movements, despite his concern to catalogue the strikes and violence of organized operatives.[42] One is left with the feeling that Chadwick's reforming vision was shaped by a determination to ensure that crime did not undermine the motive to industry on the part of the labouring poor, not by fear of a subversive dangerous class. And, again, this evidence corresponds with the generally accepted view that the Rural Police Act 1839 owed its origin to the grudging recognition on the part of the rural gentry that a new police would better maintain the daily peace, not to the fear of an alliance between criminals and 'physical force' Chartists.[43]

Belief in 'the existence of a class of persons who pursue crime as a calling', expressed by Matthew Davenport Hill, Recorder of Birmingham, in his July 1839 charge to the grand jury, was, it is clear, firmly rooted in middle-class discourse before the vocabulary of 'les classes dangereuses' arrived.[44] How, then, was the French formulation received in England? In the early 1840s, Honore Frégier's *Des classes dangereuses* was reviewed, although not widely, in the quarterly press.[45] Henry Milton in the *Quarterly Review* emphasised Frégier's assumption that 'it is from the poor and vicious of the *operative classes* that the criminal portion of the community is chiefly recruited', while the reviewer for the

---

40   See E. Yeo, 'Social Science and Social Change: A Social History of Some Aspects of Social Science and Social Investigation in Britain, 1830-1890', Ph.D. thesis, Sussex University, 1972, pp. 88-102; Randall E. McGowen, 'Rethinking Crime: Changing Attitudes Towards Law-Breakers in Eighteenth and Nineteenth-Century England', Ph.D. thesis, Illinois University, 1979, pp. 202-3; Lawrence Goldman, 'The Origins of British "Social Science". Political Economy, Natural Science and Statistics, 1830-1835', *Historical Journal*, vol. 26, 1983 , pp. 589-90.

41   First Report of the Commissioners appointed to inquire as to the best Means of establishing an efficient Constabulary Force in the Counties of England and Wales, *PP* 1839, XIX (169), p. 73. Chadwick's associate, W. A. Miles, did much to promote the image of criminals as 'a Race "sui generis", different from the rest of Society': Second Report from the Select Committee of the House of Lords appointed to inquire into the Present State of the Several Gaols and Houses of Correction in England and Wales, *PP* 1835, XI (439), p. 583. See also HO 73/16, papers of W. A. Miles.

42   Cf. Himmelfarb, *Idea of Poverty*, pp. 383-4 & 397. See also A. P. Donajgrodzki, '"Social Police" and the Bureaucratic Elite: A Vision of Order in the Age of Reform' in idem, *Social Control in Nineteenth Century Britain* (London, 1977), pp. 65-7.

43   Cf. A. Brundage, 'Ministers, Magistrates and Reformers: The Genesis of the Rural Constabulary Act of 1839', *Parliamentary History*, vol. 5, 1986, p. 62. Charles Dickens' *Oliver Twist* (1837-38) probably reinforced the image of a criminal milieu, separate from that inhabited by the labouring poor, separate even from that of the workhouse pauper.

44   M. D. Hill, *Suggestions for the Repression of Crime contained in Charges delivered to Grand Juries of Birmingham* (London, 1857), p. 7.

45   The full title of Frégier's social survey was *Des Classes dangereuses de la Population dans les Grandes Villes, et des Moyens de les rendre meilleures* (Paris, 1840), 2 vols. Frégier was a bureau chief in the headquarters of the Paris police. In a study which had the dangerous classes as its brief, Frégier found himself unable to delineate clearly the labouring from the dangerous classes. See Chevalier, *Labouring Classes*, pp. 141-2.

Athenaeum was struck by how in cities, 'poverty and crime, which should have no necessary connexion, are so inextricably intermingled as to be perpetually mistaken the one for the other'.[46] French example had the greatest impact on the historian, staunch tory, and sheriff of Lanarkshire, Archibald Alison. His articles in *Blackwood's Edinburgh Magazine* in 1844 represent the high water mark of British attention to the political consequences of what Alison called 'this prodigious and unrestrained increase of crime and depravity among the working classes in the manufacturing districts', which, he alleged, would so multiply '"les classes dangereuses" as they have been well denominated by the French, as, on the first serious political convulsion, may come to endanger the state.'[47] Urban and mining populations were especially demoralized, in Alison's opinion, by strikes that kept the labouring poor idle. He had in mind the Plug riots in England and the strikes in Scotland in 1842, the latter requiring Alison's personal intervention at the head of a band of soldiers and police.[48] He was particularly pained by the fact that nothing was being done to remedy the evils:

> Meanwhile, destitution, profligacy, sensuality, and crime, advance with unheard-of rapidity in the manufacturing districts, and the dangerous classes there massed together combine every three or four years in some general strike or alarming insurrection.[49]

These statements have been used by historians to suggest that the forties witnessed a 'criminalization' of the entire body of non-respectable urban poor, and to argue that the Victorians lumped together the 'criminal class', the 'pauper', and the 'labouring poor'. The times were certainly ripe for such an amalgam, particularly in London. Migrants flooded into the capital in the 1840s, one in six from Ireland, many of whom fetched up in unskilled labouring jobs. In 1848, London was hit by depression, cholera paid another grim visit, Ireland and the Continent were turbulent, and metropolitan Chartism was at its most insurrectionary.[50] Predictably, Alison's fears found an echo of sorts in the capital. In 1847, Captain William John Williams, a prison inspector, told a House of Lords Committee that had transportation been stopped some years back, the condition of London 'would have been similar to Paris; for we know that a criminal Population collected together in Hordes are always ready Instruments of popular violence'.[51] Edmund Antrobus warned that London Chartists, 'whose ranks are

---

46   *Quarterly Review*, vol. LXX, June 1842, pp. 1-44; *Athenaeum*, 4 April 1840, *PP* 267-91.

47   *Blackwood's Edinburgh Magazine*, vol. LV, May 1844, pp. 544-5.

48   See Sir Archibald Alison, 1792-1867, *DNB*, vol. 1 (London, 1968), p. 288.

49   *Blackwood's Edinburgh Magazine*, vol. LVI, July 1844, p. 2. The first example of 'dangerous classes' in the *OED* is from Sir Arthur Helps, *Friends in Council*, set. 11 (London, 1859), vol. 1, p. 131: 'I admit that in most of the European nations there are dangerous classes, dangerous because uncared for and uneducated; but surely there is no state in Europe in which an army of one hundred thousand soldiers could not keep down the dangerous classes, if the bulk of the people were reasonably well affected to the government.'

50   See Lynn Lees, 'Metropolitan Types. London and Paris compared' in H. J. Dyos and M. Wolff (eds.), *The Victorian City* (London, 1973), vol. 1, pp. 414-15; D. Goodway, *London Chartism, 1838-1848* (Cambridge, 1982), pp. 68-9; Saville, *1848*, pp. 93, 96-9.

51   Second Report from the Select Committee of the House of Lords appointed to inquire into the Execution of the Criminal Law, especially respecting Juvenile Offenders and Transportation, *PP* 1847, VII (534), q. 2720, p. 300.

always swelled by a vast proportion of the 30,000 idlers and thieves which infest the town', were said to be arming.[52] For some, clearly, the Chartist, rioter, and petty criminal were indivisible.

Yet even in the forties, and even in London, where a huge concentration of urban poverty stood adjacent to the largest concentration of wealth and property of any European city, the imagery of an Archibald Alison was more than offset by the beginnings of a debate on juvenile delinquency, and by statements that cautioned against an indiscriminate amalgamation of different social strata. Sir Charles Shaw, for example, the Manchester police chief, insisted in 1843 that the classes which figured in the criminal statistics 'must not be confounded with the Working Classes, for the former consist of what the French call "Les Classes Dangereuses."'[53] Even Alison took comfort from the fact that 'nine-tenths of the crime, and nearly all the professional crime' came from the lowest class — 'this dismal substratum, this hideous *black band of society*'.[54] His view was unchanged when rioting broke out in Glasgow in March 1848. The disturbances left 'the most respectable of the working people' untouched; they were caused, he informed the Home Office, by 'Chartist oratory working on the passions of the unemployed', but no subversive intent was evident, 'except in the very lowest and most depraved class in which it is synonymous with the wish for Plunder'.[55] Here we seem closer to the saturnalia of crime portrayed by Dickens in *Barnaby Rudge* (1841) or to the brutalized, degraded outcasts of Disraeli's *Sybil* (1845) and Reynolds' *The Mysteries of London* (1845-48) than to political revolution. There are important distinctions, then, which historians need to respect, between Alison's 'dangerous classes … [who] combine every three or four years in some general strike or alarming insurrection' and Dickens' 'scum and refuse of London, whose growth was fostered by bad criminal laws, bad prison regulations, and the worst conceivable police'.[56] Dickens' fear of urban revolt essentially came down to a criminal class, a species apart, living in isolated 'rookeries', overshadowed by the new police and the new penitentiaries. In this matter, Charles Dickens' vision was in accord with the dominant contemporary discourse.

III

In the aftermath of Chartism, and in an era of greater economic and political stability, the 'dangerous classes' were subjected to further classification. They were no longer endowed with any subversive potential; nor were they seen, except very intermittently, to pose a problem of disorder at all. Lawyers, charity workers, and social investigators turned their attention instead to the presentation of an

---

52 Edmund Edward Antrobus, *London, Its Danger and Its Safety* (London, 1848), p. 16.

53 *Manufacturing Districts. Replies of Sir Charles Shaw to Lord Ashley M. P. regarding the Education, and Moral and Physical Condition of the Labouring Classes* (London, 1843), pp. 20, 23.

54 *Blackwood's*, vol. LVI, July 1844, p. 12.

55 Cited in Saville, *1848*, pp. 254-5, note 30.

56 Charles Dickens, *Barnaby Rudge* (London, 1991), p. 441; G. W. M. Reynolds, *The Mysteries of London* (London, 1846), vol. II, pp. 187-9. For Disraeli, see L. Cazamian, *The Social Novel in England 1830-1850* (London, 1973), pp. 203-5.

increasingly detailed taxonomy of what was now called the 'criminal classes', and to its embodiment in institutional and legislative forms. In the minds of many mid-Victorians, the 'dangerous classes' became practically synonymous with the 'criminal classes', a body supposedly separated by a deep moral and social gulf from the honest labouring poor, and needing to be ever-more constrained by the instruments of criminal justice.

The vocabulary of the 'dangerous classes' did not, of course, disappear overnight. The slum life literature of the 1850s continued to take readers on tours of the 'swamps' and 'wilds' of London, where felons, prostitutes, tramps, and 'the hordes of Irish' lurked, ready to issue forth at times of popular rebellion; and where 'the honest and the hard-working labourer' was compelled to live among and be infected by these 'dangerous classes'.[57] Even that quintessential text of mid-century optimism, *Meliora*, contained a description of the 'substratum of society', composed of paupers and criminals, 'the throes and the heavings' of which might one day occasion society's overthrow.[58] Nor were more sober analysts of the crime problem yet exempt from using the terminology in its widest sense. Thomas Beggs, whose *idée fixe* was the evil influence of intemperance, opened his 1849 enquiry into 'juvenile depravity' with an estimate of the numbers of the 'dangerous class' — 'comprising thieves, paupers, vagrants, prostitutes, imposters, and mendicants'.[59] Such statements, however, were eye-catching prefaces to studies which, like many others between 1846 and 1852, identified what Mary Carpenter called the 'perishing and dangerous classes' (or incipient and actual delinquents), a group roaming the streets like 'city arabs' and, claimed Lord Ashley, 'distinct from the ordinary poor'.[60]

It was through this coterie of specialists, and particularly their first conference in Birmingham in late 1851, which met to consider the question of preventive and reformatory schools, that the actual term 'criminal class' entered 'criminological' parlance.[61] The accolade of 'semantic' forerunner, however, probably belongs to Leeds reformer, Thomas Plint. Over one-third of the crime of large towns, said Plint in 1851, could be traced to the 'criminal class', whose origin and natural history urgently needed investigation. A number of fallacies had to be abandoned. The 'criminal class' was not a product of the factory system; it was not recruited from the ranks of industrial workers.

> May it not be said of the class that it is *in* the community, but neither *of* it, nor *from* it? Is it not the fact
> that a large majority of the class is so by descent, and stands as completely isolated from the other

---

57 See, e.g. , Thomas Beames, *The Rookeries of London* (London, 1850), pp. 119-20, 209-14.

58 Viscount Ingestre (ed.), *Meliora: Or Better Times to Come* (London, 1853), p. 21.

59 Thomas Beggs, *An Inquiry into the Extent and Causes of Juvenile Depravity* (London, 1849), p. 26. Cf. Jelinger C. Symons, *Tactics for the Times: as regards the Condition and Treatment of the Dangerous Classes* (London, 1849), p. 1.

60 Mary Carpenter, *Reformatory Schools, for the Children of the Perishing and Dangerous Classes and for Juvenile Offenders* (London, 1851); Report from the Select Committee on Criminal and Destitute Juveniles, *PP* 1852, VII (515), p. 98; 3 *Hansard* XCIX, 6 June 1848, col. 431 (Ashley).

61 See S. J. Stevenson, 'The "criminal class" in the mid-Victorian city: a study of policy conducted with special reference to those made subject to the Provisions of 34 & 35 Vict. , c. 112 (1871) in Birmingham and East London in the early years of registration and supervision', D. Phil. thesis, 1983, p. 1.

classes, in blood, in sympathies, in its domestic and social organization … as it is hostile to them in the whole '*ways and means*' of its temporal existence?'[62]

The 'criminal class' , said Plint, was a '*pariah* and exotic tribe', morally distinct from the 'operative classes':

> No exact analysis of crime can be obtained, until the exact proportion of this class to the indigenous and really working population … which is separate and distinct from what must be considered a foreign, or, … a non-indigenous body — is ascertained.[63]

Plint was intent to concentrate crime within a clearly demarcated section of the urban community: the 'criminal or dangerous classes'.

Plint reminds anyone familiar with the *Communist Manifesto* (1848) of the 'dangerous class', the 'ragged proletariat' or 'lumpenproletariat' of Marx and Engels. The comments made by these two political thinkers on the lowest stratum of urban society had little or no influence on the mid-Victorian mind, since they only became available in translation years later. But it surely enhances the credibility of bourgeois social attitudes and categorization to recognise that Marx and Engels followed them closely. Engels' view of crime as a primitive form of insurrection, the earliest phase of the 'social war', inscribed in his study of the English working class in the mid-forties, quickly gave way to the view that criminals, vagrants and prostitutes formed a 'dangerous class', 'which in all big towns forms a mass sharply differentiated from the industrial proletariat', indeed even from the lowest pauper classes, and which was a danger to the working-class struggle since it could be 'bought' by counter-revolutionary forces.[64] The contempt displayed by Marx and Engels for the 'lumpenproletariat' stemmed partly, of course, from their theoretical commitment to the 'working proletariat'.[65] But their description of the 'lumpen', depicting it even as a nomadic tribe or race, bears a striking resemblance to the bourgeois depiction of a foreign and exotic world within urban society.[66] As such, the Marxist concept of the 'lumpenproletariat' paralleled contemporary social categorization, and likewise, albeit for different reasons, drew a strict line of demarcation between the working and dangerous classes.

It was Henry Mayhew, much more than Marx, who fashioned the mid-Victorian image of the 'dangerous classes'. In *London Labour and the London Poor* (1861-2), Mayhew concentrated on the street-folk, mostly street sellers or totters, who were an atavistic 'wandering tribe', with their own

---

62 Thomas Plint, *Crime in England. Its Relation, Character, and Extent as developed from 1801 to 1848* (London, 1851), p. 153.

63 Ibid. , p. 122. Cf. Rev. J. Edgar, *The Dangerous and Perishing Classes* (Belfast, 1852).

64 F. Engels, *The Condition of the Working Class in England* (Harmondsworth, 1987), pp. 156, 224; *The Communist Manifesto* (Harmondsworth, 1987), p. 92; K. Marx, *Capital* (London, 1928), p. 711. See also H. Draper, 'The Concept of the "Lumpenproletariat" in Marx and Engels', *Economies et societes*, vol. 6, 1972, p. 2294.

65 See P. Q. Hirst, 'Marx and Engels on law, crime and morality', *Economy and Society*, vol. 1, 1972, pp. 40-1.

66 See R. L. Bussard, 'The "Dangerous Class" of Marx and Engels: The Rise of the Idea of the "Lumpenproletariat"', *History of European Ideas*, vol. 8, 1987, p. 687; P. Stallybras, 'Marx and Heterogeneity: Thinking the Lumpenproletariat', *Representations*, no. 31, 1990, pp. 70-2.

physiognomy, moral conventions and mode of life. The first three volumes of *London Labour* dealt with those who earned an honest livelihood; the final volume examined those 'which are in reality the dangerous classes, the idle, the profligate, and the criminal'.[67] In this volume, and in *The Criminal Prisons of London* (1862), Mayhew offered 'a scientific classification of the criminal classes'. Criminals were divisible, he said, into two classes, the habitual and the casual; habituals committed burglary, robbery, and larceny from the person, all of which were 'regular crafts requiring almost the same apprenticeships as any other mode of life.'[68] As for causes, Mayhew rejected the ones commonly advanced — drink, ignorance, poverty and vagrancy — and instead echoed the *Constabulary Report*, in thinking that crime was due 'to that innate love of a life of ease, and aversion to hard work'. Thus, Mayhew built on the base of Chadwick's 1839 Report, which he considered still 'the most trustworthy and practical treatise on the criminal classes',[69] to construct an image of

> a large class, so to speak, which belongs to a criminal race, living in particular districts of society ... these people have bred, until at last you have persons who come into the world as criminals, and go out as criminals, and they know nothing else.[70]

This was an image of the criminal problem that reached its apogee in the 1860s.

In the sixties, periodical articles dealing with crime and punishment were crop-full of references to the 'criminal classes'. One reason for this was that the end of the system of transportation, and the new task, as an essayist put it, 'of washing our foul linen at home', forced a major reappraisal of the 'convict question'.[71] Another factor was that from 1857 the judicial statistics included tables on the numbers of 'known thieves and depredators, receivers of stolen goods, prostitutes, vagrants, etc.', in each police district; these data lent credibility to the notion of an identifiable class of criminals.[72] Thirdly, the public panic caused by a rash of violent robberies in London in 1862, which the press and parliament blamed on convicts released on licence (or tickets-of-leave), magnified the image of a separate 'criminal class'.[73] And finally, the Punishment and Reformation section of the newly-founded Social Science Association, made up of lawyers, prison administrators, and penologists, fixed its investigative gaze on the study and treatment of the 'criminal class'.[74]

---

67   H. Mayhew & J. Binny, *The Criminal Prisons of London* (London, 1862), opening advertisement. See also K. Williams, *From pauperism to poverty* (London, 1981), pp. 260-2.

68   Ibid., pp. 45, 87.

69   Ibid., pp. 84, 386.

70   Second Report from the Select Committee on Transportation, *PP* 1856, XVII (296), q. 3531, p. 343. Cf. *Criminal Prisons*, pp. 89, 413.

71   'How to deal with the Dangerous Classes', *Leisure Hour*, 1 January 1869, p. 54.

72   See V. A. C. Gatrell & T. B. Hadden, 'Criminal Statistics and their interpretation' in E. A. Wrigley (ed.)), *Nineteenth Century Society* (Cambridge, 1972), p. 348.

73   See J. Davis, 'The London Garotting Panic of 1862: A Moral Panic and the Creation of a Criminal Class in mid-Victorian England' in Gatrell *et al, Crime and the Law*, pp. 190-1, 212; R. Sindall, *Street Violence in the Nineteenth Century: Media Panic or Real Danger?* (Leicester, 1990), *passim*.

74   See L. Goldman, 'The Social Science Association, 1857-1886: a context for mid-Victorian Liberalism', *English Historical Review*, vol. CI, 1986, p.

Two different, not to say contradictory, images of the 'criminal class' are present in this literature. The first is of a group of rational, calculating, 'habitual criminals', whose organization, according to William Pare, 'is as complete … as that of any other class in society, both in their business and social arrangements'. The practices of this business were governed 'by the selfsame economic principles that govern ordinary trading operations'. There were operatives (the thieves) trained to the craft from an early age, there was a division of labour ('mobsmen', 'shofulmen'), and there were capitalists (landlords, receivers) whose money was the 'life-blood of the system'.[75]

The second image of the 'criminal class' was of an irrational, degenerate 'race', marked by distinct physical and mental traits. While Mayhew described 'a criminal race', James Greenwood evoked 'a wily, cunning man-wolf', and Mary Carpenter discovered 'a peculiar low expression, unlike that of the labouring portion of society'.[76] The view that the 'criminal class' was 'as distinctly marked off from the honest industrial operative as "black-faced sheep are from the Cheviot breed"', was firmly endorsed in the 1870s by many prison officials. Dr. Bruce Thomson, resident surgeon at Perth prison in Scotland, described 'a set of demi-civilized savages, who in hordes prey upon society … and, only connecting themselves with those of their own nature and habits, … must beget a depraved and criminal class hereditarily disposed to crime'.[77] Lieut.-Col. Edmund Du Cane, the man in charge of the convict prison system, pondered the suggestion of Dr. Gover, surgeon of Millbank prison, that habitual criminals and vagrants 'are examples of the race reverting to some inferior type … the type of what Professor Darwin calls "our arboreal ancestors"', a view that the use of photography in penal administration seemed to authenticate.[78] This medical and biological discourse came to fruition in Cesare Lombroso's theory of 'l'uomo delinquente' or the 'born criminal'. The theory *qua* theory gained few adherents in Britain, but the language of degeneration prevailed, thereby buttressing assumptions about the existence of a 'criminal class'.[79]

IV

As befitted practical workers in the realm of criminal justice, the authors of much of this literature

---

99. L. Radzinowicz and R. Hood in *A History of English Criminal Law* (London, 1986), vol. 5, pp. 73-84, examine the 'criminal classes', but their account relies substantially on Kellow Chesney's *The Victorian Underworld* (Harmondsworth, 1976), which in turn drew heavily on Henry Mayhew.

75 William Pare, 'A Plan for the Suppression of the Predatory Classes', *Transactions of the National Association for the Promotion of Social Science*, 1862, p. 474; Edwin Hill, *Criminal Capitalists* (London, 1872).

76 Second Report from S. C. on Transportation, p. 343; J. Greenwood, *The Seven Curses of London* (London, 1869), p. 86; H. Martineau, 'Life in the Criminal Class', *Edinburgh Review*, vol. 122, October 1865, p. 342 (quoting Carpenter).

77 James Bruce Thomson, 'The Hereditary Nature of Crime', *Journal of Mental Science*, vol. XV, January 1870, pp. 489-90.

78 E. F. Du Cane, 'Address on the Repression of Crime', *Trans. NAPSS*, 1875, pp. 302-3.

79 See Daniel Pick, *Faces of Degeneration. A European Disorder, c.1848-c.1918* (Cambridge, 1989), pp. 182-3. See also W. D. Morrison, *Crime and its Causes* (London, 1891), p. 198.

proposed taking what they saw as the 'war against crime' to the enemy. 'Criminals may be considered like a hostile army which is engaged in carrying on war against society', said Du Cane in his 1875 address to the Social Science Association, 'and the law lays down the plan of the campaign against them'.[80] In the treatment of habitual criminals, he continued,

> very great advances have been made of late years; we have in principle recognised the existence of a criminal class, and directed the operations of the law towards checking the development of that class, or bringing those who belong to it under special control.[81]

Already in 1868, in discussion of Sir Walter Crofton's address on the 'criminal classes' to the S.S.A., Lord Houghton had posed the rhetorical question:

> Was it possible for any person to go about with the police through the criminal portions of London without saying that these dangerous classes were as completely in the hands of the police — as completely watched every hour of their life as they could be in any way whatever?

The very residential concentration of these 'dangerous classes', Houghton observed, 'gave the police absolute power over them'.[82] These statements alert us to the need to examine the degree to which the law and its administration assisted the creation of both the stereotype of the 'criminal class' and the life histories or criminal careers that exemplified the stereotype.

It is apparent from the research of the past fifteen years that, whatever Victorians thought, very few Victorian criminals were full-time 'professionals'. Most crimes were committed by ordinary working people who supplemented their meagre income with thefts of food, fuel or clothing. Nor were most offenders different in social and cultural stamp from the bulk of the 'honest poor.'[83] Yet this research also reveals how public perceptions and attitudes interacted with law enforcement strategies to reinforce the notion of a 'criminal class'. An axiom of policing history is that the day-time patrolling of the Victorian police sought to impose a new standard of social discipline. More strictly, the police used their discretionary powers under the Vagrancy Act 1824 and the Metropolitan Police Act 1839 to intensify the supervision of members of marginal street economies (costers, hawkers, prostitutes), ragged children and juveniles, and vagrants. Most of those arrested or summoned for non-indictable crimes throughout the entire nineteenth century were deemed to be drunks, prostitutes or vagrants.[84] Historians are beginning to question whether the police had the manpower or willpower to attack working-class street life so vigorously, and to uncover judicial opposition to police campaigns against

---

80 Du Cane, 'Address', p. 272. See also McGowen, 'Rethinking Crime', p. 285.

81 Ibid., p. 275. See also M. D. Hill, *Suggestions*, pp. 155-6; W. Crofton, *The Present Aspect of the Convict Question* (London, 1864), pp. 15-20.

82 See discussion of W. Crofton, 'Address on the Criminal Classes and their Control', *Trans. NAPSS*, 1868, p. 306.

83 See Philips, *Crime and Authority*, chs. 6-8; Jones, *Crime, protest*, chap. 4.

84 See Storch, 'The Plague of the Blue Locusts', p. 84; Goodway, *London Chartism*, pp. 103-4; C. Steedman, *Policing the Victorian Community* (London, 1984), pp. 56-9.

barrow-boys or prostitutes.[85] Yet it does seem that urban policing responded to the stereotype of the 'criminal and dangerous classes' by targetting the economically marginal elements, whose lives were lived in the street, and the 'rookeries' of crime and vice.[86] Studies of juvenile crime and of prostitution reveal how the police assisted in the transformation of delinquents and street-walkers into identifiable outcast groups.[87] The notion of a distinct 'criminal area' provided a map for the police to locate the crime problem. The more the police focused on these communities, the more the detection and hence the apparent incidence of crime increased, thus confirming the emerging perception of these areas and their inhabitants. In these ways, the police played a part in 'making' a criminal or outcast class, which public ideology had first fashioned.[88]

Did mass imprisonment likewise create an identified 'delinquent' group? Michel Foucault would have said that it did. Prison, he argued, manufactures delinquents, both by the study of the criminal type, whose pathological character and habitat distinguishes him from the non-delinquent, and by converting offenders into recidivists or career criminals (the subsequent object of police surveillance). This served the crucial political purpose, Foucault maintained, of driving a wedge between the criminal and working classes. Foucault argued, indeed, that the prison's only true success was in constructing a 'criminal class', with a monopoly on crime, and one distinct from and shunned by the working-class community.[89] The evidence for all this is not overwhelming. Repeated imprisonment, with restrictions on visits, letters and other forms of outside contact, may well have served to isolate the criminal from his family, neighbourhood and class. The penal regimes of the time, moreover, in undermining the physical and mental health of prisoners and in releasing them ill-equipped to find work, consigned them to the 'lumpenproletariat'. But these are more the *un*intended consequences of imprisonment. It seems unlikely that the creation of a 'criminal class' was a deliberate ploy in a strategy of 'divide and conquer'. A more plausible thesis is that the prisoner identified with the 'inmate subculture', emerging from incarceration as a confirmed 'ex-convict', condemned to membership of the social 'residuum'.[90]

85 J. Davis, 'A Poor Man's System of Justice: The London Police Courts in the Second Half of the Nineteenth Century', *Historical Journal*, vol. 27, 1984, p. 328; S. Inwood, 'Policing London's Morals: The Metropolitan Police and Popular Culture, 1829-1850', *London Journal*, vol. 15, 1990, pp. 129-44.

86 See J. Davis, 'From "Rookeries" to "Communities": Race, Poverty and Policing in London, 1850-1985', *History Workshop*, issue 27, 1989, pp. 68-70; idem, 'Jennings' Buildings and the Royal Borough. The construction of the underclass in mid-Victorian England' in D. Feldman & G. Stedman Jones (eds.), *Metropolis London* (London, 1989), pp. 11-31; idem, 'Urban Policing and its Objects: Comparative Themes in England and France in the Second Half of the Nineteenth Century' in C. Emsley and B. Weinberger (eds.), *Policing Western Europe* (New York, 1991), pp. 9-14.

87 S. Margarey, 'The Invention of Juvenile Delinquency in Early Nineteenth-Century England', *Labour History*, no. 34, 1978, pp. 17-24; J. Walkowitz, *Prostitution and Victorian Society* (Cambridge, 1980), chap. 10.

88 The weight of policing continues to bear more heavily on the social 'residuum' or 'underclass', whom the police invidiously term the 'slag' or 'scum', and whom they persist in seeing as their main clientèle: D. J. Smith & J. Gray, *Police and People in London* (Aldershot, 1985), pp. 120, 434-6.

89 Foucault, *Discipline and Punish*, part 4, chs. 1-2. Cf. Ignatieff, 'A Critique', pp. 172-3.

90 See D. Garland, *Punishment and Welfare. A history of penal strategies* (Aldershot, 1985), p. 39; idem, *Punishment and Modern Society. A Study in*

But what of the policy to punish and supervise the habitual criminal, a policy encouraged by the violent robbery or 'garotting' panic of 1862? The Royal Commission on Penal Servitude of 1863 identified 'a class of persons who are so inveterately addicted to dishonesty, and so averse to labour', that there was no chance of their abstaining from a life of crime.[91] Hence, the Penal Servitude Act of 1864 provided for mandatory, monthly reporting to the police by ticket-of-leave men, and gave the police power to arrest any licence holder suspected of having committed a crime, or having broken a condition of his licence. The next step was to extend such surveillance to the larger number of habituals released from local prisons. Under the 1869 Act (as amended by the Prevention of Crimes Act 1871), any person twice convicted of a felony and sentenced to imprisonment (as distinct from penal servitude) could be subject to police supervision for seven years. This legislation also inaugurated a system of registration and identification of a 'criminal class' of habituals.[92]

Enforcement of these Acts was decidedly spotty. In London the law was null and void, since the stipendiary magistrates called upon the Commissioner of Police in person to inform the court each time a licence holder failed to report to the police. The metropolitan police had a difficult time supervising criminals who were, claimed the Police Commissioner, 'a most migratory class'.[93] The register of every person convicted of felony — and by 1876 there were almost 180,000 persons in it — was so bulky as to be beyond monitoring. Even the slimmer Register of Habitual Criminals, with some 7-8,000 names in twelve volumes, was 'perfectly useless', according to a London detective superintendent.[94] It is safe to conclude only that the habitual criminals legislation strengthened the public perception that a 'criminal class' existed, and that by inhibiting the re-integration of the hardened criminal into working-class life (doing for habitual criminals what the Contagious Diseases Acts of the 1860s did for the common prostitute), it gave some substance to this perception.[95]

Social Theory (Chicago, 1990), p. 173.

91 Report of the Commissioners appointed to inquire into the operation of the Acts relating to Transportation and Penal Servitude, *PP*, 1863, XXI (6457), p. 25 (para 36).

92 See M. W. Melling, 'Cleaning House in a Suddenly Closed Society: the Genesis, Brief Life and Untimely Death of the "Habitual Criminals Act, 1869"', *Osgoode Hall Law Journal*, vol. 21, 1983, p. 326; Radzinowicz & Hood, *History*, vol. 5, pp. 254-6.

93 HO 45/9442/66692, 'Report of the Departmental Commission to inquire into the Detective Force of the Metropolitan Police', January 1878, q. 5183, p. 208 (E. Henderson). See also S. J. Stevenson, 'The "habitual criminal" in nineteenth-century England: some observations on the figures', *Urban History Yearbook*, 1986, p. 48.

94 Ibid., q. 1860, p. 66 (J. Thomson). See also PRO, PRI. COM 2/404, Register of Habitual Criminals, 1869-76.

95 Cf. Stevenson, 'The criminal class', p. 375; Melling, 'Cleaning House', p. 355. The legislation also perhaps contributed to a late-century prison population which was older than the population at large, and more hardened by previous prison sentences: Gatrell & Hadden, 'Criminal statistics', pp. 378-85. For discussion of the important possibility that popular value-systems, themselves, recognised and reinforced the demarcation between the working and dangerous classes, see Ignatieff, 'A Critique', pp. 173-4.

V

In the mid-Victorian years, the 'dangerous classes', which had only rarely been prominently profiled, were pared down further to a problem of an habitual 'criminal class', or, at most, to a 'residuum' of criminals, vagrants and 'roughs'.[96] The confidence in being able so to classify, subdivide and diminish the size and threat of the 'dangerous classes' was challenged, however, on two separate occasions (1866-67 and the mid-1880s) by a metropolitan-based fear that, in circumstances of renewed political turmoil, the dangerous and labouring classes were closing ranks. Yet both sets of events, in their own way, revealed the immutability of boundaries drawn over a longer period.

In a setting of trade depression, unemployment, the return of cholera, and bread riots (blamed on 'roughs and juvenile thieves from Kent-street and the Mint'), the reform bills of 1866-67 raised the political temperature once more.[97] Not since the 1840s had there been so much nervousness about political change and expectation of political violence. The worst fears of the alarmists were confirmed by the events of July 1866, when Reform League demonstrators, having been forbidden access to Hyde Park, forced an entry. This symbolic violation of boundaries, and the subsequent days of disorder, led Matthew Arnold to complain bitterly that the erosion of authority had emboldened the 'residuum' into 'marching where it likes, meeting where it likes, bawling what it likes, breaking what it likes'.[98] Such incidents, however, impelled politicians, radical and conservative alike, to emphasise that the vote would not be given to 'the residuum ... of almost hopeless poverty and dependence'.[99] Only the 'respectable working class' had the moral qualities and civic virtue to deserve incorporation into the constitution. These arguments gave political blessing, then, to the social construct, 'respectable artisan', and to its moral antithesis, the 'residuum' or 'dangerous class'.[100] As such, the crisis helped to narrow the definition of the 'dangerous class', confining it largely to a residue of 'roughs' and the 'criminal classes'.[101]

The second metropolitan challenge to mid-Victorian certainties came in the 1880s. Once again,

---

96   The *OED* defined 'rough' as 'a man or lad belonging to the lower classes and inclined to commit acts of violence or disorder.' The first example of 'rough' in the *OED* is dated 1837; ten years later, the *Illustrated London News* rendered 'rough' as 'an electioneering name for ruffians.' The mid-Victorian gloss was of men who worked at particular unskilled and casual occupations (navvies, bricklayers' labourers, dockers); they were not necessarily criminal, though amateur thieves were thought to be among their number.

97   *The Times*, 26 January 1867, p. 5.

98   M. Arnold, *Culture and Anarchy* (Cambridge, 1950), p. 105.

99   3 *Hansard* 186, 26 March 1867, cols. 636-37 (John Bright). The *OED* cites this reference to the 'residuum', a term 'applied to persons of the lowest class.'

100 See E. P. Hennock, 'Poverty and social theory in England: the experience of the eighteen eighties', *Social History*, vol. 1, 1976, pp. 78-79; G. Crossick, 'From gentlemen to the residuum: languages of social description in Victorian Britain' in P. J. Corfield (ed.), *Language, History and Class* (Oxford, 1991), pp. 161-63.

101 For the contemporaneous attempt to distinguish between the unemployed (in casual jobs and decaying trades) and the semi-criminal 'incompetent class', see Alsager Hill, *Our Unemployed* (London, 1868), pp. 8-10.

economic depression and unemployment, exacerbated by a new crisis in the provision of working-class housing, aroused fears of an insurrectionary alliance between the 'residuum' and the 'respectable working class'. The residential mixing of the criminal and working classes, of which witnesses informed the Royal Commission on the Housing of the Working Classes in 1884, especially endangered the social and moral boundaries drawn in the 1860s.[102] Once again, an outbreak of disorder in central London brought mounting middle-class fears to the surface. The Trafalgar Square riot of 8 February 1886 provoked the journalist, Alexis Krausse, to fear the conjunction of the 'vast criminal population' of London (a section of which 'sacked the West-end a few weeks ago'), the 'unprincipled individuals' who preached revolution and riot, and the large number of 'hungry men … with honest hearts and of respectable antecedents, their stomachs empty, their children sickly, their future a blank'.[103] But these fears were not widely shared. As I have argued elsewhere,[104] the standard interpretation of the riots affirmed the established distinction between the 'real working class', including those who were unemployed, and the 'residuum', what Engels called 'the masses of the Lumpenproletariat whom Hyndman [leader of the Social Democratic Federation] had taken for the unemployed'.[105] The social differentiation inscribed in the 1867 Reform Act held fast, even in the face of the Trafalgar Square riot.

At the end of the 1880s, moreover, the 'residuum' or 'dangerous class' was further reduced in size and menace by the initial volume of that leviathan social survey, orchestrated by Charles Booth, *Life and Labour of the People in London*, and by the London dock strike. Booth's first category of social classification, Class A, was described as '[t]he lowest class, which consists of some occasional labourers, street-sellers, loafers, criminals and semi-criminals'. From this largely hereditary, 'savage semi-criminal class of people', including the inmates of common lodging houses, whose children were the 'street arabs', came

> the battered figures who slouch through the streets, and play the beggar or the bully, or help to foul the record of the unemployed … [these are] the ready materials for disorder when occasion serves.[106]

Booth put their numbers at roughly 11,000 or 1.2 per cent of the East End population. These figures were the foundation of his legendary statement that

> The hordes of barbarians of whom we have heard, who, issuing from their slums, will one day overwhelm modern civilization, do not exist. There are barbarians, but they are a handful, a small and decreasing percentage: a disgrace but not a danger.[107]

---

102 See G. Stedman Jones, *Outcast London* (London, 1971), chap. 11.

103 A. S. Krausse, *Starving London* (London, 1886), pp. 163-4. Cf. H. Solly, 'Our Vagrant and Criminal Classes', *Leisure Hour*, 1887, pp. 761-67.

104 See chap. 2 above.

105 Engels to Bebel, 15 February 1886, *Correspondence of Marx and Engels* (1934), p. 447.

106 Charles Booth, *Life and Labour of the People in London* (London, 1892), pp. 37-8, 174.

107 Ibid., p. 39. Here Booth was pointedly replying to Henry George's *Progress and Poverty* (New York, 1898 ed. 1st. pub. 1879), vol. II, p. 535. Cf. what Sir William Harcourt, the prominent Liberal MP told the House of Commons: 'I do not share the opinion of those who hold that, apart from

This paragraph seized the imagination of reviewers. The *Spectator* extrapolated from Booth's figures an estimate for the entire city: 'most assuredly it does not amount to more than 1 per cent of the total population of London — or only fifty thousand in five millions'.[108] As the reviewer noted, Booth would leave the police to harry the 'residuum' or 'criminal scum' out of existence.

In the summer of 1889, the strike of 100,000 dock workers, by running its course (including a mass demonstration through the West End) without disorder, served to show that the London dockers, and by extension the casual labour force, were not the demoralised, semi-criminals of middle-class imagination. It proved, too, according to one contemporary evaluation of the strike,

> that the hordes of East End ruffians who have been supposed (did they but know their power) to hold the West in the hollow of their hands, were a fantastic myth: for this Great Strike would have been their opportunity.[109]

The few small-scale disturbances that did occur were invariably attributed by the metropolitan police to the 'roughs', not striking dockers.[110] The dock strike had the undoubted effect, therefore, of promoting a large number of casual workers — those in Booth's Class 'B' — to the ranks of the working class proper, and thus of detaching them from 'the gutter proletariat', in Engels' evocative phrase.[111] The problem of the 'residuum', said Hubert Llewellyn Smith, one of Booth's assistants, would become 'essentially one of the treatment of social disease', and could be safely left to the social administrator.[112]

VI

The image of deviance embodied in the language of the 'criminal and dangerous classes' overshadowed the Victorian debate on crime and punishment. Crime was thought to be embedded in the lowest sectors of the social order; it was seen as a product of an alien, almost an outcast, group. Encoded in this language was a set of values which verified the tenets of political economy; criminals were masterless men without gainful employment, attracted by the ease of a life of crime. By denying that crime was an integral feature of working-class life, induced by poverty or unemployment, the discourse exonerated the process of economic production and the inequitable distribution of wealth, incriminating instead

---

the criminal classes, there is a large floating population of what is called 'the dangerous classes.' I do not believe in the existence of the dangerous classes to any very great extent in the Metropolis.' 3 *Hansard* 330, 14 November 1888, col. 1165.

108 *Spectator*, 20 April 1889, pp. 535-6. In fact, the figures for Class A that Booth's survey eventually submitted were: 37,610 or 0.9 per cent of London's population. See G. Himmelfarb, *Poverty and Compassion* (New York, 1991), p. 108.

109 H. Llewellyn Smith & Vaughan Nash, *The Story of the Dockers' Strike Told by Two East Londoners* (London, 1889), p. 6. Cf. H. H. Champion, *The Great Dock Strike in London* (London, 1890), p. 6.

110 Joan Ballhatchet, 'The Police and the London Dock Strike of 1889', *History Workshop*, issue 32, Autumn 1991, p. 57.

111 Quoted in Himmelfarb, *Poverty and Compassion*, p. 53.

112 Llewellyn Smith and Nash, *The Story of the Dockers' Strike*, p. 165.

urban dislocation and moral indiscipline. Instrumental in the elaboration of this discourse were the 'urban gentry', who in government reports, Social Science Association addresses, and the periodical press, defined the boundaries between the 'dangerous' and working classes, whittled down the collective construct of the 'dangerous classes' to that of an encircled 'criminal class', and contributed 'solutions' to the very problem their language framed. Their formulations shaped the content of policing and punishment, and thus law enforcement reinforced the concept of the social 'residuum'.

More significantly, however, the Victorian fabrication of deviance took place as an integral feature of the structural and moral differentiation of the working classes. The early stages of industrialization and mass urbanisation, in conjunction with some serious challenges from political radicals, led middle-class observers to discern the emergence of a 'dangerous class' and, occasionally, even links between the dangerous and labouring classes. Their fears of an insurrectionary alliance were never, in my view, as strong or as widespread as many historians of police and prisons have maintained. But the idea of a marginal group of paupers, prostitutes, beggars and thieves gave point to the task of separating the labouring poor from the dependent paupers, the honest poor from the habitual criminal. The elite perception of the 'dangerous classes' in the first half of the nineteenth century is intelligible only in relation to this larger project of partitioning the working population, the better to forestall the moral contagion of pauperism and criminality.

After 1850, economic stabilisation, the demise of radical possibilities, and the 'disciplines' of moral reform, factory labour, and 'self-help' led middle-class observers to postulate the existence of a 'respectable working class' that was segregated from its economic and moral antithesis, the urban 'residuum', of which an habitual criminal class was the cornerstone. This 'dangerous class' was seen less as a threat to public order and more as evidence of the moral boundary between those who could be granted full citizenship and those deemed unfit for membership of the 'political nation'. The incorporation of the 'respectable working class' reduced the 'residuum' to a politically insignificant stratum, a problem amenable to policing and social administration. This, then, is the broader political and cultural context in which the language of the 'criminal and dangerous classes' must be set. Only by constructing an historically-thick account of the way Victorian society's language of social description assisted the invention of deviance can one appreciate the full significance of social distinctions that have shaped beliefs and behaviour from that day to this. It remains to be seen whether the growth of a semi-permanent, increasingly black 'underclass' in our present inner cities,[113] representing the 'de-incorporation' of sections of the working class and from which the riots of the 1980s drew their force, will undermine the set of social distinctions constructed by the Victorians.

---

113 See R. Dahrendorf, *Law and Order* (London, 1985), pp. 106-8; J. K. Galbraith, *The Culture of Contentment* (New York, 1992), chap. 3.

Prisoners Going to Dinner, Wormwood Scrubs Prison, London, 1901

5

English Prisons, Penal Culture, and the Abatement of Imprisonment, 1895-1922

The prison method is callous, regular and monotonous and produces great mental and physical strain. The deprivation of liberty is extremely cruel and if it is attended with treatment that deadens the spiritual nature and fails to offer any stimulus to the imagination, that coarsens and humiliates, then it stands condemned. (Arthur Creech Jones, conscientious objector, Wandsworth Prison, 1916-19)[1]

I

The nineteenth century was the century of the penitentiary. Public and physical punishments (from whipping to the death penalty) were gradually replaced by the less visible, less corporal sanction of imprisonment. By the start of the Victorian era, imprisonment was the predominant penalty in the system of judicial punishments. For every 1,000 offenders sentenced at higher and summary courts in 1836 for serious (or indictable) offences, 685 were punished by imprisonment in local prisons.[2] By mid-century, moreover, sentences of penal servitude in convict prisons were plugging the gap left by the end of transportation to Australia. The three hundred or so local prisons in the 1830s, to which offenders were sent for anywhere between one day and two years (though typically for terms of less than three months), were locally controlled until 1877 and were less than uniform in regime. The separate system of prison discipline (or cellular isolation) increasingly prevailed over the silent system (or associated, silent labour), but it was subject to considerable local modification. Convict prisons were run

I am grateful to the University of Kansas for a General Research Fund award which made it possible to complete this article. I would also like to thank John Beattie, Joanna Innes, Randall McGowan, Elaine Reynolds, Nancy Scott, and Martin Wiener for their valuable comments on an initial draft of the article, the participants of the Social History Society conference at Putteridge Bury, Bedfordshire, January 1994, who braved snow and ice to give me a critical audience, and the graduate students in my modern British colloquia on whom the arguments were first inflicted.

1 Papers of Arthur Creech Jones, Rhodes House Library, Oxford, MS British Empire S 332, box 1, file 2, fols. 194-7, n.d.; manuscript account of his thoughts in Wandsworth prison; quoted with permission from Violet Creech Jones.

2 In addition, 33 were punished by death, 21 were fined, and 245 were transported; see Leon Radzinowicz and Roger Hood, *The Emergence of Penal Policy*, vol. 5 of *A History of English Criminal Law and Its Administration from 1750* (London, 1986), p. 777. In a move to privatise punishment, public executions were abandoned in 1868; thereafter, hanging took place behind prison walls; sec V. A. C. Gatrell, *The Hanging Tree: Execution and the English People, 1770-1868* (Oxford, 1994), pp. 589-611; R. McGowan, 'Civilizing Punishment: The End of the Public Execution in England', *Journal of British Studies* 33 (July 1994), pp. 257-82.

by central government with less variability. Offenders sentenced to the longer terms of penal servitude spent the first nine months separately confined in a prison like Pentonville, the symbol since its foundation in 1842 of the penitential ideal, and the bulk of the sentence at a 'public works' prison like Dartmoor, working silently in association, until release on license. These differences aside, the regime behind the tall perimeter walls of most Victorian prisons inclined to one of hygienic and routinised order, cellular surveillance, and religious indoctrination.[3]

The first rays of reformist zeal were soon obscured by the clouds of deterrence that rolled in during the 1860s. One commission of inquiry after the next advised government to make the prisons more repressive, more deterrent, more feared. The task of making the prison regime exacting and uniform went to Edmund Du Cane, chairman of the Directors of Convict Prisons and an administrative martinet. From 1869 until his retirement in 1895, Du Cane turned the convict prison system into 'a huge punishing machine', in the words of the Irish Fenian Michael Davitt,[4] and from 1877, when the Prison Act brought local prisons under central government control, he unified and streamlined the local prison structure. Two features distinguished Du Cane's penology: an inflexible adoption of deterrence as the primary aim of punishment, and a rigid adherence to the uniform enforcement by the prison authorities of the court-ordered punishment. Thus, Du Cane put into practice what the 'classical school' of criminal law and penal policy had preached since the eighteenth century. Since individuals had freedom of choice in deciding whether or not to commit crime, they should be deemed to be responsible; hence punishment, to be effective, should deter, and it should be strictly proportionate to the gravity of the crime. On the surface, the results of 'classical' penal policy were impressive. Between 1879 and 1894, the daily average population in convict prisons fell by over half, from 10,880 prisoners to 4,770, and the population of local prisons fell by one-third, from 20,833 prisoners to 13,850. The drop in the prison population was probably less a function of prison discipline, however, than of the fall in recorded crime, a reduction in the minimum duration of penal servitude (from 7 years to 3 years), and an increasing resort by courts to non-custodial penalties. For every 1,000 offenders sentenced at higher and summary courts in 1896 for indictable crimes, 516 were imprisoned, 19 sentenced to penal servitude, 194 fined, 120 bound over in their recognizances, and 34 sent to reformatory and industrial

---

3   See U. Henriques, 'The Rise and Decline of the Separate System of Prison Discipline', *Past and Present*, no. 54 (1972), pp. 61-93; Victor Bailey, ed., *Policing and Punishment in Nineteenth Century Britain* (London, 1981), pp. 11-24; Michael Ignatieff, 'State, Civil Society, and Total Institutions: A Critique of Recent Social Histories of Punishment', in *Crime and Justice: An Annual Review of Research*, ed. M. Tonry and N. Morris, vol. 3 (Chicago, 1981), pp. 153-92; S. McConville, *A History of English Prison Administration, 1750-1877* (London, 1981), chaps. 6-8, 11-13; M. DeLacy, *Prison Reform in Lancashire, 1700-1850* (Stanford, Calif., 1986); J. A. Sharpe, *Judicial Punishment in England* (London, 1990), pp. 61-87; Clive Emsley, 'The History of Crime and Crime Control Institutions, c. 1770-c. 1945', in *The Oxford Handbook of Criminology*, ed. M. Maguire, R. Morgan, and R. Reiner (Oxford, 1994), chap. 4. Pentonville was initially used for convicts aged 18 to 35, who were sentenced to transportation for their first offence. They spent 18 (later reduced to 9) months in separate confinement before going to the penal colony. The period of separate confinement was applied to all penal servitude sentences after 1857.

4   Quoted in Radzinowicz and Hood, p. 545.

schools.[5] As the century of the prison drew to a close, the confidence in deterrent imprisonment was decidedly on the wane.

In 1895, two events brought the secret world of the Du Cane regime to public attention. The Departmental Committee on Prisons, under the chairmanship of Herbert Gladstone, issued its report, and Oscar Wilde, found guilty of homosexual acts, began a sentence of two years' imprisonment with hard labour.[6] In both cases, the medium that brought prison conditions to public attention was the press.[7] The Liberal newspaper the *Daily Chronicle* had taken the lead in January 1894 with a set of articles entitled 'Our Dark Places'.[8] It has long been presumed that the author of these articles was the assistant chaplain of Wandsworth prison, W. D. Morrison, but it now seems certain that the assistant editor, H. W. Massingham, wrote them, having toured a number of Her Majesty's prisons in the previous autumn.[9] Likewise, news of Oscar Wilde's prison treatment appeared in the columns of the *Daily Chronicle*, as did Wilde's two letters on prison reform written on release from Reading Gaol.[10] Massingham followed Wilde's case closely and urged W. T. Stead, editor of the *Pall Mall Gazette*, to do the same. 'Don't forget the horror of the [prison] system', wrote Massingham, 'which continually presses on my imagination since I went the round of the prisons. The whole thing is torture & nothing but torture. Oscar Wilde is being slowly starved to death, & is now little better than an hysterical imbecile.'[11]

The main burden of the indictment against the Du Cane regime was that a highly centralized system of prison administration gave attention to 'organization, finance, order, health of the prisoners, and prison statistics' but treated prisoners 'as a hopeless or worthless element of the community.'[12] A prison regime characterized by inflexible discipline, rigid uniformity, and separate confinement was not even

---

5   See ibid., chap. 16, and p. 777; Sharpe, pp. 66-7, 85; V. A. C. Gatrell, 'The Decline of Theft and Violence in Victorian and Edwardian England', in *Crime and the Law*, ed. V. A. C. Gatrell, B. Lehman, and G. Parker (London, 1980), chap. 9. Du Cane's rigorous administration of the local prison system is exhaustively detailed in Sean McConville, *English Local Prisons, 1860-1900: Next Only to Death* (London, 1995), chaps. 4-10. For the 'classical school', see Ian Taylor *et al.*, *The New Criminology* (London, 1973; 4th impression, London, 1977), pp. 2-5.

6   Herbert Gladstone was first commissioner of works in the Liberal government and previously parliamentary under-secretary at the Home Office.

7   Report from the Departmental Committee on Prisons, C. 7702, *PP*, 1895, vol. 56, p. 5. For a full account of the vigorous public campaign for a prison inquiry, see McConville, *English Local Prisons*, Chap. 13. The Irish nationalists in Parliament, many of whom had been imprisoned for political offences, were also critical of prison administration. Their influence was strong enough to get one of their number, Arthur O'Connor, onto the Departmental Committee. See Michael Davitt, *The Prison Life of Michael Davitt, Related by Himself* (Dublin, 1882), pp. 10-18, and 'Criminal and Prison Reform', *Nineteenth Century* 36 (December 1894): 875-89; *Hansard*, 3d ser., vol. 39 (August 22, 1887), col. 1485 (Arthur O'Connor).

8   See John Stokes, *In the Nineties* (Chicago, 1989), pp. 96-9; A. F. Havighurst, *Radical Journalist: H. W. Massingham* (1860-1924) (Cambridge, 1974), p. 65.

9   See McConville, *English Local Prisons*, pp. 554-77; Stokes, p. 96; Radzinowicz and Hood, p. 574. See also W. D. Morrison, 'Are Our Prisons a Failure?', *Fortnightly Review* 55 (April 1894), pp. 459-69. For Morrison's evidence to the Gladstone Committee, see *Minutes of Evidence to the Departmental Committee on Prisons*, C. 77024, *PP*, 1895, vol. 56, pp. 158-84.

10   Letters, *Daily Chronicle* (May 27, 1897; March 24, 1898), reprinted in Oscar Wilde, *The Soul of Man and Prison Writings* (Oxford, 1990), pp. 159-67, 190-6. Wilde completed his sentence on May 19, 1897.

11   Quoted in Havighurst, p. 67. See Richard Ellmann, *Oscar Wilde* (New York, 1988), pp. 479-532.

12   Report from the Departmental Committee on Prisons, C. 7702, *PP*, 1895, vol. 56, p. 11, par. 23.

acting as an effective deterrent: prisons held, nay manufactured, increasing numbers of recidivists. The present principles of prison discipline, the Reverend Morrison charged, were so 'debilitating', as evinced by the amount of insanity and suicide in local prisons, that they turned the casual offender into 'a gaol-made criminal, the most dangerous class of all, and the most incorrigible.'[13] In response to the growing dissatisfaction with the prison regime, the Gladstone Committee expressed the cautious hope that deterrence and reform could be pursued at one and the same time as the 'primary and concurrent objects' of prison treatment within a prison structure in which unproductive hard labour would be eliminated, the time spent in separate confinement reduced, and educational and trade-training services developed. More radical proposals followed for young offenders and recidivists, characterized by longer detention and special institutions.[14]

Meanwhile, between June 1895 and May 1897, Oscar Wilde served his sentence of two years' hard labour, a term that the Gladstone Committee judged to be more than a man could endure and that the 1898 Prison Act would ultimately abolish. Each day during the first month, prisoners climbed the equivalent of 6,000 feet on the treadmill, a purely penal form of labour. Wilde was declared unfit for first-class labour by the medical officer and so was excused from the treadmill. Each night, however, he slept on a bare plank bed. After the first month, Wilde worked in silence stitching mailbags or picking oakum (tearing old rope to pieces for the loose fibre used in caulking). In silence, too, he attended chapel each morning (twice on Sunday) and took daily exercise in single file for an hour in the open air. After the first three months, he could write four letters a year, all vetted and censored before they were dispatched, and see friends four times a year for no more than twenty minutes each time.[15] An attack of dysentery put Wilde into the prison infirmary for two months and led to some improvement in his dietary lot. Additional relief came in the shape of the Liberal lawyer, R. B. Haldane, who, as a member of the Gladstone Committee, had the authority to enter any prison and make the governor produce any prisoner. He visited Wilde in Pentonville and agreed to get him books of his choice. He also visited the prisoner in Wandsworth and subsequently persuaded the home secretary to transfer Wilde to Reading, where he was assigned to light work in the garden and in book distribution. For his troubles, Haldane later received a copy of Wilde's celebrated work, *The Ballad of Reading Gaol* (1898), written on his release from prison.[16]

The rise of the prison as the main, not to say symbolic, form of punishment in the nineteenth century has concentrated the minds of a number of historians in the past twenty-five years. One

---

13   Morrison, 'Are Our Prisons a Failure?', p. 468. See Christopher Harding, "The Inevitable End of a Discredited System'? The Origins of the Gladstone Committee Report on Prisons, 1895', *Historical Journal* 31 (1988): pp. 598-600; McConville, *English Local Prisons*, pp. 559-61, 581-3.

14   See W. R. Cornish and J. Hart, *Crime and Law in Nineteenth Century Britain* (Dublin, 1978), pp. 38-9; Radzinowicz and Hood (n. 2 above), pp. 576-9; McConville, *English Local Prisons*, chap. 15.

15   See Ellmann, p. 480; Wilde's letter to the *Daily Chronicle* (March 24, 1898), in Wilde, *The Soul of Man*, pp. 193-4.

16   R. B. Haldane, *An Autobiography* (London, 1929), pp. 166-7; Ellmann, p. 495; Wilde, *The Ballad of Reading Gaol*, lines 559-70, in Wilde, *The Soul of Man*, pp. 186-7; McConville, *English Local Prisons* (n. 5 above), pp. 593-9.

question, above all, has guided their work: why, between 1780 and 1840, was the penitentiary conceived and constructed? And one explanation has taken centre stage: the origins of this revolution in punishment are to be found less in the humanitarian sensibility of prison reformers, whether evangelical or utilitarian (which an older historiography underlined), and more in the desire of elite groups to isolate the criminal class, to shape a disciplined workforce, and to cope with the social dislocations of a new industrial order. Humanitarian sensibility is traced back to its supposed source in economic interest or the will to power.[17] Twelve years ago, however, David Garland's *Punishment and Welfare* (1985) offered a new approach to the origins of the modern English penal system.[18] In particular, Garland converted the blueprint offered by the Gladstone Report (1895) into the starting point of the 'modern penal complex' and, in so doing, shifted the timing of the transition to 'modern penality' from the birth of the penitentiary to the Edwardian period. Between 1895 and 1914, according to Garland, the conceptual domain defined by the 'classical' jurisprudential principles of individual moral responsibility, deterrence, and just proportion between crime and punishment, and the Victorian penal structure that rested on these principles, were replaced by a new 'positivist' criminology and by the 'modern penal complex.'[19]

The main tenets of 'positivist' criminology were, first, that criminal behaviour was determined by factors and processes that could be discovered by observation, measurement, and inductive reasoning, the methods used by the natural and social sciences. Second, since people were impelled to commit crime by constitutional and environmental forces beyond their control and, thus, were not responsible for their actions, treatment, not punishment, was the most appropriate legal response. Third, the delinquent was fundamentally different from normal, law-abiding citizens. In the twenty years following Cesare Lombroso's *L'Uomo delinquente* (1876), the founding text of positivist criminology, numerous congresses, associations, and journals promoted a positivist diagnosis of criminal behaviour and linked it to a new model of criminal justice. Proportionate punishment was rejected in favour of a system of sanctions adapted to the reformability or 'dangerousness' of the individual offender. An exclusively deterrent system of criminal justice was rejected in favour of one that would prevent, treat, and eliminate delinquency.[20] The proponents of this scientific criminology, along with advocates of the eugenic program (who claimed that criminality, like feeble-mindedness and alcoholism, was a heritable 'degenerate' characteristic), and prison administrators all took part, according to Garland, in the

17   See Michel Foucault, *Discipline and Punish: The Birth of the Prison* (1975; reprint, London, 1977); M. Ignatieff, *A Just Measure of Pain: The Penitentiary in the Industrial Revolution, 1750-1850* (New York, 1978). See also chap. 4 above.

18   David Garland, *Punishment and Welfare: A History of Penal Strategies* (Aldershot, 1985).

19   Ibid., chap. 1. See also David Garland, 'The Criminal and His Science: A Critical Account of the Formation of Criminology at the End of the Nineteenth Century', *British Journal of Criminology* 25 (April 1985), pp. 109-37.

20   Cesare Lombroso, *L'Uomo delinquente* (Milan, 1876). See L. Radzinowicz, *Ideology and Crime* (New York, 1966), pp. 50-6; David Matza, *Delinquency and Drift* (1964), chap. 1; Taylor *et al.* (n. 5 above), pp. 10-23; D. Garland, 'Of Crimes and Criminals: The Development of Criminology in Britain', in Maguire *et al.*, eds. (n. 3 above), pp. 37-42.

complex administrative and legislative process that lay the foundations of modem penality. The notable milestones on this twenty-year legislative road were the Prison Act (1898), the Inebriates Act (1898), the Prevention of Crime Act (1908), and the Mental Deficiency Act (1913). Under these enactments, special institutions were established for the extended training or segregation of 'habitual drunkards', 'habitual criminals', and the 'mentally defective'. The new penal forms, finally, were part of a much wider social and political transformation, according to Garland. The new penality was tightly linked to the social principles and strategies that would become known as the Welfare State.[21]

Punishment and Welfare owes an obvious, if largely unacknowledged, intellectual debt to Michel Foncault's *Discipline and Punish* (1975). Garland and Foucault examined different fault lines, but they adopted the same method of sinking a shaft into the culture of a particular period and excavating its *episteme* or the deep structure of knowledge at work in that society. Moreover, Garland translated Foucault's conception of change by radical shifts from one discursive formation or *episteme* to another, into a recognizable historical and political reality. And last, Garland shared Foucault's view that the reforms we tend to describe as rational, progressive, and humanitarian in fact constituted a new strategy for the more effective exercise of social control: 'Not to punish less, but to punish better … to insert the power to punish more deeply into the social body.'[22]

More recently, Martin Wiener's *Reconstructing the Criminal* (1990), while critical of Garland's exclusively political interpretation of criminal policy, and while concerned to show the role of culture, values, and sensibilities in the shaping of penal history, presented an account of the transformation of criminal justice from the penal crisis of the 1890s to the outbreak of war in 1914 that differed little in essentials from that of Garland. In the last quarter of the nineteenth century, according to Wiener, society lost confidence in the inherent responsibility of individuals. Crime was increasingly ascribed, not to wilful utilitarian calculation, but to inherited mental or physical deficiency. Accordingly, reformers no longer sought to 'remoralize' the criminal — to develop the moral character necessary for leading a law-abiding life — but to 'demoralize' the criminal — to uncover the physiological and environmental (or 'natural') roots of criminal behaviour. Wiener, like Garland, contended that the new image of criminal man owed a good deal to the force of the human sciences and, notably, positivist criminology. And the network of penal measures grounded on this new image of man represented, for Wiener, too, a major structural change in the penal complex.[23]

---

21 Garland, *Punishment and Welfare*, chaps. 3-5, and *Punishment and Modern Society: A Study in Social Theory* (Chicago, 1990), pp. 206-9. And see Harding, p. 608. In recent years, Garland has enriched his approach to the history of 'penality' by incorporating discussion of the links between penal institutions and cultural phenomena; see *Punishment and Modern Society*, chaps. 9-11. Nonetheless, he stands by his original conception of a new Edwardian 'penal-welfare complex', characterized by 'its distinctively positive approach to the reform of deviants, its extensive use of interventionist agencies, its deployment of social work and psychiatric expertise, its concern to regulate, manage, and normalize rather than immediately to punish, and of course its new 'welfarist' self-representation'. (ibid., p. 128).

22 Foucault, p. 82.

23 Martin J. Wiener, *Reconstructing the Criminal: Culture, Law, and Policy in England, 1830-1914* (Cambridge, 1990), chap. 6.

The shift in 'mental frame' and the enactment of positive penology owed not a little, argued Wiener, to changes in Home Office personnel and to the reforming Liberal governments of 1906-14. The first generation of career civil servants, 'less moralistic or legalistic than their predecessors ... more attracted to the idea of scientific administration', assumed positions of influence in the Home Office and Prison Commission in the 1890s.[24] A case in point was Evelyn Ruggles-Brise, who entered the Home Office in 1881 and replaced Du Cane as chairman of the Prison Commission in 1895. Likewise, a new generation of politicians took the tiller. Herbert Gladstone, who chaired the Gladstone Committee, became home secretary in the 1906 government and enacted the committee's two proposals concerning habitual criminals and young adult offenders. His successor, Winston Churchill, was more visionary still, instructing his officials to draft plans for a scientific penal system. By 1914, then, as Wiener concluded, 'the rationales of deterrence and disciplinary moralization were yielding to those of welfarist administration. After the First World War, the seeds planted in the late Victorian and Edwardian years came to fruition, and the criminal justice system was thoroughly reorganized according to the new vision of criminality and its solution.'[25]

I wish to offer a different interpretation of the years 1895-1914, and, by extension, to 1922, one that seeks, first, to argue for a more limited alteration in the structure of criminal justice, second, to reconstruct the penal culture of this period in its full complexity, and third, to highlight what I take to be the truly significant change in penal practice in the quarter century following the Gladstone Report, the massive abatement of imprisonment.[26] These years are simply not intelligible in terms solely of an emerging positivism or medicalism. David Garland and Martin Wiener, in my view, placed far too much emphasis on positivist criminology and the associated alterations in the practice of criminal justice. The intellectual roots of what happened, and what failed to happen, in the realm of penality need to be sought elsewhere: in a radical humanitarianism, in the writings of the Philosophical Idealists, and in ethical socialism.[27] The most critical change in these years — the recognition of the worthlessness of short-term imprisonment, and the related 'decentring' of the prison in the system of judicial punishments — needs greater emphasis and evaluation than it has received. I begin this reassessment of the changes and continuities in the penal policy and practice of late Victorian and Edwardian England by arguing that alterations in the structure of the penal complex have been

---

24 Ibid., p. 339.

25 Ibid., p. 379. McConville, *English Local Prisons*, chap. 12, also emphasizes the contribution of a new generation of Home Office clerks, including Ruggles-Brise, to penal change. McConville makes no attempt, however, to engage with the important discussion of the influence of positivist criminology on English penal policy and administration. Lombroso is mentioned only in relation to Du Cane's penal thought (p. 182); positivism is referred to but once, with regard to W. D. Morrison (p. 562, n. 59); Garland receives three inconsequential footnotes, Wiener none. Indeed, Wiener's *Reconstructing the Criminal* does not even figure in McConville's bibliography.

26 In this I have built on the suggestive remarks to be found in Radzinowicz and Hood (n. 2 above), chaps. 1, 17; and W. J. Forsythe, *Penal Discipline, Reformatory Projects and the English Prison Commission, 1895-1939* (Exeter, 1990), chap. 1.

27 See Jose Harris's convincing reassessment of the role of Idealist thought in the development of the welfare state: 'Political Thought and the Welfare State, 1870-1940: An Intellectual Framework for British Social Policy', *Past and Present*, no. 135 (May 1992), pp. 117-39.

exaggerated in recent scholarship.

II

The first legislative response to the Gladstone Committee's report — a report that simply proposed ameliorating the cruelty and inhumanity of prison discipline, and the grafting of a limited number of treatment and training initiatives to the existing body of punishment and moral improvement — was the Prison Act, 1898. The primary object of the measure, according to the home secretary, Matthew White Ridley, was 'the creation of powers for applying differential treatment or classification ... to our prison population.'[28] The act established three separate divisions for those sentenced to imprisonment without hard labour. Prisoners placed in the first division, for example, were excused the first month of separate confinement. Yet significantly — and in fairness, the point is not lost on David Garland — a classification that was meant to determine the conditions under which an offender would serve his sentence was left, *pace* the positivist program, to the sentencing court, not the prison executive. The criteria to be followed by the courts, moreover, included both individualization — the offender's 'character' and 'antecedents' — and neoclassical concerns — the 'nature of the offense' and 'special provocation'. Undaunted, Garland described the act's classifications as a 'discursive bridgehead to later and more fundamental changes.'[29] In fact, the experiment was a failure since the courts seldom used any but the third and most severe classification. In 1912-13, thirty-seven males and one female were placed in the first division, mainly for offences against the Elementary Education Acts; 869 males and 246 females got the second division, or roughly 1 percent of persons admitted into local prisons.'[30]

The 1898 act also conferred on the home secretary the power to make rules for prison administration without seeking fresh legislation, abolished all forms of penal labour (including the treadmill and hand-crank), and allowed local prisoners to earn remission of up to one-sixth of their sentence.[31] Of all the minor improvements made prior to the war, however, the most important concerned the term of solitary or separate confinement endured by every convict prisoner for the first few months of a penal servitude sentence and by every local prisoner sentenced to hard labour for the

---

28 *Hansard*, 4th ser., vol. 55 (March 24, 1898), col. 837. See Garland, *Punishment and Welfare* (n. 18 above), pp. 216-17. The most complete account of the 1898 Prisons Bill, and of the unsuccessful press and parliamentary campaign to deepen its reforming effect on the prison system, is in McConville, *English Local Prisons* (n. 5 above), chap. 17. The Second Reading of the Bill prompted Oscar Wilde to write to the *Daily Chronicle* (March 24, 1898), to catalogue what he termed the 'three permanent punishments authorised by law in English prisons': hunger, insomnia, and disease. See Wilde, *The Soul of Man* (n. 10 above), pp. 190-6. See also McConville, *English Local Prisons*, pp. 708-10, 755-6.

29 Garland, *Punishment and Welfare*, p. 217. See W. D. Morrison, 'Prison Reform: I. Prisons and Prisoners', *Fortnightly Review* 63 (May 1898), pp. 781-9.

30 See *Report of the Indian Jails Committee, 1919-20*, Cmd. 1303, *PP*, 1921, vol. 10, pp. 447-50.

31 See the Advisory Council on the Penal System, *Sentences of Imprisonment: A Review of Maximum Penalties* (London, 1978), p. 64.

first month.[32] The playwright John Galsworthy first concentrated the official mind in an 'Open Letter to the Home Secretary' in the *Nation* in May 1909, in which he charged that solitary confinement was detrimental to mental, moral, and physical health to no deterrent purpose.[33] Ruggles-Brise countered by arguing that solitary confinement was not retained on grounds of deterrence but 'in order to give the necessary penal character to a sentence of penal servitude in the same way as a month's separate confinement is maintained in local prisons as the penal element of the sentence of hard labour.'[34] He was willing, however, to limit the duration of strict cellular isolation to three months for all classes serving a sentence of penal servitude. Gladstone, now home secretary, agreed; hence, Galsworthy was told that a uniform term of three months' separate confinement for all convicts would come into force on April 1, 1910. For Galsworthy, it was 'a big step in the right direction', but not the end of the campaign.[35] Winston Churchill's appointment as home secretary brought fresh hope.

As Churchill took up the reins of office, Galsworthy urged him 'to strike the finishing blow at a custom which continues to darken our humanity and good sense.' Churchill asked the prison commissioners for the main arguments against the total abolition of the system of separate confinement.[36] But Galsworthy left nothing to chance. He highlighted the detrimental effects of such confinement in his new play *Justice*, first produced in February 1910. The play's high point is a three-minute prison scene in which a young clerk, imprisoned for forgery, beats helplessly on his cell door, racked by the mental torture of solitary confinement. The scene, in which no word is spoken, profoundly affected the audience. Both Churchill and Ruggles-Brise went to see the play, the latter concluding that it was unfair because 'it makes an abnormal case typical of the system.'[37] Churchill, however, insisted on a reduction in the term of separate confinement, and a compromise was reached with the Prison Commission whereby separate confinement would be limited to one month for all convicts, except for 'old lags', who would continue to serve three months. If unsuccessful in his quest for abolition, Galsworthy took comfort from the reckoning that his writings had helped 'to knock off 1000 months of Solitary Confinement per year.'[38]

This change aside (which brought no improvement for the large body of *local* prisoners), the

---

32 More strictly, the period of separate confinement undergone by convicts was three months for the 'Star' class, six months for 'Intermediates', and nine months for recidivists and revokees.

33 *Nation* (May 1, 8, 1909). The *Nation* was the main mouthpiece of the New Liberalism.

34 P. Com. 7/308; E. Ruggles-Brise memo, June 10, 1909, P.Com. 7/309.

35 P. Com. 7/309; H. V. Marrot, T*he Life and Letters of John Galsworthy* (London, 1935), pp. 250, 677; E. Garnett, ed., *Letters from John Galsworthy, 1900-1932* (London, 1934), p. 174.

36 Marrot, pp. 676-8.

37 J. Galsworthy, *Justice* (New York, 1910), pp. 81-4; E. Ruggles-Brise to W. Churchill, March 21, 1910, P. Com. 7/309. C. F. G. Masterman, parliamentary under-secretary at the Home Office, told Galsworthy at a *Nation* lunch in April that 'he had turned the Home Office upside down with *Justice*'; quoted in Havighurst (n. 8 above), p. 163. Galsworthy kept up the pressure with a Penal Reform League leaflet, *The Spirit of Punishment* (London. 1910).

38 Marrot, p. 266; *The Times* (July 23, 1910), p. 4, letter from Galsworthy; P. Com. 7/310. See Paul Addison, *Churchill on the Home Front, 1900-1955* (London, 1992), p. 113

Victorian prison system remained essentially inviolate. Nothing better illustrates how the new rules introduced under the 1898 Prison Act were simply a development, on less repressive lines, of the older system of prison discipline, than the fact that twenty years on from the act, prison administration came under a barrage of criticism quite as heavy as that which had provoked the appointment of the Gladstone Committee. And it emerged that little had truly changed.

Ruggles-Brise's regime came under the critical scrutiny of the 'absolutist' conscientious objectors, 'unaccustomed travellers into this valley of shadow', as Margery Fry, Quaker secretary of the Howard League for Penal Reform, so appositely termed them.[39] Over 16,000 men were conscientious objectors during the First World War, but only the 1,350 who took up an 'absolutist' position and refused alternative work were subject to the treadmill of arrest, court martial, prison, release, and arrest. The practice quickly developed of commuting the original sentence of two years' imprisonment with hard labour to 112 days, which, with 'good conduct', meant just over three months in prison. Repeated sentences — and some conscientious objectors served three, four, and even five such sentences — meant that many conscientious objectors served more than two years' hard labour, the maximum sentence that could normally be imposed.[40] It also meant that conscientious objectors underwent the first month's separate confinement at regular intervals; a first month of spare diet, bare wooden plank for a bed, work done in cellular isolation, and no contact with the world outside.[41] There was little advance here on Oscar Wilde's treatment! The 'first month' regulation, in fact, was abandoned for second and subsequent terms as the war dragged on, and from January 1918 some conscientious objectors were permitted to talk during exercise.[42]

Not surprisingly, perhaps, conscientious objectors were horrified by the inhumanity of the prison regime, and especially by the dehumanizing effects of the silence rule. No conversation was allowed either with other prisoners or with prison warders, except to answer a warder's question or to make an official request. For rebelling against the silence rule, Fenner Brockway, the young socialist who, with Clifford Allen, had formed the No-Conscription Fellowship (which orchestrated the movement of resistance to conscription and acted as the guardian of the conscientious objectors), received eight months' solitary confinement and three months' bread and water.[43] If some conscientious objectors complained of the semi-starvation diet, some the intense cold, and some the monotony of sewing post

---

39 S. Margery Fry, 'The State in Its Relation to Law-Breakers', *Friends Fellowship Papers* (May 1920), p. 67. She also mentioned the prison experiences of the militant suffragists.

40 Philip Viscount Snowden, *An Autobiography* (London, 1934), I, p. 410; T. C. Kennedy, 'Public Opinion and the Conscientious Objector, 1915-1919', *Journal of British Studies* 12 (May 1973), p. 113.

41 See David Boulton, *Objection Overruled* (London, 1967), p. 220

42 See J. W. Graham, *Conscription and Conscience: A History, 1916-1919* (London, 1922), pp. 298-9.

43 See Boulton, p. 223; Hubert W. Peet, 'Some Fruits of Silence', *Friends Quarterly Examiner* (April 1920), pp. 127-60. Most of the leadership and the rank and file of the No-Conscription Fellowship were from the ILP and the Quaker Society of Friends; see Kennedy, 'Public Opinion and the Conscientious Objector, 1915-1919', p. 107.

office mailbags, all conscientious objectors bore witness to the silence rule as the most arduous of all prison regulations.[44] Let Arthur Creech Jones, a junior civil servant, socialist, and conscientious objector stand proxy for them all. At some date between 1916 and 1919, Creech Jones smuggled out his uncensored thoughts in prison. 'The whole system', he declared, 'is based on fear.' You want to live a normal healthy life while in prison, he continued:

> But instead you meet your friends and you dare not speak. You dare not show any comradeship or even geniality. Often to speak pleasantly to an officer is to earn his rebuke. You must live in complete isolation, your self all hedged round as if you were a thing without a personality or soul. You must ever be stoical, never laugh, hum, whistle, sing or speak in case you are punished by bread & water diet and solitary confinement in a bare cell without work or reading material. The general result is that you are made cunning and crafty & adopt all manner of subterfuge to escape the vigilance of the warders. You go to church and have to sit under eyes that watch you as if they were hawks, you march 3 yards apart at exercise under the eyes of 3 or 4 officers, you work after your first month of solitary confinement under the stern face of an officer who stands on a raised platform, you sit in your cell and never sew but some eyes are not watching you through the spy hole in the door. ... It is this feeling of isolation at the worst and most miserable moments that ever come to men, this feeling of eternal surveillance, this deprival of initiative and stripping of men of their personality, this submission to ignorance and abuse which make men bitter and anti-social.[45]

By war's end, many of the conscientious objectors were broken in health.[46] But many also were eager to publicize further the state of English prisons and to effect some reform.

Margaret Hobhouse was the first to use letters written from prison. In *I Appeal unto Caesar* (1917), most of which was ghost written by Bertrand Russell, acting on behalf of the No-Conscription Fellowship, Hobhouse pleaded the case of the absolutists, one of whom, Stephen, was her son.[47] Of greater importance was the Prison System Enquiry Committee established in January 1919, by the executive of the Labour (formerly Fabian) Research Department. Instrumental in the appointment of this Committee was Mrs. Hobhouse's younger sister, Beatrice Webb; the final report, published as

---

44 See R. C. Wallhead, 'In Jail', *Socialist Review* 15 (April-June 1918), p. 175; Martin Gilbert, *Plough My Own Furrow: The Story of Lord Allen of Hurtwood as Told through His Writings and Correspondence* (London, 1965), pp. 62, 66-3; E. Williamson Mason, *Made Free in Prison* (London, 1918), pp. 134-5, 191-2, T. Corder Catchpool, *On Two Fronts* (London, 1918), p. 171; S. Hobhouse, *An English Prison from Within* (London, 1919), pp. 29, 33; A. Fenner Brockway, 'Prisons as Crime Factories' (ILP pamphlet, London, 1919), pp. 4-8. If the silence rule were truly enforced, said Brockway, 90 percent of prisoners would lose their reason within a few months. See the comments made by the Poplar councillors imprisoned in September 1921 in N. Branson, *Poplarism, 1919-1925: George Lansbury and the Councillors' Revolt* (London, 1979), pp. 67-8.

45 Papers of Arthur Creech Jones, Rhodes House Library, Oxford, MS British Empire S 332, box 1, file 2, fols. 194-7, n.d.: account of his thoughts in Wandsworth prison, quoted with permission from Violet Creech Jones. Creech Jones also noted: 'We were always in touch with the ordinary prisoners. Many of them were incorrigible, infirm, maimed; some almost utterly depraved.'

46 Nine conscientious objectors died in prison; approximately sixty others died later from the after-effects of prison treatment. See John Rae, *Conscience and Politics: The British Government and the Conscientious Objector to Military Service, 1916-1919* (London, 1970). p. 226.

47 Mrs. Henry Hobhouse, *I Appeal unto Caesar* (London, 1917), pp. 44-70; Jo Vellacott, *Bertrand Russell and the Pacifists in the First World War* (Brighton, 1980), pp. 210-12.

English Prisons To-Day, was edited by two absolutists, Stephen Hobhouse and Fenner Brockway.[48] With Arthur Creech Jones's assistance, Hobhouse collected information from official documents (including a pirated copy of prison standing rules), from questionnaires completed by some fifty prison officials (until the Prison Commission nipped that in the bud), from agents of Discharged Prisoners' Aid Societies, and above all from 290 ex-prisoners, mainly ex-conscientious objectors.[49]

Witnesses who went to prison as a form of political demonstration, and who were more sensitive in mind and body than the average felon, were not, the Home Office complained, the best judges of the prison system.[50] Hobhouse defended the first-hand testimony, however, on the grounds that conscientious objectors could readily communicate their prison experiences and 'that the mental effects observed in the course of imprisonment can be more easily isolated from the consequences of previous habits of crime, congenital abnormalities, and such concomitants of imprisonment as social ostracism.' As the finishing touches were being applied to the report, an official appraisal appeared in the form of Ruggles-Brise's *English Prison System* (1921).[51] The contrast was telling: one displayed a defensive parental pride in the achievements of the past twenty-five years, while the other presented an unassailable case for the prosecution.

English Prisons To-Day was an exhaustive report of 728 pages (or a quarter of a million words), describing and evaluating the various forms of imprisonment, the different kinds of prisoner, prison food and work, and medical and sanitary treatment. At times, indeed, the excess of detail detracts from the report's effectiveness. The report is certainly longer on exposure of prison conditions than on proposals for a thoroughgoing alternative. The latter were precluded, however, by divisions in the Prison System Enquiry Committee.[52] Once again, the silence rule, the first rule on the card that hung in every prisoner's cell, was named as the most pernicious feature of prison life.[53] But the silence rule was, the authors insisted, 'only characteristic of the whole system. Self-respect is systematically destroyed and self-expression prevented in every phase of prison existence.'[54] The effects of imprisonment, they claimed, 'are of the nature of a progressive weakening of the mental powers and of a deterioration of the character in a way which renders the prisoner less fit for useful social life, more predisposed to crime, and in consequence more liable to reconviction'.[55] The distinctive feature of prison life 'is the

---

48 See A. F. Brockway, *Inside the Left* (London, 1942), pp. 126-8, and *Towards Tomorrow: The Autobiography of Fenner Brockway* (London, 1977), p. 61. See also S. Hobhouse and A. F. Brockway, *English Prisons To-Day: Being the Report of the Prison System Enquiry Committee* (London, 1922). For details of the membership of the Prison System Enquiry Committee, and for more on Hobhouse and Brockway, see pp. 138-9 below.

49 See Stephen Hobhouse, *Forty Years and an Epilogue. An Autobiography* (London, 1951), p. 176; Gordon Rose, *The Struggle for Penal Reform* (London, 1961), pp. 108- 9, HO 45/11543/357055/33.

50 HO 45/11543/357055/33.

51 Hobhouse and Brockway, p. 482; E. Ruggles-Brise, *English Prison System* (London, 1921).

52 Brockway, *Inside the Left*, p. 129; personal interview with Fenner Brockway, June 1980.

53 Hobhouse and Brockway, pp. 561-62.

54 Ibid., p. 356.

55 Ibid., p. 561. Another continuing feature of prison administration was its dreary uniformity, encapsulated by Ruggles-Brise's 1911 comment,

sense of being in the grip of a huge machine which is felt to be repressive at every point, inhuman, aimless, tyrannical.' In all, *English Prisons To-Day* proclaimed that the guiding principles and effect of the Ruggles-Brise regime were barely distinguishable from those of its predecessor, the Du Cane regime. There could be no greater indictment of a quarter century during which the Gladstone Report had been implemented.[56]

English Prisons To-Day, according to Margery Fry of the Howard League, became 'the Bible of penal reformers.'[57] It inspired a number of parliamentary questions concerning insanity among prisoners and the suicide rate in prisons.[58] More important, Sir Maurice Waller, the new chairman of the Prison Commission (as of August 1921), studied the volume and then, claimed Stephen Hobhouse, consulted both Sir William Clarke Hall (progressive London magistrate and Hobhouse's brother-in-law) and Margery Fry. Moreover, a member of the Prison System Enquiry Committee, Alec Paterson, who had helped draft the section on Borstal training, was appointed to the Prison Commission and was 'the guiding and most beneficent spirit of that powerful body, revolutionising a large part of prison treatment by substituting educational methods for the rigid and stupid punitive regime.'[59] This all perhaps exaggerates the direct influence of *English Prisons To-Day* since the new prison commissioners were already committed to a less repressive regime, and some of their immediate changes anticipated the recommendations of the Prison System Enquiry Committee.

To the end of a more humane treatment of prisoners, Waller persuaded the home secretary in late 1921 to abolish the close cropping of convicts' hair and to allow prisoners to see visitors without intervening wire or bars.[60] But the volume doubtless strengthened Waller's arm when it came to ending the rigours of the silence rule and separate confinement. A month after the book's publication, all prison governors were instructed to allow conversation between prisoners at labour and between warders and prisoners.[61] A few months later, convinced that solitude led to morbid introspection, revengeful feelings, and suicidal tendencies, the Prison Commission got Home Office approval to suspend, for an experimental period of six months, the stage of separate confinement at the start of every convict's sentence. These arrangements were ultimately made permanent.[62] And, finally, a statement of aims in the annual reports for 1924 and 1925 illustrated the new approach of the prison commissioners. Their

---

quoted in Hobhouse and Brockway, p. 97: 'It is now 4-30 in the afternoon and I know that just now, at every Local and Convict Prison in England, the same things in general are being done, and that in general they are being done in the same way.'

56 It should be added, however, that there had doubtless been a change in expectations since the Gladstone Report, sufficient to sharpen the postwar critique.

57 Enid Huws Jones, *Margery Fry: The Essential Amateur* (London, 1966), p. 113.

58 For example, *Hansard*, 5th ser., vol. 156 (July 11, 1922), col. 1040. See also HO 45/11543/357055/54 and 55.

59 Hobhouse, *Forty Years and an Epilogue* (n. 49 above), pp. 178-9. For Paterson, see Victor Bailey, *Delinquency and Citizenship: Reclaiming the Young Offender, 1914- 1948* (Oxford, 1987), pp. 195-6.

60 HO 45/11033/428541.

61 See Rose, *The Struggle for Penal Reform* (n. 49 above), p. 111; PRO, P.Com. 7/475.

62 HO 45/13658/185668/21; Lionel W. Fox, *The English Prison and Borstal Systems* (London, 1952), p. 68.

object was to restore prisoners 'to ordinary standards of citizenship' by promoting self-respect and a sense of personal responsibility. This in turn would require 'vigorous industrial, mental, and moral training, pursued on considered lines by officers, teachers, and prison visitors of character and personality.'[63]

Yet if improvements in prison administration were evident, helped forward by Hobhouse and Brockway, by some eighteen MPs who shared the status of ex-prisoner, and by a reconstructed Prison Commission, the pace of penal change remained decidedly halting.[64] In many prisons, claimed Fenner Brockway in 1926, the new interpretation of the silence rule had yet to find full expression.[65] In the case of men sentenced to imprisonment with hard labour, moreover, the preliminary period of separate confinement (reduced from 28 to 14 days in 1919) still obtained. In September 1924, Waller pressed for its abolition, but the home secretary demurred, and the issue was dropped.[66] Not until 1931 was the period of cellular confinement entirely abolished. And the prison commissioners failed to get the Royal Commission on Prisons and Borstals they clearly wanted. An inquiry would, they believed, arouse public interest in the treatment, education, and reclamation of social failures. It would also give them the opportunity to argue that people ought not to be sent to prison at all if it could be avoided. In August 1922, the Treasury made money available for the public inquiry. Alas, the government changed, and the next home secretary felt public demand was too weak to justify a review of the prison system.[67] In short, this entire catalogue of evidence should give pause to those who insist that the Edwardian years witnessed the emergence of a new penal structure.

III

Garland is perhaps on firmer ground when it comes to the separate treatment of distinct categories of offender, recommended by the Gladstone Committee for young offenders aged sixteen to twenty-three and for habitual criminals. Lengthy discussions, and some experimentation, preceded the Prevention of Crime Act, 1908, which brought into being the sentence of preventive detention, to rid society of the habitual criminal, and the Borstal training sentence, to stem the flow of new habitual offenders. Both measures are typically seen as basic components of the positivist restructuring of the penal system; both measures reflect the influence of the principles of individualization and indeterminacy. Even here, however, caution is required.

---

63 Quoted in Fox, pp. 70-1.

64 For details of ex-prisoner MPs, see Snowden (n. 40 above), p. 410; Lord Pethick-Lawrence, *Fate Has Been Kind* (London, 1942), p. 130; K. Robbins, 'Morgan Jones in 1916', *Llafur* 1 (Summer 1975): pp. 38-43. Another influence on penal change, particularly in staff conditions, was the unrest among prison officers, which found expression in the growth of the National Union of Police and Prison Officers, and in the 1919 strike.

65 A. F. Brockway in *Socialist Review* (September, October, and December 1926).

66 HO 45/13658/185668/21.

67 See HO 45/11543/357055/71; 'Editorial', *Howard Journal* 1 (1922), pp. 4-5.

For habitual offenders, the 1908 act settled on a so-called 'dual track' system.[68] In an awkward alliance of classicism and positivism, those deemed to be habitual criminals first paid for their crime in the coinage of just deserts (penal servitude), after which they were detained for their habitual criminality in the new currency of social defence (preventive detention). What looked to the judiciary like double sentencing made judges so uneasy that they became extremely averse to using the measure. By 1921, only 577 convicts had been sentenced to preventive detention.[69] The low number was a result not only of judicial scepticism but also of Churchill's determination, when home secretary, to restrict preventive detention to the dangerous professional criminal. The act, he believed, had pressed too largely on the persistent minor offender.[70] Churchill's intervention gave the kiss of death to this new form of detention. In 1911, only 53 men were sentenced to preventive detention, as compared with 177 in the previous year.[71] If the sentence of Borstal training was less troubled by a conflict of penal philosophies, it fell well short of a full-blooded positivist transplant. Ruggles-Brise saw Borstal as an alternative to penal servitude for the dangerous criminal between sixteen and twenty-one years of age and hence insisted on a regime that would build character via strict discipline, obedience, and uniform treatment. Up to and for some years beyond 1918 the conditions and regime of Borstal training were only one step removed from those of a convict prison.[72]

If the net is cast wider to include the Inebriates Act, 1898 (establishing state reformatories for habitual drunkards), and the Mental Deficiency Act, 1913, the overall conclusion persists. The first-mentioned statute reflects the shift of policy toward extended custody and medical treatment of habitual drunkards.[73] The other measure was one for which the eugenics movement could legitimately claim responsibility. Mental deficiency was thought to be hereditary, to be largely incurable, and to require the compulsory segregation of the 'feeble-minded', not to mention limitation of their right to reproduce.[74] Two points establish the overall conclusion. First, evidence of the origins and workings of these acts suggest that Garland's notion of a shift in criminological understanding from the 'moral' to the

---

68 For discussion of the definition of habitual criminality adopted by the 1908 act — one that failed to distinguish clearly between the habitual professional and the habitual petty nuisance — see Wiener (n. 23 above), p. 347; Radzinowicz and Hood (n. 2 above), pp. 266-7.

69 S. Petrow, *Policing Morals: The Metropolitan Police and the Home Office, 1870- 1914* (Oxford, 1994), p. 111.

70 See pp. 147-9 below for Churchill's critical approach to preventive detention.

71 Radzinowicz and Hood, p. 286. See also N. Morris, *The Habitual Criminal* (Cambridge, Mass, 1951), p. 80; Forsythe, *Penal Discipline, Reformatory Projects and the English Prison Commission, 1895-1939* (n. 26 above), p. 243, and 'Reformatory Projects in British Prisons, 1780-1939: Recent Writings and Lessons from the Past', in *History and Sociology of Crime*, ed. P. Robert and C. Emsley (Pfaffenweiler, 1991), p. 54.

72 See Bailey, *Delinquency and Citizenship* (n. 59 above), pp. 186-91, esp. p. 189.

73 See Wiener, p. 188; Radzinowicz and Hood, pp. 308-13.

74 Eugenics, based on the belief that the physical and mental condition of the population was determined more by heredity than environment, had an influential following up to 1914. Eugenists predicted race degeneration if the 'unfit' were allowed to reproduce themselves more rapidly than the 'fit'. See G. R. Searle, *Eugenics and Politics in Britain, 1900-1914* (Leyden, 1976); M. Freeden, 'Eugenics and Progressive Thought: A Study in Ideological Affinity', *Historical Journal* 22 (1979), p. 658; Jose Harris, *Private Lives, Public Spirit: A Social History of Britain 1870-1914* (Oxford, 1993), pp. 244-5.

'medical' is overdrawn. Inebriate reformatories and mental deficiency institutions were used predominantly for females.[75] Most of the committals to inebriate reformatories were for either neglect or cruelty to children or drunk and disorderly behaviour.[76] The most convincing explanation of this policy is that, because women, in their role as mothers, were identified as the biological source of inebriety and feeble-mindedness, female offenders became subject to a process of medicalization. But these new medical and psychiatric interpretations of female crime, and this is the point of importance, were, according to Lucia Zedner, 'suffused with a highly moral view of what constituted deviance and what constituted normality in women.'[77] These theories, she argues, 'fitted only too well with the long-standing belief that criminal women not merely broke the law but tended to exhibit fundamental flaws of character.' And she concludes by saying that historians have neglected the extent to which medical responses were erected on 'the foundation of older, culturally derived assumptions about women's character and behavior.'[78]

The second point relates to the abiding strength of the 'tariff' principle of sentencing. The judiciary either committed offenders to inebriate reformatories only for terms similar to those they would have served in prison or refused to make use of them at all. The figures speak for themselves. There were approximately a quarter of a million committals to prison for drunkenness *annually* before 1914. Yet the total number of committals to inebriate reformatories between 1899 and 1913 was 4,590 (3,741, or 81 percent, of whom were women). The daily average population never reached 1,000. By 1921, all the reformatories had closed.[79] The experiment of subjecting habitual drunkards to prolonged detention had proved a colossal failure. Only by a large stretch of the imagination, then, can penal measures that were full of philosophical ambiguity, that dealt with only a few hundred cases each year, and that were surrounded on all sides by more traditional forms of punishment be seen as composing a major alteration in the structure of criminal justice.

As a brief coda to this section, it is useful to refer to the failure, also, to establish penal labour colonies for those convicted of vagrancy. Garland struggles to explain this failure to establish the compulsory segregation of the 'unemployable', which he sees as an essential deterrent underside to the 'social security program' of labour exchanges and social insurance. He posits the undocumented interpretation that policy makers realized that they could instead employ the network of Borstals,

---

75 See H. G. Simmons, 'Explaining Social Policy: The English Mental Deficiency Act of 1913', *Journal of Social History* 11 (1977-78), p. 399; G. Hunt, J. Mellor, and J. Turner, 'Wretched, Hatless and Miserably Clad: Women and the Inebriate Reformatories from 1900-1913', *British Journal of Sociology* 40 (June 1989), p. 246.

76 C. Harding and L. Wilkin, "The Dream of a Benevolent Mind': The Late Victorian Response to the Problem of Inebriety', *Criminal Justice History* 9 (1988), p. 198.

77 L. Zedner, 'Women, Crime, and Penal Responses: A Historical Account', in *Crime and Justice: A Review of Research*, ed. M. Tonry, vol. 14 (Chicago, 1991), p. 308.

78 Ibid., pp. 343, 353. See Simmons, p. 393.

79 Hunt *et al.*, p. 246; Radzinowicz and Hood (n. 2 above), pp. 311-14.

preventive detention prisons, inebriate reformatories, and mental deficiency institutions.[80] I prefer the more prosaic explanation that the labour colony scheme expired because a sentence of three years' detention, even as a maximum, for the crime of vagrancy was deemed unduly drastic. Thus the failure of the penal labour colony squares with the conclusion that judges (and public opinion) consistently adopted an extremely circumspect approach to the new scientific knowledges, and they remained stubbornly reluctant to impose long preventive sentences.

IV

The way we see criminal offenders, understand their motivations, and dispose of them as cases is heavily influenced by the intellectual frameworks of the time. What patterns of thought guided the ways in which criminals were seen, understood, and treated in the Edwardian era? Garland and Wiener reply that a traditional 'moral' discourse retreated before the wave of scientific determinism. They argue that these years witnessed a major sea change in criminological discourse, from classical jurisprudence to positivist medicalism, which in turn led to a tectonic shift in penal structures.[81] This is not how I read the evidence. I am not convinced that a new positivist discourse, underwritten by the human sciences, dominated what could be seen, thought, and performed in the penal domain. I am not convinced that 'demoralization', or a diminishing faith in the efficacy of individual willpower, was as pronounced or advanced as Garland and Wiener contend. Their interpretation underestimates the continued influence of humanitarianism as a causal factor in penal change, utterly ignores the Idealist framework of social and legal thought, and relegates the force of ethical and Christian socialism to a footnote. It is to these other discourses that I turn in order to document the complexity of Edwardian penal culture and to underline the continued and vital role of moral character in Edwardian penal thought.[82]

Most historians would now accept that cultural mentalities and sensibilities affect the ways in which we think about offenders. Yet too often these important moral, religious, and emotional forces are mere ghosts at the table of penal change. If we truly wish to include sensibilities in our explanatory framework, then humanitarianism should be seen not as surface rhetoric, masking more fundamental economic or political interests — the line taken by Foucault when he dismissed humanitarianism as 'so much incidental music' — but as a causal factor in penal change. The humanitarian sensibility altered in character over the Victorian period. Early Victorian humanitarianism was a form of benevolence that regarded the 'lower orders' with a charitable and superior eye. By the last quarter of the nineteenth century, humanitarians were no longer so seized by the personal moral inadequacies of those they would

---

80 Garland, *Punishment and Welfare* (n. 18 above), pp. 227-8.

81 Wiener (n. 23 above), p. 186.

82 I am not arguing that ideological forms were the only influence on the penal system; I am arguing that positivism was only one, and not the most important, framework of social and political thought in the Edwardian debate on prisons.

redeem. Newer humanitarian feelings were emerging. Humanitarians encouraged a compassion for the weak and infirm precisely because they were weak and infirm.[83]

In 1891, humanitarian ranks were bolstered by the arrival of the Humanitarian League. It was founded by the socialist pacifist Henry Salt, a former master of Eton public school who retired to a Thoreau-inspired, simple life in the Surrey countryside. There he became the centre of a progressive literary circle, the most famous members of which were the Fabian socialist George Bernard Shaw and the ethical socialist Edward Carpenter. The League was particularly concerned with criminal law reform, the abolition of corporal punishment, and preventing cruelty to animals and children. In 1896, the League established a criminal law and prisons department to advocate improvements in prison conditions and penal policy. The department sought to humanize the conditions of prison life and to affirm that the true purpose of imprisonment was the reformation, not the mere punishment, of the offender.[84]

The most striking feature of the Humanitarian League is the way it acted as an unofficial hub of penal reform between the Gladstone Report of 1895 and the Prison System Enquiry Committee's volume, *English Prisons To-Day* (1922). One spoke of the reform wheel radiated out to the agitation that led to the Gladstone Report and the 1898 Prison Act. The League's activities were guided by W. D. Morrison, chaplain of Wandsworth prison, Christian socialist, and criminologist, and were supported by the Irish nationalist MP Michael Davitt, who was on the committee of the League's criminal law and prisons department.[85]

A second spoke led to the circle of progressives — Edward Carpenter, Havelock Ellis — who sought to live the new Ideal of Humanity, and who, with Morrison, condemned existing prisons — 'whited sepulchres full of dead men's bones', in Carpenter's telling biblical allusion — and acted as conduits for a more 'scientific' view of crime.[86] Carpenter and Ellis represented advanced opinion in the 1890s. Carpenter's lifestyle was a revolt against the oppressive conventionalities of Victorian life. He crusaded for a new ideal of social brotherhood and the honest human relation. Salt's friendship drew

---

83 For the early nineteenth-century, humanitarian concern for the protection from abuse of prisoners and lunatics, see T. W. Laqueur, 'Bodies, Details, and the Humanitarian Narrative', in *The New Cultural History*, ed. Lynn Hunt (Berkeley, 1989), p. 179; Andrew Scull, *The Most Solitary of Afflictions: Madness and Society in Britain, 1700-1900* (New Haven, Conn, 1993), p. 380. See also Martin Wiener, ed., 'Special Issue: Humanitarianism or Control? A Symposium on Aspects of Nineteenth Century Social Reform in Britain and America', *Rice University Studies*, vol. 67 (Winter 1981). And see T. L. Haskell, 'Capitalism and the Origins of the Humanitarian Sensibility, Parts 1 & 2', *American Historical Review* 90 (April and June 1985), pp. 339-61, 547-66.

84 See Rose, *The Struggle for Penal Reform* (n. 49 above), pp. 56-7; Garland, *Punishment and Welfare*, p. 109; Wiener, p. 335. Salt and the Humanitarian League supported the *Daily Chronicle*'s 1894 campaign for a prison inquiry; see McConville, *English Local Prisons* (n. 5 above), p. 580. For Salt's and the league's agitation against cruel sports, and for Carpenter's opposition to vivisection, see Brian Harrison, *Peaceable Kingdom: Stability and Change in Modern Britain* (Oxford, 1982), pp. 91, 108, 150.

85 See Henry S. Salt, *Seventy Years among Savages* (London, 1921), p. 140; George Hendrick, *Henry Salt: Humanitarian Reformer and Man of Letters* (Urbana, Ill., 1977), p. 77; Forsythe, *Penal Discipline, Reformatory Projects and the English Prison Commission, 1895-1939* (n. 26 above), p. 23; Dan Weinbren, 'Against *All* Cruelty: The Humanitarian League, 1891-1919', *History Workshop Journal* 38 (Autumn 1994), pp. 92-5.

86 E. Carpenter, *Prisons, Police and Punishment* (London, 1905), p. 120.

him into the Humanitarian League and into speaking and writing on behalf of penal reform. The prisons, Carpenter advised, should be transformed into 'Industrial Asylums' in which prisoners would be educated for citizenship.[87] Havelock Ellis was a member of the Fellowship of the New Life, a group that viewed individual moral regeneration as the key to social reform (and from which the Fabian socialists had broken away in 1884). Ellis's Contemporary Science Series, in which his own contribution to 'criminal anthropology', *The Criminal*, appeared in 1890, introduced Cesare Lombroso, the 'criminal type', biological determinism, and the indeterminate sentence to an English audience. Not surprisingly, his remedy for crime was resolutely positivist: to replace the word 'crime' with that of 'disease', in the belief that criminals needed individualized treatment.[88]

Positivism also attracted W. D. Morrison. The Criminology Series he edited included the work of European positivists such as Lombroso and Enrico Ferri, and Morrison's own studies stressed the deterministic (particularly biological) sources of delinquency. But Morrison's criminology was, in fact, an eclectic, often contradictory, mix of positivism, practical prison experience, and Christian socialism. To judge from his introductions to the translations of continental theorists, moreover, Morrison's attraction to positivism grew out of deep dissatisfaction with the existing prison system, and hence his main approach was to mine the new theory for scientific sanction to the humanitarian-cum-evangelistic campaign for penal reform. Anyway, Morrison's enthusiasm for positivism gradually waned. He could not ultimately accept the Lombrosian theory of degenerate 'criminal man'. Nor could he support the indeterminate sentence, so foreign was it, he felt, to the English liberal tradition.[89]

A third spoke of the reform wheel ran from the Tolstoyans and humanitarians in the Penal Reform League to the socialists and pacifists of the Prison System Enquiry Committee. The Penal Reform League was founded in 1907, an outgrowth of the prison experience of the suffragettes and the new humanist spirit. It stood for the reclamation of criminals by a curative and educational prison system. The founder and first secretary was Arthur St. John, a Tolstoy disciple and a believer, with Salt and Carpenter, in the good in every individual. In truth, the league was a small body with no money to speak of and had little influence on the course of penal reform before 1914. This was not for want of trying. League leaflets, written by such humanitarians as the playwright John Galsworthy, advocated penal reform. St. John led deputations to the Home Office, where he complained that the prison system was having a disastrous effect on the minds and souls of prisoners and declared that the country needed a

---

87 See E. Carpenter, *England's Ideal and Other Papers on Social Subjects* (London, 1895), pp. 1-22, and *Prisons, Police and Punishment*, pp. 61-77; C. Tsuzuki, *Edward Carpenter, 1844-1929* (Cambridge, 1980), p. 113.

88 Havelock Ellis, *The Criminal* (London, 1890). See Phyllis Grosskurth, *Havelock Ellis* (New York, 1980), pp. 69, 114-16; R. E. McGowen, 'Rethinking Crime: Changing Attitudes towards Law-Breakers in Eighteenth and Nineteenth-Century England' (Ph.D. diss., University of Illinois at Urbana-Champaign, 1979), pp. 311-14.

89 See McGowen, 'Rethinking Crime', pp. 301-11; Radzinowicz and Hood (n. 2 above), pp. 86-8; W. D. Morrison, 'The Study of Crime', *Mind*, no. 4 (Oct.1892), pp. 489-517; David Garland, 'British Criminology before 1935', *British Journal of Criminology* 28 (Spring 1988), p. 7; C. Lombroso and W. Ferrero, *The Female Offender* (New York, 1916), introduction by W. D. Morrison, pp. v-xx.

different spirit in prison administration.[90] Predictably, St. John was asked to join the Prison System Enquiry Committee in 1919. Other committee members included the ubiquitous W. D. Morrison, Margery Fry, the secretary of the Howard League for Penal Reform (a 1921 amalgamation of the Howard Association and the Penal Reform League), Alexander Paterson, secretary of a voluntary society to assist discharged prisoners, Sidney and Beatrice Webb, and the guild socialist G. D. H. Cole. The chairman of the committee was Fabian socialist, Sydney Olivier, a friend of the Salts and fellow humanitarian.[91]

The secretary of the Prison System Enquiry Committee was Stephen Hobhouse. He emerged from prison determined to bear witness to the defects of prison conditions. 'If some of our predecessors in the Society [of Friends] have a heavy responsibility fixed on them for assisting in the establishment of the false methods of today', wrote Hobhouse, in a reproachful reference to his Quaker forebears, 'we may perhaps atone for this want of imagination by helping to inaugurate a new and more Christ like treatment of our erring fellow-creatures.'[92] After two years' work on the report, Hobhouse was close to a nervous breakdown. Hence Beatrice Webb asked Fenner Brockway to join her nephew, Stephen, as joint editor. A year later a report appeared under the title, *English Prisons To-Day*. The two authors converted the searing personal testimony of the conscientious objectors into an impeachment of the prison administration of the Prison Commission chairman, Sir Evelyn Ruggles-Brise. If one thread held together *English Prisons To-Day* it was that, whatever the prevailing theory of punishment, 'the Prison System ought not to result in the brutalisation, deterioration, or devitalisation of the criminal, but should, as far as possible, be humane in the best sense of the word.'[93]

The humanitarian or 'moral' approach of these various reform bodies was, for David Garland, little more than rhetoric that either served to mask power or provided legitimacy for the use of power. Thus, humanitarian values, he suggests, facilitated the acceptance by a conservative political and administrative elite of positivist penal measures.[94] This reductive approach underestimates the contribution of humanitarianism to penal debate and change. Humanitarianism exists at a different level than coherent and articulated theories like positivism, idealism, or socialism; it is at once more popular,

---

90 See Galsworthy, *The Spirit of Punishment* (n. 37 above); Arthur St. John, *Prison Regime* (London, 1913), and *Reception Houses* (London, [1918?]); HO 45/11543/357055/16.

91 HO 45/11543/357055/33; Stephen Hobhouse, *Forty Years and an Epilogue* (n. 49 above), pp. 133-44; Hendrick, p. 161. For the contribution of conscientious objectors to the Prison System Enquiry Committee, see pp. 130-1 above.

92 S. Hobhouse, 'The Silence System in British Prisons', *Friends' Quarterly Examiner* (July 1918), p. 263.

93 HO 45/11543/357055/33; A. Fenner Brockway, *Inside the Left* (n. 48 above), chap. 13.

94 Garland, *Punishment and Welfare* (n. 18 above), pp. 108-9, 123. In fairness, Garland states that the approach of the penal reform groups to the 'criminological programme' was 'mediated by Christian evangelicalism, which allowed a large degree of policy support, but prohibited any total endorsement of the programme as a whole' (ibid., p. 109). In more recent work, moreover, Garland acknowledges the need to include sensibilities in the examination of penal policy and speculates on the contribution of humanitarian values to change in penal laws and institutions; see David Garland, *Punishment and Modern Society* (n. 21 above), p. 198, 'Sociological Perspectives on Punishment', in Tonry, ed. (n. 77 above), p. 142, and 'Criminological Knowledge and its Relation to Power: Foucault's Genealogy and Criminology Today', *British Journal of Criminology* 32 (Autumn 1992), pp. 411-12.

vague, and elusive. Yet if humanitarianism's weight was felt less rationally, it was an essential feature of the emotional and intellectual environment of these years. It is misleading, moreover, *pace* Foucault, to see humanitarianism as the antithesis of social science. Rather, the Edwardian years point to a more complex relationship between the two. A reinvigorated humanitarianism accompanied the rise of positivist criminology. As a result, humanitarians began to use more deterministic language and to propose more 'scientific' remedies. Yet humanitarians also modified and limited the effect of positivist theory by their emphasis on the suffering and dignity of individual prisoners. The gravamen of the reformers' critique was that the existing prison system manifestly failed to believe in, or to revive, the good in every prisoner. No one would wish to accept at face value all the claims of the humanitarian bodies, but humanitarian sensibility deserves full recognition in an explanation of Edwardian penal debate and change.

V

The penal culture of these years was also deeply touched by the ideas of the Philosophical Idealists, notably the work of the Oxford professor of moral philosophy, T. H. Green. This should occasion no surprise, given the considerable influence that Idealism is known to have exerted on social thought and public policy in the late Victorian and Edwardian years.[95] Yet Garland and Wiener make little or no mention of it. It is time to repair the neglect, starting with the bare essentials of this philosophical approach.[96]

Green believed that every man had the capacity for moral choice and the will to behave responsibly and that every man had to be encouraged to cultivate his 'best self'. For a man to realize his 'best self', he had to will it; social institutions could not enforce self-realization. However, the state had an obligation to help the individual to further his 'best self'; the state had a key role to play in creating the conditions for moral advancement. A framework of law guaranteeing certain rights (such as access to education) was the *sine qua non* of an individual's moral development. Rights, that is, were the powers given by the state to permit each individual to develop his moral character and contribute his best to society. In pursuing his 'best self', the individual also contributed to the 'common good'. Moral

---

95 See Melvin Richter, *The Politics of Conscience: T. H. Green and His Age* (London, 1964), p. 13, and 'T. H. Green and His Audience: Liberalism as a Surrogate Faith', *Review of Politics* 18 (October 1956), p. 444. For the most recent assessment of the influence of Idealist thought on the structural transformation of welfare provision, see Jose Harris, 'The Webbs, the Charity Organisation Society and the Ratan Tata Foundation: Social Policy from the Perspective of 1912', in *The Goals of Social Policy*, ed. M. Bulmer *et al.* (London, 1989). pp. 51-5, and 'Political Thought and the Welfare State, 1870- 1940' (n. 27 above).

96 The next paragraph is based on G. Himmelfarb, *Poverty and Compassion: The Moral Imagination of the Late Victorians* (New York, 1991), chap. 17; Adam B. Ulam, *Philosophical Foundations of English Socialism* (Cambridge, Mass, 1951), pp. 34-8; A. Vincent and R. Plant, *Philosophy, Politics and Citizenship: The Life and Thought of the British Idealists* (Oxford, 1984), pp. 2, 40, 52; J. Harris, *Private Lives, Public Spirit* (n. 74 above), pp. 248-50.

improvement, then, was the motor of social progress. Social transformation depended on the moral improvement of individual citizens. Two notions relevant for our purposes flowed from this philosophy.

One was a non-deterministic approach to human behaviour. 'Idealist man' willed his own destiny 'instead of being driven this way and that by external forces.'[97] Though the state had the job of creating conditions that would enable men to realize their moral potential, state intervention was meant not to diminish individual responsibility but rather to offer a new way to promote it. The second notion was the cult of citizenship. Idealism dignified all men, even the poorest, as citizens capable of self-realization. The disadvantaged had to be helped to achieve self-development, either by state assistance or, more suitably, by voluntary social service. This belief in active citizenship underpinned the work, for example, of the university settlement movement.[98] These two notions contributed to the debate on Edwardian penal policy. The insistence on individual responsibility reinvigorated the classical philosophy and practice of punishment and provided an antidote to the excesses of positivism. The secular religion of citizenship converted a number of key prison reformers and practitioners to the belief that they had a civic duty to create penal environments in which prisoners could fit themselves for citizenship.

Idealism offered a philosophy of punishment and, indirectly, an image of 'criminal man'. Not for the Idealist, Lombroso's 'born criminal', nor the notion of crime as degeneracy or disease requiring prolonged, if not indefinite, detention. Rather, the criminal was a moral and responsible being who had violated someone else's rights. Punishment was the state's way of securing 'the future maintenance of rights'. Among the rights to be maintained, however, 'are included rights of the criminal himself'. Green argued that 'this consideration limits the kind of punishment which the state may justly inflict. It ought not in punishing to sacrifice unnecessarily to the maintenance of rights in general what might be called the reversionary rights of the criminal, rights which, if properly treated, he might ultimately become capable of exercising for the general good.'[99] To be just, then, punishment ought to be proportionate to the importance of the right violated, and it ought to be 'reformatory' in the sense that 'it must tend to qualify the criminal for the resumption of rights.'[100] A similar theory of punishment was presented by Bernard Bosanquet, except that he warned against the tendency in 'reformation theory' to treat the offender 'as a 'patient', not as an agent.'[101] In this manner, Bosanquet claimed, 'it leads to the notion that

---

97   T. H. Green, 'Principles of Political Obligation', par. 7, in *Works of Thomas Hill Green*, ed. R. L. Nettleship, vol. 2 (1886; 5th impression, London, 1906).

98   See J. Morrow, 'Ancestors, Legacies and Traditions: British Idealism in the History of Political Thought', *History of Political Thought* 6 (Winter 1985), p. 510; S. Meacham, *Toynbee Hall and Social Reform, 1880-1914* (New Haven, Conn., 1987), pp. 12-14. See also Clement Attlee, *The Social Worker* (London, 1920)

99   Green, par. 205.

100   Ibid., par. 206. See H. B. Acton, *The Philosophy of Punishment* (London, 1969), p. 11; Paul Harris, 'Moral Progress and Politics: The Theory of T. H. Green', *Polity* 21 (Spring 1989), p. 542. See also Henry Jones, *The Working Faith of the Social Reformer* (London, 1910), p. 254.

101   B. Bosanquet, *The Philosophical Theory of the State* (London, 1910), p. 223.

the State may take hold of any man, whose life or ideas are thought capable of improvement, and set to work to ameliorate them by forcible treatment.'[102] In a later work, Bosanquet argued that 'the reformatory theory, in its purity, *is* arbitrary and cruel', for 'Revenge may be exhausted by a term in prison; it is the work of reformation to the duration of which no sane man can profess to set a limit.' In words that have contemporary resonance, he asked rhetorically: 'Could anything be conceived more brutalising, arbitrary, and oppressive? … You want to annul the bad will, and in doing so, to help the offender against it so far as within reasonable limits you can. But to bind a man under the jurisdiction of some official expert in morals — say a gaol chaplain — till the latter should be satisfied of his reformation, would be a tyranny to which I find it hard to conceive a parallel.'[103] Punishment, in all, was 'a negation of an evil will which has been realised in action'; 'deterrence and reformation are subordinate aspects implied within it.'[104] The correction of the young was a different matter, however, since it involved 'imperfect wills, which have not entered upon complete responsibility.'[105]

The import of all this is that the Idealist movement, a dominant intellectual force by the 1890s, reinstated retribution as the key justification for punishment, with all that that entailed: individual responsibility, just proportion, and the quest for uniformity in sentencing.[106] Moreover, the judiciary (which, strangely, Garland never includes within his 'penal complex') was confirmed in its tendency to see the criminal law as an embodiment of the fundamental moral principles of the community and to guard against moves to limit their applicability. Attachment to classical notions of criminal justice was not a judicial peculiarity but was endemic among the prison service, even including prison doctors and psychiatrists. While top penal administrators were willing to accept that criminality might have a physical basis in 'degeneracy', particularly in 'feeble-mindedness', at the level of the prison medical officer continuity prevailed. Prison medical officers were preoccupied still with separating the malingerer from those who were unfit for prison discipline. Few of the 'weak-minded', however, were transferred elsewhere, even after 1913 and the Mental Deficiency Act, and a more thoroughgoing mental diagnosis and treatment of prisoners was a rarity. For the most part, medical officers continued to serve the 'moral' mission of the prisons.[107] But let us turn to the most powerful prison administrator, the chairman of the Prison Commission and devotee of T. H. Green, Evelyn Ruggles-Brise.

In explaining why this 'humane and high-minded administrator, well versed in the literature of penology', a pillar of the international Penal and Penitentiary Commission, did so little to change the

---

102 Ibid., p. 224.

103 B. Bosanquet, *Some Suggestions in Ethics* (London, 1918), pp. 200-2, emphasis in original.

104 Ibid., p. 207.

105 Ibid., p. 183.

106 See Radzinowicz and Hood (n. 2 above), pp. 18-19.

107 See S. Watson, 'Malingerers, the 'Weakminded' Criminal and the 'Moral Imbecile': How the English Prison Medical Officer Became an Expert in Mental Deficiency, 1880-1930', in *Legal Medicine in History*, ed. M. Clark and C. Crawford (Cambridge, 1994), p. 229; Hobhouse and Brockway (n. 47 above), pp. 257-85. See also Wiener (n. 23 above), p. 234; and Garland, 'British Criminology before 1935' (n. 89 above), p. 5.

principles and practice of the prison regime in response to the Gladstone Report, Lionel Fox correctly highlighted Ruggles-Brise's own statements, 'which suggest that he never really accepted the possibility of a system of treatment in which reform would hold a primary and concurrent place with deterrence.'[108] In an address to the American Prison Association in Washington in 1910, Ruggles-Brise argued forcefully against a change in the 'historic order of the factors of punishment' — to wit, retributory, deterrent and, reformatory. For support, he turned to the formula 'prescribed by one of the clearest and profoundest thinkers of the end of last century, Professor T. H. Green', whose definitions Ruggles-Brise then emulated. By 'retributory', said Ruggles-Brise, he meant 'the determination of the human consciousness that the system of rights shall be maintained, and that he who offends against it shall be punished, and that the punishment shall be of such a nature as to deter him and others from anti-social acts.' By 'reformatory', he meant 'the accepted axiom of modern penology that a prisoner has reversionary rights of humanity ... and that no effort must be spared to restore that man to society as a better and a wiser man and a good citizen.'[109] On other occasions, too, Ruggles-Brise warned against a retreat from the classical traditions of punishment.[110]

Nothing, in Ruggles-Brise's opinion, had more retarded modern penology than the idea of a 'criminal type', of persons predestined to crime. The idea challenged the entire system of punishment since the 'criminal type' was hardly likely to be amenable to deterrent or reformatory influences. Fortunately, the tide of criminal anthropology ebbed quickly, as Ruggles-Brise recorded in 1910: 'The Lombrosian theories of the criminal-né [*sic*] are exploded. Our own investigations now being conducted into the physiology of crime will, I think, fire the last shot at this deserted ship.'[111] Ruggles-Brise had commissioned Dr. Charles Goring, medical officer at Parkhurst, to test Lombroso's theory by a large-scale examination of English convicts. Happily, Goring successfully demolished the 'physical criminal type'. But ironically his finding that the English prisoner was, on average, defective, either physically or mentally, gladdened the heart of all eugenists. It required Ruggles-Brise, in his preface to *The English Convict*, to warn that Goring's 'theory of defectiveness ... must not be pressed so far as to affect the liability to punishment of the offender for his act.'[112] Ruggles-Brise also contested other planks of the positivist credo. He rejected both an entirely indeterminate sentence and anything that trenched on judicial discretion in sentencing, 'the most sacred principle of English Criminal Law.'[113]

---

108 Fox (n. 62 above), pp. 62-3.

109 E. Ruggles-Brise, *Prison Reform: At Home and Abroad* (London, 1924), p. 193.

110 See Report of the Commissioners of Prisons ... for 1912-1913, Cd. 7092, *PP*, 1914, vol. 45. pp. 22-3.

111 E. Ruggles-Brise memo, April 18, 1910, HO 45/13658/185668/6.

112 Charles Goring, *The English Convict: A Statistical Study*, abridged ed. (London, 1919), preface by E. Ruggles-Brise, p. vi. See Ruggles-Brise, *English Prison System* (n. 51 above), pp. 198-212. See also Radzinowicz and Hood, pp. 21-6; Wiener, p. 357; Piers Beirne, *Inventing Criminology: Essays on the Rise of Homo Criminalis* (New York, 1993), p. 213. Hobhouse and Brockway's *English Prisons To-Day* confirmed the view that the criminal type was manufactured by the prison system.

113 Quoted in D. A. Thomas, *Constraints on Judgment: The Search for Structured Discretion in Sentencing, 1860-1910* (Cambridge, 1979), p. 27. See Radzinowicz and Hood, p. 268, n. 17; E. Ruggles-Brise memo, July 13, 1910, HO 144/18869/196919/3.

Other features of the positivist paradigm attracted Ruggles-Brise. He endorsed the principle of 'the individualization of punishment.'[114] He recognized the merit of greater specialization in the treatment offered by each prison, adapted to different kinds of offender,[115] *apropos* of which he recommended a special institution for mentally defective prisoners requiring long, possibly permanent detention.[116] And he was generally supportive of preventive detention for habitual offenders.[117] But Ruggles-Brise's most valuable contribution was surely the urge to save young adult offenders from a career of crime. Moreover, the development of the Borstal training system owed something to positivist criminology, more to American example, but much more to the social conscience of a follower of T. H. Green. Only for young, feeble-minded, and gravely habitual offenders, those considered incapable of making moral choices, was Ruggles-Brise willing to waive the application of culpability, punishment, and moral reformation. He still saw the primary function of a humane administration to be 'to secure obedience, discipline, order, and the habit of industry.' 'These things alone', he continued, 'have a great moral value.'[118]

The Idealist movement thus influenced British legal circles and prison administration. Legal and jurisprudential thinking, reinforced by philosophical idealism, clung fast to the classical principles of moral culpability, responsibility, and of measure for measure between crime and punishment. Penal officials held tight to traditional modes of uniformly administered discipline and remained sceptical of, if also open-minded about, the positivist view of crime as the determined outcome of biological or environmental conditions.[119] The upshot, I suggest, was a neoclassical philosophy and practice of punishment, by which I mean a continued legal appraisal of behaviour in terms of moral choice, at least for sane adults (modified only by minor mitigating factors), and a departure from voluntarism with regard only to the young, the insane, and the feeble-minded — in a word, those incapable of exercising free will — whose actions were largely determined. But determinist philosophies never came close to triumphing over older legal and penological imperatives. The Edwardian debate on prisons was guided less by the new positivist discourse and more by an Idealist framework of thought, with its stress on moral responsibility, just proportion, and the role of the state and citizens to secure the general protection of rights and to help the criminal resume the exercise of rights.

---

114 Ruggles-Brise, *Prison Reform*, p. 195.

115 Edward Marsh to W. Churchill, August 23, 1910, in Randolph Churchill, *Winston S. Churchill: Companion Volume* (Boston, 1969), 2, pt. 2;1196.

116 E. Ruggles-Brise memo, April 9, 1910, HO 144/1085/193548/1.

117 Radzinowicz and Hood (n. 2 above), pp. 269-71.

118 Ruggles-Brise, *English Prison System*, p. 3. Ruggles-Brise was liverishly unsympathetic, therefore, to the Penal Reform League's 1918 complaints about degrading prison garb, 'spy hole' practice, and the exclusion of outside news; see HO 45/11543/357055/9.

119 See Forsythe, *Penal Discipline, Reformatory Projects and the English Prison Commission, 1895-1939* (n. 26 above), p. 239; Garland, 'British Criminology before 1935' (n. 89 above), p. 5. Idealism's influence might also explain, at least in part, the continued resort to voluntary agencies as an adjunct to the penal system, notably for discharged prisoners, probation, and Borstal aftercare. This feature of the penal system was of particular concern to Ruggles-Brise.

VI

The influence of 'moral character', active citizenship, and the realization of the best possible self is evident, too, in ethical socialism. A fundamental strand of the ethical socialist tradition is a belief in the power of moral character both to improve individual conduct and to build a virtuous society.[120] The important point, for present purposes, is that the moral fervour of ethical socialism contributed to the critique of Edwardian prisons by way of conscientious objection to participation in the First World War and the Prison System Enquiry Committee of the Labour Research Department.

Socialist war resisters, many from the ILP, made up three quarters of the membership of the No-Conscription Fellowship. They made common cause with Quaker Christians and libertarians, grouping around the principle of resistance to compulsion where life and death were concerned.[121] Stephen Hobhouse, a Quaker pacifist (converted by Tolstoy's *What I Believe*) and long-time social worker in London's East End, observed later that the Quakers' faith 'did not divide us in spirit from the many deeply sincere Socialists and others who were holding out against the army on grounds partly ethical and partly political.'[122] Hobhouse himself told the conscription tribunal in Shoreditch Town Hall that he chose conscientious objection 'as a disciple of Jesus Christ and as an advocate of International Socialism.'[123] The two main founders of the No-Conscription Fellowship, Fenner Brockway and Clifford Allen, were ILP socialists. Brockway edited the *Labour Leader*, the ILP's official journal. Allen, also a political journalist, opposed the 'capitalist' war from the outset. In March 1916, requesting exemption from military service, he declared, 'there is something of divinity in every human being, irrespective of the nation to which he belongs.' As the war hastened the shift toward state power, Allen was attracted to guild socialism, defined by its defiance of the state.[124] Robin Page Arnot, an ILP member, attempted to evade conscription in May 1917 as a self-proclaimed revolutionary socialist; he served eighteen months in Wormwood Scrubs prison.[125] A significant number of these conscientious objectors made up the next

---

120 For Idealism's influence on ethical socialism, see W. H. Greenleaf, *The British Political Tradition* (New York, 1983), 2:139; and Himmelfarb (n. 96 above), p. 261. See also N. Dennis and A. H. Halsey, *English Ethical Socialism* (Oxford, 1988), pp. 1-12.

121 See Clifford Allen in Julian Bell, ed., *We Did Not Fight* (London, 1935), p. 28; T. C. Kennedy, *The Hound of Conscience: A History of the No-Conscription Fellowship, 1914-1919* (Fayetteville, Ark., 1981), p. 48; Vellacott (n. 47 above), p. 29. See also *Report of the Annual Conference of the I.L.P.* (London, 1916), pp. 72-4. The treasurer of the No-Conscription Fellowship was Edward Grubb, a Quaker and former secretary of the Howard Association for Penal Reform.

122 Leo Tolstoy, *What I Believe* (Geneva, 1888). S. Hobhouse's quote is in Bell, ed., p. 167. Hobhouse was from a wealthy Quaker family, but he renounced his inheritance of the family estate. For other details, see Hobhouse, *Forty Years and an Epilogue* (n. 49 above), pp. 174-7; A. G. Rose, 'Some Influences on English Penal Reform, 1895-1921', *Sociological Review* 3 (July 1955), pp. 34-7; Martin Ceadel, *Pacifism in Britain, 1914-1945* (Oxford, 1980), p. 43.

123 S. Hobhouse in Bell, ed., p. 166.

124 Quoted in Gilbert (n. 44 above), p. 5. See J. M. Winter, *Socialism and the Challenge of War* (London, 1974), p. 129. Bertrand Russell, chairman of the No-Conscription Fellowship during the final years of the war, also turned to guild socialism; see W. B. Gwyn, 'The Labour Party and the Threat of Bureaucracy', *Political Studies* 19 (December 1971), p. 385

125 See H. E. Roberts, 'Years of Struggle: The Life and Work of Robin Page Arnot', *Labour History Review* 59 (Autumn 1994), pp. 58-63.

generation of penal reformers. Their first contribution was to the Labour Research Department's enquiry launched in 1919.

The Prison System Enquiry Committee was a heavily socialist outfit, although a number of socialisms were represented: ethical, Fabian, and guild. The chairman was Sydney Olivier, a Fabian socialist who sought a social reconstruction in accord with the highest moral possibilities. Committee members included George Bernard Shaw, the Webbs, and G. D. H. Cole, the guild socialist.[126] Hobhouse and Brockway were, of course, the joint editors of the enquiry *English Prisons To-Day*, and they were assisted by Arthur Creech Jones, secretary of the Camberwell Trades and Labour Council, member of the Liberal Christian League, and also a conscientious objector. At times of greatest despair in prison, Creech Jones had been sustained by the faith 'that humanity was one, that I was not a tool of the governing classes to slay my fellow workmen in a senseless, suicidal slaughter, that I was trying in a poor way to bear testimony to the ideals of liberty, internationalism, & fraternity.'[127]

In summary, I would submit that another strand to the penal culture of these years was an ethical-cum-Christian socialism, a socialism that appealed to the common good, to social service, and to the power of moral character to perfect the person and to reform society. The overarching conclusions to this discussion of Edwardian penal culture seem inescapable. First, the set of attitudes to crime and punishment associated with the European positivist movement succumbed to the fatal embrace of British humanitarian, idealism, and ethical thought. If positivism extended a superficial 'scientific' allure to calls for penal reform, the bedrock sensibilities remained heavily 'moral'. Second, the different groups examined here assisted the continuing adherence to a more traditional jurisprudence and penality by the overlaps and relationships between their ideas and personnel. *En bloc*, these groups remained sceptical of the brave new world of positivist criminology and contributed to the widespread public disenchantment with the use of imprisonment.

VII

Third, let me turn to what I conceive to be the significant development, not to say achievement, of the years 1895-1922: the reduction in the number passing through the prison turnstile. In evidence to the Gladstone Committee, Sir Godfrey Lushington, late permanent under-secretary at the Home Office, uttered the immortal lines: 'I regard as unfavourable to reformation the status of a prisoner throughout his whole career; the crushing of self-respect; the starving of all moral instinct he may possess; the absence of all opportunity to do or receive a kindness; the continual association with none but criminals

---

126 N. MacKenzie and I. MacKenzie, *The First Fabians* (London, 1977), p. 62. See also Margaret Olivier, ed., *Sydney Olivier: Letters and Selected Writings* (London, 1948), chap. 3. The other committee members were penal reformers; see pp. 137-8 above.

127 Rhodes House Library, Arthur Creech Jones Papers, MS British Empire S 332, box 1, file 2, fol. 142: letter from Hounslow barracks, January 9, 1917.

... the forced labour and the denial of all liberty. I believe the true mode of reforming a man or restoring him to society is exactly in the opposite direction of all these.'[128] Lushington's approach to criminal justice was shaped by a commitment to the classical Liberal ideal of the free and responsible individual. He was extremely sceptical of the reformatory claims of institutions and of the medicalization of criminal justice. The Gladstone Committee accepted the accuracy of Lushington's description but could not agree 'that all of these unfavourable features are irremovable'.[129] Nevertheless, the principal achievement of the years after Gladstone took place where Lushington pointed: outside prison. The main tendency of the period was not the expansion of preventive confinement, the emergence of new islands in the 'carceral archipelago', but the extraordinary decrease in both the number of prisoners, especially those undergoing short sentences (and of the 200,000 committals to prison in 1909, no fewer than 125,000, or 61 percent, were under sentences of two weeks or less, over half of which were imposed on first offenders),[130] and of the prison estate.

Detention in penal institutions was still the mainstay of the criminal justice system in the early twentieth century. The cardinal characteristic of the prison system was the enormous procession of persons sentenced for non-indictable (or less serious) offences or those receiving sentences in default of payment of a fine for such offences as drunkenness, minor assaults, or contravention of borough by-laws. In 1899, prison receptions were running at 175,000 per annum, and the daily average population was about 14,500 in local prisons, 4,000 in the convict prisons. By 1903, receptions were close to 200,000, and the daily average population rose to 20,000. Thereafter, the numbers fell, but still in 1914 receptions numbered 150,000, and the daily average population stood at 18,000. Yet by 1918, receptions had plummeted to 30,000, and the daily average population was below 9,000. The pre-war peaks were never again ascended.[131] A number of factors explain this enormous decrease.

The Probation of Offenders Act, 1907, gave the courts another alternative to incarceration; the Children Act, 1908, excluded those aged under sixteen from prison. Of vital importance, the Criminal Justice Administration Act, 1914, did much to keep fine defaulters out of prison by allowing magistrates to give time for payment. Between 1910 and 1921, the numbers imprisoned annually for non-payment

---

128 *Minutes of Evidence to the Departmental Committee on Prisons*, C. 7702-I, *PP*, 1895, vol. 56, question 11482, p. 459. See J. Pellew, 'Law and Order: Expertise and the Victorian Home Office', in *Government and Expertise: Specialists, Administrators and Professionals, 1860-1919*, ed. R. MacLeod (Cambridge, 1988), pp. 68-9. For a subtle and convincing assessment of Lushington's evidence to the Gladstone Committee, one that reveals that the permanent under-secretary defended the existing 'punitive and deterrent' prison system yet faulted 'the general spirit of administration', for which Du Cane was responsible, see McConville, *English Local Prisons* (n. 5 above), pp. 625-32.

129 Report from the Departmental Committee on Prisons (n. 7 above), p. 12.

130 Victor Bailey, 'Churchill as Home Secretary: Prison Reform', *History Today* 35 (March 1985), p. 11.

131 K. Neale, 'Her Majesty's Commissioners, 1878-1978' (Home Office, London, 1978, private circulation), pp. 19-20; E. H. Sutherland, 'The Decreasing Prison Population of England', *Journal of Criminal Law and Criminology* 24 (1933), pp. 880-900. The figures specifically for women tell the same story. At the tum of the century, 50,000 women were annually committed to prison, largely for prostitution and drunkenness. In 1918, commitments were 14,922, a drop of 72 percent. The daily average in local prisons fell from about 3,000 to 1,500 prisoners. See E. Ruggles-Brise memo, October 22, 1918, HO 45/11543/357055/9.

of fines dropped from 85,000 to 15,000. And the wartime combination of full employment and drinking restrictions resulted in a fall-off in the numbers imprisoned for minor offences like drunkenness and vagrancy. The downward trend of the prison population, it should be stressed, was not the result of a decrease in crime but of the legislation mentioned above, the effect of war, and perhaps most crucially, of judicial willingness to move away from custody in their sentencing practice.[132] A credible explanation of the judicial mindset would require separate investigation, but it is possible that justices were influenced by the disenchantment with prison that pervaded the press and the Home Office from the 1880s and by their own experience of the revolving doors of short-term imprisonment. In addition, home secretaries, aware of the effect that sentencing practice had on penal administration, were increasingly prepared to supervise magistrates and judges, either directly by circular or indirectly via the lord chancellor.

I am familiar, finally, with the fall-back position of the revisionist historians, which is to insist that non-custodial measures actually extended the field of intervention available to the courts. Modern criminologists speak of the 'hidden discipline' of community corrections and suggest that it amounts to a qualitatively new and different pattern of penality. Perhaps so. For my part, I simply wish to insist that the revisionists' image of a prison system ingesting ever more prisoners into its insatiable maw is a gross exaggeration. We should be impressed rather with the pre-war mood of profound scepticism about imprisonment, local and convict, a mood that one Liberal politician in particular helped to shape.

Winston Churchill, home secretary for an animated eighteen months in 1910-11, assisted the reductionist tendency. The first principle of prison reform, declared Churchill, 'should be to prevent as many people as possible getting there at all. There is an injury to the individual, there is a loss to the State whenever a person is committed to prison for the first time.'[133] His opening gambit was audacious by the standards of any former or subsequent home secretary: 'to arrange matters so that next year there will be 50,000 fewer people sent to prison than this year.'[134] He not only wanted to reduce by one-third the annual committals to prison but also to reduce by 10-15 percent the daily average prison population and to abolish all imprisonment for periods of less than one month. To reduce this 'gigantic number of useless and often pernicious committals'[135] and avoid the unnecessary familiarization of offenders with prison surroundings, four main lines of advance were explored by Churchill.

First, for the 5,000 lads aged sixteen to twenty-one who were sent to prison each year for such

---

132 For the figures cited, see Sidney Webb and Beatrice Webb, *English Prisons under Local Government* (1922; reprint, London, 1963), p. 248; Ruggles-Brise, *English Prison System* (n. 51 above), pp. 224-5; A. Rutherford, *Prisons and the Process of Justice: The Reductionist Challenge* (London, 1984), pp. 123, 130, and 'Lessons from a Reductionist Era', in Robert and Emsley, eds. (n. 71 above), pp. 59-60. The rate of indictable crime recorded by the police rose by less than 10 percent between 1900 and 1921; see F. H. McClintock and N. H. Avison, *Crime in England and Wales* (London, 1968), pp. 18-24.

133 *Hansard Parliamentary Debates*, 5th ser., vol. 19 (July 20, 1910), col. 1344.

134 W. S. Blunt, *My Diaries* (New York, 1922), pt. 2, p. 335.

135 W. Churchill minute, August 13, 1910, HO 144/18869/196919/1.

offences as gaming and stone throwing, Churchill proposed a system of 'defaulters' drill', or physical exercise, to be administered at the police station. Second, there was to be time to pay fines. Third, imprisonment for debt was to be abolished. Finally, Churchill proposed a 'suspensory sentence' of imprisonment for petty offenders. As a result, first or infrequent offenders would never go to prison for less than one month.[136] Once the prisons were emptied of their dead-weight of petty criminals, Churchill envisaged a radical reorganization of the penal system. The prison population was to be classified into twenty main categories and distributed for specialized treatment to 'a regular series of scientifically graded institutions.'[137] Prisoners would be so distributed by a board of classification since no 'scientific uniform system' could be administered through the courts. Churchill was in office too briefly to bring more than a few of his many planned reforms to fruition. Accordingly, his contribution to keeping people out of prison was characterized more by promise than accomplishment. Nonetheless, Churchill contributed to the mood of disenchantment with short-term confinement in 'the general mixed prison', a mood that was rekindled in the postwar years by *English Prisons To-Day*.[138]

Churchill's tenure at the Home Office also serves to underscore a central ambivalence running through Edwardian Liberalism. The impulse toward scientific medicalization was continually balked by deep-rooted commitments to morality and liberty. This was noticeably evident in Churchill's approach to sentencing. Indeed, Churchill was more interested in the techniques of sentencing and commitment than in the administration of penal custody. His letters are far more concerned with who should or should not go to prison, and for how long, than what happened to them after they arrived. His thinking was dominated, moreover, by classical notions of justice, notably a just proportion between crime and penalty. He would have liked to set down a uniform scale of penalties for judges to follow. He had to make do with revising sentences piecemeal, searching the criminal calendars for cases of injustice, and exercising the prerogative of mercy to influence sentencing practice.[139]

Churchill was particularly disturbed by what he termed 'the first fruits of the [Preventive Detention] Act': 'It has greatly increased the severity of the criminal law, and the inequality of sentences', he wrote in June 1910.[140] Through new administrative rules, Churchill sought to mitigate the inequalities arising from the working of the act and to restrict the act's scope to the criminal who was a 'danger to society', whose newest crime was a serious offence.[141] So, too, Churchill insisted that Borstal detention be

---

136 Cabinet paper, 'Abatement of Imprisonment', in R. Churchill (n. 115 above), 2, pt. 2:1198-1203; HO 45/10613/194534. For the full history of imprisonment for debt, see G. R. Rubin, 'Law, Poverty and Imprisonment for Debt, 1869-1914', in *Law, Economy and Society, 1750-1914: Essays in the History of English Law*, ed. G. R. Rubin and D. Sugarman (Abingdon, 1984), pp. 241-99.

137 HO 144/18869/196919/1.

138 See also Webb and Webb, p. 248. And see Robert Badinter, *La prison républicaine (1871-1914)* (Paris, 1992): the penal reforms introduced in France (suspended sentence, conditional release, educational solutions for juveniles) all had as their aim the avoidance of the prison, not its reformation.

139 See Radzinowicz and Hood (n. 2 above), pp. 770, 773; Addison (n. 38 above), pp. 112-17; Thomas (n. 113 above), pp. 40, 46-7.

140 HO 45/10589/184160/23.

141 HO 45/10589/184160/25a. See also Thomas, pp. 41-5; Addison, pp. 118-19.

reserved for those who had committed serious offenses, by which he meant rape, robbery with violence, and burglary. Some check must be imposed, he minuted, on the increasing tendency of the courts to inflict sentences of three years' imprisonment at Borstal for offences that would ordinarily receive six months or less. And linking both provisions of the Prevention of Crime Act, 1908, together, Churchill wrote: 'Within proper limits both the Borstal and Preventive Detention systems are desirable as being beneficial and humane refinements upon the ordinary prison system. Beyond those limits they cannot be defended and will quickly draw upon themselves a current of public displeasure. I should certainly not consent to be responsible for any system which can be shown to aggravate the severity of the Penal Codes.'[142]

Churchill *was* ready to sanction prolonged detention (of up to two years) in curative labour colonies for habitual offenders convicted repeatedly of vagrancy and drunkenness, and he inclined to the eugenic in proposals to deal with the feeble-minded.[143] This could be expected of a young politician who had donned the coat of the New Liberalism in all its progressive and welfarist colours. The influence of positivist criminology was never such, however, as to shake Churchill's dependence on the classical principles of deterrence, just proportion, and uniformity of treatment. In the face of 'scientific reform', he displayed a meticulous regard for what he termed 'the rights of convicted criminals against the State.'[144] He resisted the advance of indeterminate detention, the emblem of the new penology, except with regard to the segregation of mental defectives.[145] And he curbed the excesses, as he saw them, of the semi-indeterminate sentences of preventive detention and Borstal training.

VIII

The debate on English prisons between 1895 and 1922 was framed by the unchanging structures of a harsh prison system and the related determination to diminish the number of persons passing through prison gates. Despite the good intentions of the Gladstone Committee, the pace of progress in humanizing prisons was glacial. The prison discipline meted out to conscientious objectors during the war was almost identical to that suffered by Oscar Wilde, a quarter century before: 'Deprived of books, of all human intercourse, isolated from every humane and humanising influence, condemned to eternal silence, robbed of all intercourse with the external world, treated like an unintelligent animal, brutalised

---

142 HO 144/18869/196919/2.

143 See HO 144/A60866/4; HO 45/10520/138276/57; Radzinowicz and Hood, pp. 372-5; Addison, pp. 123-6; Searle (n. 74 above), pp. 107-8. According to his friend, William Scawen Blunt, Churchill was 'a strong eugenist'; see Blunt, p. 399 (entry for October 20, 1912). When the Cabinet discussed the issue of 'the unfit' in December 1911, Churchill presented Dr. A. F. Tredgold's article, 'The Feeble-Minded — a Social Danger', which warned of the peril of 'national degeneracy'. See Ted Morgan, *Churchill: Young Man in a Hurry, 1874-1915* (New York, 1982), p. 289.

144 *Hansard Parliamentary Debates*, 5th ser., vol. 19 (July 20, 1910), Col. 1354.

145 HO 45/1085/193548/1.

below the level of any of the brute-creation, the wretched man who is confined in an English prison can hardly escape becoming insane.'[146] Is this Oscar Wilde or Hobhouse and Brockway? It hardly matters, since it could serve as an accurate description of the prison regime both in 1895 and 1921. The special measures proposed by the Gladstone Committee met with no greater success than the attempts to improve prison conditions. If Borstal training was lauded as a progressive step in the treatment of young adult offenders, the various forms of preventive detention for habituals, defectives, inebriates, and vagrants met with considerable judicial, administrative, and public scepticism, so much so that all withered on the vine. To see all this as a new penal structure, as an integral part of a 'modern penal complex', seems terribly wide of the mark.

Nor is it any more convincing to see positivism as the main ideological inspiration of the limited changes that did take place. Judges, prison administrators, and penal reformers were generally familiar with the ideas of individualization, classification, and indeterminacy, but true converts were thin on the ground, and their ranks became thinner as the first flush of enthusiasm dissipated. The new scientific knowledges, whether Lombrosian positivism or British eugenics, far from being incorporated into penal practice, were held at arm's length. Judges and prison officials remained loyal to the classical credo of moral culpability, a just measure of punishment, and uniformly administered discipline. In this they were guided by a jurisprudence and a civic consciousness that drew inspiration from philosophic idealism. Lombrosian criminal man was born, his action the determined outcome of biological inheritance, his fate to be incarcerated in perpetuity to protect society against his dangerousness. By contrast, Idealist criminal man was a responsible agent, his action the willed violation of an explicit social right, his fate to have his bad will annulled by a punishment proportionate to the importance of the right violated. As such, the prisoner possessed an individual human worth, and the state had the duty to safeguard his 'reversionary rights' by sending him out better fitted to assume the role of citizen. This philosophy shaped the *idée fixe* of a host of administrators, reformers, and social workers in the early twentieth century, and, as I have argued elsewhere, was the predominant influence on the patterns of criminal policy and practice in the 1920s and 1930s.[147]

If there was a sea change in prison policy and practice between 1895 and 1922, then it was surely the massive reduction in the number of short-sentence prisoners. The tightening of urban regulations in the nineteenth century had brought growing numbers of citizens into conflict with the law through drunkenness and street offences and growing numbers into the prisons, either directly or in default of fine payment. In their campaigns to make inroads into this mass of petty imprisonments, the reformers were aided by the pre-war Liberal home secretaries, Herbert Gladstone and Winston Churchill, by a war that for various reasons reduced the size of the social 'residuum' from which much of the short-stay

146 Wilde, *The Soul of Man* (n. 10 above), p. 193.

147 Bailey, *Delinquency and Citizenship* (n. 59 above).

prison population was drawn, and by a change in judicial sentencing practice about which we still know too little. From the vantage point of the present day, when the number of prisoners continues to rise inexorably, the steep drop in both prison receptions and daily average population in the first quarter of the 20th century is remarkable. It was this statistical change, based in turn on a change in the judicial, prison, and political temper, on which Sidney and Beatrice Webb concluded their historical study of the administration of English prisons, published simultaneously with Hobhouse and Brockway's *English Prisons To-Day*. Echoing Sir Godfrey Lushington's evidence to the Gladstone Committee, the Webbs wrote:

> The reflection emerges that, when all is said and done, it is probably quite impossible to make a good job of the deliberate incarceration of a human being in the most enlightened of dungeons. Even the mere sense of confinement, the mere deprivation of liberty, the mere interference with self-initiative — if in any actual prison the adverse regimen were, in practice, ever limited to these restrictions — could hardly ever, in themselves, have a beneficial result on intellect, emotions or character. We suspect that it passes the wit of man to contrive a prison which shall not be gravely injurious to the minds of the vast majority of the prisoners, if not also to their bodies. So far as can be seen at present, the most practical and the most hopeful of 'prison reforms' is to keep people out of prison altogether![148]

---

148 Webb and Webb (n. 132 above), pp. 247-8.

A notice is posted outside Pentonville Prison in London, to announce the execution of Neville Heath, 16 October 1946

6

The Shadow of the Gallows

The Death Penalty and the British Labour Government, 1945-51

It is queer to look back and think that only a dozen years ago the abolition of the death penalty was one of those things that every enlightened person advocated as a matter of course, like divorce reform or the independence of India. Now, on the other hand, it is a mark of enlightenment not merely to approve of executions but to raise an outcry because there are not more of them.

George Orwell

The punishment prescribed by English law for murder in the first half of the twentieth century was death. A judge had to pronounce this sentence upon a person convicted of murder, except in two special classes of cases: persons under eighteen years of age at the time of the offence and pregnant women.[1] He had no discretion to impose any less severe sentence. While retribution survived only in a symbolic form elsewhere in the criminal law, capital punishment, as Oxford criminologist Max Grunhut maintained, was a 'powerful relic of retaliation in kind'. The law still reflected the ancient concept that every murderer forfeits his life because he has taken another's life: 'He that smiteth a man, so that he die, shall be surely put to death'.[2]

In practice, the rigidity of the law was mitigated by the exercise of the royal prerogative of mercy, which rested in the hands of the home secretary, the government minister responsible, among other things, for the police and prison services. The effect of a reprieve, before 1948, was to reduce the sentence to penal servitude for life.[3] In the fifty-year period from 1900 through 1949, 1,210 persons

I am grateful to the University of Kansas for the General Research Fund award that made it possible to complete this article. I would also like to thank Sheila Blackburn, Karl Brooks, Jonathan Clark, Ken Morgan, Elaine Reynolds, Lisa Steffen, the members of the British Seminar at Kansas University, and the anonymous reviewers for their valuable comments on an earlier draft of this article.

1   From 1887, executions for those under eighteen were virtually abolished by use of the prerogative of mercy. The Children Act, 1908, formally abolished the death penalty for persons under sixteen; the Children and Young Persons Act, 1933, confirmed the existing practice of reprieve by ending capital punishment for those under eighteen. The Sentence of Death (Expectant Mothers) Act, 1931, prohibited the death sentence on a pregnant woman. In addition, by the 1922 Infanticide Act, a woman charged with the death of her 'newly born' — a term undefined in the Act, and narrowly interpreted by the courts, but enlarged in 1938 to apply to the death of a child under twelve months of age — would be punished for the commission of manslaughter rather than murder. This change meant little in practice, because no woman had been executed for the murder of her baby since 1849. It simply brought law and practice into conformity. See Gordon Rose, *The Struggle for Penal Reform* (London, 1961), pp. 202, 206; Christopher Hollis, *The Homicide Act* (London, 1964), p. 13; P. G. Richards, *Parliament and Conscience* (London, 1970), p. 37.

2   Max Grunhut, 'Murder and the Death Penalty in England', *Annals of the American Academy of Political and Social Science* 284 (1952), p. 158; Exodus 21:12.

3   This sentence did not typically mean life, of course. Of the 253 commuted death sentence cases where release was authorized between 1920 and

were sentenced to death in England and Wales (1,080 men and 130 women). Five hundred and fifty-three, or 45.7 percent, had their sentences commuted or respited.[4] A larger percentage of female murderers (90.8 percent) benefited from the prerogative of mercy than males (40.3 percent). The first figure indicates considerable reluctance to apply the death penalty to a woman. The remaining 632 (or 52.2 percent of those sentenced to death) were executed for murder (621 men and 11 women), making an execution rate of 13 a year between 1900 and 1949.[5] The annual number of hangings was in large part, then, a function of the use of the reprieve power.

The law reformers of the early nineteenth century had successfully whittled the number of capital offences down to the four that remained in the twentieth century: murder, treason, piracy with violence, and arson in government dockyards and arsenals. But they and their successors, while restricting the application of the death penalty to the gravest crimes, had failed to secure the complete abolition of capital punishment. The only proposal of the Royal Commission on Capital Punishment (1864-66) to be accepted was the prohibition of public execution; from 1868, executions were carried out within prison confines. The six subsequent attempts between 1866 and 1891 to divide murder into two degrees, capital and non-capital, which the Royal Commission had also proposed (on the model widely used in the United States), all failed. By 1918, the influence of the abolitionists was at its nadir. But from that point on, things improved rapidly. The emergence of the Labour Party in 1906, and its rise to become the main opposition to the Conservative Party by the 1920s, changed the parliamentary dynamics of the capital punishment debate. For the first time, abolitionists had the sympathetic ear of a principal political party.

The achievements of the first two Labour governments of 1924 and 1929-31 were limited. Nonetheless, by the end of the 1930s, the number executed each year was at an all-time low; support for abolition in Parliament and among the public was arguably at an all-time peak. Little wonder that hopes ran high in abolitionist circles when the first Labour government with a parliamentary majority was elected in 1945, at the end of the Second World War, on a flood-tide of popular support for a juster, more humane society. It was confidently expected that the 1938 Criminal Justice Bill, which had been

---

1948, 58 (or 23 percent) were released after less than five years' detention, 141 (or 56 percent) after less than ten years' detention, and 236 (or 93 percent) after less than sixteen years' detention. See *Home Office, Capital Punishment*, Cmd. 7419 (London, 1948), 1.

4 Forty-seven were certified insane (respited to Broadmoor); 506 were reprieved (their sentence commuted to penal servitude).

5 Twenty-three had their conviction quashed by the Court of Appeal. The figures in this paragraph are drawn from *Royal Commission on Capital Punishment, 1949-1953*, Cmd. 8932 (1953; reprint, 1965), 13 (table 3), 19, and 298-301 (appendix 3, table 1); Select Committee on Capital Punishment, Parliamentary Papers (*PP*), 1930-31, VI (15), Report, 14; Harry Potter, *Hanging in Judgment: Religion and the Death Penalty in England* (New York, 1993), pp. 143, 243, n. 4. The death penalty was, in practice, confined to murder, except for wartime executions for treason. In addition, eighteen U.S. soldiers (over half of whom were African Americans) were executed for murder or rape (or a combination of the two) in England during the Second World War, under the Visiting Forces Act, 1942. See J. Robert Lilly and J. Michael Thomson, 'Executing US Soldiers in England, World War II', *British Journal of Criminology* 37 (1997): 262-88. Between 1900 and 1965, the year when capital punishment for murder was suspended, 780 civilians were hanged in Britain after being convicted of murder. See Christie Davies, 'The British State and the Power of Life and Death', in *The Boundaries of the State in Modern Britain*, ed. S. J. D. Green and R. C. Whiting (Cambridge, 1996), p. 342.

abandoned at the outbreak of war in 1939, would be resurrected, and that a clause eliminating the death penalty for murder would find a place in the new version. The 1947 Criminal Justice Bill, though shaped almost entirely by pre-war thought, was part and parcel of the postwar Labour government's program to reconstruct the social and economic framework of the country. Like its 1938 predecessor, the postwar bill concentrated upon two categories: young and persistent offenders. It sought to keep young offenders out of prison, especially by providing new alternatives to imprisonment, and to keep recidivists either in long-term 'preventive detention' or under 'corrective training'. It also abolished corporal punishment (except in prisons), swept away the anachronistic nomenclature of 'hard labour' and 'penal servitude', and provided for improvements in the organization and staffing of the probation service. In all, the 1947 bill, like its precursor, aimed to eclipse the idea of retribution by further extending the principle that punishment should fit the criminal, not the crime. What better moment to abolish capital punishment, the last relic of a barbarous penal code, the one punishment in which reformation has no place? As the *News Chronicle* declared at the height of the ensuing battle over the death penalty, abolition 'has been regarded as a pinnacle of criminal reform which we must attain before we can hold up our heads in the modern world'.[6]

Thus, there were great expectations; abolitionists felt victory to be within their grasp. In November 1945, the executive committee of the National Council for the Abolition of the Death Penalty advised members that the end of the war and the election of a Labour government 'should bring success to our efforts for Abolition within the next few years', to ensure which 'we must create from one end of the country to the other a public opinion insistently demanding Abolition'. Yet three years later, following intense discussion of the subject both within and without Parliament, the abolitionists were disappointed, divided, and almost empty-handed. Anticipating the end of the death sentence for murder, abolitionists had to settle for a Royal Commission on Capital Punishment (1948-63), whose terms of reference restricted it to the possible means of limiting the operation of the death penalty, as distinct from its abolition. Few abolitionists expected an unimpeded procession toward abolition. They knew they still had worthy opponents in the senior judges, some of the principal Home Office mandarins, and the entire House of Lords. Yet few abolitionists expected the death penalty to become the paramount issue in the parliamentary debates on the Criminal Justice Bill and in the press and public discussion of the impending penal reform. Few would have forecast that the only revolt of Labour MPs (or the Parliamentary Labour Party) seriously to embarrass the Attlee government would arise over capital punishment. Few would have predicted that one of the two issues on which the House of Lords would exercise its delaying power would be capital punishment.[7] Clearly, something went

---

6   *News Chronicle*, June 2, 1948, p. 2. For details of the 1938 and 1947 Criminal Justice Bills, see Victor Bailey, *Delinquency and Citizenship: Reclaiming the Young Offender 1914-1948* (Oxford, 1987), pp. 255-65, 291-302.

7   NCADP, miscellaneous publications, MSS 16B/ADP/4/4/9/1, Modern Records Centre, University of Warwick Library. The other issue on which the Lords used their delaying power was the nationalization of iron and steel. See K. O. Morgan, *Labour in Power, 1945-51* (Oxford, 1985), pp.

terribly wrong for the abolitionists.

Exactly what went wrong and why is the theme of this article. How and why did the Labour government, despite its massive majority in Parliament and a long-standing commitment to abolition, fail to get rid of the death penalty? Why was this 'window of opportunity' to abolish capital punishment shut for another decade and a half? The answers to these questions will be sought primarily in the realm of government and Parliament. This is not as limiting as it may sound. An enduring condition of the conflict over capital punishment was that its crucial battles were fought in the main legislative fora. To *limit* the use of the death penalty, executive fiat in the form of more reprieves would suffice; but to *abolish* the penalty required changes in the law of murder that only Parliament could make. Moreover, the subject evoked such widespread lay interest, not to say passion, that the struggle over it had to be fought out in full view of the public. Accordingly, the answers to these questions have an essentially political character. Above all, the Labour government failed to take full responsibility for the death penalty. This, in turn, arose from the inclination of the government to see capital punishment as peripheral to its main business, as an issue best left to the private conscience of individual MPs, and hence to a free rather than a 'whipped' vote of the House of Commons.[8] The bulk of the government's troubles flowed from these peculiarities of the debate over the death penalty. There is, however, an additional explanation of the government's failure, one particular to the 1940s, yet one that lends wider significance to the entire evaluation.

The postwar world was much less hospitable to penal reform than the abolitionists had anticipated. For a start, the war crimes trial at Nuremberg, which began on November 20, 1945, affected the postwar mood. Judgement on the twenty-two war criminals was delivered in October 1946; twelve of the accused were sentenced to death, and ten were immediately hanged.[9] For some people, Nuremberg lent justification to a retributive approach to indigenous murder. More influential was the rise in officially recorded crime and the 'moral panic' the figures generated.[10] The press was full of the

---

62, 84; R. F. V. Heuston, *Lives of the Lord Chancellors, 1940-1970* (Oxford, 1987), p. 127.

8   The members of Parliament who have the job of delivering each party's vote in the House of Commons are known as 'whips'; hence, a 'whipped' vote is one in which MPs have no choice but to vote for their party; a free vote is when MPs are allowed to vote the way their conscience dictates. The free vote is generally permitted when the subject is deemed to be an issue of public morality that cuts across party lines. Any divisions are not taken as votes of confidence in the government. Almost all bills dealing with capital punishment have been put to free votes on some or all of their stages. It is arguable, however, that capital punishment rarely cut across party lines, despite the pretence that it did. For most of this century, Labour and Liberal MPs have typically voted against capital punishment, while Conservative MPs have typically voted in favour. See Davies, 'Power of Life and Death', p. 343.

9   One of those condemned to death — Martin Bormann — was sentenced *in absentia*; Hermann Goring cheated the hangman by committing suicide. See Peter Calvocoressi, *Nuremberg: The Facts, the Law and the Consequences* (New York, 1948); Werner Maser, *Nuremberg: A Nation on Trial* (New York, 1979).

10   See Harold L. Smith, ed., *Britain in the Second World War* (Manchester, 1996), pp. 16-18; Terence Morris, *Crime and Criminal Justice since 1945* (Oxford, 1989), pp. 34-7, 96 (table 7.2). For the concept of the moral panic, see Stanley Cohen, *Folk Devils and Moral Panics: The Creation of the Mods and Rockers* (London, 1972). See also, Stanley Cohen and Jock Young, eds., *The Manufacture of News: Social Problems, Deviance, and the Mass Media* (Beverly Hills, 1973).

senseless violence of juvenile gangs and of the sordid and meaningless nature of contemporary homicide, a theme taken up by George Orwell in his 1946 essay on the changed character of murder.[11] This crime-wave narrative had an effect upon penal thought, notably by reinvigorating the belief that punitive measures could not be surrendered. The reforming tide of the 1920s and 1930s can be exaggerated, but there is no doubt that this tide was turned back in the 1940s, at least to some degree, by the combined pressure of the senior judges, the lord chancellor, and the House of Lords, and with the effective deployment of majority public opinion. Inevitably, the debate over the abolition of the death penalty became embroiled in this pronounced attack upon reformist sentiment. The fact that at one of the most propitious moments for abolition, an impassioned debate ended with the survival of this retributive symbol, should tell us something about the political, judicial, and popular resistance to the reforming ethos in punishment. In the post-war struggle to lay the axe once and for all to the gallows tree, a struggle that, as James Christoph affirmed, 'cut more deeply into British life ... than at any time since the first two decades of the nineteenth century', we have one of the more instructive moments in the history of modern British penology.[12]

I

In February 1810, Sir Samuel Romilly addressed the House of Commons on the subject of the frequency of capital punishment. '[T]here [is] no country on the face of the earth', he declared, 'in which there [have] been so many different offences according to law to be punished with death as in England'.[13] In Romilly's day, there were some 220 capital offences. Every felony, with the exception of petty larceny and maiming, was capital. As Fowell Buxton reminded the Commons in 1821, 'the law of England has displayed no unnecessary nicety, in apportioning the punishments of death. ... Kill your

---

11 Orwell contrasted the 'domestic poisoning dramas' of the pre-war era with the *cause célèbre* of the war years, the Cleft Chin Murder, in which an American army deserter and an eighteen-year-old ex-waitress murdered a taxi driver with £8 in his pocket. 'The background', explained Orwell, 'was not domesticity, but the anonymous life of the dance-halls and the false values of the American film'. See 'Decline of the English Murder', in *George Orwell, Decline of the English Murder and Other Essays* (Harmondsworth, 1965), p. 12. Of course, Orwell had a penchant for drawing a contrast between the ordered stability of the past and the awfulness of the present. See also Harry Hopkins, *The New Look: A Social History of the Forties and Fifties in Britain* (London, 1963), pp. 207-8; Peter Hennessy, *Never Again: Britain, 1945-51* (New York, 1994), pp. 445-6.

12 James B. Christoph, *Capital Punishment and British Politics* (London, 1962), p. 190. I readily concede that a full measurement of the last point would require a broad-ranging penological and cultural analysis. I am currently preparing such a study, under the provisional title, *The Rise and Demise of Rehabilitation: Punishment, Culture and Society in Modern Britain*.

13 Parl. Deb., Commons, 15, Feb. 9, 1810, 366. The history of capital punishment has attracted considerable attention in recent decades. For the most important contributions, see Leon Radzinowicz, *A History of English Criminal Law and Its Administration from 1750*, vols. 1-4 (London, 1948-1968); Douglas Hay *et al.*, (eds.), *Albion's Fatal Tree* (London, 1975); E. P. Thompson, *Whigs and Hunters: The Origin of the Black Act* (London, 1975, reprinted Breviary Stuff, 2013); J. M. Beattie, *Crime and the Courts in England, 1660-1800* (Princeton, 1986); Peter Linebaugh, *The London Hanged* (London, 1991); V. A. C. Gatrell, *The Hanging Tree: Execution and the English People, 1770-1868* (Oxford, 1994). See also Elizabeth O. Tuttle, *The Crusade against Capital Punishment in Great Britain* (London, 1961), pp. 3-13; Potter, *Hanging in Judgment*, chaps. 1-3; B. P. Block and John Hostettler, *Hanging in the Balance: A History of the Abolition of Capital Punishment in Britain* (Winchester, 1997), chaps. 1-4.

father, or catch a rabbit in a warren — the penalty is the same! Destroy three kingdoms, or destroy a hop-bine — the penalty is the same!'[14] The Bloody Code, as it was known, provided the most extensive capital jurisdiction in Europe. Only a small and declining proportion of those capitally condemned were actually executed, thanks to the regular use of the prerogative of mercy, but this only induced reformers like Romilly to assert that the non-execution of the law was not the best way to mitigate the law's severity. The reformers pressed, instead, to exempt from capital punishment as many offences as possible. This alone, they argued, would improve the detection, conviction, and punishment of delinquents. A stubborn rearguard action by the main representatives of *ancien régime* justice — Lord Chief Justice Ellenborough and Lord Chancellor Eldon — slowed the amelioration of the penal code, but limb after limb of the Fatal Tree dropped away.[15] At Victoria's accession in 1837, the number of capital crimes had fallen to fifteen, and over the next twenty-five years the remaining capital offences were reduced to the four that came down to the twentieth century. Just the trunk of the gallow's tree was left, on which alone was strung the murderer.

The succeeding phase in the crusade against capital punishment was much less effective. For abolitionists, the next fifty years were fallow ones, though they did have their moments. In 1866, the Royal Commission on Capital Punishment unanimously recommended a gradation of murder, by which many homicides then punishable by death would become non-capital, and five of the twelve Commissioners even declared themselves in favour of total abolition. No progress was made toward the establishment of degrees of murder, but an amendment to the 1868 bill providing for private executions proposed abolition. The amendment failed, at least in part because of the powerful defence of the death penalty, 'when confined to atrocious cases', by renowned liberal John Stuart Mill, who argued that 'the short pang of a rapid death' was a less cruel way of deterring the criminal from crime than 'immuring him in a living tomb'.[16] For the rest of the century, parliamentary bills were introduced to establish degrees of murder, but the difficulty of defining which murderers deserved death and which did not proved insuperable. Bills also continued to press for abolition but the opportunity had passed. The creation of the Court of Criminal Appeal in 1907, by diminishing the possibility of a fatal miscarriage of justice, further weakened the abolitionist case against the irrevocable nature of the death penalty.[17] The revival of the abolitionist cause had to wait until after the First World War.

In the early 1920s, a succession of sensational murder trials and executions focused public attention on the question of capital punishment. One such was the execution of Edith Thompson in January 1923

---

14 Parl. Deb., Commons, 5, May 23, 1821, 904.

15 See Gerald Gardiner and Nigel Curtis-Raleigh, 'The Judicial Attitude to Penal Reform', *Law Quarterly Review* 65 (1949), pp. 199-205; Derek Beales, 'Peel, Russell and Reform', *Historical Journal* 17 (1974), pp. 873-82; Boyd Hilton, 'The Gallows and Mr Peel', in *History and Biography: Essays in Honour of Derek Beales*, ed. T. C. W. Blanning and David Cannadine (Cambridge, 1996), pp. 88-112.

16 See E. Roy Calvert, *The Death Penalty Enquiry* (London, 1931), p. 3; Turtle, *Crusade*, pp. 17-20; Hollis, *Homicide Act*, 13; Parl. Deb., Commons, 191, Apr. 21, 1868, 1049.

17 See Rose, *Struggle*, pp. 27-8; Potter, *Hanging in Judgment*, chap. 8; HO 45/12914/154425/9.

for alleged complicity in the murder of her husband by her lover. Many felt she was hanged for adultery as much as for murder; and rumours began to circulate that she had gone to the scaffold in a state of semi-collapse. The governor and chaplain of Holloway prison were both deeply distressed by this harrowing execution, and the executioner attempted suicide a fortnight later. Simultaneously, weeklies like the *Spectator* began to acknowledge that 'public opinion has for some time been inclining against the death penalty'.[18] The public seemed disturbed by the irrevocability of the death penalty and especially by the idea of hanging women. Significantly, in 1922, the Infanticide Act had reduced the penalty for women who killed their 'newly-born' from murder to manslaughter, thereby ending the 'black cap folly' of judges pronouncing the death sentence on women on whom all knew the sentence would not be executed. The last and most critical ingredient for a renewed abolitionist campaign was the addition of the Labour Party. From this point on, indeed, the movement for the abolition of capital punishment became closely associated with the British labour movement.

In 1923, the annual conference of the Labour Party passed a resolution urging the party to secure 'the substitution of reformative treatment instead of the punitive treatment of criminals at present obtaining and the abolition of the death penalty'. Soon letters urging abolition were pouring into the Home Office from local Labour Party branches and Labour Churches.[19] Then, in January 1924, Labour was asked and agreed to form a ministry, though the party was in a minority in the House of Commons. According to the Howard League for Penal Reform (established in 1921), over one hundred MPs in the new Parliament, or one-sixth of the entire body, were in favour of abolition. Unfortunately, the first Labour government, which survived only until the autumn, did nothing for abolition. Home Secretary Henderson had intended to submit a memorandum to the cabinet on the question of capital punishment and was ready in February 1924 to tell the House that he would soon define the government's attitude. The prime minister, James Ramsay MacDonald, would have none of this. His office informed Henderson: 'the Government cannot, within the first few months, commit themselves to every desire they have'.[20] As a result, two private member's bills failed to make progress, and the March deputation of the Howard League, led by Labour stalwart George Lansbury, was fed the standard Home Office line: abolition had never commanded a majority in any Parliamentary division, there was little evidence of any public desire for abolition, and there was no feasible substitute for capital punishment. All Henderson added by way of encouragement was: 'You must agitate public opinion. You must get it on your side. You must raise in the House of Commons an interest which becomes compelling'.[21]

18 See Potter, *Hanging in Judgment*, p. 121; Block and Hostettler, *Hanging in the Balance*, pp. 86-8; *Spectator*, Jan. 13, 1923, p. 46. See also *Justice of the Peace*, Sept. 6, 1924, p. 536.

19 *Labour Party Conference Report, 1923* (London, 1923), 250; HO 45/12914/154425/28, 31 and 32.

20 *Howard Journal* 1 (1924), p. 114; HO 45/12914/154425/57. The home secretary told the House, therefore, that the government had come to no decision on the subject: Parl. Deb., 5th ser., Commons, 170, Feb. 25, 1924, 84.

21 HO 45/19044/455787/31; *The Times*, Mar. 25, 1924, p. 11; *Howard Journal* 1 (1925), p. 191.

The result of the first Labour government was to demonstrate the need for a central abolitionist body, capable of conducting a concerted campaign over an extended period. In 1925, the National Council for the Abolition of the Death Penalty (NCADP) was established, with Roy Calvert as secretary. Calvert was the complete abolitionist, combining passionate commitment, moral earnestness, and scientific rigour. 'My purpose is not a sentimental one', he wrote in *Capital Punishment in the Twentieth Century* (1927) — the classic statement of the case for abolition; '[m]y objection to the death penalty is based upon the conviction that it is both futile and immoral'.[22] It was Calvert's wife, however, who most accurately evoked his *modus operandi*: 'He wished to see a general advance to an enlightened and rational humanity in the treatment of all law breakers, and viewing the campaign with the eye of a strategist he saw the Death Penalty as the stranglehold which enabled the forces of reaction to keep their ground'.[23] For the rest of the decade, the NCADP held hundreds of meetings on capital punishment around the country, circulated thousands of leaflets and pamphlets, and orchestrated countless parliamentary questions. Ties with the labour movement were understandably close. In early 1927, a pro-abolitionist manifesto, signed by twenty-six Labour leaders and sent to 7,000 Labour Party branches and kindred bodies, helped to bring the issue before the party's rank and file. In late 1928, the bill to abolish capital punishment, sponsored by the NCADP, which was read for a first time in the Commons, was supported by most of the Labour leadership, including J. R. Clynes, the next Labour home secretary. This was the first occasion, moreover, on which Parliament had voted against capital punishment, albeit by a margin of one (119 to 118).[24] Also in the course of the 1920s, a campaign orchestrated by Labour and Liberal MPs, including future Labour Prime Minister Clement Attlee, succeeded in abolishing the death penalty for military offences (except for treachery, mutiny, and desertion to the enemy).[25]

The inter-war peak of the abolitionist campaign was reached in October 1929 with the first full-scale debate in the twentieth century on the abolition of the death penalty, culminating in the appointment of the Select Committee on Capital Punishment. The precondition of this ascent was the election of a new House of Commons in 1929, believed by the NCADP to contain a 'substantial abolitionist majority', and of a new Labour ministry, with a home secretary, J. R. Clynes, who was thought to be 'personally sympathetic' to abolition. In late October 1929, William Brown presented a

---

22 E. Roy Calvert, *Capital Punishment in the Twentieth Century* (London, 1927), preface to the first edition. For Calvert, see Rose, *Struggle*, pp. 203-5.

23 Foreword to Calvert, *Capital Punishment*, 5th ed. (1936), quoted in E. H. Jones, *Margery Fry* (London, 1966), p. 124.

24 *Howard Journal* 2 (1927), p. 124; Second Annual Report of the NCADP (1926-27), p. 3; Parl. Deb., 5th sen, Commons, 223, Dec. 5, 1928, 1220-6; Fourth Annual Report of the NCADP (1928-29), p. 4. This vote was of no practical import, since the majority in favour of abolition was too small to persuade the government to give the necessary parliamentary time for the remaining stages of the bill.

25 See Davies, 'Power of Life and Death', pp. 349-51; J. H. Brookshire, *Clement Attlee* (Manchester, 1995), p. 155. This campaign is described more fully in John McHugh, 'The Labour Party and the Parliamentary Campaign to Abolish the Military Death Penalty, 1919-1930', *Historical Journal* 42 (1999), pp. 233-49.

motion in the House of Commons for abolition. Home Secretary Clynes immediately indicated that even if the motion passed, no bill would be introduced by the government until after a committee of inquiry. Brown reluctantly accepted Sir Herbert Samuel's amendment for the appointment of a Select Committee.[26] Abolitionists were bewildered and for long believed that the resolution against capital punishment would have been carried by the House, had not Clynes and Samuel muddied the water.[27] But they were soon mobilizing to win the argument before the Select Committee.

The committee consisted of members of the different parties in proportion to their strength in the House: seven Labour, six Conservative, and two Liberal MPs. All the Conservative representatives held retentionist views, even though possibly as many as a quarter to a third of all Conservative MPs were of abolitionist persuasion. Of the thirty-one British witnesses who gave evidence, ten advocated abolition, thirteen retention, and eight favoured a reduction in the number of death sentences and executions. Pointedly, the committee refused to hear from the judges because their opposition to reform was a foregone conclusion.[28] Of the twenty-three acting or retired government officials to give evidence, only four favoured abolition. Sir Alexander Paterson, the most reform-minded of the Prison Commissioners, was not among them. Echoing John Stuart Mill's speech, Paterson gave it as his opinion that death was more humane than the 'rotting death' of a long prison term, though this hardly squared with his other main point, that six out of every seven persons sentenced to death should be reprieved, given that the average term served by a man undergoing life imprisonment was then over thirteen years. The primary fact that emerged from the enquiry was that abolition had been successful in the European countries that had tried it.[29] Unfortunately, however, the committee divided on strictly party lines, the Conservatives refusing to accept the final report. The Labour majority reported against the possibility of grading murders into two or more degrees and instead proposed the total suspension of capital punishment for a trial period of five years. Abolitionists hailed the result as the first recommendation by a public committee that the death penalty should be abolished; but the press, the opposition, and the Home Office all argued that the report was not representative of the views of its members. The Labour government, before it fell in August 1931, consistently refused to grant time for the Commons to discuss the report, though Clynes himself never wished to block debate on the subject.[30]

---

26 Fourth Annual Report of the NCADP (1928-29), 5; A. Fenner Brockway to J. R. Clynes, June 28, 1929, in HO 144/19045/455787/71; Howard League executive committee meeting, July 12, 1929, Howard League Minute Books, MSS 16B/1/1, Modern Records Centre, Warwick University Library; Parl. Deb., 5th ser., Commons, 231, Oct. 30, 1929, 241- 66.

27 See E. Roy Calvert to J. R. Clynes, May 12, 1931 in HO 45/15739/546977/36. Cf. *Law Journal* 68 (1929), p. 284.

28 See Calvert, *Death Penalty Enquiry*, p. 27; Hollis, *Homicide Act*, pp. 14-15; Select Committee on Capital Punishment, *PP*, 1930-31, VI(15), Report, pp. 1-99; Arthur Koestler, *Reflections on Hanging* (New York, 1957), p. 26.

29 Calvert, *Death Penalty Enquiry*, p. 27; Hollis, *Homicide Act*, p. 103. The abolitionist countries were Belgium, Denmark, Holland, Italy, Norway, Sweden, and Switzerland. See Calvert, *Death Penalty Enquiry*, p. 109.

30 See HO 45/17481/584763/16; HO 45/15739/546977/32. In the mid-1930s, the Labour Party Conference passed a resolution, introduced by renowned suffragist Frederick Pethick-Lawrence, that urged the next Labour government to give legislative effect to the Select Committee's recommendation for the abolition of the death penalty.

In the thirties, opinion in favour of abolition continued to ripen. An influential advocate was the archbishop of York, William Temple, a member of both the NCADP and the Labour Party, and a rare example of a Church of England leader willing to declare for abolition. Temple had impressed upon the 1930 Select Committee that capital punishment devalued rather than sanctified human life. In 1935 he wrote an essay on the death penalty, subsequently reprinted in pamphlet form by the NCADP, in which he insisted that the debate over the death penalty had an importance that went beyond the subject itself. Retention or abolition, he said, 'must depend upon the moral principles accepted by the community for the government of its penal code'. He concluded by declaring that 'few public actions would at the present time so much demonstrate and secure an advance in the ethics of civilization as the abolition of the Death Penalty'. The archbishop also believed that public opinion, in many cases, was against the execution of criminals. The barrister Gerald Gardiner was similarly convinced that, since the publication of the evidence given before the Select Committee, 'there has been a marked change of opinion among the members of the Bar', though Lord Chief Justice Hewart remained adamantly retentionist.[31] In response, perhaps, to the state of public opinion, the proportion of reprieves increased steadily. In the years on either side of the thirties, 60 percent of those sentenced to death were executed; between 1930 and 1939, the figure fell to 43 percent. Moreover, the average of 8.2 executions each year in the thirties was the lowest of any decade in the twentieth century.[32]

There was another important way of developing parliamentary opinion. Every Wednesday in the House of Commons backbenchers could make private members' motions. The government was not bound by the result, but since the 'whips' were not on, MPs could vote without the restraint of party loyalty. In November 1938, Conservative MP Vyvyan Adams, who was also a member of the executive committee of the NCADP, tried his hand with a motion welcoming legislation to abolish the death penalty for five years. He launched the first full-scale Commons debate on capital punishment since 1929. The under-secretary of state at the Home Office, Geoffrey Lloyd, opposed the motion on the grounds that the experimental period was too short to enable the effect of abolition to be measured; that the difficulties involved in an alternative penalty would not reveal themselves in a five year period; and that opinion in favour of abolition had not increased. Even so, the division (ayes 114, noes 89) showed a majority in favour of the legislation. Among the abolitionists were ten future Labour ministers, including James Chuter Ede, home secretary in the postwar Labour government. But the present National Government, led by Conservative Prime Minister Neville Chamberlain, refused to embrace the

31 The Archbishop of York, 'The Death Penalty', *Spectator*, Jan. 25, 1935, p. 112; Tuttle, *Crusade*, p. 49; Potter, *Hanging in Judgment*, chap. 11. Temple was made archbishop of Canterbury in 1942. His death in 1944 prevented his involvement in the postwar debate over the death penalty. His successor, Geoffrey Fisher, was cut from a different cloth. See also G. Gardiner to Sir John Gilmour, April 16, 1935, in HO 45/17481/584763/213B; Lord Hewart, 'The Sentence of Death. Why It Still Remains a Necessity', *News of the World*, cutting in HO 45/17481/584763/27A.

32 See Parl. Deb., 5th ser., Commons, 416, Nov. 29, 1945, 1753-54.

principle of abolition, contending that since the resolution was passed in a thinly attended House on a private members' day, it expressed the view neither of the House nor of the country on this question.[33]

Fortunately for the abolitionists, another opportunity arose within the year. The Conservative politician, Sir Samuel Hoare, whose great-grandfather had been an abolitionist in Romilly's time, insisted on going to the Home Office in May 1937 in order to advance the cause of penal reform. He wished to introduce legislation that would incorporate the findings of several committees (namely those on young and persistent offenders and on corporal punishment) and the ideas of Prison Commissioner Sir Alexander Paterson. As for the death penalty, Hoare later recorded: 'I was instinctively drawn towards the total removal from the Statute Book of a punishment that was altogether out of keeping with the kind of penal reforms that I had at heart'. Alas, he also believed that to avoid a controversy that might endanger the rest of the Criminal Justice Bill, he had to exclude a clause to abolish the death penalty. The issue, he maintained, needed a separate bill upon which Parliament could come to a decision. The heated exchanges on the abolition of *corporal* punishment, which the House of Lords would have opposed had the war not intervened, give some credence to Hoare's position. The abolitionists still saw a chance, however, of raising the issue. When the Criminal Justice Bill was under consideration in standing committee in the spring of 1939, a new clause was presented proposing abolition for a five year period. In view of Home Secretary Hoare's opposition, the committee rejected the new clause.[34] When war broke out a few months later, criminal justice reform was by consent shelved until after the war.

An abolitionist balance sheet of the inter-war years would have to include both debit and credit entries. The grand prize had certainly eluded them, despite the best efforts of a new abolitionist body and campaign and the support of one of the two main political parties in Parliament. A worrying trend was already evident, moreover, for Labour's leadership tended to be more enthusiastic abolitionists when in opposition than when in government. In office, Labour seemed more concerned to follow parliamentary opinion than to lead it. Nonetheless, abolitionists could take heart from the Report of the Select Committee, which demonstrated that capital punishment could be successfully relinquished in Britain, as it had been in much of western Europe. Public opinion was also surely moving towards abolition. In a November 1938 Gallup poll, to the question 'Should the death penalty be abolished?' 45 percent of those who held an opinion answered Yes, 55 percent said No, while 11 percent expressed no opinion. Furthermore, executions were becoming rare events. Even J. S. Mill had accepted that if the time came when home secretaries, 'under pressure of deputations and memorials', shrank from their duty, 'and the threat becomes ... a mere *brutum fulmen*; then, indeed, it may become necessary ... to

---

33   Parl. Deb., 5th ser., Commons, 341, Nov. 16, 1938, 954-1012. The other abolitionists who became Labour ministers included A. V. Alexander, Aneurin Bevan, James Griffiths, F. W. Pethick-Lawrence, Emanuel Shinwell, and Joseph Westwood. See also HO 45/18066/ 677344/34.

34   Viscount Templewood (Samuel J. G. Hoare), *The Shadow of the Gallows* (London, 1951), p. 10; Bailey, *Delinquency*, pp. 143-6; Hollis, *Homicide Act*, p. 15.

abrogate the penalty'.[35] And there was yet another straw in the wind: abolition of capital punishment now ran in tandem with the movement to carry through long-needed reforms in criminal law and its administration. Indeed, the abolition of the death penalty became for many penal reformers a deeply symbolic test of the country's commitment to the reformative treatment of prisoners.

Whichever party had been in power in 1945 would have been obliged to introduce a Criminal Justice Bill. The reformers were doubtless hoping, however, that Labour would be in government, and for good reasons. As early as 1942, when the war was far from over, Herbert Morrison, socialist home secretary in the Coalition Government, considered appointing a committee on the reformative treatment of prisoners. He turned for advice to the political scientist, and member of the Labour Party's National Executive Committee, Harold Laski. The latter submitted a strident report on behalf of a Royal Commission to create an effective public opinion in favour of a Criminal Justice Bill. He drew attention to the 'painfully small part played by the judges in the reform of the Criminal Law' and to their hostility to 'the revision of penal concepts in the light of advancing medical knowledge'. Consequently, Laski warned against a commission with a judge as chair 'and a flock of barristers and solicitors among its members'.[36] In the event, the idea of a Royal Commission was superseded by the appointment of the Advisory Council on the Treatment of Offenders, with a particular brief to examine juvenile delinquency. But this did nothing to diminish Morrison's desire to prepare for legislation. In April 1944, he asked Prime Minister Winston Churchill if he could reintroduce the Criminal Justice Bill. Though Churchill advised waiting on the subject, Morrison stood firm, asking again to 'stake out a claim for a Penal Reform Bill in our legislative programme of social reconstruction after the war'.[37] The issue would not brook postponement, he insisted; all the penal reform groups, at war's end, would press the government to reintroduce the Criminal Justice Bill.

A year later, the war was over, and a Labour government had indeed been elected, with a majority of 146 over all other parties (393 MPs out of 640). Britain now became a laboratory of social engineering. Over one-fifth of the economy was taken into public ownership; the framework of the welfare state was erected. 'Not since the Washington of the early New Deal in 1933', declared historian Ken Morgan, 'had the governmental agencies in a democratic country been so caught up in experimentation and social advance'.[38] The socialist tide flowed strongly until mid-1947, when economic problems and a reinvigorated Conservative opposition forced Labour to retrench. For three years, however, the country had witnessed a torrent of reformist legislation. The condition of criminal justice, moreover, was an integral part of this postwar reform program.

---

35   George H. Gallup, ed., *The Gallup International Public Opinion Polls: Great Britain, 1937-75* (New York, 1976), 1:11; Parl. Deb., Commons, 191, April 21, 1868, 1051.

36   June 13, 1942, in HO 45/21948/884452/1. For Laski, see K. O. Morgan. *Labour People* (Oxford, 1987), pp. 91-100.

37   See Bailey, *Delinquency*, pp. 287-9; HO 45/21948/884452/1.

38   K. O. Morgan, *The People's Peace: British History, 1945-1990* (Oxford, 1992), p. 30.

James Chuter Ede, the new home secretary, had the task of winning a place for penal reform in the program of reconstruction. In April 1946, he decided to introduce the Criminal Justice Bill of 1938, subject to a few modifications. At the legislation committee in early July, however, Ede was asked by Herbert Morrison, leader of the House of Commons, to withdraw the bill until the next session. Ede declined, warning that the government 'would be exposed to criticism if they concentrated entirely on economic measures and did not include ... some social and humanitarian measures'. Two days later, Ede informed the permanent secretary at the Home Office that the bill was safe. In fact, it was not. In October 1946, Morrison again asked Ede to omit the Criminal Justice Bill from the 1946-47 legislative program, and he was forced to comply.[39]

At this point, it was still an open question whether a provision to abolish or suspend the death penalty would get into the new bill. It is to this issue we now turn. The goal is to explain the Labour government's conduct in the lead up to the Second Reading of the Criminal Justice Bill in November 1947, by which time the government had decided to omit an abolitionist clause from the bill, but to allow a free vote in the House of Commons if an abolitionist amendment were introduced.[40]

II

In March 1947, the pace quickened. Morrison asked Chuter Ede to submit a policy paper on the Criminal Justice Bill. Of most significance, for present purposes, is the home secretary's view that any amendment to abolish or suspend capital punishment 'should be resisted on the ground that it is inappropriate that such a far-reaching change in the law should be included in a Criminal Justice Bill, and that, if any such change in the law were to be effected it should be after full consideration in a separate Bill dealing solely with this subject'. At the Lord President's Committee meeting held on March 7, therefore, Chuter Ede remarked that most controversy was likely to centre on the abolition of *corporal* punishment.[41]

---

39 HO 45/21950/884452/75 and 77. The press and penal reform lobby felt that a scheme of penal reform deserved a place in Labour's programme. See *The Times*, Mar. 12, 1946, 5 and HO 45/21951/884452/99.

40 In this task I have been helped by Gordon Rose, Elizabeth Tuttle, and James Christoph, all of whom, in the early 1960s, examined the Labour government's contribution to the movement to abolish the death penalty. See Rose, *Struggle*; Tuttle, *Crusade*; Christoph, *Capital Punishment*. They did so, however, before the cabinet and other official papers were available for public scrutiny. More recently, Lord Windlesham used a few of the relevant official papers in his study of penal policy making. See Windlesham, *Responses to Crime, vol. 2, Penal Policy in the Making* (Oxford, 1993), chap. 2. And Sir Leon Radzinowicz reviewed the lead-up to the Royal Commission on Capital Punishment, 1949-53, of which he was a member, but without any special inquiry into the main questions. See Radzinowicz, *Adventures in Criminology* (London, 1999), pp. 245-52. It seems worthwhile, therefore, to return to this ground in the light of the available cabinet papers, of Home Office and Lord Chancellor's Office papers, and of the memoirs of some of the main political personalities.

41 HO 45/21951/884452/99; 'Criminal Justice Bill', memo by Home Secretary, Mar. 2, 1947, LP (47) 39, attached to CP (47) 182, June 16, 1947, CAB 129/19. The lord chief justice, Lord Goddard (appointed by Prime Minister Attlee in January 1946), had already informed the home secretary that he and two of his fellow judges did not agree that corporal punishment should be entirely abolished. Goddard to Ede, Nov. 28, 1946, HO 45/21951/884452/86. The lord chancellor, Lord Jowitt, had said much the same to the attorney-general, Sir Hartley Shawcross: 'I am

Indeed, the main dispute that broke out between Home Secretary Ede and Lord Chancellor Jowitt was over corporal punishment. Ede stood his ground, reminding the meeting that on the matter of abolishing corporal punishment, 'the Labour Party were deeply committed by their attitude in 1938'.[42] He had an ally in the attorney-general, Sir Hartley Shawcross, who said he strongly supported the abolition of corporal punishment. Additionally, Shawcross argued that the bill should provide also for the abolition or suspension of the death penalty and that '[t]he attitude of the Bench to past proposals for the reform of the criminal law did not suggest that their judgment in this matter was reliable', a brave line from a young government law officer.[43] Even so, Lord Chancellor Jowitt was invited to put his reservations on paper and allowed to consult the lord chief justice and certain other senior judges about the proposals.[44]

The exchange of views at the meeting of the Lord President's Committee also spurred the law officers into action. In early April 1947, Shawcross and Sir Frank Soskice (the solicitor-general) sent a strongly worded statement to both Jowitt and Chuter Ede. The proposed abolition of flogging, the law officers proclaimed, 'carries out what has always been Labour Party policy'. Corporal punishment had neither deterrent value nor reformative effect. 'There are', they continued, 'the strongest moral objections to its use as barbarous and degrading to society'. They took the same view about capital punishment:

> If, as it is agreed, the present Bill provides a suitable opportunity for the abolition of flogging, we can see

---

one of these old-fashioned people who believe in corporal punishment though I would abolish the Cat. I would be very sorry to see the birch or the cane disappear'. LCO 2/3340. The Lord President's Committee was a sub-cabinet or general purposes committee; it had referred to it questions of domestic policy not assigned to other committees. See Herbert Morrison, *Government and Parliament* (Oxford, 1954).

42   LP (47) 8th meeting, Mar. 7, 1947, CAB 132/6. In the 1930s, the birching of young offenders (to whom corporal punishment was effectively restricted) had been almost abandoned by the courts. The wartime rise in delinquency, however, led to renewed birching, at least until 1943, when a controversial case in the Hereford juvenile court again deterred courts from ordering the birch. See Rose, *Struggle*, p. 213; Geoffrey Pearson, *Hooligan: A History of Respectable Fears* (London, 1983), p. 261, n. 92.

43   Ibid. The attorney- and solicitor-general were the chief legal advisers to the executive. The attorney-general was not a member of the cabinet, but he saw all the relevant cabinet papers, and he would attend cabinet meetings to advise upon legal or constitutional issues. See J. Ll. J. Edwards, *The Law Officers of the Crown* (London, 1964), pp. 174-5, and chap. 9, *passim*. The position of lord chancellor was something of a constitutional oddity. He participated in all three branches of government: as cabinet minister, speaker of the house of lords, and head of the judiciary. See John Griffith, *Judicial Politics since 1920* (Oxford, 1993), p. 65. The Labour Party was congenitally distrustful of the senior judiciary and legal profession. This was only intensified by the mistrust of Lord Chancellor Jowitt by the more left-wing members of the Labour government (notably Nye Bevan). The fact that Jowitt boasted in late 1947 that he had never appointed 'a member of my own Party' to be a judge corroborated the doubts about Jowitt, which had their origin in his thin socialist credentials. He generally took a detached attitude to cabinet quarrels and party-political questions. See Robert Stevens, *Law and Politics: The House of Lords as a Judicial Body, 1800-1976* (Chapel Hill, 1978), pp. 336-7, and *The Independence of the Judiciary* (Oxford, 1993), pp. 78-9, 114; 'Message from Britain: The Lord Chancellor's Address in Cleveland', *American Bar Association Journal* 33 (1947), p. 1180.

44   Jowitt was persuaded that corporal punishment had a deterrent effect and that judges should have the increased power to inflict corporal punishment 'in all cases involving violence, particularly where women and children are concerned'. See Jowitt to Lord Chief Justice, Mar. 7, 1947, LCO 2/3340; Jowitt to Ede, Mar. 28, 1947, HO 45/21951/884452/99. The lord chancellor's correspondence also reveals that he had doubts about other provisions of the Criminal Justice Bill concerning young offenders, believing that they were unduly lenient. Above all, he thought the middle of a crime wave was not the moment to shout from the housetops that juvenile criminals could not be whipped.

no reason why it should not be equally appropriate for the abolition of capital punishment if the abolition of such punishment is otherwise desirable. We do not think that the Labour Party in the House would be likely to accept the position that this matter could not be dealt with in the present Bill unless an assurance were given that special legislation would be introduced. The case in favour of abolition of capital punishment seems to us overwhelming and the grounds for its abolition very similar to those above urged for the abolition of flogging.

Moving to a loftier moral plane, they wrote feelingly:

> The knowledge that society is deliberately hunting a man to his death, and when it has caught him taking away his life with the hideous trappings of legal execution, cannot fail to lessen the respect for the sanctity of human life. … It is absolutely no answer to say that the convicted man has himself taken human life, since by carrying out the act of execution society is rendering itself culpable of precisely the same act as that for which the condemned man has been convicted.

They strongly urged, therefore, that the opportunity be taken in the bill to give effect to 'what has been for many years a humanitarian conception associated with the Labour movement. There can, we think, be no excuse for what is virtually a running away from an obvious opportunity to introduce this overdue reform'. The law officers had firmly nailed their colours to the mast. In his cover letter, Shawcross added that strong views were held in the party on corporal and capital punishment and the government could be defeated if they opposed abolition, with the whips on.[45]

In May 1947, the Criminal Justice Bill was slotted for the 1947-48 session. The abolitionists were relieved, since it would allow time in the present Parliament to override a veto of the House of Lords, which a later date would not have done. The Lords still had the power to delay a bill's passage for two years (though the government had plans to abbreviate their delaying power). The cabinet now had to resolve how they wished to deal with corporal and capital punishment. At the cabinet meeting of June 19, Ede refused to give way on the flogging issue, and Jowitt finally conceded that 'for political reasons it would be very difficult to do less than had been proposed in the Bill introduced in 1938'.[46] On the

---

45 Shawcross had been associated with the Howard League for Penal Reform in the 1920s and had been a member of the Advisory Council on the Treatment of Offenders, the body established in August 1944 by Herbert Morrison, when home secretary, to plan postwar penal reform. See *New Statesman*, Feb. 21, 1975, pp. 234-6; Bailey, *Delinquency*, p. 288. Shawcross had always opposed capital punishment, but in 1945-46, he acted as the chief British prosecutor at the Nuremberg trial. 'So far as the Nazi war criminals were concerned', Shawcross wrote many years later, 'I did feel that if ever the death sentence was deserved it was in most of the Nuremberg cases'. See Shawcross, *Life Sentence: The Memoirs of Lord Shawcross* (London, 1995), p. 130. The citations in this and the previous paragraph are all drawn from HO 45/21951/884452/102B. See also Shawcross to Jowitt, Apr. 16, 1947, HO 45/21951/ 884452/102B. Jowitt replied to Shawcross on Apr. 19, 1947: 'On corporal and capital punishment I have no doubt you are right in saying that strong views are held in the Party. I wonder how much thought and knowledge have gone to the formation of these views?' See LCO 2/ 3340. In an earlier letter to Shawcross, Jowitt had spoken to the issue of the death penalty: '… it may well be true that our Party would demand the abolition of capital punishment. I think they would be unwise in so doing, particularly at the present time. … At least let us realise that if we are going to indulge in humanitarian conceptions we may expose the ordinary citizen to added peril'. See Jowitt to Shawcross, Apr. 10, 1947, LCO 2/3340.

46 CP (47) 182, June 16, 1947, 'Criminal Justice Bill', memo by Home Secretary, CAB 129/19; minute by F. Graham-Harrison, Assistant Private Secretary to the Prime Minister, June 18, 1947, PREM 8/739; CM (47) 55th conclusions, Cabinet meeting, June 19, 1947, CAB 128/10. At first,

desirability of abolishing the death penalty, ministers were divided. Retentionists (Morrison undoubtedly, Ede and Jowitt presumably) argued that public opinion was not yet ready for abolition, that the abnormal amount of robbery with violence made abolition unwise, that the judges 'were convinced that the fear of capital punishment was a real deterrent' and an effective alternative punishment was wanting, and that abolition at home would make it hard to justify its retention in the colonies and in the British Zone of Germany. Abolitionists (Shawcross indubitably, Aueurin Bevan most probably, and Shinwell possibly) argued that there was no firm evidence of its deterrent effect (particularly in the case of unpremeditated murders), that the opinion of His Majesty's judges was unreliable, and that the government supporters in Parliament who had studied the matter were unanimously in favour of abolition. In the face of such a divergence of opinion, the prime minister suggested that the cabinet return to the issue at a later meeting.[47]

For the next month, the Home Office worked on the question. The guiding light in these internal discussions was the permanent secretary, Sir Alexander Maxwell. He was particularly concerned about the parliamentary strategy that seemed to be evolving. The plan was to introduce the bill without a clause abolishing capital punishment. Then, in the Second Reading debate, the suggestion would be made that, since the question aroused differences of opinion transcending party lines, the government would leave the matter to a free vote of the entire House. (This would, in fact, be the course ultimately followed by the cabinet.) For Maxwell, pitfalls abounded on this path. 'To leave the matter to a free vote of the House', he argued, 'would be an indication that the Government had not made up its mind on the question'. If an abolitionist clause was introduced on a free vote, this would only inspire the House of Lords to delete the clause from the bill and defend their action on the ground that the government had given no clear lead to Parliament. At that point, the government would feel unable to leave the matter any longer to a free vote and thus would have to decide 'either to propose that [the] Lords amendment be rejected or to propose it be accepted and to put the Whips on'. All this, it has to be said, bears an uncanny approximation to the difficulties that soon overtook the government.

Maxwell's main advice, therefore, was to take the bull by the horns. Unless the government was prepared to resist an amendment proposing abolition, however strong its supporters in the Commons, 'their right line would be to take the initiative and to insert in the Bill as introduced a Clause for the abolition of the death penalty. If the Government are going ultimately to accept a Clause to this effect, and to resist any attempt on the part of the House of Lords to delete it, their better course would be

---

the cabinet was dominated by Attlee, the prime minister; Herbert Morrison, lord president and leader of the Commons; Ernest Bevin, foreign secretary; Hugh Dalton, chancellor of the exchequer; and Sir Stafford Cripps, president of the Board of Trade.

47   CM (47) 55th conclusions, Cabinet meeting, June 19, 1947, CAB 128/10. The prime minister was no partisan on the question of capital punishment, even though he had been involved in securing the abolition of the death penalty for military offences (see text at note 25 above). For Attlee, I suspect, capital punishment was not a manifesto pledge, but a 'policy novelty' for which he had little time. Compare Morgan, *Labour People*, p. 140.

themselves to propose the Clause'.[48] Maxwell's thinking imposed itself on the home secretary's July 8 memorandum for cabinet discussion.[49]

At the meeting of July 15, 1947, it became crystal clear that the cabinet was trapped in a logical circle of its own creation. The discussion went something like this. Since ministers could not agree on the merits of the question, the right course was to tell the Commons that because there were differences of opinion transcending party lines, the matter would be left to a free vote of the House. If this resulted in an abolitionist amendment, however, one that was accepted by the Commons but then rejected by the Lords, the government would be in an awkward position. There was much to be said, therefore, for uncoupling the death penalty question from the Criminal Justice Bill. But such was the sentiment in the House and Party that a *quid pro quo* of an uncoupling would be a government promise of abolitionist legislation in a later session. For this, ministers had to agree that the death penalty ought to be abolished. But this was exactly what ministers could not agree upon![50]

Not until early November 1947 did the cabinet return to the issue. It then learned from Herbert Morrison that his recent meeting with the Parliamentary Labour Party (PLP) indicated that while government supporters would accept the absence in the bill of a provision for the abolition of capital punishment, they had every intention of moving an abolitionist amendment. The cabinet resolved that in these circumstances the decision on this issue should be left to a free vote.[51] The next day the bill was published.

The main principle of the Criminal Justice Bill was warmly received by the press. 'Modern penal doctrine', said *The Times*, 'has firmly established that simple retribution ... is not a proper objective of secular justice'. 'It is right', said the *Daily Telegraph*, 'that no individual with the capacity for self-redemption should be denied an opportunity to re-qualify for the privileges and responsibilities of citizenship'. There was less unanimity concerning the government's decision to omit an abolitionist clause. *The Times* inclined toward an abolitionist position. 'Capital punishment is so repulsive that no civilized people would continue it unless convinced that there is no other means of protecting life.' On the day of the bill's Second Reading, the same paper declared that the experiment of suspending capital punishment for five years 'would provide both parties to the controversy ... with the facts required for a final settlement of their difference'. Lord Templewood doubted the wisdom of retaining capital punishment. The 'savage executions that have disgraced Europe have convinced me', he said, 'that the

---

48 Minutes of June 25 and July 1, 1947, HO 45/21959/884452/203. By July 1947, the Parliamentary Penal Reform Group, organized by the Howard League, had got 187 (mostly Labour) MPs to sign a memorial to the home secretary asking him to include in the Criminal Justice Bill a provision to suspend the death penalty for a five-year experimental period. In addition, a joint deputation from the League and the NCADP met Home Secretary Ede and gained the impression that he had no firm views on the subject of capital punishment. See Christoph, *Capital Punishment*, pp. 36-7; Morris, *Criminal Justice*, p. 79.

49 CP (47) 200, July 8, 1947, 'Abolition of the Death Penalty', memo by Home Secretary, CAB 129/19.

50 CM (47) 61st conclusions, Cabinet meeting, July 15, 1947, CAB 128/10.

51 CM (47) 84th conclusions, Cabinet meeting, Nov. 3, 1947, CAB 128/10.

time has come for us to give a conspicuous example of our detestation of brutal punishments'. The secretary of the NCADP, Frank Dawtry, complained that the bill's intention to fit treatment to the criminal, not the crime, 'will seem to be contradicted if the death penalty remains, for most murderers are first offenders'. 'Who could have imagined', said C. H. Rolph in the *New Statesman*, 'that this immensely powerful Government, containing probably more idealists to the square vote than any of which there is biographical record, would reject the opportunity afforded by a great penal reform Bill to abolish the death penalty?'[52]

In the final days before the Second Reading debate, the cabinet made two more decisions: one, that the home secretary should advise the Commons that there would be serious risks in abolishing capital punishment in the unsettled conditions following a major war (which amounted to advising the House to reject the amendment abolishing the death penalty); and, two, that ministers who dissented from the government's advice should refrain from speaking in the debate, but should be free to vote according to their convictions.[53]

On November 27, 1947, the Second Reading of the Criminal Justice Bill took place. At the close of his speech, Home Secretary Ede stated the government's position on capital punishment. The reasons for retaining the death penalty were, first, that it acted as a deterrent; second, that the war and postwar rise in crime made it dangerous to experiment with abolition; and, third, that little public support existed for such an experiment. However, 'recognising that this is a matter on which very strong individual conscientious feelings are held and that the division does not follow the usual party lines', the government, said Ede, would 'leave the final decision to a free vote of the House', and 'no attempt will be made to coerce the conscience of any individual hon. Member'. (No-one thought to ask whether this meant minister as well as backbencher.) For the opposition, Osbert Peake promised that any vote on capital punishment would be free on his side of the House also. He himself felt that capital punishment should be retained in view of the increases in violent crime, ending his speech with something of a *non sequitur*: 'There were few protests, if any, about capital punishment at the time the Nuremberg Trials

---

52 *The Times*, Nov. 5, 1947; *Daily Telegraph*, Nov. 5, 1947; *The Times*, Nov. 27, 1947; *Observer*, Nov. 9, 1947, press cuttings in HO 45/21953/884452/128B. Templewood (formerly Sir Samuel Hoare) was now president of the Howard League and a publicly proclaimed abolitionist. See also *Manchester Guardian*, Nov. 11, 1947, press cutting in HO 45/21962/884452/ 263; 'Cat and Hangman', *New Statesman*, Nov. 15, 1947, p. 387.

53 CP (47) 306, Nov. 13, 1947, 'Criminal Justice Bill: Capital Punishment', memo by Home Secretary, CAB 129/22; Norman Brook minute, Nov. 14, 1947, PREM 8/739; CP (47) 310, Nov. 17, 1947, 'Criminal Justice Bill: Capital Punishment', memo by Secretary of State for Scotland, CAB 129/22. Norman Brook was the secretary of the cabinet. For Brook's influence, particularly through his 'steering-briefs' for Attlee, see Peter Hennessy, *Cabinet* (Oxford, 1986), p. 18. In Scotland, only eight death sentences were imposed in the fifteen years between 1929 and 1944. None was carried out. This situation was largely the result of the acceptance by the Scottish courts of a doctrine of diminished or impaired responsibility, which, if established, reduced the crime from murder to culpable homicide. Thus, by the attitude of the courts, and the exercise of the prerogative, the death penalty had been virtually abolished. And during this time crimes of violence did not increase. Nonetheless, the Scottish secretary, Arthur Woodburn, still felt the government should give a lead in favour of retaining the death penalty. See also CM, (47) 89th conclusions, Cabinet meeting, Nov. 18, 1947, CAB 128/ 10; Norman Brook minute, Nov. 18, 1947, PREM 8/739.

took place, and certain very depraved men were brought to a very proper end'.[54]

Sydney Silverman, a left-wing Labourite and outspoken leader of the abolitionists in Parliament, greeted the bill as 'a great act of courage and a great act of faith', before noting caustically that the increase in violent crime had led the previous (Templewood) and present (Ede) home secretaries to change their minds about capital punishment in precisely opposite directions; and that the same increase led Ede to conclude that corporal punishment (inflicted in the main for violent crime) should be abolished, while capital punishment (for a crime known to be little affected by general crime waves) should be retained. These confusions aside, Silverman acknowledged that the government 'have done wisely and generously, in agreeing to leave this matter to the free, unfettered, judgement of Members of the House'.[55] Otherwise, the Second Reading debate passed off without incident, and the crucial vote on the death penalty was postponed for several months.

What conclusions can we draw from this recital of the governments conduct? There are, I would submit, five possible explanations for its behaviour. The first is that given by the home secretary during the Second Reading debate: a cocktail of deterrence, public opinion, and crime rates. It has considerable validity. The senior judges, Lord Chancellor Jowitt, and Chuter Ede all subscribed to the deterrent efficacy of the death penalty. They also took notice of, and were not above exploiting, opinion polls that indicated there were at least two retentionists for every abolitionist. When a deputation from the NCADP came to see him in July 1947, Ede specifically asked for the council's view on the results of a recent Gallup Poll.[56] And Ede and Jowitt were not alone in underlining the war and postwar crime rise. Indeed, it is arguable that the increase in recorded crime, interpreted by many as a sign of the erosion of traditional moral standards, did more than anything to turn back the tide of abolition and of penal reform in general. The recorded incidence of murders and crimes of violence was markedly higher than before the war. No longer was the rise in juvenile delinquency reassuringly ascribed to the willingness of police and public to use the reformed system of juvenile justice, as it had been in the 1930s, but rather, as even Lord Templewood insisted in February 1947, because 'moral restraints have lost much of their power in the confused and restless world of today'.[57] The moral crisis was aggravated

---

54 Parl. Deb., 5th ser., Commons, 444, Nov. 27, 1947, 2150-51, 2161.

55 Ibid., 2186-9. Silverman made the obligatory abolitionist attack upon the judges, who 'have always been on the side of harshness, cruelty, corporal punishment, and capital punishment', and 'have always been demonstrably wrong' (2188). For Silverman, see Emrys Hughes, *Sydney Silverman: Rebel in Parliament* (London, 1969), p. 90; Christoph, *Capital Punishment*, p. 42; *Dictionary of National Biography, 1961-70* (Oxford, 1980), pp. 941-4. Silverman was something of a thorn in the government's flesh. In October 1946, he had been a critic also of the government's foreign policy, believing it to be too pro-American. See Emanuel Shinwell, *I've Lived Through It All* (London, 1973), p. 188.

56 July 7, 1947, HO 45/21959/884452. The Gallup Poll had asked: 'In this country most people convicted of murder are sentenced to death. Do you agree with this or do you think that the death penalty should be abolished?' The result was: Agree, 69 percent; Abolish, 24 percent; No opinion, 7 percent. See Gallup, ed., *Public Opinion Polls*, p. 156. Abolitionists soon realized, as Koestler remarked, 'that governments only use public opinion as a shield when it is convenient to them'. When public opinion demanded reprieves, government could just as easily disregard it. See Koestler, *Reflections*, p. 164.

57 The number of indictable (or serious) offences known to the police rose by 76 percent between 1938 and 1947. More specifically, the annual average of cases of murder (of persons aged over one year) increased from 95 between 1936 and 1939 to 121 between 1945 and 1948. Crimes of

in July by the trial of the three young men (aged 17, 20, and 23) who had shot Alec de Antiquis while robbing a south London jeweller's shop. All were found guilty of murder, and following unsuccessful appeals, the two eldest were executed on September 19, 1947. In a letter to the *Times*, three weeks before the Second Reading debate, Mr. Curtis-Bennett declared that to let such young men know 'that they can still kill, and live, is surely madness and an invitation to murder'. Tellingly, the 1947 Criminal Justice Bill, unlike the 1938 bill, provided for 'detention centres', residential institutions in which the regime would be brisk and the sentence brief, in order to apply a 'short, sharp shock' to young offenders. There seems little doubt that this new measure was a *quid pro quo* to appease a judiciary that resented being deprived of the power to order corporal punishment.[58]

There is evidence, too, for an explanation that emphasizes the desire not to lose the Criminal Justice Bill by including a clause that could arouse controversy. Like Sir Samuel Hoare in 1938, Ede and his officials did not want to endanger a bill that could improve the treatment of young and recidivist offenders, and a bill that had all-party support, by embroiling it in the contentious debate over the death penalty. Perhaps they thought that the proposal to deprive the courts of all power to impose flogging sentences would load the bill with as much controversy as it could carry in a session. Just prior to the bill's publication, Morrison and Ede appealed to Labour backbenchers to save the possible (a penal reform bill) by foregoing the perfect (a bill that also abolished capital punishment).

There is less evidence, at least before mid-1948, for a third explanation that says abolition was a potential vote-loser and had to be dropped. I would agree that Herbert Morrison's pragmatic socialism meant he believed, as Francis Williams said, 'in not getting too far ahead of public opinion'. From mid-1947, Morrison was the main advocate of 'consolidation', which sought to slow the pace of reform and included avoiding policies that unnecessarily alienated voters. He was told that the bulk of the working-class (or broadly Labour) voters favoured hanging and that abolitionism tended to be a middle-class fad. Moreover, the government had a huge social and economic program that Morrison, as leader of the House of Commons, did not want imperilled by a crisis over what seemed to him a fringe issue. Yet Morrison, by suspending the parliamentary party's standing orders, had permitted Labour backbenchers wider liberty to express disagreement with the leadership, and he was well versed in allowing backbench revolts quietly to defuse. This is doubtless what he expected to occur with the revolt

---

violence against the person (committed by persons aged seventeen and above) rose from 1,467 in 1938 to 2,952 in 1948, or from 4.7 to 8.9 per 100,000 population. Indictable sexual offences known to the police rose by 54 percent between 1945 and 1950. And the daily average prison population went up from close to 13,000 in 1944 to over 17,000 in 1947. Moreover, since the prevalence of crime had not yet been politicized, it could still influence all the political parties. See Rose, *Struggle*, p. 215; Morris, *Criminal Justice*, p. 96. For the 1930s, see Bailey, *Delinquency*, chap. 5; Pearson, *Hooligan*, pp. 46-7. For Templewood's lecture to the newly formed Department of Criminal Science in the School of Law, Cambridge University, see *The Times*, Feb. 1, 1947.

58 *The Times*, July 26, July 29, Sept. 4, Sept. 20, and Nov. 3, 1947. See also Bailey, *Delinquency*, pp. 291-302; Rose, *Struggle*, p. 231; Morris, *Criminal Justice*, pp. 74-7.

over capital punishment.[59]

Nor is a 'bureaucratic' explanation of the government's behaviour fully persuasive. The home secretary, it is claimed, became captive of the 'departmental view', more strictly of the supposedly retentionist views, of Sir Alexander Maxwell, the permanent secretary, and Sir Frank Newsam, the deputy under-secretary. The predilections of the senior Home Office officials were reinforced, it is said, by the associations working on behalf of prison and police officers. The permanent officials in the Home Office called attention, of course, to the security aspects of the question. In early July 1947, Maxwell told Ede that many police and prison officers believed that criminals would be more likely to use lethal weapons if the penalty for murder were imprisonment rather than death and that those serving life sentences for murder would feel less restraint about killing prison officers. A related concern was a satisfactory alternative to death. Alexander Paterson, the former prison commissioner, told the 1930 Select Committee on Capital Punishment that imprisonment for terms beyond ten years was less humane than the death sentence. Paterson's views were possibly dear still to the permanent officials. But security considerations were only one dimension of departmental discussion, and not always the most important.[60]

When it comes to the supposedly retentionist views of department officials, the 'bureaucratic' explanation is hard to sustain, at least for the most senior figure, Maxwell. In 1961, Gordon Rose implied that Maxwell and Newsam both shared the retentionist views of the former permanent secretary, Sir John Anderson (1922-1932). James Christoph reached no firm conclusion, but he pointed out that, in an interview, Ede had claimed that both officials were 'at heart' abolitionists. Fenton Bresler maintained that Newsam was a decided retentionist and hence unpopular with the abolitionists. Herbert Morrison's biographers declared in 1973 that Maxwell 'was a strong believer in the abolition of capital punishment'. For my part, I have found nothing in the evidence to suggest that Maxwell was anything other than abolitionist in sentiment.[61] Maxwell's advice, moreover, was essentially to avoid the free vote strategy, for a number of politically sound reasons, and instead to do one of two things: either resist an abolitionist amendment, or include abolition and back it to the hilt. The presumption must be that, above all, Maxwell simply wanted the government to take a consistent and defensible course of action, whether for or against abolition.

---

59 See Francis Williams, *Socialist Britain* (New York, 1949), p. 80; Morgan, *Labour People*, pp. 179, 183, 187; Steven Fielding, Peter Thompson, and Nick Tiratsoo, *"England Arise!" The Labour Party and Popular Politics in 1940s Britain* (Manchester, 1995), pp. 175-9, 216; Bernard Donoughue and G. W. Jones, *Herbert Morrison: Portrait of a Politician* (London, 1973), p. 309. See also R. K. Alderman, 'Discipline in the Parliamentary Labour Party 1945-51', *Parliamentary Affairs* 18 (1965), pp. 296-7.

60 Maxwell minute, July 1, 1947, HO 45/21959/884452/203; Select Committee on Capital Punishment, *PP*, 1930-31, VI (15). Minutes of Evidence, pp. 599-601 (Alexander Paterson). The department also believed, for example, that there was still no general trend of public opinion in favour of abolition.

61 Rose, *Struggle*, p. 215; Christoph, *Capital Punishment*, p. 70, n. 10; Fenton Bresler, *Reprieve. A Study of a System* (London, 1965), p. 75; Donoughue and Jones, *Morrison*, p. 310.

And to what extent was Chuter Ede a captive of the 'departmental view'? The character of the man points in that direction. Ede was a moderate, cautious, and practical politician, certainly no innovator, and, as such, likely to listen to his permanent officials. He tended to steer clear of controversy within the party, preferring the part of conciliator, and the capital punishment debate cannot have been to his liking. It is a telling point against him, moreover, that he was abolitionist both before and after his stint as home secretary, but retentionist when in office. Margery Fry, vice-president of the Howard League and a member of the Advisory Council on the Treatment of Offenders, claimed a few months later that 'the conversion of the Home Secretary in favour of capital punishment seems unfortunately likely to be a reflection of one section of Home Office views'. Above all, Ede believed that so disputatious a subject as capital punishment required separate legislative treatment, as did officials in the Home Office and the Cabinet Office.[62] Perhaps, then, Ede was more than a mite 'captive'.

The preceding account of cabinet thinking leads me to suggest a fifth and final explanation for the government's behaviour, one that underscores the incompatibility between a Parliamentary Labour Party chock-full of radical idealists and abolitionists, on the one hand, and a cabinet with only a few committed abolitionists, on the other.[63] Only Shawcross and Soskice had 'fire in their bellies' on this issue. They were up against the leader of the house, the home secretary, and a lord chancellor wielding the club of His Majesty's judges. Yet if the abolitionists were out-gunned, the combination of strong backbench support for abolition and ministerial division together scuppered the idea of a separate bill to suspend or abolish the death penalty and impelled the strategy of the free vote in the House of Commons. The cabinet sought to find a way out of its difficulties by throwing the burden on the House by a free vote.

In early December 1947, abolitionists from the major parties (though predominantly Labour members) decided to press for a five-year suspension of the death penalty rather than its complete abolition, presumably because this coincided with the recommendation of the 1930 Select Committee on Capital Punishment and would attract a wider body of parliamnetary support. The scene was set for a free debate and free vote on the Report Stage of the Criminal Justice Bill, on the most controversial, and for some the most crucial, reform in the penal system. It would soon become clear that, by gambling on a free vote, the government had opened a Pandora's box of political troubles.[64]

---

62 S. Margery Fry, 'The Criminal Justice Bill', *Political Quarterly* 19 (1948), pp. 115-16. For more on Ede, see Francis Williams, 'Chuter Ede', *Spectator*, Oct. 1, 1948, pp. 423-4, and *Nothing So Strange* (London, 1970), p. 233; Morgan, *Labour in Power*, pp. 54-5; Kevin Jefferys, ed., *Labour and the Wartime Coalition: From the Diary of James Chuter Ede, 1941-1945* (London, 1987), pp. 8-9. Ede revised his views on capital punishment in the 1950s when serious doubts were raised about the conviction of Timothy Evans, who was executed on Ede's watch. Ede began to campaign for abolition of the death penalty and for a posthumous free pardon for Evans. See Jefferys, *Labour and the Wartime Coalition*, pp. 15-16.

63 Norman Brook's minute of Nov. 18, 1947, PREM 8/739, indicated that not more than five cabinet ministers would vote for abolition, while ten or eleven supported the view that the time was not opportune to abolish the death penalty. But as for the Parliamentary Labour Party, one should not underestimate the pro-hanging views of many of the trade union or working class MPs, who made up some 38 percent of all Labour MPs.

64 Christoph, *Capital Punishment*, p. 42. The twenty-two abolitionists (led by Silverman) who met in the Commons also agreed to confine the change

III

In mid-March 1948, Prime Minister Attlee agreed, at Herbert Morrison's prompting, that the cabinet ought again to discuss the question of whether ministers should be free to vote according to conscience on the amendment for the abolition of the death penalty. The previous cabinet decision — that ministers should be free to vote for abolition — had the disadvantage that the division list would show afterwards that government members were not united in support of the advice given the Commons by the home secretary. At the cabinet meeting of April 8, Morrison argued that even on an issue like capital punishment, ministers who shared a collective responsibility ought not to vote in different lobbies, especially since it was 'not wholly a matter for the individual's conscience ... it also involved questions of law and order for which the Government had a collective responsibility'. He recognized that some of his colleagues held such strong views on the moral issues involved that they could not vote against abolition, but he wondered if their views 'would not be sufficiently met if they abstained from voting'. The cabinet agreed that members of the government who could not vote for retention of the death penalty should abstain from voting. All ministers and junior ministers outside the cabinet were so informed, as was the PLP.[65] This was a heavy blow to the Silverman group, who were banking on the votes of sympathizers in the ministry. Ministers began to search their consciences. James Griffiiths, minister of national insurance, informed Attlee: 'as all through my life I have been for the abolition of the death penalty, I feel constrained to abstain from voting tonight'. Kenneth Younger, under-secretary at the Home Office, and Ede's main assistant in steering the bill through the Commons, was allowed by Ede to abstain.[66]

At the Report Stage of the bill on April 14, the first order of business was the Silverman amendment, by now bearing the signatures of 147 MPs, proposing that for a period of five years (which might be extended by Order in Council on a prayer by both Houses) the death penalty should be suspended and sentence of life imprisonment substituted. This is not the place to review exhaustively the debate that took place in a packed House of Commons. Suffice it to say that Silverman tried to show the contradictory nature of the government's case. He took their case to be that the death penalty was,

---

to the crime of murder (rather than all existing capital offences) and to advocate as an alternative to hanging the usual sentence of life imprisonment. Between the Second Reading and the Report Stage, the various extra-parliamentary bodies (including the police and prison officers' associations and the NCADP) were busy canvassing MPs. See Christoph, *Capital Punishment*, pp. 42-4. Some abolitionists were by now less optimistic about the outcome. In January 1948, Margery Fry told Professor Kinberg: 'I'm very much afraid we are going to be defeated. A tremendous rise in crime ... has made people jumpy and vindictive'. Quoted in Jones, *Margery Fry*, p. 220.

65 CM (48) 27th conclusions, Cabinet meeting, Apr. 8, 1948, CAB 128/12; Norman Brook minute, Mar. 19, 1948, PREM 8/739. At a stormy meeting of ministers outside the cabinet, many objected strongly to the abandonment of the free vote. See Windlesham, *Responses to Crime*, p. 60.

66 Griffiths to Attlee, Apr. 14, 1948, PREM 8/739; Donoughue and Jones, *Morrison*, p. 430. The abolitionist cause was probably further weakened by a series of shocking murders in the months prior to the vote, including the murder of a police constable, all of which were given banner headlines in the press. See Christoph, *Capital Punishment*, p. 45.

in principle, mistaken and ought to be abolished, but that it was 'the wrong moment in which to live up to those principles'. '[I]t is impossible to my mind', said Silverman, 'to argue at one moment that the thing ought to be abolished some day because it is not a deterrent, but ought to be retained today because it is a deterrent'. He also brought attention to the absence from the Front Bench at that moment of the chancellor of the exchequer (Stafford Cripps), the minister of health (Nye Bevan), and the four law officers of the Crown (which included Shawcross and Soskice).[67]

For a number of speakers in the debate, wartime events had manifestly reinforced their moralist convictions. Supporters of capital punishment argued that if it was morally right to hang war criminals, then it was right to use the death penalty for murderers at home. 'We have just been hanging our defeated enemies after the trials at Nuremberg', said Quintin Hogg, Conservative MP for Oxford, and the attorney-general had prosecuted them 'not as an act of war but as an act of what was claimed to be justice'. If we were going to say that it was wrong in all circumstances to take life, Hogg continued, 'then the time to say so was before Nuremberg and not immediately after'. By contrast, opponents of capital punishment underlined the penchant for Britain's wartime enemies to use the death penalty. 'It is not insignificant', said Elwyn Jones, who had been a member of the prosecution team at Nuremberg, 'that one of the first acts of the Nazi Government was to restore the death penalty. ... Our democracy is a democracy that does not need the terror of the death penalty'. In fine, the capital punishment debate in 1948 had a strong moral tone, whether retributive or humanitarian in sentiment.[68]

When the House divided on the Silverman clause, 245 voted yes, 222 voted no. By a slim majority, the Commons had approved a major change in the law of murder for the first time in almost a century. Immediately a roar of cheers went up. R. H. S. Crossman (who voted yes) later explained the emotional outburst:

> For once the machine had been defeated by conscience; and a long-standing Party pledge had been fulfilled despite the dictates of expediency... It was a glorious victory. The violence of the jubilation revealed the frustration of a Party which longs to be able to choose between right and wrong and is constrained time after time to make do with the lesser evil.[69]

To its embarrassment, the government drew the bulk of its support from the Conservatives (no less than 134 of them). Of the 289 Labour Members who took part in the division, 215 voted for the clause (or three to one in favour). Party lines were thus clearly drawn on the issue, despite the government's

---

67 Parl. Deb., 5th ser., Commons, 449, 986, Apr. 14, 1948, 986. The amendment had been tabled by an all-party list of sponsors.

68 Ibid., 1017 (Hogg), 1066 (Elwyn Jones). And see 1015 (John Paton, Labour MP, and former secretary of the NCADP), 1093 (Reginald Paget, Labour MP). See also Lord Elwyn-Jones, *In My Time: An Autobiography* (London, 1983), chap. 10. Note, finally, that Christie Davies, *Permissive Britain: Social Change in the Sixties and Seventies* (London, 1975), pp. 36-41, used the 1948 debates to argue that the 'causalist' arguments concerning deterrence and the possibility of error, which he felt were dominant by the 1950s and 1960s, were by no means as important in the 'moralistic' 1940s.

69 *New Statesman*, Apr. 24, 1948, p. 326.

argument that opinion transcended such lines. The most remarkable fact, however, is that of the seventy-two government members in the Commons, only twenty-eight voted against the amendment, while forty-four availed themselves of the right to abstain, several pointedly remaining on the Front Bench during the division. Out of fourteen cabinet ministers eligible to vote in the Commons, nine voted against the amendment (including Attlee, Morrison, Bevin, and Ede), while Cripps, Bevan, and Harold Wilson (president of the Board of Trade) were present but abstained.[70] Another nine senior ministers not of cabinet rank and thirty-two junior ministers abstained, including all four law officers. (Indeed, none of the law officers had participated in the debate, despite the nature of the issue).[71] Government dissension was awfully palpable.

What had gone wrong? The government presumably expected to win the vote. A year later, referring to the Commons vote, the lord chancellor said: 'I frankly confess that I expected an answer in a different sense ...' And the *Daily Telegraph* stated that Morrison had believed there was a majority for the death penalty and thus the free vote would go in the government's favour.[72] It seems, then, that the government miscalculated abolitionist strength on their own benches and wrongly expected there would be enough Opposition members to see them through. One can only wonder why the government did not do more to divine the mood and intention of their own supporters.

We are on firmer ground in saying that the government had failed to think through the full consequences of a defeat. For they now had to defend a policy they disliked in the House of Lords where they had few supporters and where the Conservative majority would doubtless delete the clause. If the clause came before the Commons again, the home secretary would have to ask the House to insist on a clause that the government opposed. Those who had abstained on the first occasion would be free to vote in support of abolition, while the ministers who were against the clause on the first occasion would be compelled to vote for the abolition that they previously opposed. If the Lords held firm, moreover, the government would be faced with a clash between the two chambers. Then the Lords would be able to maintain that they were defending the opinion of the Labour government, not to mention the will of the people, against the Commons' free vote and there would be a long delay in the

---

70 The other two cabinet ministers (Arthur Creech Jones and Philip Noel-Baker) were abroad. The nine ministers who voted for retention were Attlee, Morrison, Bevin, Ede, Arthur Woodburn (Scottish secretary), A. V. Alexander (minister of defence), George Isaacs (minister of labour), George Tomlinson (minister of education), and Tom Williams (minister of agriculture). Six of them were from working-class backgrounds. Two other cabinet ministers, Lords Jowitt and Addison, were in favour of retention, but they could not vote in the Commons.

71 Mass-Observation Archive, TC 72, Box 1, File E; *The Times*, Apr. 16, 1948; Christoph, *Capital Punishment*, p. 51; Morgan, *Labour in Power*, p. 62. According to James Callaghan, a junior minister at the time, he and the following government members abstained on April 14: Arthur Blenkinsop (parliamentary secretary at the Ministry of Pensions), George Buchanan (minister of pensions), Evan Durbin (parliamentary secretary at the Ministry of Works), Geoffrey de Freitas (undersecretary of state for the Air Ministry), and John Wheatley (lord advocate). Callaghan said that he abstained 'as I could not vote as I would like to' (i.e., for abolition). He is quoted in K. O. Morgan, *Callaghan: A Life* (Oxford: Oxford University Press, 1997), p. 85. Sir Stafford Cripps was thought to have organized the passive resistance of the more than forty ministers (though Callaghan makes no mention of Cripps's influence). Margery Fry was particularly pleased that none of the law officers had voted for retention. Jones, *Margery Fry*, p. 220.

72 Parl. Deb., 5th ser., Lords, 155, April 28, 1948, 546; *Daily Telegraph*, Jun. 7, 1948.

passage of the Criminal Justice Bill. Lord Samuel surely encapsulated the government's plight when he said they 'did not chastise the Back Benchers with Whips, but they are now themselves being chastised with scorpions'.[73]

First, in the aftermath of the abolitionist triumph, ministers agreed that the government must accept the Commons' decision and must ask the House of Lords to accept the new clause. The cabinet also agreed with Ede's proposal that no death sentence for murder should be carried into effect while Parliament was still considering the Criminal Justice Bill. The House was duly told of this change in the exercise of the prerogative of mercy in capital cases, and the judges were asked to forego the black cap, the presence of the chaplain, and the 'Lord have mercy on your soul', when a sentence of death was given.[74]

Second, it became clearer still that Parliamentary opinion and public opinion were at odds on the issue of capital punishment. Three opinion polls appeared in quick succession, indicating that the abolition or suspension of the death penalty was rejected by between two-thirds and three-quarters of respondents (see table below).[75] Neither sex, age, economic class, geographic location, nor religious persuasion made much difference to the result. Mass-Observation found that there was a steady rise in approval with increasing education (though even among those with higher secondary education, only 21 percent approved of the suspension measure) and that political affiliation influenced opinion (yet only 19 percent even of Labour supporters approved of the measure).[76] Perhaps the most significant finding, for present purposes, was the discovery by Mass-Observation that 'the principle of a 'life for a life' is very much alive in many peoples' minds still ...'[77] Two-fifths of Mass-Observation's respondents

---

73 Parl. Deb., 5th ser., Lords, 156, Jun. 1, 1948, 32.

74 See CM (48) 28th conclusion, Cabinet meeting, Apr. 15, 1948, CAB 128/12. The cabinet also decided that they should review at an early date 'the existing powers of courts to impose the death penalty in the British Zone of Germany, in British Colonial territories, and in the Armed Forces of the Crown'. See also the home secretary's statement on the prerogative of mercy in capital cases in the Commons, Apr. 16, 1948, and Ede's letter to the lord chief justice, Apr. 19, in HO 45/21958/884452/202A. Ede's announcement that he intended to advise His Majesty to commute every death sentence by conditional pardon to a sentence of penal servitude for life was eventually deemed to be unconstitutional, since the home secretary was assuming a dispensing power that Parliament had taken from the executive in James II's reign. Ede was required to make another statement to the House on June 10, 1948. See CM. (48) 37th conclusions, Cabinet meeting, June 8, 1948, CAB 128/12.

75 See Mass-Observation Archive, File No. 2996, Capital Punishment Survey, Supplement No. 1, p. 14: 'Results of the Three Surveys on the Experimental Abolition of the Death Penalty'. This table was reproduced in L. R. England, 'Capital Punishment and Open-Ended Questions', *Public Opinion Quarterly* 12 (1948), p. 413 (table 1). These figures are in marked contrast to the Gallup poll of November 1938, when 45 percent chose abolition. See the text at note 56 above.

76 See *Daily Express*, Apr. 29, 1948, 1; Gallup, ed., *Public Opinion Polls*, p. 174; *Daily Telegraph*, May 28, 1948, 1; Mass-Observation Archive, File No. 2996, Capital Punishment Survey, and File No. 3001, Three Surveys on Capital Punishment; Christoph, *Capital Punishment*, pp. 43-4, 53-7. The British Gallup Poll was founded in 1937. For most surveys, Gallup Poll findings were based on samples of 1,000 interviews conducted in some 100 sampling points. Its poll findings were at this date published in the *News Chronicle*. The Mass-Observation survey interviewed over 6,000 people aged sixteen and over throughout England, Wales, and Scotland and used an 'open-end' question ('How do you feel about the death penalty for murder being given up for 5 years?'), which allowed scope for spontaneous expressions of opinions. For more on M-O, see Angus Calder, 'Mass-Observation 1937-1949', in *Essays on the History of British Sociological Research*, ed. Martin Bulmer(Cambridge, 1985), pp. 121-36.

77 Mass-Observation Archive, File No. 2996, Capital Punishment Survey, 9.

spontaneously gave a reason for their attitude. Among those who disapproved of abolition, 40 percent felt it would result in an increase of crime. This was the most frequently expressed reason. Yet 26 percent cited the principle of retribution, prompting Mass-Observation to advise the *Daily Telegraph*, which published their poll: 'It is well for both parties to know how deeply entrenched still in the minds of hundreds of thousands of citizens is the principle of retribution, quite irrespective of the merely *practical* merits or demerits of abolition'.[78]

Table 1. Experimental Abolition of the Death Penalty

Attitude	*Daily Express*	British Institute of Public Opinion (Gallup)	Mass-Observation[a]
Approve	14	26	13
Disapprove	77	66	69
Degrees of murder	-	-	7
Mixed feelings	-	-	4
Miscellaneous	-	-	2
Don't know	9	8	5

[a]Figures based only on those who had heard of the experiment. A blank indicates that this category was not included in the published results.

Third, the lord chancellor, whose job it was to persuade the Lords to accept the new clause, felt all at sea. 'The more I think about the conclusion to which the Commons came', he wrote to the lord chief justice, 'the more deeply I am disturbed by it. I don't see that we can do anything in our House for I feel sure that the Commons would resent any alteration'. Jowitt concluded: 'I am personally placed in an extremely difficult position about the whole thing and wonder what on earth I shall say about it'. Goddard, L. C. J., sympathized: 'Like you, I feel this vote is disasterous (*sic*). I believe it has no public demand behind it except a vocal body who have always agitated for abolition. One thing which I fear may result is retaliation from which, happily, this country has hitherto been free'.[79]

If the government hoped to persuade the House of Lords to accept the new clause, they could have chosen no worse advocate than the lord chancellor. Arguing in the most backhanded manner that he,

---

78 Mass-Observation Archive, TC 72, Capital Punishment Survey, Box 2, File B, May 1948 ('Mass Observation and Opinion Polls'), emphasis in the original. M-O's finding gained confirmation in August 1948 when Gallup asked the question: 'What do you think is the main reason for sentencing a murderer to death — because he deserves it, or because it will stop other people committing murders?' The result was: Desert, 45 percent; Stop others, 43 percent; Don't know, 12 percent. See Gallup, ed., *Public Opinion Polls*, p. 180.

79 Jowitt to Goddard, Apr. 19, 1948; Goddard to Jowitt, Apr. 20, 1948, LCO 2/3340. Surprisingly, the *Daily Mail*, a retentionist paper, advised the House of Lords not to reject the abolitionist clause. Hollis, *Homicide Act*, p. 17. Other responses to the free vote were more predictable. The *Police Chronicle* warned that British policemen would now need to be armed; the chairman of the Prison Officers' Association vowed to press for compensation for dependants of officers killed in prison as a result of abolition. See Christoph, *Capital Punishment*, p. 52. And Winston Churchill, Opposition leader, denounced the cabinet for having left 'this grave decision on Capital Punishment to the casual vote of the most unrepresentative and irresponsible House of Commons that ever sat at Westminster'. Speech of April 21, 1948, to the Annual Conference of Conservative Women, quoted in Martin Gilbert, *Winston S. Churchill* (Boston, 1988), 8, pp. 400-1.

the head of the judiciary, was opposed to the experiment, but that the Lords should nonetheless make it, was hardly calculated to win over such determined opponents as Lords Simon and Samuel. In the second day's debate, Jowitt was more forthright still:

> I was a party to a bargain. I agreed that this matter should be left to a free vote, and I agreed to stand by the result of that free vote. … I do not suggest for a moment, however, that your Lordships are bound … your Lordships have constitutionally … the perfect right to send the clause back to another place for further consideration if you are so minded.[80]

And, of course, many of the Lords were so minded.

Again, I will not attempt to give a comprehensive review of the four days of debate in the Lords. Suffice it to emphasize three important points. The first is that what has been called the 'law-and-order group' among the law lords, which emerged with the postwar rise in recorded crime, were in full cry. Lord Oaksey, a lord of appeal (who, as Lord Justice Lawrence, had acted as president of the Nuremberg Tribunal in 1945), was an assertive retentionist with regard to both corporal and capital punishment, for both retributive and deterrent reasons. 'Is this the time in which to introduce this change in the law?' he asked the House (shades of Lords Eldon and Ellenborough). 'It seems to me somewhat difficult to justify putting to death your enemies' (in Germany), he argued, 'and at practically the same time abolish the penalty of death in your own country'. Additionally, the time was not ripe 'because there is a lack of discipline in the country which gives rise to this wave of crime'.[81] He was ably seconded by the lord chief justice, Lord Goddard, or 'Lord God-damn', as Churchill styled him. In what was his maiden speech, Goddard delivered a furious assault on those who believed 'that punishment should never be punitive, only reformative'. Large numbers of criminals (namely professional abortionists, the homosexual who corrupts small boys, and professional receivers) were not sentenced for reformative purposes, said Goddard, but to show that such conduct would result in punitive consequences. 'I have never yet understood how you can make the criminal law a deterrent unless it is also punitive'. He continued: 'If the criminal law of this country is to be respected, it must be in accordance with public opinion … I cannot believe that the public opinion (or I would rather call it the public conscience) of this country will tolerate that persons who deliberately condemn others to

---

80 Parl. Deb., 5th ser., Lords, 155, Apr. 28, 1948, 545-46. See also Parl. Deb., 5th ser., Lords, Apr. 27, 1948, 396-99. A few years later, Jowitt told the House of Lords that when the Criminal Justice Bill came before the House, 'I was one of those who took the view and, I say quite frankly advised behind the scenes, that we should insist upon the retention of capital punishment'. Parl. Deb., 5th ser., Lords, 185, Dec. 16, 1953, 149-50. According to Lord Longford, Jowitt thought the secret of advocacy was to find the worst thing an opponent could say about your case and say it yourself. In the Lords, moreover, 'he seemed to identify himself emotionally with the huge Conservative majority'. See Frank Pakenham, Earl of Longford, Five Lives (London, 1964), p. 81. Jowitt was also said to be a poor advocate when he knew he had a difficult position. See Heuston, Lives, pp. 70, 98, 115; Shawcross, Life Sentence, p. 65.

81 Parl. Deb., 5th ser., Lords, 155, April 27, 1948, 430-1. In the later debate, Oaksey concluded his speech by declaring, 'It is all wrong to say that punishment has nothing to do with retribution. There are certain cases which shock the conscience of every ordinary man'. Parl. Deb., 5th ser., Lords, 157, July 20, 1948, 1047-8. See also Stevens, Law and Politics, pp. 360-1.

painful and, it may be, lingering deaths should be allowed to live'. The conclusion was foregone: 'I believe that there are many many cases where the murderer should be destroyed'.[82]

Second, the bishops of the Church of England provided choral backing for the legal leads. Only the Bishop of Chichester voted for abolition. A more representative figure was Mervyn Haigh, the lord bishop of Winchester. The Criminal Justice Bill, he remarked, was 'infected at some points by an excessive fear of punishment. I certainly view with some alarm the extent to which the door is opened to the opinions and influence of more medical men and more psychiatrists'. But perhaps, he continued, 'the heyday of what I might call Patersonian optimism in this matter has, at any rate for the time being, passed'. Haigh took the opportunity, therefore, to remind the Lords of 'the primitive framework whereby punishment is awarded by the State in a quite objective way':

> … I believe that the deepest point is not just whether the death penalty deters a certain number of people from committing murder … but what the effect of abolishing the death penalty on the education of the conscience of the community as a whole will be; how far it will affect the general sense of the wickedness of wickedness, the general sense of the criminality of crime, and the general sense that some crimes are infinitely more heinous than others.[83]

The death penalty, he concluded, still aroused among large numbers of people 'what I can only describe as a quasi-religious sense of awe'.[84]

Finally, a number of speakers recommended the alternative course of limiting the infliction of the death penalty to certain categories of the gravest cases. Lord Samuel, for example, suggested that all murderers should be reprieved except in four categories: political assassins, murderers of police officers, murderers of prison officers, and murders of a 'planned and callous character'.[85] Soon schemes of grading murders would be all the rage.

On June 2, the Silverman clause was defeated by 181 votes to 28.[86] The rest of the bill was approved

---

82 Ibid., pp. 490-4. Goddard also said that the twenty King's Bench judges were all in favour of retaining the death penalty. In late June, however, he had to admit that he had been in error; two judges had since told him that they supported the proposal to suspend the death penalty for five years. See *The Times*, July 1, 1948; Fenton Bresler, *Lord Goddard: A Biography of Rayner Goddard, Lord Chief Justice of England* (London, 1977), p. 184 and note. Goddard later tabled an amendment to the Criminal Justice Bill that would have limited the abolition of corporal punishment to the cat o' nine tails. Whipping with a birch rod would have remained. The amendment carried in a thinly attended House of Lords by twenty-nine to seventeen. In the Commons, the amendment was rejected, and the Lords gave way. See Parl. Deb., 5th ser., Lords, 156, June 2, 1948, 191-215.

A month after his appointment as lord chief justice, in the case of Harry John McBain, Goddard had signalled his response to the post-war crime wave. 'In the state of crime in this country the time has now come when sentences must be severe, and where a prisoner appeals against sentence this Court will not shrink from increasing the sentence if it thinks it right to do so'. *Criminal Appeals Report* 31 (1946), p. 115. Goddard retired in 1958 and died in 1971. His death prompted one of his severest critics, Bernard Levin, to declare that 'Goddard's influence on the cause of penal reform was almost unrelievedly malign'. *The Times*, June 8, 1971. And see Levin, 'Brother Savage', *Spectator*, 16 May 1958, 629. See also Shimon Shetreet, *Judges on Trial* (Amsterdam, 1976); Stevens, *Law and Politics*, p. 362.

83 Parl. Deb., 5th ser., Lords, 155, April 27, 1948, 426.

84 Ibid., 427.

85 Ibid., 415-18.

86 Ibid., 156, June 2, 1948, 102 and following. The Lords had not divided in April on the bill's Second Reading. The twenty-eight supporters of the

by the Lords, even the abolition of corporal punishment. Only hope stayed inside Pandora's box.

IV

Confronted by a Lords' revolt, what could the Labour government do? The strongest response would be to defy the Lords, namely to invoke the Parliament Act and stand behind the clause, albeit one they had originally opposed. At this time, however, the government was wary of challenging the Lords on anything. The weakest response would be to defer to the Lords, namely to accept the bill denuded of the abolitionist clause and face the wrath of many in the Parliamentary Labour Party. A third way would be either to extend the use of the royal prerogative of mercy (which abolitionists considered no advance at all) or to find a compromise clause satisfactory to both retentionists and abolitionists.

The press response to the Lords' vote gestured toward a compromise clause, establishing degrees of murder. The *News Chronicle*, for example, advised the government 'that there were comparatively few in the House of Lords who desire the permanent retention of the death penalty in its present form'. Leading the charge for a compromise clause was Lord Chancellor Jowitt. He had been struck by the archbishop of Canterbury's opinion during the Second Reading debate that the country could not now go back to the *status quo*. In addition, he wished to avoid a clash with the House of Lords at a moment when the press was waxing lyrical about how the Lords' delaying power had been used in the public interest. Jowitt feared that if the abolition clause was restored in the Commons, the Lords would again reject it, since they would know that, at a time when the Labour government aimed to reduce the Lords' veto power from two years to one, they had no better case for demonstrating their value as a revising chamber.[87]

The day following the Lords' vote, the cabinet, on the advice of the home secretary, decided to recommend to the PLP that they accept a compromise clause retaining the death penalty for certain specified classes of murder. The lord chancellor had drafted a clause to this end. Ministers were swayed by two considerations. First, 'it seemed likely that the balance of public opinion throughout the country was against the clause'. To be sure, the *Daily Telegraph* claimed that 'privately, constituency representatives submitted that votes were being lost to the party over this issue'; and closer to home, the *Daily Herald* maintained that many MPs who had either voted for suspension or abstained 'have been impressed by the volume of criticism from their constituencies'.[88] Second, if the Commons' decision no

---

Silverman clause included twenty-two Labour peers, three Conservative peers, and three others. The total number voting was large by upper chamber standards, pointing to the role of 'backwoodsmen', or Conservative peers who come out only on emotive occasions. See P. A. Bromhead, *The House of Lords and Contemporary Politics, 1911-1957* (London, 1958), pp. 47, 218, n. 2.

87 *News Chronicle*, June 4, 1948. See also *The Times*, June 3, 1948, 5; minute of S. Hoare, Assistant Under Secretary of State, June 2, 1948, HO 45/21962/884452.

88 CM (48) 35th conclusion, Cabinet meeting, June 3, 1948, CAB 128/12; *Daily Telegraph*, June 4, 1948, p. 1; *Daily Herald*, June 5, 1948, p. 1.

longer reflected the present mood of public opinion, this was not the moment to clash with the Lords on this issue. The debate on the Second Reading of the Parliament bill was underway, and the government had argued that the upper chamber 'was not competent to interpret the popular will as against the judgement of the House of Commons'. A battle with the Lords over the death penalty, which placed the peers in as strong a position with regard to public opinion as they were likely to attain, would give the lie to this argument.[89]

The cabinet hoped, finally, that a majority of the PLP might be persuaded to vote in favour of such a compromise, especially since they could be told that the clause had been unanimously approved by the cabinet. Even Cripps and Bevan were prepared to support the compromise. The attorney-general, Shawcross, was obviously not at this cabinet meeting, since, to judge from his memoirs, he felt strongly that the clause suspending the death penalty should be restored by the Commons. Browbeaten by Attlee and Morrison not to split 'on an issue on which public opinion was so clear', Shawcross agreed to vote with the government, but then resign (an act he never took).[90]

On June 9, Ede, Cripps, and Morrison persuaded the PLP to accept the compromise clause.[91] The next task, which was never likely to be easy, was to draft an acceptable clause. The new clause was eventually drafted on the basis that the penalty for murder should ordinarily be life imprisonment, but that the death penalty should be retained for those types of murder that were the main cause of public anxiety and for which the deterrent effect of the death penalty was likely to be more powerful than it was in other cases. The clause did not attempt to define degrees of murder or to distinguish between types of murder according to the moral gravity of the crime. Nor was it drawn so as to include premeditated murders and exclude unpremeditated ones.

Instead, the clause reserved the death penalty for (i) murder incidental to the commission of offences of robbery, burglary, and housebreaking, violence by gangs, offences involving the use of explosives, and sexual offences; (ii) murder committed in the course of resisting or avoiding arrest, of escaping from lawful custody, or obstructing the police or persons assisting the police; (iii) murder by the 'systematic administration' of poison; (iv) murder of a prison officer; and (v) for a second murder. In effect, the clause divided murder into two broad categories, capital and non-capital. The Home Office calculated that if this clause became law, the number of actual executions would be reduced by more than half, and the number of cases in which the sentence of death was pronounced by even more.[92]

The compromise clause was introduced in the Commons by Attorney-General Shawcross, in a more

---

89 CM (48) 35th conclusion, Cabinet meeting, June 3, 1948, CAB 128/12.

90 Shawcross, *Life Sentence*, p. 168. The *Daily Mirror*, June 7, 1948, p. 5, wrongly stated that Cripps and Bevan were pressing the cabinet to stand by the original decision of the Commons.

91 See *News Chronicle*, June 10, 1948, p. 1. Morrison urged acceptance for tactical reasons. It was much better to fight the House of Lords over the bill for steel nationalization than over capital punishment.

92 Maxwell minute, June 29, 1948, HO 45/21962/884452.

vigorous manner than might have been expected of a confirmed abolitionist. Winston Churchill, Opposition leader, and other Conservative members then had a field day pointing out the anomalies and illogicalities in the clause. 'All the most frequent types of murder', said Churchill, 'that is to say, wounding, stabbing, strangling, drowning, etc., committed for all the most wicked motives, jealousy, greed, revenge, etc., will not carry the death penalty, because that penalty will only apply in such cases if the offence is committed by three or more persons'. Both parties had issued three-line whips, so, unsurprisingly, the Commons agreed to substitute the government's new clause by 307 votes to 209.[93]

As Shawcross handed the baton to the lord chancellor, he warned that the clause was difficult to defend on its intrinsic merits. He had tried in his speech to justify the various categories for which the government had retained the death penalty, on the ground that it would operate as a deterrent in these cases:

> This argument rather breaks down in regard to the poisoning case, the truth being that we included this, and, indeed, one or two of the other categories [e.g., two murders], not because the death penalty was a deterrent, but because public opinion demands its imposition by way of retribution in these types of case. As, however, we are sticking to the view ... that the death penalty cannot possibly be justified on the ground of retribution, we can hardly admit that any of the categories in which we are retaining the death penalty are included on that ground.

He concluded his letter to Jowitt by saying: 'I am not at all sure that public feeling about the proposed abolition of the death penalty is nearly as strong as is sometimes thought. ... There is some rather ill informed public anxiety, no doubt, but I am afraid the truth is that it is being artificially stirred up in some places for political reasons'. Jowitt replied the day after the Lords' debate on the compromise clause to say he had had 'a very uncomfortable time' with the hanging clause and that 'Simon was almost unbearable, making a speech full of 'malice aforethought'.[94] Lord Simon certainly pulled no punches. '[T]his clause is simply shot to pieces', he said; 'this clause is rightly denounced as being a quite impossible and utterly absurd provision'. Alas, Templewood, the leader of the abolitionists in the Lords, also declared the clause to be unworkable. And even Jowitt, in a study of half-heartedness, conceded that possibly he had gone 'a little too far in assenting to this scheme. I daresay it is not very well drafted'.[95] Not surprisingly, the clause was decisively rejected by ninety-nine votes to nineteen.

The opposition to the compromise clause points again to the strength of the morality of blame and desert. The clause was a deliberate attempt to avoid questions of retribution and degrees of culpability. Capital murders were not defined by reference to moral guilt, for they were neither the most abhorrent

---

93 Parl. Deb., 5th ser., Corrunons, 453, July 15, 1948, 1442. A second amendment — to suspend capital punishment for five years but to leave it to the home secretary to order when the period would begin — was pressed by Labour MP, Anthony Greenwood. Even Sydney Silverman opposed the amendment on the grounds that it would place too great a burden on the home secretary's shoulders. The amendment was defeated.

94 Shawcross to Jowitt, July 19, 1948; Jowitt to Shawcross, July 21, 1948, in LCO 2/3341.

95 Parl. Deb, 5th ser., Lords, 157, July 20, 1948, 1055, 1070.

murders, nor those that had been most clearly premeditated. This entire approach stuck in the craw of all retributivists. They were not willing to accept a system in which the wicked might be more severely punished than the very wicked. To be acceptable to them, then, a compromise clause would have had to be based firmly and squarely upon degrees of heinousness.[96]

The nettle was back in the government's hand. It had four choices. First, it could put the bill through under the Parliament Act procedure, and include a provision about capital punishment. But this procedure could be applied only to the bill as it first left the Commons, the one including the Silverman clause suspending the death penalty. The government could hardly force this into law with popular support so lacking. Second, it could deal with capital punishment in a separate bill in the next session. But could the government find a suitable legislative form for this? The compromise clause had been shot out of the sky. Third, it could seek some further compromise that the Lords would accept, but Parliamentary time was running out for this expedient. And, fourth, it could accept the Lords' rejection of the compromise clause and thus ensure that the rest of the bill could pass in the present session. The cabinet chose the last course, and Ede advised the Commons on July 22 to drop the compromise clause. Morrison seconded this advice, reminding the House that the main issue was whether they were going to save a measure 'for making a big landmark in the progressive administration of criminal justice and the criminal law'. The government won the vote by 215 to 34. Only 129 of the 215 were Labour members, and thus two-thirds of the party voting strength failed to take part (including 14 senior ministers).[97] On July 30, 1948, the Criminal Justice Act received the Royal Assent.

In early November, the home secretary recommended to his colleagues the appointment of a royal commission on capital punishment. At this stage, the terms of reference included the issue of abolition. The cabinet endorsed the proposal, but restricted the enquiry to the question of whether liability to suffer capital punishment should be limited or modified. In effect, some new method of classifying murders by degrees, which the Lords had ridiculed, the Opposition in the Commons had opposed, and the abolitionists disliked, formed the royal commission's terms of reference. On November 18, Ede announced the proposal to set up a royal commission.[98] No one expected a report in the lifetime of the present Parliament, or before the 1950 election. But then delay was one of the prime virtues of a royal commission. On the same day, Stanley Joseph Clark, thirty-four, was hanged at Norwich prison for murdering a chambermaid, the first person to be executed since the controversy over the Criminal Justice Bill. The bishop of Norwich spent the last thirty minutes before execution with Clark. A day

---

96 Cf. the discussion of the 1957 Homicide Act in Christie, 'Power of Life and Death', pp. 365-7.

97 Norman Brook minute, July 21, 1948, PREM 8/739; CM. (48) 53rd conclusions, Cabinet meeting, July 22, 1948, CAB 128/13; Parl. Deb., 5th ser., Commons, 454, July 22, 1948, 707-11, 750; Mass-Observation Archive, TC 72, Box 1, File E. In the event, Attorney-General Shawcross did vote with the government, for which Attlee thanked him. See Shawcross, *Life Sentence*, p. 169.

98 See CP (48) 252, Nov. 3, 1948, CAB 129/30; CM (48) 74th conclusions, Cabinet meeting, Nov. 18, 1948, CAB 128/13; Brook minute, Nov. 6, 1948, PREM 8/739. The appointment of a royal commission took abolitionists by surprise. The NCADP no longer existed, so the Howard League had to take over. See Jones, *Margery Fry*, p. 225.

later, Peter Griffiths, twenty-two, was executed at Walton Gaol, Liverpool, for battering a three-year-old child to death.[99] The hangman was back in business.

The royal commission took until September 1953 to submit its report. Its recommendations (for example, that the statutory age for executions should be raised from eighteen to twenty-one) were incidental compared to the conclusions: that it was impossible to classify murders so as to confine the death penalty to the more heinous and that there was no convincing evidence that capital punishment had a uniquely deterrent effect in preventing murder. Though the terms of reference precluded the judgement, what the commission implicitly proclaimed was that the existing law could not be satisfactorily amended except by abolition.[100] The Conservative government of the day rejected all the main recommendations of the commission and declined to introduce legislation to amend the law of murder. Within a few years, however, in a desperate gambit to forestall outright abolition, the Conservatives conceded the 1957 Homicide Act.[101] In its forlorn attempt to distinguish between capital and non-capital murder, the act caused such confusion that even the senior judges withdrew their backing. The Homicide Act's failure, plus several controversial executions (Bentley, Ellis, and Evans — the latter case flying in the face of those who would insist that no mistaken execution had ever been carried out), so changed opinion that when Labour returned to office in 1964, abolition was assured. In 1965, capital punishment for murder was suspended for five years, at the end of which it was abolished.[102] The shadow of the gallows no longer fell across the land.

V

The outcome of the crisis between 1945 and 1948 was to leave the law of capital punishment exactly as it was. For an abolitionist movement that had anticipated the final triumph of a century-long campaign to abolish the death penalty in Britain, this was a deeply disappointing result. Abolitionists had looked forward to providing the capstone to the Criminal Justice Act, the symbolic emblem of a new penal future that 'liberal progressives' had so patiently constructed throughout the inter-war years. Instead,

---

99 *The Times*, Nov. 19, 1948, p. 5; Nov. 20, 1948, p. 3.

100 *Royal Commission on Capital Punishment, 1949-1953*, Cmd. 8932 (1953; reprint, London, 1965). See also Hollis, *Homicide Act*, chaps. 2-3.

101 The Homicide Act abolished the death penalty for all murders except those done in course of furtherance of theft, by shooting or explosion, in resisting arrest or escaping from custody, murder of a police officer, and of a prison officer by a prisoner, and for repeated murders. The penalty for all other murders was life imprisonment.

102 See Block and Hostettler, *Hanging in the Balance*, chaps. 17-19; 'Murder (Abolition of Death Penalty) Bill', Parl. Deb., 5th ser., Commons, 704, Dec. 21, 1964, 870. The vote on Second Reading was Ayes 355, Noes 170. See also 'Murder (Abolition of Death Penalty)', Parl. Deb., 5th ser., Commons, 793, Dec. 16, 1969, 1148. The vote on the motion, That the Murder (Abolition of Death Penalty) Act 1965 shall not expire, was Ayes 343, Noes 185. After 1969, the death penalty remained for treason, mutiny, and certain other offences specified in the Armed Forces Act, 1966. However, by virtue of the Crime and Disorder Act 1998, s. 36, and the Human Rights Act 1998, s. 21(5) — following the signing by the prime minister of the Sixth Protocol of the European Convention on Human Rights — the death penalty, whether for military or for civilian offences, is now abolished completely. Article 2 of the Convention permits a state to reintroduce the death penalty in wartime.

they had travelled for nine months on a Parliamentary switchback, which came to a halt at its starting point. Parliament passed the kind of law that the government had asked for in November 1947, one shorn of a clause to abolish or suspend the death penalty. The capital sentence was to be retained, if more sparingly used. It had been a tortuous journey, one marked by ironies, dilemmas, embarrassments, and recriminations. It was not the ride the abolitionists had paid for. And it could, they felt, have been avoided.

The government had a huge majority in the Commons, a large segment of which was avowedly abolitionist. The press, moreover, was far from retentionist in sentiment. In the abolitionist corner were *The Times, News Chronicle, Manchester Guardian, Daily Mirror, Daily Herald*, and *Reynolds News*, plus such weeklies as the *Observer, Spectator, Economist*, and *New Statesman*.[103] There can have been few issues raised by the postwar Labour government that attracted such widespread press backing. This was due, in part, to the merely suspensory nature of the amendment. As *The Times* argued, a five-year experiment would lead to evidence whereby a lasting decision could be taken.[104] How, then, could the government temporize in this matter, defer to the Conservative peers, and fail to offer clear leadership?

All this overlooked the peculiar character of capital punishment. It may in principle be the apex of the country's penal system, but in practice governments have treated it as a special case. The death penalty called up the strongest emotions; it touched the deepest fears and values. Few people were without opinions on the state's right to exact death; few governments were willing to go ahead of opinion on so volatile and unpredictable an issue. Fearing an emotionally charged controversy, parties and governments kept their heads down. Parties made no mention of capital punishment in their manifestos, lest a commitment either way became a hostage to fortune. When in power and when made to confront the issue, governments trusted to the free vote, to Parliament as a body of private consciences, to the fiction that capital punishment was an issue of public morality that cut across party lines.

By so refusing to treat capital punishment as an integral part of their legislative program, the Attlee administration opened a Pandora's box of troubles. Only when the government faced up to their responsibilities was the box closed, but between the opening and the closing, confusion reigned. Having decided that the death penalty should be retained, the Labour cabinet lacked the courage to make it government policy. Consequently, what the majority of ministers believed was necessary — to retain capital punishment — was left to a free vote of the Commons, which unexpectedly went in favour of abolition. A measure without strong government backing was doomed in a House of Lords where

---

103 See *The Press and Its Readers: A Report Prepared by Mass-Observation for the Advertising Service Guild* (London, 1949), pp. 81-4. Editorially opposed to the suspension of the death penalty were the *Daily Telegraph, Daily Mail, Daily Express*, and *Daily Graphic*. As the report also made clear, however, the press 'has had little opinion-forming influence on this issue'. With the single exception of the *Daily Worker*, the Communist Party newspaper, 'the majority of readers of *every* paper are against suspension', p. 82, (emphasis in original).

104 *The Times*, April 14, 1948, p. 5.

Conservative and retentionist feeling predominated. The lord chancellor's lacklustre performance was an effective nod and a wink to the peers to resist abolition. Jowitt had the sanguinary support, moreover, of His Majesty's judges, especially Lord Chief Justice Goddard, whose reign of retributive bombast was underway. The upper chamber's *lex talionis* was reinforced, finally, by the weight of public opinion. The Lords could legitimately claim that on the issue of capital punishment they were closer to the *vox populi* than the House of Commons. It was hard to deny the finding that close to three in every four people were unfavourable to abolition, other than by pleading that public opinion was uninformed, a doubtful argument for a People's Party. When the peers resisted, the government declined to face them down, adopting instead the face-saving formula of degrees of murder, so shot through with philosophic contradictions and practical illogicalities that it took the issue to new risible depths. What had gone so wrong? 'Funk Rule!' the *Daily Mirror* concluded, by which it meant the lack of clear leadership on a vital moral and legal issue.[105]

One other factor was decisive in the failure to abolish capital punishment. The postwar years proved much less propitious for reform of the criminal code than abolitionists were expecting. In the thirties, parliamentary, public, and even judicial opinion seemed to be moving towards abolition, in tandem with a strong desire to recalibrate the principles of punishment for all criminal offenders. The prison commissioners themselves were in the van of a broad-based campaign to demote retribution in favour of rehabilitation. The 1938 Criminal Justice Bill would have given legislative warrant to the reformative treatment of prisoners. Between 1939 and 1947, however, the rate of reported crime rose markedly, and the very act of homicide appeared to take on a more malevolent character. In this setting, the renewed attempt to abolish the death penalty sounded the tocsin. It aroused those who believed that the antisocial tendencies proceeding from the war had far from spent their force to proclaim that this was not the time to be weakening the penal armoury.[106] Corporal punishment could not be saved; all the more reason, then, to cleave to the sword of Damocles. Retaining the gallows was not only about deterring murder, as important as that mandate remained; it was also about satisfying, expressing, and educating the public instinct to condemn crimes that menaced the community. The lord bishop of Winchester had said as much in closing his speech on the Criminal Justice Bill in 1948: 'I urge that the question to be considered is not simply whether there will be a few more murders or a few less, but the whole attitude of the British people to what I have described as the criminality of crime, and to the majesty of the whole system of law from top to bottom'.[107]

---

105 *Daily Mirror*, June 11, 1948, p. 2. The fact that a reprise of the 1948 events was enacted in 1956, when a Conservative administration confronted the same issue, suggests that it was the character of capital punishment as much as the party handling the issue that influenced these events. See Nigel Nicolson, *People and Parliament* (1958; reprint, Westport, 1974), p. 86.

106 This is not to imply that postwar debate was sharply polarized on every issue of penal reform. The Conservative Party continued to understand juvenile crime, for example, in progressive ways. See *Youth Astray* (London, 1946). This report recommended the abolition of whipping for boys under fourteen and of imprisonment for persons under seventeen. See also Bailey, *Delinquency*, p. 290.

107 Parl. Deb., 5th ser., Lords, 155, April 27, 1948, 428.

It is this final factor that prompts the conclusion that the turbulent post-war conflict over the death penalty marks a critical moment in criminal justice history. Despite the good intentions and best efforts of administrators and penal reformers in the aftermath of the First World War, the structure of criminal justice experienced no radical transformation during this period. The 'classical' jurisprudential axioms of personal responsibility, deterrence, and a due proportion between crime and punishment retained much of their authority. In the criminal courts, rehabilitation was honoured more in the breach than the observance. Yet the tide was turning between the wars. Recorded crime rose slowly, prison populations declined, and innovations such as open prisons were introduced. A progressive reformism, which had points in common with a 'positivist' criminology, guided penal practice. And it shaped the legislative climax of the era, the Criminal Justice Bill. By rights, the postwar Labour government should have launched an era of unashamed rehabilitation, in which the gallows were dismantled once and for all. That it did not is surely testimony to the enduring political, judicial, and public resistance to the reforming ethos. It meant that for a while longer yet, penal debate would be consumed by the agitation to get rid of the last remaining human sacrifice.

Index

Ralph Anstis, Warren James and the Dean Forest Riots, *The Disturbances of 1831*
£14.00 • 242pp *paperback* • 191x235mm • ISBN 978-0-9564827-7-8

The full story of the riots in the Forest of Dean in 1831, and how they were suppressed, is told here for the first time. Dominating the story is the enigmatic character of Warren James, the self-educated free miner who led the foresters in their attempt to stave off their increasing poverty and unemployment, and to protect their traditional way life from the threats of advancing industrial change.

John E. Archer, 'By a Flash and a Scare', *Arson, Animal Maiming, and Poaching in East Anglia 1815-1870*
£12.00 • 206pp *paperback* • 191x235mm • ISBN 978-0-9564827-1-6

'By a Flash and a Scare' illuminates the darker side of rural life in the nineteenth century. Flashpoints such as the Swing riots, Tolpuddle, and the New Poor Law riots have long attracted the attention of historians, but here John E. Archer focuses on the persistent war waged in the countryside during the 1800s, analysing the prevailing climate of unrest, discontent, and desperation.

Victor Bailey, Charles Booth's Policemen, *Crime, Police and Community in Jack-the-Ripper's London*
£17.00 • 162pp *paperback* • *2 colour and 8 b/w images* • 140x216mm • ISBN 978-0-9564827-6-1

What explains the law-abidingness of late Victorian England? A number of modern historians contend that the answer lies with the effectiveness of policing, and with the imposition of a 'policeman-state' in Victorian and Edwardian England.

Exploiting the vast archive that Charles Booth amassed for his leviathan social investigation to explore the social order of London's East End, *Life and Labour of the People in London*, this volume takes issue with this answer.

The East End was notorious as a region of unalleviated poverty, crime and immorality, the district where the issue of large-scale Jewish immigration was first confronted, and where Jack-the-Ripper found his victims.

Victor Bailey reveals that historians have overestimated the extent to which policemen were able or willing to intervene in the daily behaviour of inhabitants to suppress law breaking. He shows that the commission and repression of crime were linked not only to the structures of law enforcement but also to levels of community solidarity, associational life, family integration, and parental authority.

Social order was a function less of policing than of a complex combination of informal family and community sanctions, the mixed welfare of charity and state support, the new board schools, slum clearance, and the negotiated justice of the magistrates' courts.

The conclusions should lead us to question the role of the state in the making of social order, and to reinstate the force of informal social sanctioning.

Bob Bushaway, By Rite, *Custom, Ceremony and Community in England 1700-1880*
£14.00 • 206pp *paperback* • 191x235mm • ISBN 978-0-9564827-6-1

Political philosophers (such as Gramsci) and social historians (such as E. P. Thompson) have suggested that rural customs and ceremonies have much more to them than the picturesqueness which has attracted traditional folklorists. They can be seen to have a purpose in the structures of rural society. But no historian has really pursued this idea for the English folk materials of the eighteenth and nineteenth centuries: the period from which most evidence survives.

Bringing together a wealth of research, this book explores the view that rural folk practices were a mechanism of social cohesion, and social disruption. Through them the interdependence of the rural working-class and the gentry was affirmed, and infringements of the rights of the poor resisted, sometimes aggressively.

Malcolm Chase, The People's Farm, *English Radical Agrarianism 1775-1840*
£12.00 • 212pp *paperback* • 152x229mm • ISBN 978-0-9564827-5-4

This book traces the development of agrarian ideas from the 1770s through to Chartism, and seeks to explain why, in an era of industrialization and urban growth, land remained one of the major issues in popular politics. Malcolm Chase considers the relationship between 'land consciousness' and early socialism; attempts to create alternative communities; and contemporary perceptions of nature and the environment. *The People's Farm* also provides the most extensive study to date of Thomas Spence, and his followers the Spenceans.

Malcolm Chase, Early Trade Unionism, *Fraternity, Skill and the Politics of Labour*
£14.00 • 248pp *paperback* • 191x235mm • ISBN 978-0-9570005-2-0

Once the heartland of British labour history, trade unionism has been marginalised in much recent scholarship. In a critical survey from the earliest times to the nineteenth century, this book argues for its reinstatement. Trade unionism is shown to be both intrinsically important and to provide a window onto the broader historical landscape; the evolution of trade union principles and practices is traced from the seventeenth century to mid-Victorian times. Underpinning this survey is an explanation of labour organisation that reaches back to the fourteenth century. Throughout, the emphasis is on trade union mentality and ideology, rather than on institutional history. There is a critical focus on the politics of gender, on the demarcation of skill and on the role of the state in labour issues. New insight is provided on the long-debated question of trade unions' contribution to social and political unrest from the era of the French Revolution through to Chartism.

Nigel Costley, West Country Rebels
£20.00 • 220pp *full colour illustrated paperback* • 216x216mm • ISBN 978-0-9570005-4-4

What comes to mind when you think of the West Country? Beautiful beaches and coastline perhaps, rich countryside and moorland, great historic sites such as Stonehenge or perhaps the grace of Regency Bath or the stunning design of Brunel's Clifton Suspension Bridge? You may think of the West Country as the peaceful, quiet corner of Britain where people visit for holidays or spend their retirement.

What may not spring to mind is the Western Rebellion against enclosures, the bloody battles for fair taxes, the Prayer Book Rebellion against an imposed English Bible, the turbulent years of the Civil War and the Monmouth Rebellion that ended with the ruthless revenge of Judge Jefferies. You may know little about the radical edge to the region's maritime past such as the naval mutinies, smuggling and struggle for safety.

The West Country was famous for its wool and cloth but the battles by textile workers is less well known. For generations communities around the South West organised and engaged in riot and uprising, for food, for access, for fair tax and to be heard in a society that denied most people the vote. Women were at the centre of many of these disputes and their battle with poverty and inequality is featured along with West Country women who challenged those that kept them out and held them back.

Trade unionism has many a West Country story to tell, from the Tolpuddle Martyrs in Dorset, the longest strike in Plymouth, the great china clay strike of 1913, 'Black Friday' in Bristol and the battle for rights at GCHQ in Cheltenham..

This book features these struggles along with the characters who defied convention and helped organise around dangerous ideas of freedom, equality and justice.

Barry Reay, The Last Rising of the Agricultural Labourers, *Rural Life and Protest in Nineteenth-Century England*

£12.00 • 192pp *paperback* • 191x235mm • ISBN 978-0-9564827-2-3

The Hernhill Rising of 1838 was the last battle fought on English soil, the last revolt against the New Poor Law, and England's last millenarian rising. The bloody 'Battle of Bosenden Wood', fought in a corner of rural Kent, was the culmination of a revolt led by the self-styled 'Sir William Courtenay'. It was also, despite the greater fame of the 1830 Swing Riots, the last rising of the agricultural labourers.

Buchanan Sharp, In Contempt of All Authority, *Rural Artisans and Riot in the West of England, 1586-1660*

£12.00 • 204pp *paperback* • 191x235mm • ISBN 978-0-9564827-0-9

Two of the most common types of popular disorders in late Tudor and early Stuart England were the food riots and the anti-enclosure riots in royal forests. Of particular interest are the forest riots known collectively as the Western Rising of 1626-1632, and the lesser known disorders in the Western forests which took place during the English Civil War. The central aims of this volume are to establish the social status of the people who engaged in those riots and to determine the social and economic conditions which produced the disorders.

Dorothy Thompson, The Chartists, *Popular Politics in the Industrial Revolution*

£16.00 • 280pp *paperback* • 191x235mm • ISBN 978-0-9570005-3-7

The Chartists is a major contribution to our understanding not just of Chartism but of the whole experience of working-class people in mid-nineteenth century Britain. The book looks at who the Chartists were, what they hoped for from the political power they strove to gain, and why so many of them felt driven toward the use of physical force. It also studies the reactions of the middle and upper classes and the ways in which the two sides — radical and establishment — influenced each other's positions.

The book is a uniquely authoritative discussion of the questions that Chartism raises for the historian; and for the historian, student and general reader alike it provides a vivid insight into the lives of working people as they passed through the traumas of the industrial revolution.

E. P. Thompson, Whigs and Hunters, *The Origin of the Black Act*

£16.00 • 278pp *paperback* • 156x234mm • ISBN 978-0-9570005-2-0

With *Whigs and Hunters*, the author of *The Making of the English Working Class*, E. P. Thompson plunged into the murky waters of the early eighteenth century to chart the violently conflicting currents that boiled beneath the apparent calm of the time. The subject is the Black Act, a law of unprecedented savagery passed by Parliament in 1723 to deal with 'wicked and evil-disposed men going armed in disguise'. These men were pillaging the royal forest of deer, conducting a running battle against the forest officers with blackmail, threats and violence.

These 'Blacks', however, were men of some substance; their protest (for such it was) took issue with the equally wholsesale plunder of the forest by Whig nominees to the forest offices. And Robert Walpole, still consolidating his power, took an active part in the prosecution of the 'Blacks'. The episode is laden with political and social implications, affording us glimpses of considerable popular discontent, political chicanery, judicial inequity, corrupt ambition and crime.

David Walsh, Making Angels in Marble, *The Conservatives, the Early Industrial Working Class and Attempts at Political Incorporation*

£15.00 • 268pp *paperback* • 191x235mm • ISBN 978-0-9570005-0-6

In the first elections called under the terms of the 1832 Reform Act the Tory party appeared doomed. They had recorded their worst set of results in living memory and were organizationally in disarray as well, importantly, seemingly completely out of touch with the current political mood. During the intense pressure brought to bear by the supporters of political reform was the use of "pressure from without" and in this tactic the industrial working class were highly visible. Calls for political reform had been growing since the 1760s and given fresh impetus with the revolutions in America and France respectively. The old Tory party had been resistant to all but the most glaring corruption and abuse under the pre-Reform system, not least to the idea of extending the electoral franchise to the 'swineish multitude', as Edmund Burke notoriously described the working class. Yet within five years after the passing of reform the Conservatives — the natural heirs to the old Tory party — were attempting to politically incorporate sections of the working class into their ranks. This book examines how this process of making these 'Angels in Marble', to use Disraeli's phrase from a later era, took shape in the 1830s. It focuses on how a section of the industrial working class became the target of organizational inclusion into Peelite Conservatism and ultimately into the British party political system.

Roger Wells, Insurrection, *The British Experience 1795-1803*

£17.50 • 372pp *paperback* • 191x235mm • ISBN 978-0-9564827-3-0

A re-evaluation of the hoary problem of the question of revolution in Britain and Ireland during the allegedly dying years of the Age of Revolution.

On the 16 November 1802 a posse of Bow Street Runners raided the Oakley Arms, a working class pub in Lambeth, on the orders of the Home Office. Over thirty men were arrested, among them, and the only one of any social rank, Colonel Edward Marcus Despard. Despard and twelve of his associates were subsequently tried for high treason before a Special Commission, and Despard and six others were executed on 21 February 1803. It was alleged that they had planned to kill the King, seize London and overturn the government and constitution.

Until recently this event had been almost entirely neglected by historians, principally on the grounds that it was an *isolated* occurrence, the brainchild of a disgruntled and probably insane Irishman. The incident is relegated to a footnote in the relevant volume of the *Oxford History of England* and even then only in support of First Minister Addington's habitual 'calmness'.

Apologists speedily claimed that Despard was just another dupe of the supposedly notorious hoard of informers and *agents-provocateurs* employed by the younger Pitt and his supposed lackey, Addington, to support their outrageous assault on the constitutional freedoms and rights of Englishmen. One pamphlet attacking the revelations of the infamous Oliver the Spy, typically claimed that in 1817 Oliver was 'by no means a novice in matters of treason, but … was closely and deeply implicated in the mad schemes of Colonel Despard'. These views, that any insurrectionary activity manifested by Englishmen was either the product of insane individuals or the manipulations of secret-service agents, or both, rather than an indigenous phenomenon, were also adopted by Whig and Fabian historians.

The first coherent reappraisal of the Despard affair was provided by E. P. Thompson, in his magnificent work, *The Making of the English Working Class*. An integral part of Thompson's thesis hinges on his analysis of what happened to one seminal political development in the 1790s, namely the first primarily English working-class movement for democracy. E. P. Thompson's claim that determined physical force revolutionary groupings originated after the suppression of the Popular Democratic Movement in 1795 has been seriously challenged by conventional British historians. This book offers a reinterpretation of Thompson's evidence, through a detailed overall study of post-1795 British politics. It throws new light on the organisation of government intelligence sources, Pitt's repressive policies and machinery, and oscillating popular responses; all developments, including recrudescences of the open Democratic Movement, and notably the emergence of insurrectionary conspiracies, are firmly related to both events in the critical Irish theatre, and the course of the war against France.

BREVIARY STUFF PUBLICATIONS
www.breviarystuff.org.uk

Roger Wells, Wretched Faces, *Famine in Wartime England 1793-1801*
£18.00 • 412pp *paperback* • 191x235mm • ISBN 978-0-9564827-4-7

This book reverts Malthus in a thoroughly English context. It proves that famine could, and *did*, occur in England during the classic period of the Industrial Revolution. The key economic determinant proved to be the ideologically-inspired war, orchestrated by the Prime Minister, the younger Pitt, against the French and their attempted export of revolutionary principles at bayonet point, to the rest of Europe. This international context, in part, conditioned the recurrent development of famine conditions in England in 1794-6 and again in 1799-1801. Here the multiple ramifications of famine in this country, as it lurched from crisis to crisis in wartime, are explored in considerable depth. These were repeated crises of capitalism, juxtaposed with the autocratic and aristocratic state's total commitment to war, which contrived to challenge not just the commitment to war, but both the equilibrium and the survival of the state itself. 'WANT' stalked the land; intense rioting periodically erupted; radical politicisation, notably of unenfranchised working people, proceeded apace, in part stimulated by the catastrophic events projected on the world stage by the process of the French Revolution. The book finally explains how such an oligarchic, unrepresentative government managed through determined economic interventionism, manipulation of the unique English social security system, and final resort to army rule, to preserve itself and the political structure during a key epoch within the Age of Revolutions.

Lightning Source UK Ltd.
Milton Keynes UK
UKOW04f1804240417
299810UK00001B/50/P

9 780957 000551